C# by Dissection

C# by Dissection

Ira Pohl

University of California
Santa Cruz

Addison
Wesley

Boston San Francisco New York
London Toronto Sydney Tokyo Singapore Madrid
Mexico City Munich Paris Cape Town Hong Kong Montreal

Senior Acquistions Editor	Maite Suarez-Rivas
Executive Editor	Susan Hartman Sullivan
Executive Marketing Manager	Michael Hirsch
Production Supervisor	Marilyn Lloyd
Project Management	Argosy Publishing
Copyeditor	Margaret Berson
Proofreader	Sybil Fetter
Composition and Art	Debra Dolsberry
Cover Design	Sandra Silva
Prepress and Manufacturing	Caroline Fell

Access the latest information about Addison-Wesley titles from our World Wide Web site: http://www.aw.com/cs

Many of the designations used by manufacturers and sellers to distinguish their products are claimed as trademarks. Where those designations appear in this book, and Addison-Wesley was aware of a trademark claim, the designations have been printed in initial caps or all caps.

The programs and applications presented in this book have been included for their instructional value. They have been tested with care, but are not guaranteed for any particular purpose. The publisher does not offer any warranties or representations, nor does it accept any liabilities with respect to the programs or applications.

Library of Congress Cataloging-in-Publication Data

Pohl, Ira.
    C# by dissection: the essentials of C# programming / by Ira Pohl.
      p.   cm.
    ISBN 0-201-87667-1 (alk. paper)
    1. C# (computer program language) I. Title
QA76.73.C154 P64 2003
005.13'3-dc21   2002071696

All rights reserved. No part of this publication may be reproduced, stored in a retrieval system, or transmitted, in any form or by any means, electronic, mechanical, photocopying, recording, or otherwise, without the prior written permission of the publisher. Printed in the United States of America.

ISBN 0-201-87667-1
1 2 3 4 5 6 7 8 9 10- MA-0605040302

About Ira Pohl

Ira Pohl, Ph.D., is a professor of Computer Science at the University of California, Santa Cruz. He has over 30 years of experience as a software methodologist. His teaching and research interests are in the areas of artificial intelligence, programming languages, practical complexity problems, heuristic search methods, deductive algorithms, and educational and social issues. He originated error analysis in heuristic search methods and deductive algorithms.

He is an ACM Fellow and has lectured at Berkeley, Stanford, the Vrije University in Amsterdam, the Courant Institute, Edinburgh University in Scotland, and Auckland University in New Zealand.

When not programming, he enjoys riding bicycles in Aptos, California, with his wife Debra and daughter Laura.

For My Students

TABLE OF CONTENTS

Chapter 2

Native Types, Operators, and Expressions   29

Chapter 3

Statements   81

Chapter 4
Methods: Functional Abstraction   **115**

Chapter 5
Arrays   **171**

Chapter 6
Classes and Abstract Data Types   237

Chapter 7
Constructors, Conversion, and Overloading   285

Chapter 8
Inheritance   327

Chapter 11
Container Classes   451

Chapter 12
OOP Using C#   493

Appendix E
Advanced Topics 559

Index 575

PREFACE

The C# programming language is an important new language designed and pioneered by Microsoft as part of its .NET initiative. C# comes with many useful libraries and is supported by sophisticated integrated environments. It efficiently supports object-oriented programming (OOP), the dominant contemporary programming methodology.

C# by Dissection presents a thorough introduction to the programming process by carefully developing working programs to illuminate key features of the C# programming language. Program code is explained in an easy-to-follow, careful manner throughout. C#, invented in the late 1990s, is a powerful, modern, successor language to C. C# adds to C the concept of *class*, a mechanism for providing user-defined types, also called *abstract data types* (ADTs). C# supports *object-oriented* programming by these means and by providing inheritance and runtime type binding.

DISSECTIONS

This book presents readers with a clear and thorough introduction to the programming process by carefully developing working C# programs, using the method of *dissection*. Dissection is a unique pedagogical tool first developed by the author in 1984 to illuminate key features of working code. A dissection is similar to a structured walk-through of the code. Its intention is to explain to the reader newly encountered programming elements and idioms as found in working code. Programs and functions are explained step-by-step. Key ideas are reinforced throughout by use in different contexts.

NO BACKGROUND ASSUMED

This book assumes no programming background and can be used by students and first-time computer users. Experienced programmers not familiar with C# will also benefit from the carefully structured presentation of the C# language. For student use, the book is intended as a first course in computer science or programming.

C# by Dissection is suitable as a CS1 course or beginning programming course for other disciplines. Each chapter presents a number of carefully explained programs that lead the student in a holistic manner to ever-improving programming skills. From the start, the student is introduced to complete programs, and at an early point in the text is introduced to writing functions as a major feature of structured programming. The function is to the program as the paragraph is to the essay. Competence in writing functions is the hallmark of the skilled programmer and is therefore emphasized here. Examples and exercises are plentiful in content and level of difficulty, allowing instructors to pick assignments appropriate to their audiences.

SPECIAL FEATURES

- Software engineering practices described throughout

- Dr. P's prescriptions, concise programming tips, for each chapter

- Early explanation of simple recursion to reflect its earlier introduction in beginning computer science courses

- Coverage of program correctness and type safety

- In-depth explanation of methods and parameter passing, typically stumbling blocks for the beginner

- Emphasis on object-oriented programming concepts

- UML diagrams aid in understanding object-oriented programming

- Comparison to Java and C++, as well as coordinating references to *Java by Dissection* (Ira Pohl with Charlie McDowell) and *C++ by Dissection*

CHAPTER FEATURES

Each chapter contains the following pedagogical elements:

Dissections. Major elements of the important example programs are explained through dissection. This step-by-step discussion of new programming ideas helps the reader encountering new ideas to understand them.

Object-Oriented Programming. The reader is led gradually to the object-oriented style. Chapter 6, *Classes and Abstract Data Types*, introduces classes, which are the basic mechanism for producing modular programs and implementing abstract data types. Class variables are the objects being manipulated. Chapter 8, *Inheritance*, develops inheritance and virtual functions, two key elements in this paradigm. Chapter 12, *OOP Using C#*, discusses OOP programming philosophy.

Programming Style and Software Engineering. Programming style and software methodology are stressed throughout. Important concepts such as structured branching statements, nested flow of control, top-down design, and object-oriented programming are presented early in the book. A consistent and proper coding style is adopted from the beginning with careful explanation as to its importance and rationale. The coding style used in the book is one commonly used by programming professionals working in the C# community.

Working Code. The student is introduced to full working programs from the start. With the executable code, the student can better understand and appreciate the programming ideas under discussion. Many programs and functions are explained through dissections. Variations on programming ideas are often presented in the exercises.

Dr. P's Prescriptions. A series of programming tips is based on wide experience. A concise rationale is given for each tip.

Comparison to Java and C++. Increasingly, beginning programmers start by studying Java. The roots of C#, C++, and Java are found in C. Most serious programmers end up learning all four languages. These sections are an enrichment for those readers who already know or wish to know Java or C++. If they are a distraction to others, they can be skipped. For the most part, C#, C++, and Java have equivalent elements. The text helps the student already conversant in Java or C++ to migrate to C#. Also the C# student who later takes up Java or C++ will benefit from this section. Furthermore, as the book is a companion volume to *Java by Dissection* (Ira Pohl with Charlie McDowell) and *C++ by Dissection,* the reader has access to complete explanations of the Java or C++ concepts fully utilizing this book's pedagogy.

Summary. A succinct list of points covered in the chapter reinforces the new ideas.

Review Questions and Exercises. Review questions and exercises test the student's knowledge of the language. Many exercises are intended to be done interactively while reading the text. This encourages self-paced instruction. In addition to exercising features of the language, some exercises examine a topic in more detail, and others extend the reader's knowledge to an advanced area of use.

CLASSROOM USE

This book can be used as a text in a one-semester course that teaches students how to program. Chapters 1 through 6 cover the C# programming language through the use of arrays and basic object programming. A second semester course can be devoted to more advanced data types, OOP, inheritance, file processing, and software engineering as covered in Chapters 7 through 12. In a course designed for students who already have some knowledge of programming, not necessarily in C#, the instructor can cover all the topics in the text. This book can also be used as a text in other computer science courses that require the student to use C#. In a comparative language course, it can be used with companion volumes for C, Java, and C++ that follow the same dissection approach and use many of the same examples, which are treated uniquely in each language.

INTERACTIVE ENVIRONMENT

This book is written explicitly for an interactive environment. Experimentation via keyboard and screen is encouraged throughout.

PROFESSIONAL USE

While intended for the beginning programmer, *C# by Dissection: The Essentials of C# Programming* is a friendly introduction to the entire language for the experienced programmer as well. In conjunction with *A Book on C, Fourth Edition* by Al Kelley and Ira Pohl (Addison Wesley Longman, Inc., Reading, MA, 1998), the computer professional will gain a comprehensive understanding of both languages. As a package, the two books offer an integrated treatment of the C/C# programming languages and their use that is unavailable elsewhere. Furthermore, in conjunction with *Java by Dissection* (with Charlie McDowell) and *C++ by Dissection*, this book gives the student or professional an integrated treatment of the object-oriented languages C#, C++, and Java.

SUPPLEMENTS

Support materials are available to instructors adopting this textbook for classroom use:

- Solutions to exercises and review questions

- Code for example programs

Please check online information for this book at www.aw.com/cssupport for more information on obtaining these supplements.

CONTENTS OF CD-ROM

The CD-ROM that comes with this book contains text files which contain the significant code in the text and the Microsoft® .NET Framework Software Development Kit (SDK) including Service Pack 1. The SDK is copyright 1985-2002 by Microsoft Corporation with all rights reserved.

Code: Working code is distributed in a directory for each chapter or appendix that contains significant code. The files are text files with file extensions of `.cs` for C#, `.cpp` for C++, and `.java` for Java. The file names are given in the book after the heading "In File."

SDK: No printed documentation for the SDK is included, but online help is available as part of the installed SDK. The SDK can be set up to run .NET Framework Redistributable, which runs .NET Framework applications only, or .NET Framework Software Development Kit, which builds and runs .NET Framework applications. The requirements for each option are given below:

.NET Framework Redistributable Requirements

- Personal computer with a Pentium class 90 MHZ or higher microprocessor

- OS: Windows 2000 with the latest Windows service pack and critical updates available from the Microsoft Security Web page (www.microsoft.com/security), Windows XP (Professional edition is required to run ASP.NET applications), Windows NT 4.0, Windows Millenium Edition (Windows ME), Windows 98

- Microsoft Internet Explorer 5.01 minimum

- CD-ROM drive

- Video: 800x600, 256 colors

- Microsoft Mouse or compatible pointing device

- RAM: 32 MB (96 MB or higher recommended)

- Hard disk space required to install: 160 MB

- Hard disk space required: 70 MB

.NET Framework Software Development Kit Requirements

- Processor: Intel Pentium class 133 MHz or higher

- OS: Windows 2000 with the latest Windows service pack and critical updates available from the Microsoft Security Web page (www.microsoft.com/security), Windows XP (Professional edition is required to run ASP.NET applications), Windows NT 4.0

- RAM: 128 MB (256 MB or higher recommended)

- Hard disk space required to install: 600 MB, Hard disk space required: 370 MB

- Video: 800x600, 256 colors

- Microsoft Internet Explorer 5.01 minimum

- CD-ROM drive

- Microsoft Mouse or compatible pointing device

ACKNOWLEDGMENTS

Special thanks go to Adam Bickett, Marc Mosko, Brian Hanks, and Alice Westin, who were careful readers of the technical content of this work and suggested numerous improvements, without being responsible for my errors. Thanks to our reviewers, Robert W. Miller, Stark State College of Technology; Jack C. Wileden, University of Massachusetts Amherst; David R. Kaeli, Northeastern University; and Steve Houk, Instructor of Computer Science at Santa Barbara City College. Thanks also to John dePillis, Debra Dolsberry, Molly Intersimone, and Laura Pohl who helped develop and draw many of the cartoons. Most important further thanks to Debra Dolsberry, who acted as the chief technical editor for much of the material in this book and the CD-ROM. In addition, she was largely responsible for using FrameMaker to create files suitable for typesetting this book and also helped write several of the appendices. Thanks also to Charlie McDowell and Al Kelley for writing companion volumes in C and Java. This book benefited from previous reviewers' efforts with C++ by Dissection. It shares examples and exercises with all three other Dissection series books. Many of the exercises were carefully tested and reworked by Adam Bickett.

I would also like to thank Maite Suarez-Rivas, Acquisitions Editor, Marilyn Lloyd, Production Supervisor, and Patty Mahtani, Associate Managing Editor for their enthusiasm, support, and encouragement, and Sally Boylan at Argosy, for their careful attention to the production of this book.

Ira Pohl
University of California, Santa Cruz

CHAPTER 1

WRITING A C# PROGRAM

The C# programming world is introduced in this chapter. We discuss how to program and explain a number of elementary programs thoroughly. Basic ideas presented here become the foundation for more complete explanations in later chapters. These first programs stress basic input/output for C#. Getting information into and out of a machine is the first task to be mastered in any programming language.

C# uses the methods `WriteLine()` and `ReadLine()` for output and input, respectively. The use of both of these methods is explained. Other topics discussed in this chapter include the use of variables to store values and the use of expressions and assignments to change the value of a variable.

Throughout the text many examples are given and dissected. You see in detail how each programming construct works. Topics that are introduced in this chapter are revisited in later chapters, with more detailed explanation where appropriate. This spiral approach to learning emphasizes ideas and techniques essential for the C# programmer.

C# is largely a superset of C and an alternative to C++ and Java. By learning C# you are also learning the kernel language C. This book is the fourth in a series of dissection books that include *C by Dissection: 4th edition*, by Al Kelley and Ira Pohl; *C++ by Dissection*, by Ira Pohl; and *Java by Dissection*, by Ira Pohl and Charlie McDowell. The modern programmer needs to be comfortable in all four C-based languages.

**"When grandpa Algol was your age, he had to run in only 4K of
memory and get around by paper tape!"**

1.1   GETTING READY TO PROGRAM

Programs are written to instruct machines to carry out specific tasks or to
solve specific problems. A step-by-step procedure that accomplishes a
desired task is called an *algorithm*. Thus programming is the activity of
communicating algorithms to computers. We are all used to giving instructions to someone in English and having that person carry out the instructions. The programming process is analogous, except that machines have
no tolerance for ambiguity and must have all steps specified in a precise
language and in tedious detail.

The Programming Process

1. Specify the task.

2. Discover an algorithm for its solution.

3. Code the algorithm in C#.

4. Test the code.

A computer is a digital electronic machine composed of three main components: processor, memory, and input/output devices. The processor is also called the *central processing unit*, or *CPU*. The processor carries out instructions that are stored in the memory. Along with the instructions, data is also stored in memory. The processor typically is instructed to manipulate the data in some desired fashion. Input/output devices take information from agents external to the machine and provide information to those agents. Input devices are typically terminal keyboards, disk drives, CD drives, and DVD drives. Output devices are typically terminal screens, printers, disk drives, and writable CD drives. The physical makeup of a machine can be quite complicated.

The *operating system* consists of a collection of special programs and has two main purposes. First, the operating system oversees and coordinates the resources of the machine as a whole. For example, when a file is created on a disk, the operating system takes care of the details of locating it in an appropriate place and keeping track of its name, size, and date of creation. Second, the operating system provides tools that are useful to the C# programmer. Two of these tools are of paramount importance: the text editor and the C# compiler or builder.

We assume the reader is capable of using a text editor to create and modify files containing C# code. C# code is also called *source code*, and a file containing source code is called a *source file*. After a file containing source code (a program) has been created, the C# compiler is invoked. For example, using the Microsoft Windows terminal environment we can invoke the C# compiler with the command

　　csc pgm.cs

where *csc* is the C# compile command and *pgm.cs* is the name of a file that contains a program. If there are no errors in *pgm.cs*, this command produces the *executable file pgm.exe*, which can be run, or executed.

After the programmer writes a program, the program has to be compiled and tested. If modifications are needed, the source code has to be edited again. Thus part of the programming process consists of the cycle

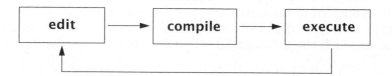

When the programmer is satisfied with the program performance, the cycle ends.

There are also a number of integrated development environment (IDE) tools available for use. These tools, such as Microsoft's Visual Studio for C#, provide an editor for creating programs along with all the tools needed to compile, debug, and run them. Appendix D, *Visual Studio .NET for C#*, describes the use of the Microsoft Visual Studio IDE.

1.2   A FIRST PROGRAM

A first task for anyone learning to program is to print on the screen. Let us begin by writing the traditional first C# program that prints the phrase *Hello, world!* on the screen. The complete program is

In file Hello1.cs

```csharp
// Hello world in C#
// by Olivia Programmer

using System;

class Hello {
  public static void Main()
  {
    Console.WriteLine("Hello, world!");
  }
}
```

The output of this program is

```
Hello, world!
```

Using the text editor, the programmer types this into a file ending in *.cs*. The choice of a file name should be mnemonic. It should remind us of the class name the file contains. Let us suppose *Hello1.cs* is the name of the file in which the program class Hello has been written.

Hey, Heidi, Alpha Centauri says 'Hello' and it's in C#!

Dissection of the *Hello* Program

■`// Hello world in C#`
`// by Olivia Programmer`

The symbol "//" is used as a rest-of-line comment symbol. Program text can be placed in any position on the page, with white space between tokens being ignored. White space, comments, and indentation of text are all used to create a well-documented, readable program, but do not affect program semantics.

■`using System;`

The C# program *hello.cs* imports any needed library definitions. In this case, the I/O library for a typical C# compiler system is found in the library *System*. The compiler knows where to find this and other system files.

On C# systems, standard C# I/O definitions are wrapped in `namespace` `System`. The `using` declaration allows names to be used without `System.` prepended to each name. For the moment treat the `using` `Namespace` as a needed convention. We leave an explanation of `namespace` to Section 6.5.1, *The Dot Operator, Namespaces, and Class Names*, on page 247.

```
class Hello {
   public static void Main()
   {
```

A C# program is a collection of classes. Here the program is the single class `Hello`. It contains the method `Main()`. Its full name is `Hello.Main` to distinguish it from any `Main`s found in other classes. The body of `Main()` starts with an open left brace {. A program begins by executing the method `Main()`. A method in C# has a return type that can be `void`, indicating that no value is to be returned. The special method `Main()` can also be declared to return an integer value to the runtime system when declared `int Main()`.

```
Console.WriteLine("Hello, world!");
```

The method `WriteLine()` is in the `System` library. It is the workhorse for displaying output. It prints out to the screen a string expression, which, for this example, is the string found inside the parentheses. This method also moves the screen cursor to a new line. Note that without the `using System` statement we could have written

```
System.Console.WriteLine("Hello, world!");
```

```
}
```

This ends the method `Main()`. In C#, braces are paired, and an open brace { can be understood as a *begin construct* and a closing brace } means *end construct*.

This program has one class, the `class Hello` and one method `Main()`. The first programs we write follow this structure. Later we write programs that have many methods and many classes. The method `Main()` in these examples is preceded by the special words `public static void`. This rule is explained in Section 4.2, *Static Method Definitions*, on page 118.

The expression `Console.WriteLine(`*string expression*`)` prints the string expression across the screen and then moves to the next line. The expression `Console.Write(`*string expression*`)` prints its string expression, but does not advance the cursor to the next line. The screen is a two-dimensional display that prints from left to right and top to bottom. To be readable, output must appear properly spaced on the screen.

Let us rewrite our program to use two output statements. Although the program differs from our first one, its output is the same.

In file Hello2.cs

```
// Hello world in C#
// by Olivia Programmer
// Version 2

using System;

class Hello {
  public static void Main()
  {
    Console.Write("Hello, ");
    Console.WriteLine("world!");
  }
}
```

Notice that the string in the first statement ends with a blank character. If the blank were not there, the words `Hello, world!` would have no space between them in the output.

As a final variation to this program, let us add the phrase *Hello, universe!* and print the statements on two lines.

In file Hello3.cs

```
// Hello universe in C#
// by Olivia Programmer

using System;

class Hello {
  public static void Main()
  {
    Console.WriteLine("Hello, world!");
    Console.WriteLine("Hello, universe!");
  }
}
```

When we execute this program, the following appears on the screen:

```
Hello, world!
Hello, universe!
```

The two output statements in the body of `Main()` could be replaced by the single statement

```
Console.WriteLine("Hello, world!\nHello, universe!");
```

In this version, the special character \n is the newline character. Inserting a newline character in an output statement has the same effect as executing either of the two following statements:

```
Console.WriteLine("");
Console.WriteLine();
```

1.3   PROBLEM SOLVING: RECIPES

Computer programs are detailed lists of instructions for performing a specific task or for solving a particular type of problem. Instruction lists, sometimes called algorithms, for problem solving are commonly found in everyday situations. Examples include detailed instructions for knitting a sweater, cooking a favorite meal, registering for classes at a university, traveling from one destination to another, and using a vending machine. Examining one of these examples is instructive. Consider this recipe for preparing a meat roast.

> Sprinkle the roast with salt and pepper. Insert a meat thermometer and place in oven preheated to 150ºC. Cook until the thermometer registers between 80ºC and 85ºC. Serve roast with gravy prepared from either meat stock or from pan drippings, if there is a sufficient amount.

The recipe is typically imprecise—what does *sprinkle* mean, where *exactly* is the thermometer to be inserted, and what is a *sufficient amount* of pan drippings? However, the recipe can be formulated more precisely as a list of instructions by taking some liberties and reading between the lines.

Cooking a Roast Algorithm

1. Sprinkle roast with 1/8 teaspoon salt and pepper.

2. Turn oven on to 150°C.

3. Insert meat thermometer into center of roast.

4. Wait a few minutes.

5. If oven does not yet register 150°C, go back to step 4.

6. Place roast in oven.

7. Wait a few minutes.

8. Check meat thermometer. If temperature is less than 80°C, go back to step 7.

9. Remove roast from oven.

10. If there is at least 1/2 cup of pan drippings, go to step 12.

11. Prepare gravy from meat stock and go to step 13.

12. Prepare gravy from pan drippings.

13. Serve roast with gravy.

These steps comprise three categories of instructions and activities—those that involve manipulating or changing the ingredients or equipment, those that just examine or test the *state* of the system, and those that transfer to a numbered step. Steps 1 and 6 are examples of the first category; the temperature test in step 8 and the pan dripping test in step 10 are instances of the second category; and the transfers in steps 5 and 8 (go to step *x*) are examples of the last category.

By using suitable graphical symbols for each of these categories, a simple two-dimensional representation of our cooking algorithm can be obtained, as shown in the following illustration.

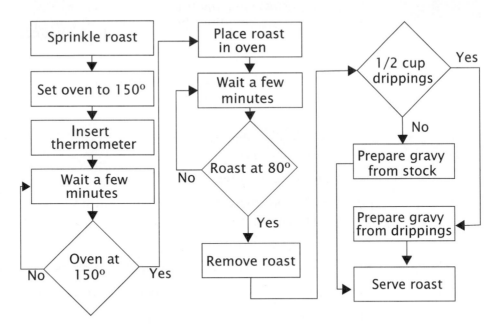

Such a figure is called a *flowchart*. To perform the program (prepare the roast), just follow the arrows and the instructions in each box. The manipulation activities are contained in rectangles, the tests are shown in diamonds, and the transfer or flow of control is determined by the arrows. Because of their visual appeal and clarity, flowcharts are often used instead of lists of instructions for informally describing programs. Some cookbook authors even employ flowcharts.

1.3.1 ALGORITHMS—BEING PRECISE

Our recipe for preparing a roast can't be executed by a computer because the individual instructions are too loosely specified. Let's consider another example—one that manipulates numbers instead of food. You need to pay for some purchase with a dollar bill and get change in dimes and pennies. The problem is to determine the correct change with the fewest pennies. Most people mechanically do this simple everyday transaction. But how do we precisely describe this algorithm?

In solving such a problem, trying a specific case can be useful. Let's say that you need to pay 77 cents and need change for a dollar. You can easily see that one dollar minus the 77 cents leaves you with 23 cents in change. The correct change having the fewest coins in dimes and pennies would be two dimes and three pennies. The number of dimes is the integer result of dividing 23 by 10 and discarding any fraction or remainder. The number of pennies is the remainder of dividing the 23 cents by 10. An algorithm for performing this change for a dollar is given by the following steps.

Change-Making Algorithm

1. Assume that the price in cents is written in a box labeled `price`.

2. Subtract the value of `price` from 100 and place it in a box labeled `change`.

3. Divide the value in `change` by 10, discard the remainder, and place the result in a box labeled `dimes`.

4. Take the integer remainder of `change` divided by 10 and place it in a box labeled `pennies`.

5. Print out the values in the boxes `dimes` and `pennies` with appropriate labels.

6. Halt.

This algorithm has four boxes, namely, `price`, `change`, `dimes`, and `pennies`. Let's execute this algorithm with the values given. Suppose that the price is 77 cents. Always start with the first instruction. The contents of the four boxes at various stages of execution are shown in Table 1.1.

Table 1.1	Change-Making Boxes				
Box	Step 1	Step 2	Step 3	Step 4	Step 5
price	77	77	77	77	77
change		23	23	23	23
dimes			2	2	2
pennies				3	3

To execute step 1, place the first number, 77, in the box `price`. At the end of instruction 2, the result of subtracting 77 from 100 is 23, which is placed in the box `change`. Each step of the algorithm performs a small part of the computation. By step 5, the correct values are all in their respective boxes and are printed out. Study the example until you're convinced that this algorithm works correctly for any price under $1.00. A good way to do so is to act the part of a computer following the recipe. Following a set of instructions in this way, formulated as a computer program, is called *hand simulation* or *bench testing*. It is a good way to find errors in an algorithm or program. In computer parlance these errors are called *bugs,* and finding and removing them is called *debugging.*

We executed the change-making algorithm by acting as an agent, mechanically following a list of instructions. The execution of a set of instructions by an agent is called a *computation.* Usually the agent is a computer; in that case, the set of instructions is a computer program. In the remainder of this book, unless explicitly stated otherwise, we use *program* to mean *computer program.*

The algorithm for making change has several important features that are characteristic of all algorithms.

Algorithms

- ■ The sequence of instructions terminates.

- ■ The instructions are precise. Each instruction is unambiguous and subject to only one interpretation.

- ■ The instructions are simple to perform. Each instruction is within the capabilities of the executing agent and can be carried out exactly in a finite amount of time; such instructions are called *effective.*

- ■ There are inputs and outputs. An algorithm has one or more outputs (answers) that depend on the particular input data.

Our description of the change-making algorithm, although relatively precise, is not written in any formal programming language. Such informal notations for algorithms are called *pseudocode,* whereas real code is something suitable for a computer. Where appropriate we use pseudocode to describe algorithms. Doing so allows us to explain an algorithm or computation to you without all the necessary detail needed by a computer.

The term algorithm originally stems from the name of a well-known Arabic mathematician of the ninth century, Abu Jafar Muhammed Musa Al-Khwarizmi. It later became associated with arithmetic processes and then, more particularly, with Euclid's algorithm for computing the greatest common divisor of two integers. Since the development of computers, the word has taken on a more precise meaning that defines a real or abstract computer as the ultimate executing agent—any terminating computation by a computer is an algorithm, and any algorithm can be programmed for a computer.

1.4   IMPLEMENTING OUR ALGORITHM IN C#

Here we implement our change-making algorithm in the C# programming language. You need not worry about following the C# details at this point; we cover them fully in the next two chapters. For now, note the similarity between the following C# program and the informal algorithm presented earlier. To write a program, you not only have to be able to formulate a recipe and make it algorithmic, you also have to express it in code.

In file MakeChange.cs

```csharp
// Change in dimes and pennies

using System;

class MakeChange {
  public static void Main()
  {
    int price, change, dimes, pennies;        // declarations
    string data;

    Console.WriteLine("Enter price (0:100):");
    data = Console.ReadLine();
    price = int.Parse(data);
    change = 100 - price;                      // how much change
    dimes = change / 10;                       // number of dimes
    pennies = change % 10;                    // number of pennies
    Console.Write("\n\nThe change is: " + dimes
                  + " dimes  ");
    Console.WriteLine(pennies + " pennies.");
  }
}
```

If we use 77 as the input, what we see on the screen is

```
Enter price (0:100):
77


The change is: 2 dimes  3 pennies.
```

Dissection of the *MakeChange* Program

```
int price, change, dimes, pennies;          // declarations
string data;
```

This program declares four integer variables. These hold the values to be manipulated. The string variable `data` is declared to hold the input obtained from the keyboard.

```
Console.WriteLine("Enter price (0:100):");
```

This line is used to prompt you to type the price. Whenever a program is expecting a user to do something, it should print out a prompt telling the user what to do. The part in quotes appears on the user's screen when the program is run.

```
data = Console.ReadLine();
price = int.Parse(data);
```

This statement obtains the input typed in from the keyboard. The string value read is stored in the variable `data`. At this point you must type in an integer price. For example, you would type 77 and then press Enter. The string needs to be understood as an `int` value. The `System` method `int.Parse()` converts the string representation of 77 to an integer and puts it in the variable `price`.

```
change = 100 - price;                       // how much change
```

This computes the amount of change from one dollar.

```
dimes = change / 10;                        // number of dimes
pennies = change % 10;                      // number of pennies
```

The number of dimes is the integer or whole part of the result of dividing `change` by 10. The symbol /, when used with two integers, computes the integer part of the division. The number of pennies is the integer remainder of `change` divided by 10. The symbol % is the integer remainder or modulo operator. So if `change` is 23, the integer part of 23/10 is 2 and the remainder or modulo of 23%10 is 3.

```
■Console.Write("\n\nThe change is :" + dimes
             + " dimes  ");
Console.WriteLine(pennies + " pennies.");
```

The quoted string prints out the characters between the quotation marks. This includes two newlines advancing the cursor down the screen. Then the value in `dimes` is converted to a string and is printed followed by the string " `dimes` ". Finally, the value of `pennies` is converted to a string and is printed followed by the string " `pennies` ". The plus symbol is string concatenation in this context. The print method `Write()` does not automatically advance the cursor to a newline. The second print method `WriteLine()` indicates that a newline should be sent to the console, ending the line of output.

1.5   WRITING AND RUNNING A C# PROGRAM

The precise steps you must follow to create a file containing C# code and then to compile and execute it depend on three things: the operating system, the text editor, and the compiler. However, in all cases the general procedure is the same. We describe in some detail how it is done in a Windows environment. This is currently the only environment for C# in wide use.

In the following discussion, we use the *csc* command to invoke the C# compiler. This uses the command-line version of the Microsoft C# compiler.

Steps for Writing and Running a C# Program

1. Using an editor, create a text file—say *Pgm.cs*—that contains a C# program. The name of the file ends with *.cs*, indicating that the file contains C# source code. For example, we would give the command

    edit Pgm.cs

    To use an editor, the programmer must know the appropriate commands for inserting and modifying text.

2. Compile the program. This can be done with the command

    csc Pgm.cs

    The *csc* command invokes the compiler, which translates the source code into an executable. If there are errors, the programmer must start again at step 1, editing the source file. Errors that occur at this stage are called *syntax errors* or *compile-time errors.* If there are no errors, the program is now ready to be executed.

3. Execute the program. This is done with the command

    Pgm or Pgm.exe

    Typically, the program completes execution, and a system prompt reappears on the screen. Errors that occur during execution are called *runtime* errors. If, for some reason, the program needs to be changed, the programmer must start again at step 1.

Different kinds of errors can occur in a program. Syntax errors are caught by the compiler, whereas runtime errors are caught only during program execution. For example, if an attempt to divide by zero is encoded into a program, a runtime error may occur when the program is executed.

C# systems, such as Microsoft Visual Studio C#, have both a command-line environment and an integrated environment. The integrated environment includes both the text editor and the compiler. This environment is discussed in Appendix D, *Visual Studio .NET for C#.*

No, Mother, I didn't say, "our secret pizza sauce code would make us rich." I said, "our secret piece of source code would make us rich."

1.5.1 INTERRUPTING A PROGRAM

You may need to interrupt, or kill, a program that is running. For example, the program may be in an infinite loop. (In an interactive environment it is not necessarily wrong to use an infinite loop in a program.) Throughout this text we assume that the user knows how to interrupt a program. In Windows, Ctrl-c is commonly used to effect an interrupt. On some systems a special key, such as *delete* or *rubout*, is used. Make sure you know how to interrupt a program on your system.

1.5.2 TYPING AN END-OF-FILE SIGNAL

When a program is taking its input from the keyboard, it may be necessary to type an end-of-file signal for the program to work properly. In Windows, Crtl-z is typed. In Unix Ctrl-d is typed.

1.6   SOFTWARE ENGINEERING: STYLE

A good coding style is essential to the art of programming. It facilitates the reading, writing, and maintenance of programs. A good style uses white space and comments so that the code is easy to read and understand, and is visually attractive. It is also important to choose names for variables that convey their use in the program to further aid understanding. A good style avoids error-prone coding habits.

Software needs to be maintained. Maintenance costs are frequently higher than the initial cost of writing the code. Programs need to be readable to aid in maintenance. Readability incorporates comments in the code, useful identifiers, and associated documentation, such as a manual page or online help.

In this text we are following a common industrial programming style. We place all `usings`, and outer class declarations at the far left.

In file Hello4.cs

```csharp
using System;

class Hello {
  public static void Main()
  {
    int n = 5;

    Console.WriteLine("Hello, world! " + n + " times.");
  }
}
```

The output of this program is

```
Hello, world! 5 times.
```

The declarations and statements in the body of Main() are indented two spaces. This visually highlights the beginning and end of the method body. There is one blank line after the using, and one between the declarations and statements in the body of Main().

An indentation of two, three, four, five, or eight spaces is common. We use two spaces. Whatever you choose for an indentation, use it consistently. To heighten readability, we put a blank space on each side of binary operators. Some programmers do not bother with this, but it is part of our book's style.

There is no single agreed-upon good style. As we proceed through this text, we often point out alternate styles. Once you choose a style, you should use it consistently. Good habits reinforce good programming.

Caution: Beginning programmers sometimes think they should dream up their own distinctive coding style. The preferred strategy is to choose a style that is already in common use.

1.6.1 DEBUGGING: SYNTAX AND RUNTIME ERRORS

When you first start programming, you may make many frustrating simple syntax errors. Syntax errors are caught by the compiler and prevent the program from being compiled into executable code. A common example of a syntax error is to leave off a closing double quote character to mark the end of a string. When the compiler sees the first ", it starts collecting all the characters that follow as a string. If the closing " is not present, the string continues to the next line, causing the compiler to complain, and resulting in the following C# compiler message:

```
Newline in constant
```

Another common syntax error is to misspell a variable name or forget to declare it. Compilers catch this kind of error readily and inform you of what is wrong. However, if you misspell the name of a method, such as `Math.Sqr()` instead of `Math.Sqrt()`, the compiler informs you that the method cannot be found. If you do not notice that the error message refers to `Math.Sqr` instead of `Math.Sqrt`, you may be quite mystified.

Even elementary errors, such as forgetting to place a semicolon at the end of a statement or leaving off a closing brace, can result in confusing error messages from compilers. As you become more experienced, some of the error messages produced by your compiler begin to make sense. Exercise 4 on page 25 suggests some programming errors you may want to introduce on purpose in order to experiment with the error message capability of your compiler. The Microsoft Visual Studio .NET IDE as explained in Appendix D, *Visual Studio .NET for C#*, provides an integrated editor and syntax error detection scheme that makes detecting and correcting such errors very convenient.

Runtime errors are errors in the logic of your program and are much harder to find and correct. For example, if in coding the `MakeChange` program you had accidentally added, instead of subtracted, in the statement:

```
change = 100 + price;
```

The program would compile and run, but the output would be incorrect. There are many strategies to prevent runtime errors and from time to time we talk about common runtime errors for given standard programming idioms. There is also specific runtime debugging support in the Microsoft Visual Studio .NET IDE as explained in Section D.6, *Tracing Program Execution*, on page 548.

A common strategy discussed in Section 1.3.1, *Algorithms—Being Precise,* on page 11, called *hand simulation* or *bench testing,* using some simple cases. If, in the example above, the price were 100 (one dollar) there would be no change. Hand simulating this on the incorrect program would lead to an output of 20 dimes in change, which is obviously wrong.

1.7   DR. P'S PRESCRIPTIONS

- Dr. P's first rule of style is *Have a style.*

- Be consistent in whatever style you choose.

- Check that your compiler supports full modern C#.

In this book we follow a style that combines traditional C and C# style pioneered by Bell Laboratories programmers such as Kernighan, Ritchie, and Stroustrup with some elements of the Microsoft C# style. Several elements of our style can be seen in our programs. Beginning and ending braces for method definitions line up under each other and under the first character of the method definition. Beginning braces after keywords, such as `do` and `while`, follow the keyword with the ending brace under the first character of that line. This style is in widespread use and makes it easy for others to read your code. The style allows us to distinguish key elements of the program visually, enhancing readability. Style should aim for clarity for both ourselves and others who need to read our code. Cleverness by its nature usually obscures and is the enemy of clarity. Hence, Kernighan and Plauger's maxim: "Write clearly—don't be too clever." Inconsistency also tends to obscure.

C# compilers, as described here, may still be incomplete. Make sure you know what the vendors support, especially when it comes to recent changes in the use of libraries.

1.8 C# COMPARED WITH JAVA AND C++

In this section we implement the change-making program from Section 1.4, *Implementing Our Algorithm in C#*, on page 13, in both Java and C++. The differences between the Java, C++, and C# implementations of the *MakeChange* program have to do with method encapsulation, how they handle I/O, and naming conventions used for methods and variables.

First, we look at the Java implementation. This is taken from *Java by Dissection,* pages 5 through 7.

In file MakeChange.java

```
// Change in dimes and pennies

import tio.*;                          // use the package tio

class MakeChange {
  public static void main(String[] args)
  {
    int price, change, dimes, pennies;

    System.out.println("type price (0:100):");
    price = Console.in.readInt();
    change = 100 - price;                  // how much change
    dimes = change / 10;                   // number of dimes
    pennies = change % 10;               // number of pennies
    System.out.print("The change is :");
    System.out.print(dimes);
    System.out.print(" dimes ");
    System.out.print(pennies);
    System.out.print(" pennies.\n");
  }
}
```

In Java, a package is a library or collection of previously written program parts that you can use. The program `MakeChange` uses information from the package `tio`. We developed this package especially for *Java by Dissection* to simplify the input and output required for Java. It allows you to write `Console.in.readInt()`. The source code is available on the Web at ftp:ftp.awl.com/cseng/authors/pohl-mcdowell/.

Here is the C++ version of the program:

In file makeChange.cpp

```cpp
// Change in dimes and pennies

#include <iostream>
using namespace std;

int main()
{
  int  price, change, dimes, pennies;

  cout << "Enter price (0:100):";
  cin >> price;
  change = 100 - price;                      // how much change
  dimes = change / 10;                       // number of dimes
  pennies = change % 10;                   // number of pennies
  cout << "\n\nThe change is :" << dimes << " dimes  ";
  cout << pennies << " pennies." << endl;
}
```

C++ requires preprocessor commands to pull in standard library declarations such as *iostream*, which works with the overloaded operators << and >> to print and read respectively. C++, being an earlier language than either C# and Java, is often more arcane and system-dependent.

C++ differs from Java or C# by allowing file scope methods—C++ programs are not encapsulated in a class. Methods, or functions as they are known in C++, can either be inside classes, where they are known as member functions, or exist independent of any class. Methods in Java and C# are always inside a class.

In Java and C++, methods, like variables, start with a lowercase letter. In C#, methods start with an uppercase letter, while variables start with lowercase. It is also common for variables or method names to be composed of multiple words. In both Java and C#, the convention is to use an uppercase letter at the start of subsequent words, whereas C++ frequently uses an underbar to separate the words:

```
writeLine()                                              // Java
WriteLine()                                               // C#
write_line()                                              // C++
```

SUMMARY

■ An algorithm is a computational procedure consisting of simple steps. Programming is the art of communicating algorithms to computers.

■ A simple program consists of a class that holds the method `Main()`. The body of the method is made up of declarations and statements written between the braces { and }. All variables must be declared before the statements that use the variables.

■ The statement `Console.WriteLine("Hello world!");` prints output to the terminal. Using the method `WriteLine()` rather than `Write()` places the cursor on a new line.

■ There are inputs and outputs. An algorithm has one or more outputs that depend on the particular input data.

■ Informal notations for algorithms are called pseudocode, whereas real code is suitable for a computer. Before coding in C#, it is useful to write pseudocode and simulate its execution.

■ Following a set of instructions by writing out the results is called *hand simulation* or *bench testing*. It is a good way to find errors in an algorithm or program. Errors are called bugs, and finding and removing them is called debugging.

REVIEW QUESTIONS

1. C# uses the method `WriteLine()` for _____.

2. A step-by-step procedure that accomplishes a desired task is called an _____.

3. An operating system has two main purposes. First, the operating system oversees and coordinates _____ of the machine as a whole. Second, the operating system provides _____.

4. The compiler takes _____ code and produces _____ code.

5. Standard C# I/O definitions are wrapped in _____ System.

6. When using `WriteLine()` the cursor is _____.

7. `int price, change, dimes, pennies;`
   This declares four _____. These hold the _____ to be manipulated.

8. This text uses _____ style. There is _____ following the `using Sys-tem`, and between the declarations and statements in the body of `Main()`. An _____ of two, three, four, five, or eight spaces is common.

9. In Windows, _____ is commonly used to effect an interrupt.

10. A common error is to _____ a variable name or forget to _____ it.

EXERCISES

1. Write a program to display on the screen the words

   `she sells sea shells by the seashore`

   (a) all on one line, (b) on seven lines, and (c) inside a box.

2. Here is part of a program that begins by having the user input three integers:

   ```
   using System;

   class EchoInts {
   public static void Main()
   {
      int   a, b, c, sum;

      Console.WriteLine("Enter three integers-1 per line:");
      .....
   ```

   Complete the program so that when the user executes it and types in 2, 3, and 7, this is what appears on the screen:

```
Enter three integers-1 per line.
2
3
7
Twice the sum of your integers plus 7 is 31 - bye!
```

3. The following program is Laura Pohl's first program:

```csharp
// Print Laura's name

using System;
class MyName {
  public static void Main()
  {
    // Print L A U R A
    Console.Write("L        A    U      U RRRRR     A\n");
    Console.Write("L       A A   U      U R   R    A A\n");
    Console.Write("L      A   A  U      U R   R   A   A\n");
    Console.Write("LLL A      A  UUUUU  R   R A       A\n");
    Console.WriteLine("\n\n\n");

    // Print P O H L
    Console.WriteLine("PPPP 00000 H    H L ");
    Console.WriteLine("P  P O   O H    H L ");
    Console.WriteLine("P P  O   O HHHHH L ");
    Console.WriteLine("P    O   O H    H L ");
    Console.WriteLine("P    00000 H    H LLLLL");
    Console.WriteLine("\n\n");
    Console.WriteLine( " By Laura Michelle Pohl ");
  }
}
```

Rewrite this program so that it prints your name instead.

4. The purpose of this exercise is to help you become familiar with some of the error messages produced by your compiler. You can expect some error messages to be helpful and others to be less so. Correct each syntax error.

```
// Full of syntax mistakes.
using System;

class SyntaxErrors (
public static float Main()
{
  int   a = 1, b = 2, c = 3,

  Consol.Writeline(a + b " = a + b");
}
```

5. Here is part of an interactive program that computes the sum of the value of some coins. The user is asked to input the number of half dollars, quarters, dimes, etc.

```
using System;

class Money {
public static void Main()
  {
    int   h,                        // number of half dollars
          q,                        // number of quarters
          d,                        // number of dimes
          n,                        // number of nickels
          p;                        // number of pennies
    .....

    Console.WriteLine("Your change is computed.");
    Console.WriteLine("Enter how many half dollars:");
    .....
    Console.WriteLine("Enter how many quarters:";
    .....
```

Complete the program, causing it to print out relevant information. For example, you may want to create output that looks like this:

```
You entered:   0 half dollars
               3 quarters
               2 dimes
               17 nickels
               1 pennies
The value of your 23 coins is
equivalent to 181 pennies.
```

Notice that `pennies` appears twice. The `1 pennies` should be `1 penny`. After you learn about the `if-else` statement in Section 3.3, *The `if` and `if-else` Statements*, on page 85, you can modify your program so that its output is grammatically correct.

6. Modify the program that you wrote in the previous exercise so that the last line of the output looks like this:

```
The value of your 23 coins is $1.81
```

7. The purpose of this exercise is to find out what happens on your system when a runtime error occurs. Try the following code:

```
using System;
class RunTimeErrors {
  public static void Main()
  {
    int  a = 1, b = 0, c;

    c = a/b ;
    Console.WriteLine("c = " + c);
  }
}
```

If you are using Visual Studio, see how to find this out with the debugger. See Section D.6, *Tracing Program Execution*, on page 548.

8. Here is a two-class version of *hello world*. In this version the `class OneHello` provides a method for writing "Hello world." The second class `CallHello` uses the `WriteHello()` method from the first `class OneHello`. This gives the program a more object-oriented flavor. Modify this program to write "Hello world" n times.

```
using System;

class OneHello {
  public static void WriteHello()
  {
    Console.Write("Hello, ");
    Console.WriteLine("world!");
  }
}
```

```
class CallHello {
  public static void Main()
  {
    Hello.CallHello();
  }
}
```

CHAPTER 2

NATIVE TYPES, OPERATORS, AND EXPRESSIONS

This chapter provides an introduction to programming in C# using its *native types*. A native type is one provided by the language directly. In C#, this includes the simple types, such as character, integer, and floating-point types; the boolean type; and derived types, such as array and string types, which are aggregates of the simple types. This chapter focuses on the native simple data types.

The intent of this and the next few chapters is to enable beginning programmers to use the kernel or core language, that subset of C# that comes closest to forming a traditional imperative language such as C or FORTRAN. Careful study of the simple types is also important to understand how to use the sophisticated object-oriented features of C#. An important object-oriented feature is type extensibility, which is the ability within the programming language to develop new types suitable to a problem domain. For this extensibility to work properly, the new type should work like the native types of the kernel language. Object-oriented design of user-defined types should mimic the look and feel of the native types, one reason why it is important to understand the design and use of the native types.

For the experienced C or C++ programmer, most of this chapter's material should be skimmed and read mainly with an eye for differences between C or C++ and C#, which are summarized in Section 2.9, *C# Compared with Java and C++*, on page 70.

2.1 ▸ PROGRAM ELEMENTS

A program is composed of elements called *tokens*, which are collections of characters that form the basic vocabulary the compiler recognizes. Table 2.1 shows the C# character set.

Table 2.1   Character Set
a b c d e f g h i j k l m n o p q r s t u v w x y z
A B C D E F G H I J K L M N O P Q R S T U V W X Y Z
0 1 2 3 4 5 6 7 8 9
+ = _ - ( ) * & % $ # ! | <> . , ; : " ' / ? { } ~ \ [ ] ^
white space and nonprinting characters, such as newline, tab, blank

In C#, tokens can be interspersed with white space and with comment text that is inserted for readability and documentation. There are five kinds of tokens: keywords, identifiers, literals, operators, and punctuators.

C# distinguishes between uppercase and lowercase. As we shall see, C# uses lowercase in its keyword list.

As a historical note, ALGOL60 was an ancestor language to C and C#, but has not been used in any substantial way since the 1970s. It was the core language of Simula67, which was the first real object-oriented language.

2.1.1 COMMENTS

C# supports three kinds of comments: single-line, multiline, and XML documentation comments.

C# has a single-line comment, written as *rest-of-line.*

```
// C# by Dissection Chapter 2 - Example

#define DEBUG               // preprocessor flag for debugging
```

A multiline comment is written as */* possible multiline comment */*. Everything between /* and */ is a comment. Multiline comments do not nest.

```
/*  Multiline Comments are Frequently Introductory
    Programmer:  Laura Pohl
    Date:        January 1, 1989
    Version:     DJD v4.3
*/
```

XML documentation comments are written as *///rest-of-line.* The compiler turns these comments into an XML file. XML comments are supported as well by Visual Studio.NET (see Appendix D, *Visual Studio .NET for C#*).

```
/// <summary>
/// Hello World Demo Program
/// Compare to C and C++
/// </summary>
```

2.1.2 KEYWORDS

Keywords in C# are explicitly reserved words that have a strict meaning and may not be used in any other way. They include words used for type declarations, such as `int`, `char`, and `float`; words used `for` statement syntax, such as `do`, `for`, and `if`; and words used for access control, such as `public`, `protected`, and `private`. Table 2.2 shows the keywords in current C# systems. We list `set`, `get`, and `value` because they have special meaning when used in the context of creating properties. In other contexts these can be used as ordinary identifiers.

Table 2.2	Keywords		
abstract	event	namespace	static
as	explicit	new	string
base	extern	null	struct
bool	false	object	switch
break	finally	operator	this
byte	fixed	out	throw
case	float	override	true
catch	for	params	try
char	foreach	private	typeof
checked	*get	protected	uint
class	goto	public	ulong
const	if	readonly	unchecked
continue	implicit	ref	unsafe
decimal	in	return	ushort
default	int	sbyte	using
delegate	interface	sealed	*value
do	internal	*set	virtual
double	is	short	void
else	lock	sizeof	volatile
enum	long	stackalloc	while

2.1.3 IDENTIFIERS

An identifier in C# is a sequence of letters, digits, and underscores. An identifier cannot begin with a digit. Uppercase and lowercase letters are treated as distinct. It is good practice to choose meaningful names as identifiers. One- or two-letter identifiers can be used when it is obvious what the name is being used for. Avoid using identifiers that are distinguished only by case differences. In principle, identifiers can be arbitrarily long, but many systems distinguish only up to the first 31 characters. Table 2.3 shows examples of identifiers.

Table 2.3	Valid Identifiers
n	typically an integer variable
count	meaningful as documentation
bufferSize	C# style—capital separates words
buffer_size	C and C++ style—underline separates words
q2345	bad practice—obscure
Console	used in the System standard library
CountScores	a capital usually starts a method name

Table 2.4 has examples of illegal identifiers:

Table 2.4	Invalid Identifiers
for	keyword
3q	cannot start with digit
-count	do not mistake - for _
Console.Write	two identifiers dotted

**No wonder she never gets asked out:
No one can remember her name or what she does!**

2.1.4 LITERALS

Literals are constant values, such as 1 or 3.14159. There are literals for each C# data type. Table 2.5 contains arithmetic literals.

Table 2.5	Arithmetic Literals
5	an integer literal
5u	u or U specifies unsigned
5L	l or L specifies long
05	an integer literal written as octal
0x5	an integer literal written as hexadecimal
5.0D	a floating-point literal treated as double
5.0	a floating-point literal treated as double
5.0F	f or F specifies float—typically single precision
5.0M	m or M specifies decimal

There are three special literals which are also keywords as shown in Table 2.6. The keywords true and false may be assigned to variables of type bool. The default value for any variable of type bool is false. The value null is the default value for a reference type meaning that it does not refer to an object.

Table 2.6	Boolean and Reference Literals
true	a bool literal
false	a bool literal
null	a reference literal

Character literals are written between single quotes. Special characters can be represented with the backslash character \. Table 2.7 has examples of character literals. (See Appendix A, *Unicode and ASCII Character Codes*, for a more complete list.) The ASCII values are between 0 and 127 and can be used to represent the characters on the standard American keyboard.

Table 2.7	Character Literals
'5'	character literal—ASCII value 53
'A'	letter capital A—ASCII value 65
'a'	letter small a—ASCII value 97
'\0'	null character—terminates strings
'\t'	character printing a tab space
'\n'	character printing a new line

String literals are series of characters which represent string constants. The double quote character that delimits a string can be represented inside strings by escaping the double quote character with a backslash character \". In addition, string literals can also be designated as verbatim string literals by using the @" characters to delimit the beginning of the string. In verbatim string literals, the backslash does not act as a special escape character, and spaces and new lines are treated as part of the literal. Everything enclosed within the double quotes following the @ is therefore treated as the string literal. Table 2.8 shows string literals and the characters they include.

Table 2.8	String Literals	
"abc"	3 characters	a b c
"a\tb\n"	4 characters	a *tab* b *newline*
"1 \\"	3 characters	1 *space* \
@"1 \\"	4 characters	1 *space* \ \
@"234 5"	5 characters	2 3 4 *newline* 5
"\""	1 character	"

When printed, these strings would produce effects required by the special characters. Thus, the second string prints a followed by a number of white-space characters as determined by the tab setting, then b followed by a newline character.

String literals that are separated only by white space are implicitly concatenated into a single string.

```
"This is a single string, "
"since it is separated only "
"by white space."
```

The character literals are usually represented as themselves. So the character `'A'` stands for the uppercase letter A. It also has an integer representation of 65. This can be written as the hexadecimal representation `'\x041'` or the Unicode representation `'\u0041'`. Unicode provides values between 0 and 32,767. This provides a basis for numerically representing the symbol set for all the important languages in use. For example, the Hebrew Alef in Unicode is value `'\u05D0'` which in decimal is the integer value 1488. A browser or operating system capable of printing in Hebrew would print this value as א.

Some nonprinting and special characters, such as blank or newline, require an escape sequence, as shown in Table 2.9.

Table 2.9	Escaped Characters
\a	alert
\\	backslash
\b	backspace
\r	carriage return
\"	double quote
\f	formfeed
\t	tab
\n	newline
\0	null character
\'	single quote
\v	vertical tab
\x	hexidecimal (followed by 1–4 hex digits)
\u	Unicode (followed by 4 hex digits)
\U	Unicode (followed by 8 hex digits)

A more extensive list of escape sequences is given in Appendix A, *Unicode and ASCII Character Codes*.

Floating-point literals can be specified either with or without signed integer exponents, as illustrated in Table 2.10.

Table 2.10	Floating-Point Literals
0.1234567	`double` is default floating-point literal
1.234F	`float` is smallest floating-point literal
3. 3.0 0.3E1	all express `double` 3.0
300e-2	also 3.0

2.1.5   OPERATORS AND PUNCTUATORS

C# allows operators, punctuators, and white space to separate language elements. Table 2.11 lists some C# operators.

Table 2.11	Some C# Operators				
+	–	*	/	%	arithmetic operators
&&	||				logical operators
=	+=	*=			assignment operators
(*type*)					cast operator
new					memory allocation operator

Operators are used in expressions and are meaningful when given appropriate arguments. C# has many operators. Certain symbols stand for different operators, depending on context; for instance, – can be either unary or binary minus. A unary operator is an operator on one argument, and a binary operator is an operator on two arguments. The unary minus expression –(*expression)* is equivalent in value to the binary minus expression 0 – *expression*. A complete list of operators with their precedence is presented in Appendix B, *Operator Precedence and Associativity*.

Punctuators include parentheses, braces, commas, and colons, and are uscd to structure elements of a program. For example, the following contain punctuators in C#:

```
Test(a, 7, b + 8)           // comma-separated argument list
{ a = b; c = d; }           // {starts statement list or block
```

2.2   CONSOLE INPUT/OUTPUT

C# input/output (I/O) is not directly part of the language, but rather is added as a set of routines found in a standard library. We discuss I/O in detail in Chapter 9, *Input/Output*. Until then we rely largely on the simple use of the methods `Console.Write()` and `Console.WriteLine()` for output. Both methods print to the console, and `WriteLine()` additionally advances the cursor to a new line. What is especially nice about this method is that it can automatically convert a value to a string representation for display on the console. For input, we rely on `Console.Read-Line()`. This obtains a string literal as entered on the keyboard. That string is terminated by pressing the Enter key. We see how both of these methods are used in the following program.

In file BasicIO.cs

```csharp
using System;

class BasicIO {
  public static void Main()
  {
    int i;
    double x;
    string data;

    Console.WriteLine("Enter a double:");
    data = Console.ReadLine();
    x = double.Parse(data);
    Console.WriteLine("Enter a positive integer:");
    data = Console.ReadLine();
    i = int.Parse(data);
    while (i < 1) {
      Console.WriteLine("error i = " + i );
      Console.WriteLine("Enter a positive integer:");
      data = Console.ReadLine();
      i = int.Parse(data);
    }
    Console.WriteLine("i * x = " + i * x );
  }
}
```

Here is some sample output:

```
Enter a double:
2.556
Enter a positive integer:
156
i * x = 398.736
```

In this example, the user entered the floating-point 1.2 and the integer 3 with the result being output as the double value 3.6.

Dissection of the *BasicIO* Program

```
■int i;
  double x;
  string data;
```

The program uses three variables i, x, and data. It is usual in short programs to place declarations at the head of the block. In longer programs variables are often declared near to their first use. The string variable data is used to read in an input line typed at the console. This string is then converted to either integer or floating-point values.

```
■Console.WriteLine("Enter a double:");
  data = Console.ReadLine();
  x = double.Parse(data);
```

If we run this program, the first output statement in the preceding code places a string on the screen. This string, "Enter a double:", prompts the user for an input value of appropriate type. The second statement gets a string input typed at the keyboard. The string needs to represent a value that is either a double or assignment-convertible to a double. If the input is correct the third statement parses the string to extract the appropriate double value to be assigned to x.

```
Console.WriteLine("Enter a positive integer:");
data = Console.ReadLine();
i = int.Parse(data);
while (i < 1) {
    Console.WriteLine("error i = " + i);
    Console.WriteLine("Enter a positive integer:");
    data = Console.ReadLine();
    i = int.Parse(data);
}
```

Again we obtain an input string. The third statement parses the string to extract the appropriate `int` value to be assigned to `i`. Notice how the `while` statement insists on getting a positive integer value for input. When programs are to be heavily used, it is important to test that the input is correct. For example, if -1 was entered the following would be printed:

```
error i = -1
    Enter a positive integer:
```

```
Console.WriteLine("i * x = " + i * x);
}
```

The last statement prints the string `i * x = `, followed by the `double` value of the expression `i * x`. It is important to be careful in such expressions to make sure the precedence is correct. In this case `+` is as expected the string operator concatenate. In case of any confusion, it is good practice to use parentheses as in `"i * x = " + (i + x)` where the first plus sign is concatenate and the second plus sign is addition.

2.2.1 FORMATTING THE OUTPUT

Both the `Write()` and `WriteLine()` construct a string of the arguments passed and output that string to the console. An empty argument list may be used with `WriteLine()` to output a newline. We have already seen the use of the newline character `'\n'` to force a line feed. Another commonly used character is the tab `'\t'`. There are several other escaped characters used specifically for formatting:

Table 2.12	Formatting Characters
\n	carriage return and newline
\t	tab
\r	carriage return only
\v	vertical tab
\f	form feed

In addition to the single string arguments we have used thus far, both `Write()` and `WriteLine()` can produce formatted output by using a string containing formats followed by list of arguments. A *format* is a description of how an argument is to be printed. Some of the concepts here are advanced and are covered in more detail in Section 9.3.2, *Creating a User-Defined Format*, on page 385. For now, we present a simplified explanation so that you can use the `Write()` and `WriteLine()` to produce nicely formatted output. A simple example of their use would be to replace from the last program

```
Console.WriteLine("i * x = " + i * x);
```

with

```
Console.WriteLine("i * x = {0}", i * x);
```

Notice that embedded in the string is the format specification {0}. This means look for the 0th argument that is immediately to the right of the comma, namely, `i * x` and place its string representation at this point in the output string.

The general form is

```
Write(string, args)
WriteLine(string, args)
```

where *string* contains a string with embedded format parameters and *args* may be 0 or more variables to be formatted. Some of the format options include specifying how many characters to output, padding with blanks, filling with leading zeroes, aligning left or right, specifying the number of decimal places to output, and specifying that the number be output as a currency, percentage, or comma-delimited number.

The format parameter has the general form

{N, M:C}

where:

> *N* is a zero-based integer indicating the argument to be formatted. An argument is ignored if it is not referenced by a formatting parameter in the string, but a missing argument results in a runtime exception being thrown. The argument list need not be invoked in order, and an argument may be referenced by more than one formatting parameter.
>
> *M* is an optional integer indicating the width of the region to contain the formatted value, padded with spaces. If the sign of M is negative, the formatted value is left-justified in the region; if the sign of M is positive, the value is right-justified. If M is too small to represent the number, M is ignored and the entire value is output according to formatting code specified.
>
> *C* is an optional string of formatting codes.

Table 2.13 shows some of the more frequently used formatting codes.

Table 2.13	Some Standard Formatting Codes
Conversion character	How the corresponding argument is printed
C, c	as currency
D, d	as a decimal integer
X, x	as an unsigned hexadecimal integer
E, e	as a floating-point number
F, f	as a fixed-point number (defaults to 2 places)
G, g	in the e-format or f-format, whichever is shorter
S, s	as a string
N, n	a numerical fixed point format with embedded commas

The following program demonstrates the use of formatting.

In file FormatUse1.cs

```
using System;
public class FormatUse {
  public static void Main()
  {
    double x = 12.3456789;
    int y = 78;
    Console.WriteLine("One: {0} Two: {1}.", x, y);
    Console.WriteLine("One: {0:F2} Two: {1:C2}.", x, y);
    Console.WriteLine("One: {0,15:F4} Two: {1:F}.", x, y);
    Console.WriteLine("One: {1,-15} Two: {0:F3}.", x, y);
  }
}
```

The output is

```
One: 12.3456789 Two: 78.
One: 12.35 Two: $78.00.
One:         12.3457 Two: 78.00.
One: 78               Two: 12.346.
```

Dissection of the *FormatUse* Program

```
■double x = 12.3456789;
 int y = 78;
 Console.WriteLine("One: {0} Two: {1}.", x, y);
```

This `WriteLine()` has three arguments: the defining string argument and the two numeric arguments x and y. The string argument "One: {0} Two: {1}." contains two format parameters, namely, {0} and {1}. Format parameters have the general form {*N*, *M*: *C*}, where *N* is the number of the argument in the following argument list, *M* is the optional size of the resulting substring to produce, and *C* is the formatting code. You can think of the output string as being constructed by taking the string argument and putting a placeholder, say @, in where there is a format parameter. In this example, we have

```
"One: @ Two: @."
```

The format parameter {0} says output x and {1} says output y. Since only the number of the argument (counting from 0) is given in the format parameter, the arguments x and y are output with a default formatting based on their type producing the string

```
"One: 12.3456789 Two: 78."
```

■WriteLine(One: {0:F2} Two: {1:C2}.);

This `WriteLine()` also has three arguments: the defining string argument and the two numeric arguments x and y, but the format parameters now contain a format code. (See Table 2.13 for a list of format codes). {0:F2} indicates that the 0th argument, x, is to be output as a floating-point number to 2 decimal places. {1:C2} indicates that y should be output as a currency to two decimal places.

■WriteLine("One: {0,15:F4} Two: {1:F}.", x, y);

In {0,15:F4}, 0 corresponds to the 0th argument following the string. The 0th argument is x, so {0,15:F4} is applied to x.

The 15 indicates that x is output in 15 characters total with blank padding on the right. The F4 means that the number is to be output as a decimal with four significant digits, padded on the right with zeroes if needed.

Similarly, {1:F} indicates that y should be output as a floating-point number. The default is to output to 2 decimal places, making the resulting string output for y be "78.00".

■WriteLine("One: {1,-15} Two: {0:F3}.", x, y);

The format parameter {1,-15} results in the output of y as a 15 character string representation padded on the left with blanks. The {0:F3} acts on x to output a floating-point number with 3 decimal places. If we attempt to display x with {0:D}, an error results because it would attempt to output the floating-point number as an `int`, losing information. Note also that x and y were referenced y first, then x, despite the comment to the contrary.

The following program further illustrates the use of formatting in output strings.

In file FormatUse2.cs

```
using System;

public class FormatUse {
  public static void Main()
  {
    double x = 12.3456;
    int y = 78;

    Console.WriteLine("$ !{0,8:C2}!{1,8:C2}!", x, y);
    Console.WriteLine("xG!{0,8}!{0,8:G3}!{0,-8:G3}!", x);
    Console.WriteLine("xF!{0,8:F}!{0,8:F3}!{0,-8:F3}!", x);
    Console.WriteLine("yG!{0,8}!{0,8:G3}!{0,-8:G3}!", y);
    Console.WriteLine("yF!{0,8:F}!{0,8:F3}!{0,-8:F3}!", y);
    Console.WriteLine("yD!{0,8:D}!{0,8:D3}!{0,-8:D3}!", y);
    Console.WriteLine("\nOver write !\rUnder");
  }
}
```

The output of this program is

```
$ !   $12.35!   $78.00!
xG!  12.3456!      12.3!12.3      !
xF!    12.35!  12.346!12.346     !
yG!       78!        78!78        !
yF!    78.00!  78.000!78.000     !
yD!       78!       078!078       !

Underwrite !
```

In this example we used the field width property to align the output nicely in 8 character fields. Note also how the G option works: it displays the value up to the maximum number of digits specified without zero fill. The last line of text is somewhat mysterious because of the embedded control character \r that causes an overwrite of the word Over. As noted in Table 2.12, \r outputs a carriage return, without advancing to a new line. Hence, \r positions the output to the beginning of the current line, thus overwriting any underlying characters.

2.3 PROGRAM STRUCTURE

A program is a collection of methods and declarations. C# is block structured, and variables declared within blocks are allocated automatically on block entry. Unless otherwise specified, parameters are call-by-value as discussed in Section 4.8, *Invocation and Call-By-Value*, on page 140. The following program computes the greatest common divisor of two integers:

In file Gcd.cs

```csharp
// Gcd greatest common divisor program

using System;
class GreatestCommonDivisor {
  public static int Gcd(int m, int n)        // definition
  {                                          // block begin
    int  r;                       // declaration of remainder
    while (n != 0) {                          // not equal
      r = m % n;                          // modulus operator
      m = n;                                 // assignment
      n = r;
    }                                       // end while loop
    return m;                      // exit Gcd with value m
  }

  public static void Main()
  {
    int  x, y, howMany;
    string data;

    Console.WriteLine("PROGRAM Gcd in C#");
    Console.WriteLine("Enter how many:");
    data = Console.ReadLine();
    howMany = int.Parse(data);
```

```
    for (int i = 0; i < howMany; ++i) {
      Console.WriteLine("\nEnter two integers:");
      Console.WriteLine("One per line");
      data = Console.ReadLine();
      x = int.Parse(data);
      data = Console.ReadLine();
      y = int.Parse(data);
      Console.WriteLine("\nGcd({0}, {1}) = {2}",
                             x, y, Gcd(x, y));
    }
  }
}
```

Here is some sample output for 2 pairs of values:

```
PROGRAM Gcd in C#
Enter how many:
2

Enter two integers:
One per line
394815
48

Gcd(394815, 48) = 3

Enter two integers:
One per line
12
96

Gcd(12, 96) = 12
```

C# compilers can compile multifile programs. Large C# programs are prepared as separate files where each file is conceptually a module that contains one or more classes. So,

csc Class1.cs Class2.cs MainClass.cs

is the C# compile command acting on three files: *Class1.cs*, *Class2.cs*, and *MainClass.cs*. If compilation shows no errors, an executable *MainClass.exe* is produced. Further compilation overwrites the previous *MainClass.exe*.

Note that we use the file naming convention that starts file names with an uppercase letter with new words starting also with an uppercase letter and ends with the *.cs* file extension.

Dissection of the *Gcd* Program

```
int Gcd(int m, int n)
```

The core language relies on functional encapsulation to produce well designed modular programs. The method name should be chosen to be meaningful. In this case Gcd is a standard abbreviation for greatest common divisor. The method has two integer arguments passed by value. See Section 4.8, *Invocation and Call-By-Value*, on page 140.

```
{                                      // block begin
   int  r;                  // declaration of remainder
```

Method definitions are blocks. A block begins with an open (left) brace and includes declaration and executable statements. In C#, declaration statements can occur anywhere in a block. In small blocks, it is usual to place all declarations at the head of the block. In large blocks, it is often the case that declarations appear just before the first use of the associated variable.

```
while (n != 0) {                            // not equal
   r = m % n;                        // modulus operator
   m = n;                                // assignment
   n = r;
}                                      // end while loop
```

The while statement is a basic looping construct controlled by a bool expression. In this case as long as the expression "n is not equal to zero" is true, the statement block after the while expression is executed. The statement block is any number of contiguous statements between a matching set of braces. In this case, there are three assignment statements that constitute the heart of the greatest common divisor algorithm. The operator % is the integer modulo operator, meaning in this case, r is assigned m modulo n.

```
■   return m;                           // exit Gcd with value m
```

The `return` statement terminates the method. Here, the `return` statement returns an integer value as the value of `Gcd()` at the point the method was called in `Main()`.

```
■public static void Main()
{
  int  x, y, howMany;
  string data;

  Console.WriteLine("PROGRAM Gcd in C#");
```

The `Main()` method initiates the running of a C# program calling any subsidiary method, such as `Gcd()`. Here `Main()` prints out a message calling attention to its use. It is important to have input/output be clear and robust so that an untrained user of a program can readily use it without detailed knowledge of the program's components.

```
■Console.WriteLine("Enter how many:");
data = Console.ReadLine();
howMany = int.Parse(data);
for (int i = 0; i < howMany; ++i) {
```

The `for` statement is a loop that is executed `howMany` times. Here just before the loop, the user is prompted for the value of `howMany`. Note that the `for` loop variable `i` is declared inside the `for` statement; this is not possible in C.

```
■Console.WriteLine("\nEnter two integers: ");
Console.WriteLine("One per line");
data = Console.ReadLine();
x = int.Parse(data);
data = Console.ReadLine();
y = int.Parse(data);
```

Inside the loop, the user is asked for two integer values. These are stored in the `x` and `y` variables.

```
Console.WriteLine("\nGcd({0}, {1}) = {2}",
                   x, y, Gcd(x, y));
}
```

The variables x and y are used as arguments to Gcd(). The final brace ends the loop. The output uses formatting. We could also have written the argument to WriteLine() as a concatenated string:

```
Console.WriteLine("\nGcd(" + x + ", " + y +") = " +
                   Gcd(x, y));
```

It is easier to see the form of the intended output and what is being output when the arguments are written as arguments at the end of the statement that uses formatting.

2.3.1 REDIRECTION

On most systems, input can be *redirected* from a file. Assume the *Gcd* program has been compiled into an executable file called *Gcd*. The command

Gcd < Gcd.dat

takes its input from the file *Gcd.dat* and writes the answers to the screen. Test this with a file containing

```
4    4  6  6  21  8  20  15  20
```

On most systems, output can also be redirected to a file. The following command

Gcd > Gcd.ans

places its output in the file *Gcd.ans,* taking its input from the keyboard. Note that the messages prompting the user for input also go to that file, and the user has to know what to do without being prompted on the screen.

Enter the same data as before and check the file *Gcd.ans* to see that it has the four correct answers. The two redirections can be combined as follows:

Gcd < Gcd.dat > Gcd.ans

This command line takes its input from the file *Gcd.dat* and places its output in the file *Gcd.ans*. Test this on your system. Redirection is a very useful system feature.

2.4 SIMPLE TYPES

Some representative *simple native types* in C# are `bool`, `int`, `double`, `char`, and `byte`. These types have a set of values and representation that makes them appropriate for different variables used in a computation. You need to choose the simplest and most efficient type for the job. The `bool` type provides a native boolean type, and `char` provides a two-byte Unicode character type, used for representing character sets requiring more than the standard ASCII characters.

C# integral simple types include `short`, `int`, `long`, `ushort`, `uint`, and `ulong`. They represent, from `short` to `long`, integer types that can represent bigger ranges of values. The types prefaced by `u` are the unsigned types. They are used to represent integers whose values are 0 or positive. Table 2.14 lists these types, from shortest to longest. Bytes here refers to the number of bytes used to store the type.

Table 2.14	Simple Native Integer Types	
Basic Type	Bytes	Values
short	2	(-32768, 32767)
ushort	2	(0, 65535)
int	4	(-2147483648, 2147483647)
uint	4	(0, 4294967295)
long	8	(-9223372036854775808, 9223372036854775807)
ulong	8	(0, 18446744073709551615)

C# floating-point simple types include `float`, `double`, and `decimal`. They are used to represent real numbers whose values are often only approximated on a computer to a certain number of significant digits. Table 2.15 lists these types, from shortest to longest. Bytes here refers to the number of bytes used to store the type.

Table 2.15		Simple Native Floating Types
Basic Type	Bytes	Values
float	4	$(\pm 3.4 \times 10^{38})$ 7 significant digits
double	8	$(\pm 1.7 \times 10^{308})$ 15–16 significant digits
decimal	16	Fixed precision up to 28 or 29 digits in the range 1.0e-28 to 7.9e+28. Need to use "m" or "M"

Unlike in C and C++, but like in Java, in C# these byte sizes are system independent.

As a rule, use the `int` type for most integer arithmetic, and `double` for most floating-point arithmetic. These types are the most efficient for their particular machines and compilers. Shorter types can be used if memory space is a priority. Longer types should be used when range of values or precision is needed.

2.4.1 DECLARATION AND INITIALIZATION

A variable declaration associates a type with the variable name. A declaration can also initialize the value of the variable. Initialization is expressed by following the identifier name with an initializer. For simple variables, this expression has the form

type id = expression

In C# a variable must be initialized or assigned before it is used. If it is not, the compiler complains. This is a very useful error indicator as uninitialized variables in languages that allow them, such as C, cause many hard-to-detect runtime bugs. The following program contains some examples of declarations.

In file SimpleVariables.cs

```
// Declaring and initializing variables.

using System;
class SimpleVariables {
  public static void Main()
  {
    int     i = 5;                        // i is initialized to 5
    char    c1 = 'B', c2;                 // c2 is uninitialized
    double  x = 0.777, y = x + i;

    Console.WriteLine("i = " + i);            // print i = 5
    Console.WriteLine("x = " + x);        // print x = 0.777
    Console.WriteLine("y = " + y);             // y =5.777
    Console.WriteLine("c1 = " + c1);       // print c1 = B
    c2 = c1;                           // c2 assigned before use
    Console.WriteLine("c2 = " + c2);        // print c2 = B
  }
}
```

The output of this program is

```
i = 5
x = 0.777
y = 5.777
c1 = B
c2 = B
```

Dissection of the *SimpleVariables* Program

```
■{
    int     i = 5;                   // i is initialized to 5
```

This is a typical declaration of a simple variable. It says that within the block started by the open left brace, the variable i is of type `int` and has initial value set to 5.

```
char    c1 = 'B', c2;              // c2 is uninitialized
double  x = 0.777, y = x + i;
```

In a declaration statement, you can declare and initialize several variables of the stated type. For example, both c1 and c2 are declared to be char. The variable c2 is uninitialized. It is later assigned a value before its actual use. Initialization can involve an arbitrary expression, provided that all of the variables and methods used in the expression are defined. In the preceding example, y is initialized in terms of the just-defined x and i. As a rule of thumb, when there is a choice, it is better to initialize a variable than to define it as uninitialized and assign it a value later. Initialization makes the code more readable, less error-prone, and more efficient.

```
  c2 = c1;                           // c2 assigned before use
  Console.WriteLine("c2 = " + c2 );   // print c2 = B
}
```

C# requires that variables have values before they are first used. This was not true of C and C++. This rule enforced by the compiler as a syntax error prevents many runtime mistakes. Here c2 is assigned a value which is printed in the following statement.

Syntactically, C# declarations are themselves statements, and can occur intermixed with executable statements. This differs from C, in which declarations are not syntactical statements and must be either in global scope or at the head of a block. In the previous code, we could have placed the char declarations after the first two WriteLine statements without affecting the output.

```
. . . . .
char    c1 = 'B', c2;                    // c2 is uninitialized
Console.WriteLine("c1 = " + c1 );            // print c1 = B
c2 = c1;                              // c2 assigned before use
Console.WriteLine("c2 = " + c2 );            // print c2 = B
```

2.4.2 IMPLICIT CONVERSIONS

The expression x + y has both a value and a type. For example, if x and y are both variables of type int, x + y is also an int. However, if x and y are of different types, x + y is a *mixed expression*. Suppose that x is a short and y an int. The value of x is converted, or *coerced*, to an int, and the expression x + y has type int. The value of x as stored in memory is unchanged. It is only a temporary copy of x that is converted during the computation of the value of the expression. These conversions occur when there are numeric types of different ranges. The conversions widen to a type that can best accommodate the resulting value. The general rules are straightforward.

Automatic Arithmetic Expression Conversions

1. For the signed types the following hierarchy exists:

   ```
   sbyte < short < int <  long
         <  float    <  double < decimal
   ```

2. For the unsigned types the following hierarchy exists:

   ```
   byte < ushort < uint <  ulong
   ```

   The unsigned types can also convert to next longest signed type, so byte becomes short, ushort becomes int, uint becomes long, and ulong becomes float.

3. The char type widens to either ushort or int.
   The operand of the lower type is promoted to that of the higher type, and the value of the expression has that type.

To illustrate implicit conversion, Table 2.16 makes declarations and lists a variety of mixed expressions along with their corresponding types.

Table 2.16	Declarations		
char c;	long lg;	double d;	
short s;	float f;	uint u;	int i;
Expression	**Type**	**Expression**	**Type**
c - s / i	int	u * 3 - i	long
u * 3.0 - i	double	f * 3 - i	float
c + 1	int	3 * s * lg	long
c + 1.0	double	d + s	double

An automatic conversion can occur with an assignment. For example, d = i causes the value of i, which is an int, to be converted to a double and then assigned to d; double is the type of the expression as a whole. A promotion, or *widening*, such as d = i, is usually reliable, but a demotion, or *narrowing*, such as i = d, can lose information. Demotions are illegal as implicit conversions. Narrowings can be performed by using the explicit cast operator.

2.4.3 EXPLICIT CONVERSIONS CALLED CASTS

In addition to implicit conversions, which can occur across assignments and in mixed expressions, there are explicit conversions called *casts*. Casting is usually done for narrowing conversions. An example is if i is an int,

```
(double)i
```

casts the value of i so that the expression has type double. The variable i itself remains unchanged. Some more examples are:

```
char y = (char)('A' + 1);
int i = (int)(1.2 * y + 0.5);
Console.WriteLine("1/2 = " + 1/2);                     // 0
Console.WriteLine("(double)1/2 = " + (double)1/2);     // 0.5
```

The next program converts pounds to kilograms and then computes body mass index.

In file BodyFat.cs

```
// Pounds to Kilograms and Body Mass Index BMI
using System;

class BodyFat {
  public static void Main()
  {
    const double   kiloToPound = 2.2046,
                   inchToMeter = 39.370;
    int  weight, height;            // in pounds and inches
    double kilograms, meters;
```

```
Console.WriteLine("Enter weight in pounds:");
string data = Console.ReadLine();
weight = int.Parse(data);
kilograms = weight / kiloToPound;
Console.WriteLine("\nThis is approximately "
                    + (int) kilograms + "kg.");

Console.WriteLine("\nEnter height in inches:");
data = Console.ReadLine();
height = int.Parse(data);
meters = height/inchToMeter;

Console.WriteLine("\nYour BMI is approximately "
    + kilograms/(meters * meters)
    + ". \nUnder 25 is good." );
    }
}
```

Here is an example output of this program

```
Enter weight in pounds:
121

This is approximately 54kg.

Enter height in inches:
63

Your BMI is approximately 21.4341022380036.
Under 25 is good.
```

Dissection of Casting in the *BodyFat* Program

■`const double  kiloToPound = 2.2046,`
              `inchToMeter = 39.370;`

The variables `kiloToPound` and `inchToMeter` are initialized to the values `2.2046`, and `39.370`, respectively. The `const` modifier means these values are nonmodifiable. As a result, the identifiers are mnemonic and provide useful documentation. A `const` variable must be initialized on definition.

■`int  weight, height;               // in pounds and inches`
`double kilograms, meters;`

The variable names are chosen for specific meanings they convey.

■`Console.WriteLine("\nThis is approximately "`
                `+ (int) kilograms + "kg.");`

The `double` value of the variable `kilograms` is narrowed to an `int`. The cast `(int)(kilograms)` truncates the `double` value to an `int` value. Without this explicit cast, the variable `kilometers` would have printed as a `double`.

■`Console.WriteLine("\nYour BMI is approximately "`
    `+ kilograms/(meters * meters)`
    `+ ". \nUnder 25 is good." );`

The output of the BMI number is a double, which may output more precision than you want. Alternatively, you can narrow the BMI to an `int` with

   `(int)(kilograms/(meters * meters))`

but this loses some information.

2.5 ENUMERATION TYPES

The keyword `enum` is used to declare a distinct value type with a set of named integer constants called *enumerators*. Consider the declaration

```
enum Suit { Clubs, Diamonds, Hearts, Spades }
```

This declaration creates an integer type with the four suit names—`Clubs`, `Diamonds`, `Hearts`, and `Spades`—as integer constants, whose values are 0, 1, 2, and 3, respectively. These values are assigned by default, with the first enumerator being given the constant integer value 0. Each subsequent member of the list is one more than its left neighbor. The identifier `Suit` is now its own unique type, distinct from other types. C# style is to capitalize this type identifier as well as the enumerator names.

Enumerators can be defined and initialized to arbitrary integer constants.

```
enum Ages { Linda = 29, Chet, Dan = 16,
            Ben = Dan - 5, Max }
```

The enumerators can be initialized to constant expressions. Note that the default rule applies when there is no explicit initializer; therefore, in the example, `Chet` is 30, `Ben` is 11, and `Max` is 12.

The `enum` name and the enumerators must be distinct identifiers within scope. The values of enumerators need not be distinct. Enumerations can be explicitly converted to ordinary integer types.

2.6 EXPRESSIONS

In C#, there are many special characters with particular meanings. Examples include the arithmetic operators:

```
+      –      *      /      %
```

which stand for the usual arithmetic operations of addition, subtraction, multiplication, division, and modulus, respectively. In mathematics, the value of *a* modulus *b* is obtained by taking the remainder after dividing *a* by *b*. Thus, for example, 5 % 3 has the value 2, and 7 % 2 has the value 1. In a program, operators can be used to separate identifiers. Although not required, for style reasons we put white space around binary operators to heighten readability.

```
a + b                                    // a added to b
-a                      // -a is unary minus equal to 0 - a
```

Some special characters are used in different ways in different contexts, and the context determines which way is intended. For example, parentheses are sometimes used to indicate a method name; at other times, they are punctuators. Another example is given by the expressions

```
a + b                              // binary operator add
++a                         // ++ unary operator increment
a += b          // += add-assignment operator means a = a + b
```

All of these expressions use + as a character, but ++ is a single operator, as is +=. Having the meaning of a symbol depend on context makes for a small symbol set and a terse language.

2.6.1   PRECEDENCE AND ASSOCIATIVITY OF OPERATORS

Operators have rules of *precedence* and *associativity* that determine precisely how expressions are evaluated. Because expressions inside parentheses are evaluated first, parentheses can be used to clarify or change the order in which operations are performed. Consider the expression

```
1 + 2 * 3
```

The operator * has higher precedence than +, causing the multiplication to be performed first, followed by the addition. Hence, the value of the expression is 7. An equivalent expression is

```
1 + (2 * 3)
```

On the other hand, because expressions inside parentheses are evaluated first,

```
(1 + 2) * 3
```

is different; its value is 9. Now consider the equivalent expressions

```
1 + 2 - 3 + 4 - 5    and    (((1 + 2) - 3) + 4) - 5
```

Because the binary operators + and – have the same precedence, the associativity rule *left to right* is used to determine how it is evaluated. This means the operations are performed from left to right. Thus, they are equivalent expressions.

The following table gives the rules of precedence and associativity for the operators of C#. Table 2.17 is an important reference and is repeated in Appendix B, *Operator Precedence and Associativity*, for ease of reference. We use pieces of this table when dealing with subcategories of expressions, such as the logical expressions.

Table 2.17 Operator Precedence and Associativity						Associativity
func() [] typeof(*e*) checked	(*postfix*) ++ sizeof(*e*) unchecked	(*postfix*) -- (*e*) new	name.name			left to right
++ (*prefix*) + (*unary*)	-- (*prefix*) - (*unary*)	! (*type*)(*e*)	~			right to left
*	/	%				left to right
+	-					left to right
<<	>>					left to right
<	<=	>	>=	is	as	left to right
==	!=					left to right
&						left to right
^						left to right
|						left to right
&&						left to right
||						left to right
?:						right to left
= += -= *=	/= %= >>=	<<= &= ^=	|=			right to left

All operators on a given line, such as *, /, and %, have equal precedence with respect to one another, but have higher precedence than all the operators on the lines below them. The associativity rule for all the operators on a given line appears on the right side of the table. These rules are essential information for every C# programmer.

C# operators include nearly all the C operators, but also several not found in C, such as the memory management operator `new` and the type identifier operator `typeof`.

From the preceding table, we see that the unary operators have higher precedence than binary plus and minus. In the expression

```
- a * b - c
```

the first minus sign is unary, and the second, binary. Using the rules of precedence, we see that

```
((- a) * b) - c
```

is an equivalent expression.

C# has many operators and expression forms. Arithmetic expressions in C# are normally consistent with C practice. For example, in both C# and C, the results of an operator, such as the division operator /, depend on its argument types.

```
3 / 2;                        // evaluates to integer value 1
3 / 2.0;                      // evaluates to double value 1.5
```

2.6.2 THE DOT OPERATOR

We have lots of names (or identifiers) in any C# program. Some we make up for use in our program, and some are names for standard classes and methods. For example we often use the method `Console.WriteLine()`. A name that is a series of dotted-together identifiers is called a *qualified name.* Let us look at names in the following class.

In file PrintSuit.cs

```
// Suit and dot -qualified names

using System;

class PrintSuit {
   public enum Suit { Clubs, Diamonds, Hearts, Spades }
```

```
public static void Main()
{
  Suit d = Suit.Clubs;
  if (d == Suit.Clubs)
    Console.Write("clubs");
  else if (d == Suit.Diamonds)
    Console.Write("diamonds");
  else if (d == Suit.Hearts)
    Console.Write("hearts");
  else if (d == Suit.Spades)
    Console.Write("spades");
  else
    Console.Write("unknown");
}
}
```

The output of this program is

```
clubs
```

The names d, Console.Write, Suit, Main, Clubs, and Suit.Clubs all appear in this code. These names appear in a given class PrintSuit. From outside of this class the qualified name PrintSuit.Suit is used to refer to the enumerated type Suit.

Dissection of the *PrintSuit* Program

```
■class PrintSuit {
   public enum Suit { Clubs, Diamonds, Hearts, Spades }
```

We have the declaration of the enumerated type Suit inside the class PrintSuit. The complete name for this enumerated type is Print-Suit.Suit. The four enumerators have integer constant values where Clubs is 0, Diamonds is 1, Hearts is 2, and Spades is 3.

```
public static void Main()
{
  Suit d = Suit.Clubs;
```

The enumerator `Clubs` is inside the type `Suit`. To refer to it we need its qualified name using the dot operator, namely `Suit.Clubs`.

```
if (d == Suit.Clubs)
    Console.Write("clubs");
  else if (d == Suit.Diamonds)
    Console.Write("diamonds");
  else if (d == Suit.Hearts)
    Console.Write("hearts");
  else if (d == Suit.Spades)
    Console.Write("spades");
  else
    Console.Write("unknown");
```

This statement is an `if-else` statement described in detail in Section 3.3, *The if and if-else Statements*, on page 85. Basically, the `if-else` statement lets you selectively execute statements based on a test or series of tests.

2.6.3   RELATIONAL, EQUALITY, AND LOGICAL OPERATORS

Just as with other operators, the relational, equality, and logical operators have rules of precedence and associativity that determine precisely how expressions involving them are evaluated. C# systems use the `bool` values `true` and `false` to direct the flow of control in the various statement types. Table 2.18 contains the C# operators that are most often used to affect flow of control.

Table 2.18 Relational, Equality, and Logical Operators		
Relational operators	less than	<
	greater than	>
	less than or equal to	<=
	greater than or equal to	>=
	type match test	is
Equality operators	equal to	==
	not equal to	!=
Logical operators	(unary) negation	!
	logical and	&&
	logical or	||

The negation operator ! is unary. All of the other relational, equality, and logical operators are binary, operate on expressions, and yield a bool value, either false or true.

A common C# programming mistake is to code something like

```
if (i = 1)
  // do something
```

intending

```
if (i == 1)
  // do something
```

The first if statement assigns 1 to i and evaluates to 1. The compiler catches this syntax error because a bool expression is required to control an if statement. In C, this would be a runtime bug. This is one of the many safety improvements in C#.

The logical operators !, &&, and ||, when applied to expressions, yield the bool value true or false. Logical negation can be applied to an arbitrary expression. If an expression has value false, its negation yields true.

The precedence of && is higher than ||, but both operators are of lower precedence than all unary, arithmetic, and relational operators. Their associativity is left to right.

In the evaluation of expressions that are the operands of && and ||, the evaluation process stops as soon as the outcome true or false is known. This is called *short-circuit* evaluation. For example, suppose that *expr1* and *expr2* are boolean expressions and that *expr1* has value `false`. In *expr1* && *expr2*, the expression *expr2* is not evaluated, because the value of the logical expression is already determined to be false. Similarly, if *expr1* is `true`, then *expr2* in *expr1* || *expr2* is not evaluated, because the value of the logical expression is already determined as `true`. Table 2.19 shows some examples in C#.

Table 2.19	Declarations and Initialization	
`int a = 1, b = 2, c = 0;`		
C#	**Parenthesized Equivalent**	**Value**
`(a > 5) && (b == 2)`	`((a > 5) && (b == 2))`	false
`!(a < b) && (c < 3)`	`((!(a < b)) && (c < 3))`	false
`(a != b)||(c == 0)`	`((a!= b)|| (c == 0))`	true

Short-circuit evaluation is an important feature. The following code illustrates its importance in a typical situation:

```
// Compute the roots of: a * x * x + b * x + c
.....
discr = b * b - 4 * a * c;
if ((discr >= 0) && (sqrtd = Math.Sqrt(discr)) != 0) {
  root1 = (-b + sqrtd) / (2 * a);
  root2 = (-b - sqrtd) / (2 * a);
}
else if (discr == 0)
  root1 = root2 = -b / (2 * a);

else {                                          // complex roots
  .....
}
.....
```

The `Math.Sqrt()` method would fail on negative values, and short-circuit evaluation protects the program from this error.

The conditional operator `?:` is unusual in that it is a ternary operator. It takes three expressions as operands.

expr1 `?` *expr2* `:` *expr3*

In this construct, *expr1* is evaluated first. If *expr1* is `true`, then *expr2* is evaluated and the result is the value of the conditional expression as a whole. If *expr1* is `false`, *expr3* is evaluated, and the result is the value of the conditional expression as a whole. The following example uses a conditional operator to assign the smaller of two values to the variable x:

```
x = (y < z) ? y : z;
```

Because the conditional operator has precedence over the assignment operator, the parentheses are not necessary, but they help make clear the nature of the test.

The type of the conditional expression

expr1 ? *expr2* : *expr3*

is determined by *expr2* and *expr3*. If they are different types, the usual conversion rules apply. The conditional expression's type cannot depend on which of the two expressions *expr2* or *expr3* is evaluated. The conditional operator ?: associates right to left.

C# provides bit-manipulation operators, shown in Table 2.20, which operate on the bit representation of integral operands. For example, the operand ~ changes an integral operand bit-representation into its one's complement. These operators can be ignored by programmers who don't manipulate underlying bit representations.

Table 2.20	Bitwise Operators
~	unary one's complement
<<	left shift
>>	right shift
&	and
^	exclusive or
|	or

C# considers *method call* ( ) and *indexing* or *subscripting* [ ] to be operators.

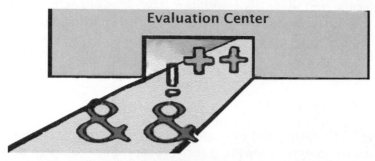

I know we were here first, but he has higher precedence!

2.7   SOFTWARE ENGINEERING: DEBUGGING

Getting your code to work correctly is crucial. A key skill in software development is how to avoid or find errors. The general term for finding errors in programming is *debugging*.

Correct choice and use of type is one of the programmer's main techniques in avoiding errors. Languages that are strongly typed are safer to program in than languages that are weakly typed. C is considered a weakly typed, and therefore error-prone, language. C# is a strongly typed language.

A classic C or C# error is an expression of the form

```
double x, y = 2.5;
int i = 5;

x = y + i / 3;
Console.WriteLine("x = " + x);              // prints x = 3.5
```

when the programmer's intention was to have i / 3.0. With the denominator being a double, the division would be double and x would equal 4.13333. All C# expressions should be examined for suspicious conversions. Also, the programmer should test code on some simple data for which the results are already known. This technique, called hand simulation, was discussed in Section 1.3.1, *Algorithms—Being Precise*, on page 11.

Section D.6, *Tracing Program Execution*, on page 548, is an extensive section on using the integrated debugger in Visual Studio .NET. This allows you to run your program line-by-line and, most importantly, watch variable values change.

2.8   DR. P'S PRESCRIPTIONS

- Use parentheses to make expressions readable.

- For readability, add space after each token except the semicolon and unary operators.

- Avoid side-effect operators, such as ++, in complex expressions unless they are used in a known idiomatic style.

- Avoid the use of `set`, `get`, and `value` as ordinary identifiers.

Parentheses in expressions can be used to aid clarity by making grouping and precedence clear. For example, if the return expression statement is complicated, it should be parenthesized for readability. Spaces around operators within expressions make them easier to read. Parentheses clarify associativity and precedence in expressions where these can be difficult to follow. They can also aid readability.

Starting global statements and preprocessing directives at the far left is consistent with historic practice, where in the earliest C systems preprocessor directives had to be in column 1. Also, because of indentation and rest-of-line comments, this gives the most room to lay out code neatly.

Using both prefix and postfix increment operators can be confusing. Stick to one most of the time. The same applies to the autodecrement operators. Idiomatic cases are code fragments that are seen repeatedly in standard texts. An example might be:

```
// idiomatic use of increment
// to advance in both arrays and test equality
while (c[i++] == d[i++]) {
// do something
}
```

The identifiers `set`, `get`, and `value` can be used outside the context of properties, but this use can be misleading and should be avoided. I would speculate that the C# language designers chose such a dual use because pre-existing class code frequently makes use of `set` and `get` methods. So this is a case where language complexity arises from a need to be backward compatible with other code.

2.9   C# COMPARED WITH JAVA AND C++

Let's start with a comparison of keywords. The following table shows keywords that exist only in C#, and are not C++ or Java keywords:

Keywords Existing Only in C#			
as	base	checked	decimal
delegate	event	fixed	foreach
*get	implicit	in	internal
is	lock	null	object
out	override	params	readonly
ref	sbyte	sealed	*set
stackalloc	string	typeof	uint
ulong	unchecked	unsafe	ushort
*value			

The starred entries are not strictly C# keywords.

This is a very significant set of differences, since keywords represent critical concepts in a programming language. In many cases the keyword is only notationally different. For example `uint` is C# for `unsigned int` in C++ and Java. But `unsafe` has no corresponding idea in Java or C++. It is a modifier that lets the C# coder use pointer arithmetic. Using pointer arithmetic is strictly disallowed in Java. It is available routinely in C++ but without any explicit designation.

The primitive types in a C# program can be `bool`, `char`, `sbyte`, `byte`, `decimal`, `short`, `ushort`, `int`, `uint`, `long`, `ulong`, `float`, and `double`. As in Java, these types are always identically defined regardless of the machine or system they run on. For example, the `int` type is always a signed 32-bit integer, unlike in C++, where `int` can vary from system to system. The `bool` type is not an arithmetic type and cannot be used in mixed arithmetical expressions. The `char` type uses 16-bit Unicode values. The `sbyte`, `short`, `int`, and `long` are all signed integer types, with length in bits of 8, 16, 32, and 64, respectively. Unsigned types are provided in C#, but unlike in C++ where the keyword `unsigned` is used, C# has keywords `ushort`, `uint`, `ulong`, and `sbyte`. In Java, unsigned types are not provided. The floating types comply with IEEE754 standards and are `float`, a 32-bit size, and `double`, a 64-bit size. C# introduces the type `decimal`, for up to 28 digits of precision.

C#, C++, and Java have the same basic set of operators, with a few exceptions. Java does not have the `sizeof` operator and has the two additional operators `instanceof` and `>>>`. C# and Java do not have the `delete` operator, the scope resolution operator `::`, or the pointer-to-member operator `->*`, all found in C++.

To illustrate, we write a program, *Moon*, in C#, Java, then C++, to convert to kilometers the distance in miles from Earth to the moon. In miles, this distance is, on average, 238,857 miles. This number is an integer. To convert miles to kilometers, we multiply by the conversion factor 1.609, a real number.

Our conversion program uses variables capable of storing integer values. The variables in the following program are declared in `main()`. Java and C# cannot have variables declared as `extern` (in other words, as global or file scope variables). Note that in Java, C, and C++ `main()` is lower case, whereas the convention in C# is to use uppercase.

In file Moon.cs

```
// Distance to the moon converted to kilometers
using System;

public class Moon {
  public static void Main()
  {
    int moon = 238857;
    int moonKilo;

    Console.WriteLine("Earth to moon = " + moon
                      + " mi.");
    moonKilo = (int)(moon * 1.609);
    Console.WriteLine("Kilometers = "
                      + moonKilo +" km.");
  }
}
```

```
// Distance to the moon converted to kilometers

public class Moon {
  public static void Main()
  {
    int moon = 238857;
    int moonKilo;

    Console.WriteLine("Earth to moon = " + moon
                        + " mi.");
    moonKilo = (int)(moon * 1.609);
    Console.WriteLine("Kilometers = "
                        + moonKilo +" km.");
  }
}
```

The output of this program is

```
Earth to moon = 238857 mi.
Kilometers = 384320 km.
```

The Java version is nearly identical.

In file Moon.java

```
// Distance to the moon converted to kilometers

public class Moon {
  public static void main()
  {
    int moon = 238857;
    int moonKilo;

    System.out.println("Earth to moon = " + moon
                        + " mi.");
    moonKilo = (int)(moon * 1.609);
    System.out.println("Kilometers = "
                        + moonKilo +" km.");
  }
}
```

C++ does not require class encapsulation for the function `main()`.

In file moon.cpp

```cpp
// Distance to the moon converted to kilometers

#include <iostream>
using namespace std;

int main()
{
  int moon = 238857;
  int moonKilo;

  cout << "Earth to moon = " << moon << " mi." << endl;
  moonKilo = (moon * 1.609);
  cout << "Kilometers = " << moonKilo << " km." << endl;
}
```

The major differences are between C++ and Java and C#. C++ does not require the program to be enclosed in a class, output differs among the systems, and casting is not required in C++.

The narrowing conversions that are implicit in C++ are not done in C# or Java. C# and Java, as in this case, are more type-safe than C++ and C. The following C++ program converts pounds to kilograms and then computes the body mass index. It can be compared to the C# implementation found in Section 2.4.3, *Explicit Conversions Called Casts*, on page 56.

In file body_fat.cpp

```cpp
// Pounds to Kilograms and Body Mass Index BMI

#include <iostream>
using namespace std;

// conversion constants

const double    lbs_to_kg = 2.2046,
                inches_to_meter = 39.370;
```

```
int main()
{
  int  weight, height;                   // in pounds and inches
  double kilograms, meters;

  cout << "\nEnter weight in pounds: ";
  cin >> weight;
  kilograms = weight / lbs_to_kg;
  cout << "\nThis is approximately "
       << static_cast<int>(kilograms) << "kg."
       << endl;
  cout << "\nEnter height in inches: ";
  cin >> height;
  meters = height/inches_to_meter;
  cout << "\nYour BMI is approximately "
       << "body fat ratio is  "
       << kilograms/(meters * meters)
       << ". Under 25 is good."
       << endl;
}
```

Notice especially how C++ has very fancy casting syntax. C++ is much more liberal than C# or Java in what it allows as casts. Also, types are system-dependent, hence, `reinterpret_cast<>` is used when this is especially nonportable.

In C# and Java, all the primitive types are implementation-independent, so, numerically, a Java or C# program gets the same answer regardless of the system it is running on. C++ continues C's tradition of having implementation-dependent choices of primitive types, so as to optimize performance on a given machine.

SUMMARY

■ C# comments include the *rest of line comment* and the multiline bracketed comments /* *comment here* */. It has a specialized /// that the compiler turns into an XML file.

■ Keywords in C# are explicitly reserved words that have a strict meaning and may not be used in any other way. They include words used for type declarations, such as int, char, and float; words used for flow of control, such as do, for, and if; and words used for access control, such as public, protected, and private.

■ C# has native types, such as int, double, char, and bool and literals appropriate to each type.

■ The Main() method initiates the running of a C# program calling any subsidiary method, such as Gcd() or Console.WriteLine().

■ C# relies on a standard library to provide input/output. The information the program needs to use this library resides in the *System* namespace. In C#, a typical output expression is

Console.WriteLine(*string expression*);

Note that Console and WriteLine are not keywords. They are identifiers used in a standard library. They should not be declared for other use.

■ In addition to implicit conversions, which can occur across assignments and in mixed expressions, there are explicit conversions, called casts, with a form: (*type*) *expression.*

■ The keyword enum is used to declare a distinct integer type with a set of named integer constants, called enumerators.

REVIEW QUESTIONS

1. Name three integer types. Discuss a situation where each might be the preferred integer type.

2. What token does the new XML comment style in C# involve? Why should it be used?

3. What two literal values does the `bool` type have? Can they be assigned to `int` variables? With what result?

4. What happens when an `int` variable is assigned to a `double`? What happens when a `double` is assigned to an `int`?

5. For `int i, double d`, show the syntax for explicitly casting from `int` to `double`.

6. Complete the following table.

Text	Legal ID	Why or Why Not
3xyz	No	Digit is first character.
xy3z		
a = b		
Main		
Count		
class		

7. What does the symbol = do in C#?

8. True or false? A multiline comment can be placed anywhere white space could be placed.

9. True or false? Keywords can also be used as variables, but then the special meaning of the keyword is overridden.

10. In the code `int i = 1, j = 0; j = i++;` what are the values of `i` and `j`?

11. For the type `enum What { Zip, Zap, Hip = 9, Hap }`, what values do the enumerators have?

12. Give an example showing how short-circuit evaluation works using &&.

13. List two keywords in C# that are not in C++. Tell their meanings if you know them.

14. Fill in the following table:

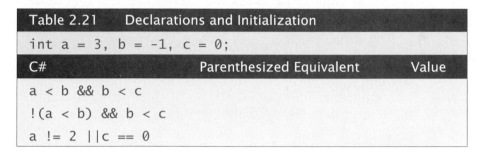

Table 2.21	Declarations and Initialization	
`int a = 3, b = -1, c = 0;`		
C#	**Parenthesized Equivalent**	**Value**
`a < b && b < c`		
`!(a < b) && b < c`		
`a != 2 || c == 0`		

EXERCISES

1. Write a program that requests that you enter your name from the console. It then prints a message, such as, "Have a nice day Laura Pohl."

2. Write a program that takes three integers as input from the console. The program should compute their sum and average and print these results.

3. Write a program that solves the seventh-grade pre-algebra problem: Given rate and time, find distance. Have rate and time be initialized to the values 75.5 and 2.5, respectively.

4. Computers are good for repetitive problem solving. Redo the last problem to ask the user to enter rate and time from the console. In this way you do not have to recompile the program when you want to compute distance.

5. Rewrite the previous exercise to avoid the Ctrl-c interrupt. This is safer than relying on the user to terminate the program by Ctrl-c. Do this by testing the rate to see if it is 0 or negative. If the user enters such a phony value, have the program terminate. Such a value is known as a *guard* or *sentinel* value.

6. Write a program that finds the maximum and minimum integer value of a sequence of inputted integers. The program should first prompt the user for how many values are to be entered. The program should print this value out and ask the user to confirm this value. If the user fails to confirm the value, she must enter a new value.

7. Rewrite the *BodyFat.cs* program to not use any casts. Convert everything to variables of type `double`. Add some input/output that further customizes the program, such as asking for the person's name and age. Think of how you would write a patient profile program that asked a patient for data for evaluating their health.

8. Write a program that produces pounds-per-inch as the output for analyzing whether a person is over- or underweight. Experiment with it and see what would be a healthy range for a typical person.

9. In the C# world, more flexible file I/O is available by using the `Streams` classes from the *System.I/O* library as described in Section 9.7, *Files*, on page 394. Convert the *Gcd* program streams. The program should get its arguments from the command line, as in

   Gcd   Gcd.dat   Gcd.ans

10. The statement `Console.WriteLine("error i = " + i);` can be replaced by `Console.WriteLine("error i = {0}",i);` In this form of I/O the `{0}` means substitute the 0th argument as text here. Rewrite the *Gcd* program in Section 2.3, *Program Structure*, on page 46 using this argument substitution based I/O. See Section 9.2, *Formatted Output*, on page 378 for more details on its use.

11. Use `Console.ReadLine()` to read in one double precision floating-point number and then print the results of calling `Math.Sin()`, `Math.Cos()`, `Math.Asin()`, `Math.Exp()`, `Math.Log()`, and `Math.Round()` with the input value as a parameter. Be sure to prompt the user for input and label the output.

12. Write a program to read two double precision floating-point numbers. Print the sum, difference, product, and quotient of the two numbers. Try two very small numbers, two very large numbers, and one very small number with one very large number. You can use the same notation used for literals to enter the numbers. For example, `0.123e-310` is a very small number.

13. Write a program to compute the area of a circle given its radius. Let `radius` be a variable of type `double` and use `Console.ReadLine()` to read in its value. Be sure that the output is understandable. The class `Math` contains definitions for the constants `E` and `PI`, so you can use `Math.PI` in your program.

14. Extend the previous program to write out the circumference of a circle and the volume of a sphere given the radius as input. Recall that the volume of a sphere is

$$V = \frac{4 \times \pi r^3}{3}$$

15. Write a program that reads in an integer and prints it as a character. Remember that character codes can be nonprinting.

16. Write a program using `Console.Read()` to read in a character and print its integer value. This `Console` method returns an integer value, so it need not be cast from a `char` to an `int`.

17. Write a program capable of converting one currency to another. For example, given U.S. dollars it should print out the equivalent number of French francs. Look up the exchange rate and use it as input.

18. (Marc Mosko) The rules for conversions are far more subtle than the simplification presented in the text. Write a program that uses

```
uint a = 1, b = 2, c = 0, d = 0, e = 0;
c = a - b;                                    // compiles
d = a + -b;            // unary minus - but doesn't compile
e = b - a;
```

Explain what goes wrong.

In order to understand the various implicit conversions, use the technique of calling `WriteLine((expression).GetType()` to display the expression type.

CHAPTER 3

STATEMENTS

T his chapter explains the various statements that C# uses. C# has a
large variety of statement types, including an expression statement.
For example, the assignment statement in C# is syntactically an
assignment expression followed by a semicolon. C# has assignment
statements, procedure statements, transfer statements, conditional statements, selection statements, and iterative statements. Syntactically C#
treats declarations as statements, allowing them to be almost anywhere in
blocks. In C#, declarations can also occur in the initializer part of the for
loop.

For the experienced Java, C, or C++ programmer, most of this chapter's
material should be skimmed and read mainly with an eye for differences
between Java, C, or C++ and C#.

Programming can be usefully compared to writing a coherent essay. In an
essay, we use words to form coherent thoughts. These are on a lowest level
organized as sentences. Statements are the sentences of a programming
language. They must follow a syntax to be legal. They must be semantically
coherent to achieve a key step of implementing a portion of an algorithmic
recipe.

3.1   ASSIGNMENTS AND EXPRESSIONS

The assignment statement is the workhorse of the C# programming language. Its key use is to assign a value to a variable. An assignment is an expression, while an expression followed by a semicolon is an expression statement.

```
a = b + 1;                    // a simple assignment statement
```

This expression evaluates the right-hand side of the assignment and converts it to a value compatible with the variable on the left-hand side. This value is assigned to the left-hand side. The left-hand side must be an *lvalue*, a location in memory where a value can be stored or retrieved. Simple variables are lvalues.

C# allows multiple assignments in a single statement.

```
a = b + (c = 3);
```

C# provides assignment operators that combine an assignment operator and some other operator.

```
a += b;        is equivalent to        a = a + b;
a *= a + b;    is equivalent to        a = a * (a + b);
```

C# also provides increment (++) and decrement (--) operators in both prefix and postfix form. In prefix form, the increment operator adds 1 to the value stored at the lvalue it acts on, and returns the result. Similarly, the prefix form autodecrement operator subtracts 1 from the value stored at the lvalue it acts on, and returns the result.

```
++i;           is equivalent to        i = i + 1;
--x;           is equivalent to        x = x - 1;
```

The postfix form behaves differently from the prefix form, changing the affected lvalue after the value has been returned.

```
j = ++i;       is equivalent to        i = i + 1; j = i;
j = i++;       is equivalent to        j = i; i = i + 1;
```

Note: These are not exact equivalencies. The compound assignment operators evaluate their left-hand side expression once. Therefore, for complicated expressions with side effects, results of the two forms can be different.

The null statement is written as a single semicolon, and causes no action to take place. A null statement is usually used where a statement is required syntactically but no action is desired. This situation sometimes occurs in statements that affect the flow of control.

3.2   THE STATEMENT BLOCK

A *statement block* in C# is a series of statements surrounded by braces { and }. The chief use of the statement block is to group statements into an executable unit. The body of a C# method, for example, is always a statement block. Wherever it is possible to place a statement, it is also possible to place a statement block. It is also usual to call a statement block a *compound statement.*

```
{
    // a block statement that inputs a double and prints
    // its square root
    double x, y;

    Console.WriteLine("Enter a positive double:");
    string data = Console.ReadLine();
    x = double.Parse(data);
    y = Math.Sqrt(x);
    Console.WriteLine("Sqrt({0}) = {1}", x, y);
}
```

The statement block can be usefully compared to a paragraph. It is a way of coherently organizing a set of related elements. A method can be thought of as a named block.

Converting the above block into the definition of the method `Main()` and placing it in a class allows us to have a fully testable C# program.

In file FindSquareRoots.cs

```
// Turning a block into a program
using System;
class FindSquareRoots {
  public static void Main()
  {
    double x, y;

    Console.WriteLine("Enter a positive double:");
    string data = Console.ReadLine();
    x = double.Parse(data);
    y = Math.Sqrt(x);
    Console.WriteLine("Sqrt({0}) = {1:F4}", x, y);
  }
}
```

```
Enter a positive double
34.55
Sqrt(34.55) = 5.8779
```

Dissection of the *FindSquareRoots* Program

■{
```
  double x, y;
```

A block is the scope for locally declared variables. The variables x and y are declared inside this block. In effect they "live" in this block. They appear upon being declared and the disappear when the block is exited. This is discussed further in Section 4.4, *Scope of Variables*, on page 125. Notice these variables are uninitialized.

■Console.WriteLine("Enter a positive double:");
```
  string data = Console.ReadLine();
```

This program processes input from the console. Always prompt the user with an appropriate message. The second statement is a declaration statement. The variable data is created local to this block and is initialized to the line of text that was inputted from the console.

```
■x = double.Parse(data);
```

The `string data` now contains must be parsed as a `double`. If this is illegal, the program dies with the system complaining. For example try inputting the text "1,000". This fails because the comma is not syntactically allowed in a C# `double`.

```
■y = Math.Sqrt(x);
Console.WriteLine("Sqrt({0}) = {1:F4}", x, y);
```

The answer is printed to the console. Notice how the `WriteLine()` limited the output of the resulting square root to 4 significant digits.

3.3   THE `if` AND `if-else` STATEMENTS

The general form of an `if` statement is

`if` (*condition*)
   statement

If *condition* is `true`, then *statement* is executed; otherwise, *statement* is skipped. After the `if` statement has been executed, control passes to the next statement. A *condition* is an expression that selects flow of control. It must evaluate to a `bool` value. Here is an example of an `if` statement.

```
if (temperature > 32)
  Console.WriteLine("Above Freezing!");
Console.WriteLine("Fahrenheit is " + temperature);
```

`Above Freezing!` is printed only when `temperature` is greater than 32. The second statement is always executed.

The expression in an `if` statement is usually a relational, equality, or logical expression. Here is an example with a logical-and expression.

```
if (grade > 70 && grade < 80) {
  Console.WriteLine(" you passed ");
  letterGrade = 'C';
}
```

Notice how the statement that is executed is a statement block. This allows one controlling `if` expression to execute a sequence of statements. In C# *condition* evaluates as a `bool`.

Closely related to the `if` statement is the `if-else` statement, which has the general form

```
if (condition)
   statement1
else
   statement2
```

If *condition* is `true`, then *statement1* is executed and *statement2* is skipped; if *condition* is `false`, then *statement1* is skipped and *statement2* is executed. After the `if-else` statement has been executed, control passes to the next statement. Consider the following code.

```
if (x < y)
   min = x;
else
   min = y;
Console.WriteLine("min = " + min);
```

If x < y is `true`, then min is assigned the value of x; if x < y is `false`, min is assigned the value of y. After the `if-else` statement is executed, min is printed.

"Which way should I go next?"

It is not just rats that get lost in a maze of if-else clauses. Programmers must be careful to test their flow-of-control logic and make sure it conforms to expectations.

In the next program we show how these statements can be used in a complete program. The program takes as input an integer grade and prints out a message and the equivalent letter grade. If the entered grade was outside the normal range, a grade of Z is printed. Notice how the if-else structure works to designate a series of logical cases. The last else is the error case. This is a frequent coding idiom, and the good programmer must master this form of decision making.

In file Grades1.cs

```csharp
// For printing out grade meanings

using System;

class Grades {
  public static void Main()
  {
    string data;
    int grade;                          // from 0 to 100
    char letterGrade = 'Z';         // is A, B, C, D, F or Z

    Console.WriteLine("Enter Your Grade:");
    data = Console.ReadLine();
    grade = int.Parse(data);

    if (grade == 100) {
      Console.WriteLine("First in Class!");
      letterGrade = 'A';
    }
    else if (grade >= 90 && grade < 100) {
      Console.WriteLine("Congratulations!");
      letterGrade = 'A';
    }
    else if (grade >= 80 && grade < 90) {
      Console.WriteLine("Very Good");
      letterGrade = 'B';
    }
    else if (grade >= 70 && grade < 80) {
      Console.WriteLine("Okay");
      letterGrade = 'C';
    }
```

```
      else if (grade >= 60 && grade < 70) {
        Console.WriteLine("Work harder");
        letterGrade = 'D';
      }
      else if (grade >= 0 && grade < 60) {
        Console.WriteLine("Sorry you failed");
        letterGrade = 'F';
      }
      else {
        Console.WriteLine("Not a recognizable grade");
      }
      Console.WriteLine("Your grade was  " + letterGrade);
    }
}
```

Here is some sample output

```
Enter Your Grade:
88
Very Good
```

Dissection of the *Grades* Program

```
■   string data;
    int grade;                          // from 0 to 100
    char letterGrade = 'Z';       // is A, B, C, D, F or Z
    Console.WriteLine("Enter Your Grade:");
    data = Console.ReadLine();
    grade = int.Parse(data);
```

The program converts an integer grade to a letter grade. The letter grade Z is reserved for an illegal integer grade. When asking a user for input, always prompt the user properly. Initializing a variable to an improper value is a useful technique to catch errors.

```
■ if (grade == 100) {
    Console.WriteLine("First in Class!");
    letterGrade = 'A';
  }
  else if (grade >= 90 && grade < 100) {
```

In a nested if-else statement, we have a series of if-else expressions. Here each if-else expression brackets a grade range.

```
■ else if (grade >= 0 && grade < 60) {
    Console.WriteLine("Sorry you failed");
    letterGrade = 'F';
  }
  else {
    Console.WriteLine("Not a recognizable grade");
  }
```

The very last clause is an else part. This frequently takes care of irregular or illegal values. Here it is an action for grades outside the range 0 to 100. Because the else block has a single statement, the braces could have been left off, but are put in for clarity.

```
■   Console.WriteLine("Your grade was  " + letterGrade);
  }
```

The if selection picks a grade of A, B, C, D or F, and assigns it to the variable letterGrade. If no grade is selected, the default value Z prevails. The output statement prints the grade in an understandable phrase.

3.4   THE while STATEMENT

The general form of a while statement is

while (*condition*)
  statement

First, *condition* is evaluated. If it is true, *statement* is executed, and control passes back to the beginning of the while loop. The result: the body of the while loop, namely, *statement,* is executed repeatedly until *condition* is false. At that point, control passes to the next statement. In this way, *statement* can be executed zero or more times.

An example of a while statement follows.

In file WhileUse.cs

```
using System;

class WhileUse {
  public static void Main()
  {
    Console.WriteLine("Simple while in C#");
    int i = 1, sum = 0;

    while (i <= 10) {
      sum += i;
      ++i;
    }                              // after exiting while i is now 11
    Console.WriteLine("Sum for 1 to 10 is " + sum);
  }
}
```

```
Simple while in C#

Sum for 1 to 10 is 55
```

Dissection of the *WhileUse* Program

■ ```
Console.WriteLine("Simple while in C#");
int i = 1, sum = 0;
```

It is customary to use variables named i, j, k, m, and n for integer variables needed in looping. This harkens back to conventions found in the original FORTRAN language invented by John Backus at IBM in 1954. It also conforms to conventions used in mathematical expressions where i is used for an integer variable and x is used for a real variable.
```

```
while (i <= 10) {
    sum += i;
    ++i;
}                          // after exiting while i is now 11
```

If you are a beginner, it is important to carefully hand-simulate this loop. Write down what i and sum are each time through the loop. Notice how the bool expression or condition i <= 10 is evaluated before the block that constitutes the statement being executed each time the condition is true.

The while loop increments the value of sum by the current value of i, and then increments i by 1. After the body of the loop has been executed 10 times, the value of i is 11, and the value of the condition i <= 10 is false. Thus, the body of the loop is not executed, and control passes to the next statement. When the while loop is exited, the value of sum is 55.

This while loop is a very important idiomatic example. It is crucial in programming to master use of iteration. That, after all, is why we use computers—namely, to perform the same actions repeatedly. What happens in the above program if the while condition was i <= 0 or i <= 1 or i < 10?

3.5 THE for STATEMENT

Consider the general form of a for statement:

```
for (for-init-statement; condition; for-iterator)
    statement
```

First, the *for-init-statement* is evaluated, and may be used to initialize variables used in the loop. Then *condition* is evaluated. If it is true, *statement* is executed, *for-iterator* is evaluated, and control passes back to the beginning of the for loop again, except that evaluation of *for-init-statement* is skipped. This iteration continues until *condition* is false, at which point control passes to the next statement.

The *for-init-statement* can be an expression statement or a simple declaration. If it is a declaration, the declared variable has the scope of the for statement. Often where more than one variable is declared in the *for-init-*

statement part, the *for-iterator* part has a comma-separated list of iterator expressions (see Exercise 3 on page 110).

The `for` statement is an iterative statement, typically used with a variable that is incremented or decremented. As an example, the following code uses a `for` statement to sum the integers from 1 to 10:

In file ForUse.cs

```
// A typical for statement

using System;

class ForUse {
  public static void Main()
  {
    int  sum = 0;

    for (int i = 1; i <= 10; ++i)
      sum += i;                          // loop and compute sum
    Console.WriteLine("Sum of 1 to 10 is "  + sum);
  }
}
```

The output for this loop is

```
Sum of 1 to 10 is 55
```

Any or all of the parts inside the parentheses of a `for` statement can be missing, but the two semicolons must remain. If *for-init-statement* is missing, no initialization step is performed as part of the `for` loop. If *expression* is missing, no incrementation step is performed as part of the `for` loop. If *condition* is missing, no testing step is performed as part of the `for` loop. The special rule for when *condition* is missing is that the test is always `true`. Thus, the `for` loop in the code

```
for (int i = 1, sum = 0;/* no test !? */ ; ++i)
  sum += i;
```

is an infinite loop.

Sartre was right; there is no exit.

The `for` statement is one common case in which a local declaration is used to provide the loop control variable, as in

```
for (int i = 0; i < N; ++i)
  sum += i;                           // sum i = 1 upto i = N-1
```

Here, the `int` variable `i` is local to the given loop. This form of local declaration is not possible in C, but it can be simulated as follows:

```
{
  int i;                              // local to block
  for (i = 0; i < N; ++i)
    sum += i;
}
```

3.6   THE do STATEMENT

The do statement can be considered a variant of the `while` statement. However, instead of making its test at the beginning of the loop, the do statement makes it at the end. The do statement always executes its body at least once. An example is

```
sum = i = 0;
do {                                        // execute
  sum += i;
  Console.WriteLine(i + '\t');
  Console.WriteLine("Enter an int or 0 to terminate:");
  data = Console.ReadLine();
  i = int.Parse(data);
} while (i == 0);                           // then test
```

In this code fragment we loop until the value 0 is assigned i. The value 0 is called a *guard* or *sentinel* value. The loop watches for this guard value and then terminates. Notice i starts off as zero, but the do loop statement is always executed the first time through.

Consider the general form of a do statement:

```
do
   statement
while (condition);
```

First, *statement* is executed, and then *condition* is evaluated. If it is true, control passes back to the beginning of the do statement, and the process repeats itself. When the value of *condition* is false, control passes to the next statement. As an example, suppose that we want to add ten positive numbers, such as the last ten readings of your blood pressure. We need to read in each integer and require that it be positive. The following code accomplishes this:

In file DoUse.cs

```
// Use of typical do statement

using System;

class DoUse {
  public static void Main()
  {
    int  sum = 0, n;
    string data;
    Console.WriteLine("Sums 10 positive integers");
```

```
for (int i = 0; i < 10; ++i) {
  // loop until a positive integer is entered
  do {
    Console.WriteLine("Enter a positive" + " integer:");
    data = Console.ReadLine();
    n = int.Parse(data);
  } while (n <= 0);
  sum = sum + n;
}
Console.WriteLine("Sum of 10 positive numbers is "+sum);
  }
}
```

Sample output skips some prompting of integers following the pattern

```
Sums 10 positive integers
Enter a positive integer:
10
Enter a positive integer:
20

    . . .
Enter a positive integer:
90
Sum of 10 positive numbers is 550
```

The user is prompted for a positive integer. A negative or zero value causes the loop to be executed again, asking for another value. Control exits the inner do loop only after a positive integer has been entered.

Dissection of the *DoUse* Program

```
■for (int i = 0; i < 10; ++i) {  // loop positive integer
    do {
```

Here we have a nested loop. The beginning programmer needs to carefully hand-simulate this program. The outer loop is the for loop and the inner loop is the do loop. Notice that the loop-control variable i is declared and initialized to zero as part of the *for-init-statement*. This again is idiomatic. The scope of i is constrained to the block statement that this for loop controls.

```
■  Console.WriteLine("Enter a positive" + " integer:");
   data = Console.ReadLine();
   n = int.Parse(data);
} while (n <= 0);
```

The inner loop is used to ensure that the inputted value is a positive integer. It is good programming practice to plan for incorrect user input. This reminds the user that the data entered was incorrect.

```
■  sum = sum + n;
   }
Console.WriteLine("Sum of 10 positive numbers is "
                     + sum);
```

The outer loop executes when n has been assigned a positive integer value. It uses the accumulation idiom to find the sum.

3.7   THE break AND continue STATEMENTS

In C#, the break and continue statements are used to interrupt ordinary iterative flow of control in loops. In addition, the break statement is most importantly used within a switch statement, which can select among several cases. To interrupt the normal flow of control within a loop, the programmer can use the two special statements

break;   *and*   continue;

The following example illustrates the use of a break statement. A test for a negative value is made. If the test is true, the break statement causes the for loop to be exited. Program control jumps to the statement immediately following the loop.

```
for (i = 0; i < 10; ++i) {
  data = Console.ReadLine();
  x = double.Parse(data);
  if (x < 0.0) {
    Console.WriteLine("All done");
    break;                        // exit loop if value is negative
  }
  Console.WriteLine("Sqrt is = " + Math.Sqrt(x));
}
// break jumps to here
.....
```

In this use of a `break` statement, a special condition is tested for inside the loop, and if the condition is met, the loop is exited.

The `continue` statement causes the current iteration of a loop to stop, and causes the next iteration of the loop to begin immediately. The following code processes all characters except digits.

```
for (i = 0; i < howMany; ++i) {
  data = Console.ReadLine();
  c = char.Parse(data);
  if (char.IsDigit(c)) {
    Console.WriteLine(c);                         // echo digit
    .....                                         // do more stuff
    continue;                           // end current iteration
  }
  // process other characters
  countNonDigits++;
  .....                                           // do more stuff
}
```

When the `continue` statement is executed, control jumps to just before the last closing brace in the `for` loop, causing the loop to begin execution at the top of the `for` loop again. Notice that the `continue` statement ends the current iteration, whereas a `break` statement would end the loop.

A `break` statement can occur only inside the body of a `for`, `while`, `do`, or `switch` statement. The `continue` statement can occur only inside the body of a `for`, `foreach`, `while`, or `do` statement. The `foreach` statement is an advanced form of iterator construct explained in Section 5.5, *The foreach Statement*, on page 184.

3.8 THE `switch` STATEMENT

The `switch` statement is a multiway conditional statement generalizing the `if-else` statement. The general form of the `switch` statement is given by

```
switch (expression)
    statement
```

where *statement* is typically a statement block containing `case` labels, and optionally a `default` label. Typically, a `switch` is composed of many cases, and the *expression* in parentheses following the keyword `switch` determines which, if any, of the cases are executed.

A `case` label is of the form

`case` *constant integral or string expression*:

In a `switch` statement, each `case` label must be unique. The action taken after each `case` label ends with a `break` or `goto` statement. If no `case` label is selected, control passes to the `default` label, if there is one. No `default` label is required, but including one is recommended. If no `case` label is selected, and if there is no `default` label, the `switch` statement is exited. The keywords `case` and `default` cannot occur outside a `switch`. To detect errors, include a `default`, even when all of the expected cases have been accounted for.

C and C++ do not require a `break` or `goto` in each non-empty case. *Fall-through* to the next case is allowed, but is considered bad style because it is error-prone. C# improves on its ancestor languages by requiring safer practices and disallowing fall-through semantics.

The Effect of a `switch` Statement

1. Evaluate the integral or string expression in the parentheses following `switch`.

2. Execute the `case` label having a constant value that matches the value of the expression found in step 1. If no match is found, execute the `default` label. If there is no `default` label, terminate the `switch`.

3. Terminate the `switch` when a `break` is encountered.

The following `switch` statement replaces the earlier `if-else` nested statement in the *Grades* program in Section 3.3, *The `if` and `if-else` Statements*, on page 87.

In file Grades2.cs

```csharp
// Program for printing out grade meanings
// use of switch - can use string constants
// also cannot have ordinary fall thru -- need goto

using System;

class Grades {
public static void Main()
  {
    string data;
    int grade;                              // from 0 to 100
    char letterGrade = 'Z';         // is A, B, C, D, F or Z

    Console.WriteLine("Enter Your Grade:");
    data = Console.ReadLine();
    grade = int.Parse(data);
    switch (grade/10) {
      case 10: Console.WriteLine(" First in Class!");
        letterGrade = 'A'; break;
      case 9: Console.WriteLine(" Congratulations!");
        letterGrade = 'A'; break;
      case 8: Console.WriteLine(" Very Good");
        letterGrade = 'B'; break;
      case 7: Console.WriteLine(" Okay");
        letterGrade = 'C'; break;
      case 6: Console.WriteLine(" Work harder");
        letterGrade = 'D'; break;
      case 5: case 4: case 3: case 2: case 1: case 0:
        Console.WriteLine(" Sorry you failed");
        letterGrade = 'F'; break;
      default: Console.WriteLine(" Not a recognizable"
          + " grade"); break;
    }                                           // end switch
    Console.WriteLine(" Your grade was  " + letterGrade);
  }
}
```

We again input 88 as the grade and we see the following

```
Enter Your Grade:
88
  Very Good
  Your grade was   B
```

Dissection of the *Grades* Program

■`switch (grade/10) {`

The `switch` expression must be an integral expression. The various cases are a selection of the possible values computed here. In this case, the expression should evaluate to the integers from 0 to 10. Other values are considered illegal.

■`case 8: Console.WriteLine("Very Good");`
  `letterGrade = 'B'; break;`

A typical case: the `case` label is followed normally by one or more actions and ended by the `break` statement. A `switch` case can be written with a `goto`, but this is a dangerous practice because it can result in error-prone, unmanageable code.

■`case 5: case 4: case 3: case 2: case 1: case 0:`
  `Console.WriteLine("Sorry you failed");`
  `letterGrade = 'F'; break;`

It is permissible to have a series of `case` labels. Here the program gives the same grade for scores less than 60.

■`default: Console.WriteLine("Not a recognizable"`
  `        + " grade"); break;`
  `}                                          // end switch`

The `default` case usually takes care of irregular or illegal values.

3.9 THE goto STATEMENT

The goto statement, the most primitive method of interrupting ordinary control flow, is an unconditional branch to an arbitrary labeled statement in the method. The goto statement is considered a harmful construct in most accounts of modern programming methodology because the statement can undermine all of the useful structure provided by other flow-of-control mechanisms (for, while, do, if, and switch).

A label is an identifier. By executing a goto statement of the form

goto *label*;

control is unconditionally transferred to a labeled statement.

label: *statement*

Both the goto statement and its corresponding labeled statement must be in the body of the same method. In general, goto should be avoided.

3.10 SOFTWARE ENGINEERING: DEBUGGING

C# has changed C's rule on where declarations can occur. Use of local declarations are allowed in the for loop, for example. It is perfectly acceptable to declare simple variables, including variables used for looping, at the head of a block, most likely the beginning of a method definition.

Following this advice yields C# code that would be similar to C++ and Java. For example, here is an iterative version of the Fibonacci method. Fibonacci numbers are defined as follows:

$$f_0 = 0, \quad f_1 = 1, \quad f_n = f_{n-1} + f_{n-2}$$

In file Fibonacci1.cs

```
// Fibonacci with declarations at the head of a block
using System;

class FibonacciNumbers {
  public static void Main()
  {
    Console.WriteLine("{0,6}{1,13}",           // align output
                      "Number", "Fibonacci");
    for (uint i = 1; i < 45; ++i)
      Console.WriteLine("{0,4}{1,13}", i, Fibonacci(i));
  }

  public static uint Fibonacci(uint n)
  {
    uint i, sum = 0, f0 = 0, f1 = 1;

    for (i = 0; i < n - 1; ++i) {
      sum = f0 + f1;
      f0 = f1;
      f1 = sum;
    }
    if (n > 1)
      return sum;
    else
      return n;
  }
}
```

```
     Number    Fibonacci
        1            1
        2            1
        .....
       12          144
       13          233
        .....
       25        75025
       26       121393
        .....
       43    433494437
       44    701408733
```

Using the fact that declarations are allowed in the *for-init-statement*, we recode the `Fibonacci()` method as follows:

In file Fibonacci2.cs

```
// Idiomatically correct C#
public static uint Fibonacci(uint n)
{
  uint sum = 0;

  for (uint i = 0, f0 = 0, f1 = 1; i < n-1; ++i) {
    sum = f0 + f1;
    f0 = f1;
    f1 = sum;
  }
  if (n > 1)
     return sum;
  else
     return n;
}
```

Dissection of the `Fibonacci()` Method

■`uint Fibonacci(uint n)`

By using `uint`, we get a larger range of integer values that can be correctly calculated without causing overflow.

■`uint sum = 0;`
`for (uint i=0, f0=0, f1 = 1; i < n-1; ++i) {`

In this version of `Fibonacci()`, we have declarations both at the head of block and inside the `for` statement. It is usual to declare and initialize the loop counter variable `i` as the first part of a `for` statement.

```
if (n > 1)
   return sum;
else
   return n;
```

The variable sum was declared outside of the `for` loop because the `return` statement is outside of the `for` loop.

Notice what happens if we make the following coding error:

In file FibonacciError.cs

```
// ERROR because of scopes

public static uint Fibonacci(uint n)
{
  uint sum;

  for (uint i = 0, f0 = 0, f1 = 1, sum = 0; i < n-1; ++i){
    sum = f0 + f1;
    f0 = f1;
    f1 = sum;
  }
  if (n > 1)
    return sum;
  else
    return n;
}
```

In this last piece of code, an error was introduced by initializing `sum` in the `for` loop. This declares a second variable `sum` because it is interpreted by the compiler as part of the list of variables declared following the keyword `uint`. The variable `sum` declared at the head of the block is not initialized, and its value is the one that gets returned. The Visual Studio C# compiler issues the following compile error:

```
FibonacciError.cs(20): A local variable named
'sum' cannot be declared in this scope
because it would give a different meaning to
'sum', which is already used in a 'parent or
current' scope to denote something else
```

3.11   DR. P'S PRESCRIPTIONS

- One statement to a line, except for very short statements that are conceptually related, which can be on the same line.

- A statement block brace comes on the same line as its controlling expression. Its matching terminating brace is lined up under the initial letter of the keyword starting the statement. A method body is a statement block and starts on its own line.

- Everything after the opening (left) brace is indented a standard number of spaces—for example, as in this text, two spaces. The matching, closing (right) brace causes subsequent statements to be lined up under it.

- Declarations at the head of a block are followed by a blank line.

- Parenthesize the `return` expression if it is not a simple expression.

- To detect errors, include a `default` in the `switch` statement, even when all the expected cases have been accounted for.

- When possible, use `break` or `continue`, rather than `goto`.

These spacing and layout guidelines conform to standard industry practice, and are used to enhance readability. For example, a uniform indentation makes it easier to follow flow of control. One statement to a line gives adequate white space for easy readability.

It is customary in C#, as it is in C and C++, to place an opening brace on the same line as the starting keyword for a statement, such as an `if` or `for`. The closing brace lines up with the first character of this keyword. In the ALGOL and Pascal community, the practice was to put the equivalent to braces (begin-end tokens) on their own line. This practice is also acceptable. Whichever brace policy is followed should be adhered to by the entire programmer team at a project or company.

Starting global statements and preprocessing directives in column 1 is consistent with historic practice, where in the earliest C systems preprocessor directives had to be in column 1. Also, because of indentation and rest-of-line comments, this gives the most room to lay out code neatly.

In most cases, you should write short method definitions. Keeping all declarations at the head of such blocks makes it easy to see what variables the method employs. These declarations should be separated for visual clarity from executable statements that follow them.

The `goto` is largely unnecessary in C#. Other structured flow-of-control statements can be used better to maintain clear flow of control. In many instances, `break` and `continue` can be used. The `goto` can also be avoided by properly constructing `if-else` statements.

3.12   C# COMPARED WITH JAVA AND C++

The flow-of-control statements—`if`, `if-else`, `while`, `do-while`, `for`, and `switch`—available to C# are also available in Java and C++. Although `goto` is a reserved word in Java, the `goto` statement is not allowed. However, Java extended the `break` and `continue` statements so that they can use labels.

C# does not allow fall-through semantics for a `switch` statement. It does allow strings as case labels. As already noted, fall-through semantics are allowed for non-empty case statements in both C++ and Java.

The basic statement types of C#, C++, and Java derive from C; hence there is considerable similarity in their use among all these languages.

As we shall see in Section 5.5, *The foreach Statement*, on page 184, C# has a `foreach` statement in that the other languages do not have.

SUMMARY

- C# has assignment, procedure, transfer, conditional, selection, and iterative statements. C# uses `bool` expressions to control flow-of-control statements, and C# allows declarations as statements instead of requiring that declarations be at the head of blocks as in C.

- In C#, assignment occurs as part of an assignment expression. The expression evaluates the right-hand side of the assignment and converts it to a value compatible with the variable on the left-hand side. This value is assigned to the left-hand side.

- The `if-else` statement has the general form

  ```
  if (condition)
      statement1
  else
      statement2
  ```

  If *condition* is `true`, then *statement1* is executed and *statement2* is skipped; if *condition* is `false`, then *statement1* is skipped and *statement2* is executed. After the `if-else` statement has been executed, control passes to the next statement. The condition must evaluate to a `bool` value.

- The general form of a `while` statement is

  ```
  while (condition)
      statement
  ```

  First, *condition* is evaluated. If it is `true`, *statement* is executed, and control passes back to the beginning of the `while` loop. The condition must be an expression that evaluates to a `bool` value.

■   The general form of a `for` statement is

`for` (*for-init-statement*; *condition*; *for-iterator*)
    statement

First, the *for-init-statement* is evaluated and may be used to initialize variables used in the loop. Then *condition* is evaluated. It is of type `bool`. If it is `true`, *statement* is executed, *for-iterator* is evaluated, and control passes back to the beginning of the `for` loop again, except that evaluation of *for-init-statement* is skipped. This iteration continues until *condition* is `false`, whereupon control passes to the next statement.

■   The *for-init-statement* can be an expression statement or a simple declaration. Where it is a declaration, the declared variable has the scope of the `for` statement.

```
for (int i = 0; i < N; ++i)
  sum += a[i];                 // sum a[0] + ····· + a[N - 1]
```

The semantics are that the `int` variable `i` is local to the given loop.

■   The `switch` statement is a multiway conditional statement generalizing the `if-else` statement. The general form of the `switch` statement is given by

`switch` (*condition*)
    statement

where *statement* is typically a statement block containing `case` labels, and optionally a `default` label.

REVIEW QUESTIONS

1. The assignment statement is an assignment expression followed by a
   _____.

2. When should you use a goto statement?

3. What happens when you omit the condition part of the for statement?

4. In the statement

   ```
   if (a < b)
      Console.Write("true");
   else
      Console.Write("false");
   ```

   what gets written when a = 1 and b = 1?

5. In the switch statement each case ends with a _____ statement.

6. In the code

   ```
   int s = 0;
   for (int i = 1; i < 5; ++i)
     s = s + i;
   ```

   what values are i and s just after the loop exits.

7. In the code

   ```
   int s = 0;
   for (int i = 1; i < 5; ++i)
     if (i % 2 == 0)
       s = s + i;
   ```

   what values are i and s just before the loop exits?

8. Good style is to write _____ per line.

9. What is the minimum number of times the do-while loop is executed?

10. What is the minimum number of times the for loop is executed?

EXERCISES

1. Write a program to convert temperatures from Celsius to Fahrenheit. The program should use integer values and print integer values that are rounded. Recall that 0 Celsius is 32 degrees Fahrenheit and that each degree Celsius is 1.8 degrees Fahrenheit.

2. Write a program that prints whether water at a given Fahrenheit temperature would be solid, liquid, or gas. In the computation, use an enumerated type:

   ```
   enum State { Solid, Liquid = 32, Gas = 212 };
   ```

3. Simplify the following code:

   ```
   for (sum =i = 0, j = 2, k = i+j; i < 10 || k < 15;
        ++i, ++j, ++k)
     sum += (i < j)? k : i;
   ```

   Remember that comma expressions are sequences of left-to-right evaluations, with each comma-separated subexpression evaluated in strict order.

4. Write a program that reads in four integers, prints out yes if the numbers were entered in increasing order, and otherwise prints out no.

5. Write a program that prompts for the length of three line segments as integers. If the three lines could form a triangle, the program prints "Is a triangle." Otherwise, it prints "Is not a triangle." Recall that the sum of the lengths of *any* two sides of a triangle must be greater than the length of the third side. For example, 20, 5, and 10 can't be the lengths of the sides of a triangle because 5 + 10 is not greater than 20.

6. Write a program that tests whether the formula $a^2 + b^2 = c^2$ is true for three integers entered as input. Such a triple is a *Pythagorean triple* and forms a right-angle triangle with these numbers as the lengths of its sides.

7. A mildly exotic operator is the conditional operator `?:`. This operator takes three arguments and has precedence just above the assignment operators, as for example in

```
s = (a < b)? a : b;

// (a < b) true then s assigned a else s assigned b
```

Rewrite the code:

```
static int Max(int a, int b)
{
  if (a < b)
    return b
  else
    return a;
}
```

to eliminate the `if-else` statement.

8. Write a program that reads in integers entered at the console until a value of 0 is entered. A *guard* or *sentinel* value is used in programming to detect a special condition. In this case the sentinel value is used to detect that no more data values are to be entered. After the sentinel is entered, the program should print out how many numbers were greater than 0 and how many numbers were less than 0.

9. Write a program that reads in integers entered at the console until a sentinel value of 0 is entered. After the sentinel is entered, the program should print out the smallest number, other than 0, that was entered.

10. Write a program that reads in characters and prints their integer values. Use the *end-of-file* value −1 as a guard value to terminate the character input. For Windows systems, the end-of-file character can be generated by hitting Ctrl+z on the keyboard. For Unix systems, the end-of-file character can be generated by hitting Ctrl+d on the keyboard. Remember that `Read()` returns −1 if the *end-of-file* is encountered. This action allows you to test the end-of-file value. If you convert this value to a `char`, negative numbers would not be representable. Explain why.

11. Write a program to print every even number between 0 and 100. Modify the program to allow the user to enter a number *n* from 1 through 10 and have the program print every *n*th number from 0 through 100. For example, if the user enters 5, then "0 5 10 15 20…95 100" is printed.

12. Write a program that prints out a box drawn with asterisks, as shown.

Use a loop so that you can easily draw a larger box. Modify the program to read in a number from the user specifying how many asterisks high and wide the box should be.

13. Write a program that reads in numbers until the same number is typed twice in a row. Modify it to go until three in a row are typed. Modify it so that it first asks "how many in a row should I wait for?" and then it goes until some number is typed that many times. For example, for two in a row, if the user typed "1 2 5 3 4 5 7" the program would still be looking for two in a row. The number 5 had been typed twice, but not in a row. If the user then typed 7, the program would terminate because two 7s were typed, one directly after the other.

14. Write a program that generates all Pythagorean triples (see Exercise 6 on page 110) whose small sides are no larger than *n*. Try it with *n* < 200. (*Hint*: Use two `for` loops to enumerate possible values for the small sides and then test to determine whether the result is an integral square.)

15. Write a program that gives you a different message each day of the week. Use a `switch` statement. Take as input an integer in the range 1 through 7. For example, if 6 means Friday, the message might say, `Today is Friday, tGif.` If the user inputs a number other than 1 through 7, have the default issue an appropriate message. Use an enumerated type to represent the days of the week.

16. Write a program that gives you a fortune based on an astrological sign. Use a `switch` statement to structure the code.

17. Write a program that generates an approximation of the real number *e*. Use the formula

$$e \approx 1 + \frac{1}{1!} + \frac{1}{2!} + \frac{1}{3!} + \ldots + \frac{1}{k!} + \ldots$$

where *k*! means *k* factorial = 1 * 2 * . . . *k. Keep track of term 1/*k*! by using a `double`. Each iteration should use the previous value of this term to compute the next term, as in

$$T_{k+1} = T_k \times \frac{1}{k+1}$$

Run the computation for 20 terms, printing the answer after each new term is computed.

18. Write your own pseudorandom number generator. A pseudorandom sequence of numbers appears to be chosen at random. Say that all the numbers you are interested in are placed in a large fishbowl and you reach in and pick out one at a time without looking where you are picking. After reading the number, you replace it and pick another. Now you want to simulate this behavior in a computation. You can do so by using the formula $X_n + 1 = (aX_n + c)$ mod *m*. Let *a* be 3,141,592,621, *c* be 1, and *m* be 10,000,000,000 (see Knuth, *Seminumerical Algorithms*, Addison-Wesley 1969, p. 86). Generate and print the first 100 such numbers as `long` integers. Let $X_1 = 1$.

19. The following code prints 100 random numbers:

```
class Random100 {
  public static void Main()
  {
    int howMany = 100;
    Random t = new Random();
    Console.WriteLine(howMany + " random integers.");
    for (int i = 0; i < howMany; ++i)
      Console.Write(t.Next() + '\t');
    Console.WriteLine();
  }
}
```

Add code that determines average, maximum, and minimum values generated.

20. Alter the previous program to ask the user how many numbers should be generated. Have this be an outer loop. Exit this program when the user answers with zero or a negative number.

21. Use `NextDouble()` to generate 1,000 randomly generated heads and tails. Print out the ratio of heads to tails. Is this a reasonable test to see whether `NextDouble()` works correctly? Print out the size of the longest series of heads thrown in a row.

22. *(C++ and Java)* Rewrite the C# Fibonacci program in Section 3.10, *Software Engineering: Debugging*, on page 102, in C++/Java. Have it print out the first 40 Fibonacci numbers. Investigate the `for` loop scope rules in C++/Java.

METHODS: FUNCTIONAL ABSTRACTION

S *tructured programming* is a problem-solving strategy and a programming methodology that includes two guidelines.

- The flow of control should be as simple as possible.
- Program construction should embody top-down design.

Top-down design, also referred to as *stepwise refinement*, consists of repeatedly decomposing a problem into smaller problems. Eventually, you have a collection of small problems or tasks, each of which can be easily coded. Object-oriented programming strategy encompasses structured programming but has additional elements, which we explain later.

The method construct in C# is used to write code that solves the small problems that result from this decomposition. *Methods* are, in classical programming terms, *functions* or *procedures*. Methods are combined into further methods and ultimately used to solve the original problem. Some methods, such as `Console.WriteLine()`, are provided by the system; others are written by the programmer.

Writing methods is critical to becoming a good programmer. To return to our analogy to writing an essay, the method serves as a well-formed paragraph. In writing a reasoned, coherent essay the paragraph is a most critical construct. Once the writer has mastered the paragraph, any larger writing task is more a test of tenacity and endurance rather than of increasing skill.

Breaking up a large program into smaller programs that can be written as methods is the heart of structured programming. We illustrate structured programming and top-down design in this chapter, but first we describe the method mechanism in more detail.

4.1   METHOD INVOCATION

A simple program is made up of one or more methods contained in a class, one of them being Main(). In these simple cases, program execution begins with Main(). When program control encounters a method name followed by parentheses, the method is *called*, or *invoked*. That is, program control passes to the method. After the method does its work, program control is passed back to the calling environment, where program execution continues. As a simple example, consider the following program, which prints a message.

In file Message1.cs

```
// Simple method use

using System;

class Message {
  public static void Main()
  {
    Console.WriteLine("Hello AJ, Brad, and Craig!");
    WriteMessage();                              // method call
    Console.WriteLine("Goodbye.");
  }

  // Definition of method WriteMessage
  static void WriteMessage()
  {
    Console.WriteLine("A message for you: ");
    Console.WriteLine("Have a nice day!");
  }
}
```

The output is

```
Hello AJ, Brad, and Craig!
A message for you:
Have a nice day!
Goodbye.
```

The method definition includes the name of the method and a method body. The *method body* is a block that is executed when the method is invoked. Program execution begins in `Main()`. When program control encounters `WriteMessage()`, the method is called, or invoked, and program control is passed to it. After the two `WriteLine()` statements in `WriteMessage()` have been executed, program control passes back to the calling environment, which in this example is in `Main()`. In `Main()`, the program finishes by printing "Goodbye."

`Console.WriteLine("Hello AJ, Brad, and Craig!");` is also a method call, as are the two statements that constitute the body of the method `WriteMessage()`. Because `WriteLine()` isn't defined in the class `Message`, we need to tell the computer where to find `WriteLine()`; hence the `Console` preceding the method name. The complete sequence of calls for this program is as follows.

```
The system calls Main() to start the program.
    Main() calls Console.WriteLine().
        "Hello AJ, Brad, and Craig!" is printed.
        Console.WriteLine() returns.
    Main() calls WriteMessage().
        WriteMessage() calls Console.WriteLine().
            "A message for you: " is printed.
            Console.WriteLine() returns.
        WriteMessage() calls Console.WriteLine() again.
            "Have a nice day!" is printed
            Console.WriteLine() returns.
        WriteMessage() returns.
    Main() calls Console.WriteLine().
        "Goodbye." is printed.
        Console.WriteLine() returns.
    Main() returns to the system.
The program ends.
```

The pressure is getting to him. He doesn't want to get called.

4.2   STATIC METHOD DEFINITIONS

The simplest methods are called *static methods*. The general form for static methods is

`public static` *ReturnType Identifier (ParameterList) block*

The *block*—also known as the *method body* of the method definition—contains variable declarations and statements that are executed when the method is called. The variables declared in the method's block are said to be within the scope of the method (see Section 4.4, *Scope of Variables*, on page 125). The *ReturnType* of the method is the type of the value returned by the method. For example, `Math.Sqrt()` returns a `double` that can be used in an expression such as `Math.Sqrt(x) + y`. If nothing is returned, as in our example `WriteMessage()`, the keyword `void` is used. The optional *ParameterList* describes the number and types of the arguments that are passed to the method when it is invoked. If no arguments are passed, the list is empty.

The parameters in the parameter list are variables and can be used within the body of the method. Sometimes the parameters in a method definition are called *formal parameters* to emphasize their role as placeholders for actual values that are passed to the method when it is called. Upon method invocation, the value of the actual argument corresponding to a formal parameter is used to initialize the formal parameter, as shown in the next example.

The keyword public is optional, except with the method Main(). This requirement for public with Main() isn't part of the C# syntax; rather, it is part of the specification of how to run a C# program. We discuss public and other method *access modifiers* in Section 6.3, *Access: Private and Public*, on page 243.

To illustrate these ideas, we can rewrite the preceding program so that the method WriteMessage() has a formal parameter, or argument. The parameter is used to specify how many times the message is to be printed.

In file Message2.cs

```
// Method parameter use
using System;

class Message2 {
  public static void Main()
  {
    Console.WriteLine("HELLO Dan and Jerre!");
    WriteMessage(5);                    // actual argument is 5
    Console.WriteLine("Goodbye.");
  }

  public static void WriteMessage(int howManyTimes)
  {
    // formal parameter  is howManyTimes
    Console.WriteLine("A message for you:");
    for (int i = 0; i < howManyTimes; ++i)
      Console.WriteLine("Have a nice day!");
  }
}
```

The output of this version of the Message program is

```
HELLO Dan and Jerre
A message for you:
Have a nice day!
Have a nice day!
Have a nice day!
Have a nice day!
Have a nice day!
Goodbye.
```

Dissection of the *Message* Program

■`class Message2 {`

A simple program is a collection of methods within a class. The class `Message2` encapsulates the various method definitions. The method `Main()` begins executing first.

■`WriteMessage(5);`   `// actual argument is 5`

This line is the method call for `WriteMessage()`. The actual argument is the constant 5, which is passed to the method and used to initialize the formal parameter `howManyTimes`.

■`static void WriteMessage(int howManyTimes) {`

The return type is `void`, which tells the compiler that the method doesn't return a value. In programming language terminology such a method is called a *pure procedure* as opposed to a function, which returns a value. The parameter list is `int howManyTimes`, which tells the compiler that the method takes a single argument of type `int`. The parameters specified in the definition of a method are called formal parameters. For now, methods must be declared as `static`. We discuss nonstatic methods when we introduce object-oriented programming in Chapter 6, *Classes and Abstract Data Types*.

■`{`
```
  Console.WriteLine("A message for you:");
  for (int i = 0; i < howManyTimes; ++i)
    Console.WriteLine("Have a nice day!");
}
```

The code between the braces constitutes the body of the method definition for `WriteMessage()`. If `howManyTimes` has the value 5, the message is printed five times. When program control reaches the end of the method, control is passed back to `Main()`.

A common mistake is to forget to include `static` in the definition of a method. In Section 6.2, *Instance Methods*, on page 240 we discuss methods that don't include `static` and how they are called. If you leave `static` out of the method definition but then try to call a method following the example in this section, then you get an error message similar to

`Can't make static reference to method` *returnType*

methodName(*parameterTypes*) `in class` *YourClass.*

This message may also include some indication of where the invalid method invocation is located. This message can be confusing at first because it isn't the invocation that's at fault. The error is in the declaration of the method being invoked.

4.3   THE return STATEMENT

When a `return` statement is executed within a method, program control is immediately returned to the point right after the call to the method; if an expression follows the keyword `return`, the value of the expression is also returned to the calling environment. Some examples are

```
return;
```

```
return a;
```

```
return (a * b + c);
```

You can enclose the expression being returned in parentheses. If the expression is complicated, it is considered good programming practice to do so.

There can be zero or more `return` statements in a method. If there is no `return` statement, control is passed back to the calling environment when the closing brace of the body is encountered. This action is called *falling off the end* and is permitted only when the return type is `void`. To illustrate the use of `return` statements, we can write a program that computes the minimum of two integers.

In file Min2.cs

```
// Return expression in a method
using System;

class Min2 {
  public static void Main()
  {
    int   j = 78, k = 3 * 30;

    Console.WriteLine("Minimum of {0} and {1} is {2}",
                      j, k, Min(j, k));
  }

  public static int Min(int a, int b)
  {
    if (a < b)
      return a;
    else
      return b;
  }
}
```

The output of this program is

```
Minimum of 78 and 90 is 78
```

Dissection of the *Min2* Program

```
■public static void Main()
 {
      int   j = 78, k = 3 * 30;
```

The variables j, k, and m are declared to be of type int. The variables j and k are assigned constant expressions for test purposes. We could modify the program to request values as input. (See Exercise 2 on page 163.)

■`Console.WriteLine("Minimum of {0} and {1} is {2}",`
`                  j, k, Min(j, k));`

The values of j and k are passed as actual arguments to `Min()`. The method `Min()` returns a value, which is then printed.

■`public static int Min(int a, int b)`

This line is the *header* of the method definition for `Min()`. The return type of the method is `int`. The value returned from within the method is converted, if necessary, to an `int` before it is returned to the calling environment. The parameter list

```
int a, int b
```

declares a and b to be of type `int`. The formal parameters are used in the body of the method definition.

■`{`
```
   if (a < b)
      return a;
   else
      return b;
}
```

The code between the braces constitutes the body of the method definition for `Min()`. If the value of a is less than the value of b, the value of a is returned to the calling environment; otherwise, the value of b is returned.

Even methods with a few lines of code, such as `Min()`, provide useful structuring to the code. In a real program, there might be several places in the code where the minimum of two numbers is needed. Without the method `Min()`, we'd end up with something like

```
. . . . .
if (a < b)
  x = a;
else
  x = b;
. . . . .
if (c < d)
  y = c;
else
  y = d;
. . . . .
```

Using our method `Min()` changes this code to

```
. . . . .
x = Min(a, b);
. . . . .
y = Min(c, d);
. . . . .
```

Using method calls is shorter and easier to understand, making the overall structure of the program clearer. Another important benefit is that we need to debug the code that finds the minimum only once. In the version without the method `Min()`, because we have to type the conditional statement each time we want the minimum, we are much more likely to make an error.

If we want to modify our program so that the maximum value is also computed, we can use a method `Max()` to do so. We have to add its method definition to the class `Min2`. Here is the method definition.

```
public static int Max(int a, int b)
{
  if (a > b)
    return a;
  else
    return b;
}
```

4.4 SCOPE OF VARIABLES

Variables such as j and k in Main() for the class Min2 are called *local variables*—they can be accessed only "locally" or "nearby." For example, you can't refer to the variable j declared in Main() of Min2, from within Min().

The *scope* of a variable is the range of statements that can access the variable. The scope of a local variable extends from the point where the variable was declared (where it was first mentioned and given a type, as in int j;) to the end of the block containing the declaration. Recall from Section 2.2.1, *Formatting the Output*, on page 45 that a block is a group of statements delimited by braces. A formal parameter is essentially a special kind of local variable. Hence the scope of a formal parameter is the entire definition of the method.

If it weren't for scope's ability to limit the accessibility of local variables, we might have been tempted to write class Min2 as follows.

In file Min2Bad.cs

```
// Doesn't work because of scope
using System;

class Min2Bad {
  public static void Main()
  {
    int   j = 78, k = 3 * 30;

    Console.WriteLine("Minimum of {0} and {1} is {2}",
                  j, k, Min(j, k));
  }

  public static int Min()
  {
    if (j < k)
      return j;
    else
      return k;
  }
}
```

This code won't compile because the variables `j` and `k` can't be referenced outside method `Main()`, as we attempted to do in method `Min()`. In order for `Min()` to compare the values for two local variables in `Main()`, those values must be passed as parameters to `Min()`, as we did in the correct version earlier.

The scope of a variable declaration in the initialization portion of a `for` loop is the loop body plus the update and loop termination expressions. Declaring the index variable for a `for` loop in the `for` loop is quite common. In that case the loop index variable won't be accessible after the loop, as shown in this example.

```
double squareRoot;

for (int i = 1; i <= 10; ++i) {
  squareRoot = Math.Sqrt(i);
  Console.WriteLine("The square root of {0} is {1}",
        i, squareRoot);
}
Console.WriteLine("i = " + i);                    // Syntax error
```

Note that the use of declarations inside blocks could result in two variables with the same name having overlapping scopes. C#, however, disallows a local declaration that conflicts with another local declaration. In the following example, the second declaration of `squareRoot` is illegal because there is already a local declaration for `squareRoot` that extends into the block that is the body of the `for` statement. Likewise, the definition of `i` in the `for` statement is illegal. Also, the final print of `square` is illegal because the scope of `square` ends at the brace that ends the `for` statement.

In file SquareRootsErrors.cs

```
// Contains scope errors
using System;

public class SquareRootsErrors {
  public static void Main()
  {
    int i = 99;
    double squareRoot = Math.Sqrt(i);

    Console.WriteLine("The square root of {0} is {1}",
          i, squareRoot);
```

```
    for (int i = 1; i <= 10; ++i) {
      double squareRoot = Math.Sqrt(i);
      double square = squareRoot * squareRoot;
    Console.WriteLine("The square root of {0} is {1}",
          i, squareRoot);
      Console.WriteLine("squaring that yields " + square);
    }
    Console.WriteLine("The final value of square is " +
                      square);
  }
}
```

Here are the error messages generated by C++ Visual Studio:

```
C:\C#BD\Class1.cs(13): A local variable named 'i' cannot be
declared in this scope because it would give a different
meaning to 'i', which is already used in a 'parent or
current' scope to denote something else

C:\C#BD\Class1.cs(15): A local variable named 'squareRoot'
cannot be declared in this scope because it would give a
different meaning to 'squareRoot', which is already used in
a 'parent or current' scope to denote something else

C:\C#BD\Class1.cs(22): The name 'square' does not exist in
the class or namespace 'SquareRootsErrors'
```

Dissection of the *SquareRootsErrors* Program

```
■public class SquareRoots2 {
    public static void Main()
    {
      int i = 99;
      double squareRoot = Math.Sqrt(i);
```

The scope of these declarations extends to the end of the method
Main().

```
■for (int i = 1; i <= 10; ++i) {
    double squareRoot = Math.Sqrt(i);
```

The declaration of i in the for statement initialization part is illegal because i was already declared in this method. Likewise the declaration of squareRoot is illegal. These declarations are illegal because we can't have two local variables with overlapping scopes that have the same name. Some programming languages allow overlapping, giving precedence to the innermost definition, but C# doesn't. This restriction simplifies the language and adds to program clarity. In this program, the error can easily be eliminated by removing the type declarations so that the two lines become

```
    for (i = 1; i <= 10; ++i) {
        squareRoot = Math.Sqrt(i);
```

```
■double square = squareRoot * squareRoot;
```

The scope of this definition of square extends only to the end of the for statement.

```
■  Console.WriteLine("squaring that yields " + square);
    }
    Console.WriteLine("The final value of square is " +
                        square);
```

The first WriteLine() involving square is within the scope of square so it is fine. The second is beyond the scope of square and results in a syntax error at compile time. A solution would be to declare square before the for statement.

4.5   TOP-DOWN DESIGN

Imagine that you have to analyze some company data represented by a series of integers. As you read each integer, you want to print out the count of integers read, the integer, the sum of all the integers read up to this point, the minimum integer read up to this point, and the maximum integer read up to this point. In addition, suppose that a banner must be printed at the top of the page and that all the information must be neatly printed in columns under appropriate headings. To help you construct this program, we decompose the problem into the following subproblems.

Decomposing the Running Sum Program

1. Print a banner.

2. Print the headings over the columns.

3. Read the data and print them neatly in columns.

You can code each subproblem directly as a method. Then you can use these methods in `Main()` to solve the overall problem. Note that by designing the code this way, you can add further methods to analyze the data without affecting the program structure.

In file RunningSums.cs

```
// Main() calls methods to handle subproblems

using System;

class RunningSums {
  public static void Main()
  {
    WriteBanner();
    WriteHeadings();
    ReadAndWriteData();
  }
  // WriteBanner, WriteHeadings and ReadAndWriteData
  // definitions go here
. . . . .
}
```

This program fragment illustrates in a very simple way the idea of top-down design. Think of the tasks to be performed and code each task as a method. If a particular task is complicated, you can subdivide it into smaller tasks, each coded as a method. A further benefit is that the program as a whole is more readable and self-documenting. There may be many ways to decompose a problem into methods. Much of the art of program design lies in finding a good decomposition.

Coding the individual methods is straightforward. The first method contains a single `WriteLine()` statement.

```
public static void WriteBanner()
{
  Console.WriteLine(
  "**********************************************\n" +
  "*    RUNNING SUMS, MINIMUMS, AND MAXIMUMS    *\n" +
  "**********************************************\n");
}
```

The next method writes headings over columns. It uses \t, which is the escape sequence for a tab character. Words appear separated by a tab.

```
public static void WriteHeadings()
  {Console.WriteLine("Count\tItem\tSum\tMinimum\tMaximum");}
```

Most of the work is done in `ReadAndWriteData()`.

```
public static void ReadAndWriteData()
{
  int cnt = 0, sum = 0, item, smallest, biggest;
  string data;
  data = Console.ReadLine();
  item = int.Parse(data);
  smallest = biggest = item;
  while (item != -99999) {
    ++cnt;
    sum = sum + item;
    smallest = Min(item, smallest);
    biggest = Max(item, biggest);
    Console.WriteLine(cnt + "\t" +  item + "\t"
        + sum + "\t" + smallest + "\t" + biggest);
    data = Console.ReadLine();
    item = int.Parse(data);
  }
}
```

If we execute the program and enter data directly from the keyboard, we get the echoing of input characters and the output of the program inter-mixed on the screen. To prevent this problem, we can use redirection as we saw in Section 2.3.1, *Redirection*, on page 50. To do this on systems with redirection, such as Windows, we create a file called *data* containing the integers

```
19    23    -7    29    -11    17 -99999
```

with each integer on its own line. Most operating systems allow you to specify a file to be used for input in place of the keyboard. If you're running C# from a Windows command line, you can use the command

```
RunningSums.exe < data
```

This procedure is called file redirection because you're redirecting the program to read from a file instead of from the keyboard. In Chapter 9, *Input/Output*, we discuss how to do file I/O more generally. Here's what is printed on the screen.

```
**********************************************
*   RUNNING SUMS, MINIMUMS, AND MAXIMUMS   *
**********************************************
Count   Item    Sum     Minimum Maximum
1       19      19      19      19
2       23      42      19      23
3       -7      35      -7      23
4       29      64      -7      29
5       -11     53      -11     29
6       17      70      -11     29
```

4.6 PROBLEM SOLVING: RANDOM NUMBERS

Random numbers have many uses in computers. One use is to serve as data to test code; another use is to simulate a real-world event that involves a probability. The method of simulation is an important problem-solving technique. Programs that use random number methods to generate probabilities are called *Monte Carlo* simulations. The Monte Carlo technique can be applied to many problems that otherwise would have no possibility of solution.

A random number generator is a method that returns numbers that appear to be randomly distributed within some interval. The method NextDouble() is provided to do this for doubles in the interval 0 to 1. The method Next() is provided to do this for positive integers. These methods require a special variable of type Random. The following program displays some random numbers generated by NextDouble().

In file RandomWrite1.cs

```
// Print Random numbers in the range (0.0 - 1.0).
using System;

class RandomWrite {
  public static void Main()
  {
    int n = 10;
    Console.WriteLine("We print " + n + " random numbers");
    WriteRandomNumbers(n);
  }

  public static void WriteRandomNumbers(int k)
  {
    Random t = new Random();

    for (int i = 0; i < k; ++i)
      Console.WriteLine(t.NextDouble());
  }
}
```

We can add to this class methods for `Max()` and `Min()` from Section 4.2, *Static Method Definitions*, on page 119, which we've already discussed. We need to modify those two methods to work with `doubles` instead of `ints` by changing their arguments and return types:

```
public  static double Min(double a, double b)
public  static double Max(double a, double b)
```

We get output such as the following

```
We print 10 random numbers
0.742152205082659
0.620674013914854
0.411038709995821
0.834714038686228
0.350436510215717
0.799338899925043
0.21757754926457
0.987620887806463
0.149891693214835
0.93123007329738
```

We can then modify `WriteRandomNumbers()` to print out the largest and smallest random number found. Since the functionality of the method was expanded, we renamed it `RandomMinMax()`.

In file RandomWrite2.cs

```
public static void RandomMinMax(int k)
{
  double r, biggest, smallest;
  Random t = new Random();

  r = biggest = smallest = t.NextDouble();
  Console.Write(" " + r);
  for (int i = 1; i < k; ++i) {
    if (i % 2 == 0)
      Console.WriteLine();
    r = t.NextDouble();
    biggest = Max(r, biggest);
    smallest = Min(r, smallest);
    Console.Write(" " + r);
  }
  Console.WriteLine("\nCount: " + k
      + "\nMaximum: " + biggest + "\nMinimum: "
      + smallest);
}
```

Before we dissect this method definition, let's see what the output of the program looks like. If we run this program, the following appears on the screen.

```
We print 10 random numbers
 0.968895339858204 0.325501040241449
 0.868387508144783 0.112957243394552
 0.270304746120379 0.784853317208985
 0.926846959128439 0.859832232287076
 0.86528732900754 0.636474374512431
Count: 10
Maximum: 0.968895339858204
Minimum: 0.112957243394552
```

Dissection of the `RandomMinMax()` Method

■
```
static void RandomMinMax(int k)
{
    double r, biggest, smallest;
```

The variable `k` is a parameter declared to be an `int`. The variables `r`, `biggest`, and `smallest` are all declared to be of type `double`.

■
```
Random t = new Random();
r = biggest = smallest = t.NextDouble();
Console.Write(" " + r);
```

The method `NextDouble()` from the class `Random` is used to generate a random number. That number is assigned to the variables `r`, `biggest`, and `smallest`. The random number is between 0.0 and 1.0.

■
```
for (int i = 1; i < k; ++i) {
    if (i % 2 == 0)
        Console.WriteLine();
    r = t.NextDouble();
    biggest = Max(r, biggest);
    smallest = Min(r, smallest);
    Console.Write(" " + r);
}
```

This `for` loop is used to write the remaining `k - 1` random numbers. Because one random number has already been printed, the variable `i` at the top of the loop is initialized to `1` rather than `0`. Whenever `i` is divisible by 2, the expression

```
i % 2 == 0
```

controlling the `if` statement is true, causing a newline character to be printed. The effect of this is to print two random numbers on each line, except possibly the last, which has only one if an odd number of random numbers are printed. This idiom is commonly used for printing several values on one line.

4.7   SIMULATION: PROBABILITY CALCULATIONS

A common use of computers is to simulate some activity that goes on in the real world. Computer simulations can often be used in place of a dangerous or costly experiment. Another advantage of computer simulations is that they can compress time. Instead of taking years to watch some natural process, a simulation of that process can be done in minutes or hours. Of course, the simulation generally has to be based on some simplifying assumptions, but the results still can be useful.

Let's use a computer to simulate the repeated tossing of a coin. We want to find the probability that we can toss some number, *n*, heads in a row. In less than a second of running time, a program can simulate tossing a coin millions of times.

This program uses a sequence of random numbers between 0 and 1 to simulate the coin tosses. If the next random number in the sequence is less than 0.5, it is considered a head; if the number is greater than or equal to 0.5, it is considered a tail. We conduct many trials, each trial attempting to "toss" *n* heads in a row. If the trial succeeds by tossing *n* heads in a row, we count the trial as a success. If the trial fails, by tossing a tail before *n* heads have been tossed, we count the trial as a failure. The probability that we can toss *n* heads in a row is approximately the ratio of successful trials to total trials. By increasing the number of trials, we can increase the accuracy of our result.

The following is a pseudocode solution to the problem.

Pseudocode for Coin Toss Simulation

```
Input the number of heads in a row for a trial.
Input the number of trials to run.
Perform the specified number of trials.
Print the result.
```

We can refine how to perform the specified number of trials as follows.

Pseudocode for Performing the Specified Number of Trials

```
Initialize the number of successes to 0
While there are more trials to run
  Run one trial
  If the trial was a success
    Increment the number of successes
End while loop
Return the number of successful trials
```

Remember: Pseudocode is an informal notation intended for human beings, not computers. We use indentation to indicate nested statements. We can refine this pseudocode further by detailing how to perform one trial.

Pseudocode for Performing One Trial

```
Let numTosses be tosses for a successful trial
Initialize the number of heads tossed to zero
While number of heads tossed is less than numTosses
  Toss the coin
  If the coin comes up tails
    Return failure
  Increment the number of heads tossed
End while loop
Return success
```

At this point we are almost ready to begin writing the code. As discussed in the preceding section, we can use the method `NextDouble()` to generate random numbers for the interval 0 to 1. This method returns a value of type `double` that is greater than or equal to 0 and less than 1. If the `double` returned is less than 0.5, it is considered heads; if it is greater than or equal to 0.5, it is considered tails. The following is the complete program. We coded each section of the pseudocode as a separate method.

In file CoinToss.cs

```
// Compute the approximate probability
// of n heads in a row by simulating coin tosses.

using System;

class CoinToss {
  public static void Main()
  {
    // Input the number of tosses in a row to try for.
    int numTosses = 4;                         // 4 for testing
    // Input the number of trials to run.
    int numTrials = 10000;                 // 10000 for testing
    // Perform the specified number of trials
    int numSuccesses = PerformTrials(numTosses,numTrials);
    // Print the results
    double probability = numSuccesses / (double)numTrials;
    Console.WriteLine("Probability found in "
            + numTrials + " is  " + probability);
  }

  // return true if numTosses heads are tossed
  // before a tail
  public static bool IsAllHeads(int numTosses)
  {
    double outcome;
    Random t = new Random();
    for (int numHeads=0; numHeads < numTosses; ++numHeads){
      outcome = t.NextDouble();                // toss the coin
      if (outcome < 0.5)
        return false;                          // tossed a tail
    }
    return true;                            // tossed all heads
  }
```

```
// perform numTrials simulated coin tosses
// and return the number of successes
static int PerformTrials(int numTosses, int numTrials)
{
  Console.WriteLine("Monte Carlo " + numTosses +
                     " in a row heads");

  int numSuccesses = 0;

  for (int trials= 0 ; trials < numTrials; ++trials)
                                      // perform one trial
    if (IsAllHeads(numTosses))
      ++numSuccesses;                 // trial was a success
    return numSuccesses;
  }
}
```

Here is the output

```
Monte Carlo 4 in a row heads
Probability found in 10000 is  0.0796
```

Dissection of the *CoinToss* Program

```
■class CoinToss {
   public static void Main()
   {
     // Input the number of tosses in a row to try for.
     int numTosses = 4;                // 4 for testing
     // Input the number of trials to run.
     int numTrials = 10000;            // 1000 for testing
```

The code for Main() follows directly from the pseudocode presented earlier. The comments correspond directly to the pseudocode. When you're actually writing the code, a good first step is to put in the pseudocode as comments. Then either replace the comment/pseudocode with real code, or when appropriate, leave the pseudocode as a comment and add the real code below the comment.

In this example we decided to *hardcode* some input, that is, to insert some test values directly into the program. The comments indicate that we should be reading in the parameters for the program, but instead we simply assign some fixed value. We can easily replace these hardcoded assignments with calls to `ReadInt()` or some other input method.

```
// Perform the specified number of trials
int numSuccesses = PerformTrials(numTosses,numTrials);
```

Here we decided to create a separate method to perform the series of trials. That method needs the number of trials to perform and the number of tosses used to determine whether a trial is a success or a failure. The comment from the pseudocode is almost superfluous because the name of the method and variable names should make clear what is happening. We decided to leave the comment because it emphasizes how we derived this code from the pseudocode.

```
double probability = numSuccesses / (double)numTrials;
Console.WriteLine("Probability found in "
                + numTrials + " is  " + probability);
```

We can now compute the estimated probability of tossing numTosses heads in a row by dividing the number of successful trials by the total number of trials. Because numSuccesses and numTrials are both integers, we must first cast one of them into a double. Otherwise, the result of the integer division would always be zero in this example.

```
public static bool IsAllHeads(int numTosses)
{
  double outcome;
  Random t = new Random();

  for (int numHeads = 0; numHeads < numTosses;
      ++numHeads) {
    outcome = t.NextDouble();                // toss the coin
    if (outcome < 0.5)
      return false;                          // tossed a tail
  }
  return true;                               // tossed all heads
}
```

This method is the key to simulating tossing a coin. If the next num-Tosses are all heads, then the method returns true. If a tail is tossed before numTosses heads are tossed, then the method immediately returns false. In the exercises, we modify this routine to make other calculations, such as the probability of tossing k - 1 heads in k tosses.

```
static int PerformTrials(int numTosses, int numTrials)
  {
  Console.WriteLine("Monte Carlo " + numTosses +
                    " in a row heads");
  int numSuccesses = 0;
  for (int trials = 0; trials < numTrials; ++trials)
                                        // perform one trial
    if (IsAllHeads(numTosses))
      ++numSuccesses;                   // trial was a success
  return numSuccesses;
}
```

This method directly follows the pseudocode presented for Performing the Specified Number of Trials. Each loop iteration performs one trial by calling isAllHeads(), testing the result, and if it was a success, incrementing the count of successful trials stored in numSuccesses.

4.8   INVOCATION AND CALL-BY-VALUE

To call one method from another method in the same class, we write the name of the called method and an appropriate list of arguments within parentheses, as for example in Min(x, y). These arguments must *match in number and type* the parameters in the parameter list in the method definition. The arguments are passed *call-by-value*. That is, each argument is evaluated, and its *value* is used within the called method to initialize the corresponding formal parameter. Thus if a variable is passed to a method, the stored value of that variable in the calling environment won't be changed.

In the following example we attempt to exchange the values of two local variables using the method Swap().

In file FailedSwap.cs

```csharp
// Call-By-Value test

using System;

class FailedSwap {
  public static void Main()
  {
    int numOne = 1, numTwo = 2;

    Swap(numOne, numTwo);
    Console.WriteLine("numOne = " + numOne);
    Console.WriteLine("numTwo = " + numTwo);
  }

  public static void Swap(int x, int y)
  {
    int temp;

    Console.WriteLine("x = " + x);
    Console.WriteLine("y = " + y);
    temp = x;
    x = y;
    y = temp;
    Console.WriteLine("x = " + x);
    Console.WriteLine("y = " + y);
  }
}
```

The output of this program is

```
x = 1
y = 2
x = 2
y = 1
numOne = 1
numTwo = 2
```

Note that, although we successfully swapped the values of the formal parameters, x and y, doing so had no effect on the actual arguments, numOne and numTwo. The formal parameters are effectively local variables in the method Swap() that have their values initialized with the values of the corresponding actual arguments. Five memory locations are identified in this program for storing integers: numOne, numTwo, x, y, and temp.

4.9   CALL-BY-REFERENCE

To write a successful Swap() method that actually swaps the values of two primitive type variables passed as parameters, we must use call-by-reference. Call-by-reference arguments are designated by using the keyword ref. These reference parameters must have *definitely assigned* values, in contrast to out parameters, which can be uninitialized. The ref keyword is used both when declaring the formal parameters and when passing actual arguments. This then makes it clear in the program that these variables have their values changed by the called method.

In file Swap.cs

```
// Call-By-Reference test
using System;

class SwapTwo {
  public static void Main()
  {
    int numOne = 1, numTwo = 2;

    Swap(ref numOne, ref numTwo);
    Console.WriteLine("numOne = " + numOne);
    Console.WriteLine("numTwo = " + numTwo);
  }

  public static void Swap(ref int x, ref int y)
  {
    int temp;

    Console.WriteLine("x = " + x);
    Console.WriteLine("y = " + y);
    temp = x;
    x = y;
    y = temp;
    Console.WriteLine("x = " + x);
    Console.WriteLine("y = " + y);
  }
}
```

The output of this program is

```
x = 1
y = 2
x = 2
y = 1
numOne = 2
numTwo = 1
```

Unlike the *FailedSwap.cs* program, here we have success.

Dissection of the *Swap* Program

■`public static void Swap(ref int x, ref int y)`

The modifier `ref` on the variables `x` and `y` means the `int` variables are to be passed by reference. This allows actual parameters to be passed in and have their values changed.

■`int numOne = 1, numTwo = 2;`

`Swap(ref numOne, ref numTwo);`

When calling `Swap()` inside `Main()`, the actual parameters `numOne` and `numTwo` need the `ref` modifier. This is good programming language design as it makes it clear that those variables may be changed by `Swap()`.

4.9.1 THE out PARAMETER

A special case of call-by-reference is the `out` parameter. It uses the keyword `out` in place of the keyword `ref`. It is used for uninitialized arguments that are *definitely assigned* a value by calling the method. Consider a method that computes the average and the sum of three doubles.

In file AverageAndSum.cs

```
using System;

class AverageAndSum {
  public static void Main()
  {
    double a = 4.5, b = 6.7, c = 88.6;
    double s, avg;

    AverageAndSum(a, b, c, out s, out avg);

    Console.WriteLine("Sum is {0} Average is {1:F3}",
                        s, avg);
  }

  public static void AverageAndSum(double x, double y,
        double z, out double sum, out double average)
  {
    sum = x + y + z;
    average = sum/3.0;
  }
}
```

The output for this is

```
Sum is 99.8 Average is 33.2667
```

Notice that the variables declared as `out` were uninitialized in the method `Main()`. They could not have been called with `ref`.

A typical method using `out` parameters is one used for input or reading values from the console. Consider a method that expects to read a line from the console and return a `double` value.

```
public static void ReadDouble(out double x)
{
    string data = Console.ReadLine();
    x = double.Parse(data);
}
```

Test this method and write similar methods for other basic types.

4.10   RECURSION

A method is said to be *recursive* if it calls itself, either directly or indirectly. In its simplest form the idea of recursion is straightforward. Try the
following program.

In file Recur.cs

```csharp
// Recursive goodbye
using System;

public class Recur {
  public static void Main()
  {
    SayGoodBye(5);
  }

  static void SayGoodBye(int n)
  {
    if (n < 1)                                  // base case
      Console.WriteLine("########");
    else {
      Console.WriteLine("Say goodbye Gracie.");
      SayGoodBye(n - 1);                        // recursion
    }
  }
}
```

This program prints

```
Say goodbye Gracie.
Say goodbye Gracie.
Say goodbye Gracie.
Say goodbye Gracie.
Say goodbye Gracie.
########
```

The general form of a recursive method body is

```
if (stopping condition)                          // base case
  // do whatever at the end;
else {                                           // recursive case
  // execute recursive step
  RecursiveMethod(arguments);
}
```

A simple standard recursive method is factorial.

```
static long Factorial(int n)
{
  if (n <= 1)
    return 1;
  else
    return (n * Factorial(n - 1));
}
```

Suppose that we executed x = Factorial(4); inside method Main(). The sequence of method calls would be

```
Main() calls Factorial(4).
  Factorial(4) calls Factorial(3).
    Factorial(3) calls Factorial(2).
      Factorial(2) calls Factorial(1).
        Factorial(1) returns 1.
      Factorial(2) returns 2.
    Factorial(3) returns 6.
  Factorial(4) returns 24.
  Main() continues assigning 24 to x.
```

When the innermost call, Factorial(1), is executing, it is like having four different copies of the factorial method that have each been started but none have yet returned. Each has its own copy of the formal parameter n, and each value of n is different. Recall that a formal parameter is like a local variable in that the scope is the body of the method. For this reason, the different versions of n don't interfere with each other.

The following table shows another view of Factorial(4). First the base case is considered. Then working out from the base case, the other cases are considered.

| Table 4.1 | Factorial Values | | | |
Call				Value Returned
Factorial(1)	1			= 1
Factorial(2)	2 * Factorial(1)	or		2 * 1 = 2
Factorial(3)	3 * Factorial(2)	or		3 * 2 * 1 = 6
Factorial(4)	4 * Factorial(3)	or		4 * 3 * 2 * 1 = 24

Simple recursive methods follow a standard pattern. Typically, a base case is tested first upon entry to the method. Then there is a general recursive case in which one of the variables, often an integer, is passed as an argument in such a way as to ultimately lead to the base case. In Factorial(), the variable n was reduced by 1 each time until the base case with n equals 1 was reached.

Most simple recursive methods can be easily rewritten as iterative methods, as in

```
static long Factorial(int n) {                    // iteratively
  int product = 1;
  for ( ; n > 1; --n)
    product = product * n;
  return product;
}
```

For a given input value, both factorial methods return the same value, but the iterative version requires only one method call regardless of the value passed in. Method call is an expensive operation, so, in general, iterative versions of methods are more efficient than their recursive versions.

**"I'm the most fascinating person I know,
so I call myself all the time."**

4.11   PROBLEM SOLVING: MATHEMATICS

In science, we frequently have an equation that describes some behavior, such as Newton's law; $F = MA$, for force equals mass times acceleration. For complicated equations, we need to use computation to study their behavior. For example, we might want to visualize an equation. To do so we might graphically plot it or print a table of values for it (see Exercise 19 on page 167).

One interesting property of a function is to find a zero of a function in a given region. We try to find it by computing a function at many points in the interval and find the point $f(x_{root}) = 0$. Consider finding a root for the quadratic equation $f(x) = x^2-2$. This computation might be partly described as follows:

In file FindRootBad.cs

```
// Find the root of x*x - 2
// Version 1.0 Won't work- Why?
using System;

class SimpleFindRoot {
  public static void Main()
  {
    double a = 0.0, b = 10.0, x, step = 0.001;
    x = a;                                  // start at one end
    while (F(x) != 0.0 && x < b) {
      x = x + step;
    }
    if (x < b)
      Console.WriteLine(" root is " + x);
    else
      Console.WriteLine(" root not found");
  }

  static double F(double x) { return (x * x - 2.0); }
}
```

When we run this version, we get the following output

```
root not found
```

What's wrong with this approach? Although we are examining the interval in fairly small steps, we might not exactly hit a zero. We are more likely to identify a zero if we make locating a zero less precise. We leave modifying this code to choose the x so that $f(x)$ is nearest to zero for Exercise 16 on page 166. This new scheme is guaranteed to find a solution, but it has two weaknesses. One, it is a *brute-force* approach and is computationally expensive. Second, it can fail because a smallest $f(x)$ might not be near a true zero.

A better method searches for a smallest interval that contains a zero, which is much safer numerically. This idea is based on the *mean value theorem* of calculus. Informally, when we plot a function on the x and y axes, keeping our pen on the paper, and on one side of the interval the function is above the x axis and on the other side of the interval the function is below the x axis, the pen must cross the x axis in that interval. In other words, for a continuous function, a zero exists in an interval where $f(x)f(y) < 0$.

In our next method we make use of this observation. Further, we use the method of bisection to search the interval efficiently for a zero. This bisection problem-solving technique recurs in many areas of computer science. The idea is to check on the sign of the function evaluated in the center of the current interval and then to replace the existing search interval by one-half the size. We do so by replacing the relevant endpoint of the interval with the point just evaluated. For the code in this example, we assume that $f(a)$ is negative and $f(b)$ is positive for the initial interval endpoints, a and b. As shown in the figure, if the value of the function at the midpoint, $f((a + b)/2)$, is negative, then the left endpoint, denoted by a, is replaced with $(a + b)/2$.

In file FindRoot.cs

```
// Use bisection to find a zero
using System;

class FindRoot {
  public static void Main()
  {
    double a = 0.0, b = 10.0;
    const double epsilon = 0.00001;
    double root = 0.0, residual = 0.0;

    while (b - a > epsilon ) {
      root = (a + b) / 2.0;
      residual = F(root);
      if (residual > 0)
        b = root;                        // replace right endpoint
      else
        a = root;                        // replace left endpoint
    }
    Console.WriteLine(" root is " + root);
  }

  static double F(double x) { return (x * x - 2.0); }
}
```

The output of this program is

```
 root is 1.41421318054199
```

Note that improvement in the accuracy of the interval is guaranteed for each evaluation. This improvement works out to a binary digit of accuracy.

4.12   METHOD OVERLOADING

In Section 4.3, *The return Statement*, on page 121, we presented Min() and Max() methods that work with integer values. If we want these methods to work with values of type double, we must rewrite the methods. Here we rewrite Min() and leave the rewriting of Max() as an exercise. Instead of a and b, we use the parameters x and y, common practice when dealing with floats and doubles:

```
static double Min(double x, double y)
{
  if (x < y)
    return x;
  else
    return y;
}
```

Because C# supports method overloading, this definition of `Min()` and the one from Section 4.4, *Scope of Variables*, on page 125, that includes integer parameters can exist in the same class or program. These two definitions are distinguished by their signatures. A *method signature* is the name of the method, the number of parameters, and the types of the parameters, in that order. For example, the two `Min()` methods have differing signatures,

```
int Min(int, int)
```

and

```
double Min(double, double)
```

When the C# compiler encounters a call, such as `Min(expr1, expr2)`, the compiler can determine which of the two `Min()` methods to call, based on the types of the expressions, `expr1` and `expr2`. For example, if both expressions result in values of type `int`, then `int Min(int,int)` would be called; if both are type `double`, then `double Min(double,double)` would be called. This procedure, known as *signature matching*, is based on the types of the parameters for the method but not on the return type. This ability to define multiple methods with the same name is called *method overloading*.

Overloading is an extremely useful feature. In languages without method overloading, programmers are frequently forced to choose contrived names for methods because another method with the preferred name already exists. Overloading is what makes it possible to call `Console.WriteLine()` with a `string` or with a format string followed by a list of parameters. Actually, different `WriteLine()` methods exist for each of the different signatures.

Returning to our example `Min()`, what would happen if there was a call to `Min()` with one `int` value and one `double` value? The compiler would convert the `int` to a `double` and call the version of `Min()` that takes `double` parameters. In general, the compiler first tries to find an exact match. If it can't find an exact match, then it performs widening primitive conversions to try to find a match. A *widening primitive conversion* is a conversion from one numeric type to another that is guaranteed to maintain the sign and most significant digits of the value being converted. For example, conversions from `int` to `long` or from `int` to `float` are widening primitive conversions. The former loses no information, and the latter may lose some significant digits; however, the most significant digits and the sign are preserved. For a detailed description of widening primitive conversion, see Section 2.4.2, *Implicit Conversions*, on page 55.

Sometimes the conversions can result in more than one possible match. Multiple matches usually result in a compile-time error, and the call is said to be *ambiguous*, as in

In file AmbiguousOverload.cs

```
// Won't compile
using System;

class AmbiguousOverload {
  public static void Main()
  {
    int i = 1, j = 2;

    Console.WriteLine(Ambig(i,j));
  }

  static bool Ambig(float x, int y)
    { return x < y; }

  static bool Ambig(int x, float y)
    { return x < y; }
}
```

An `int` can be converted to a `float` by a widening primitive conversion. The ambiguity arises because we can either convert i and match the first definition of `ambig()` or convert j and match the second definition. The definitions aren't inherently ambiguous; it is the call that is ambiguous. If j was instead declared to be a float, then the ambiguity would be eliminated and only the second definition would match the call. Explicit conversions, discussed in Section 2.4.3, *Explicit Conversions Called Casts*, on page 56, can be used to resolve ambiguities such as this one. For example, changing the call to

```
Console.WriteLine(ambig((float)i, j));
```

would result in a call to the first version of `ambig()`.

Sometimes, widening conversions can lead to two matches but not be considered ambiguous. For example, suppose that signature Scall is the signature of the call and there are methods with signatures S1 and S2. If Scall can be converted to S1 using widening conversions and S1 can be converted to S2 using widening conversions, then S1 is said to be more specific than S2.

In this case the method with signature S1, the more specific signature, is called. Note that in the preceding example, *AmbiguousOverload*, neither of the two method signatures could be converted to the other by using widening conversions. In the following example, two matches can be found, but one is more specific than the other.

In file UnambiguousOverload.cs

```
// No ambiguity here
using System;

class UnambiguousOverload {
  public static void Main()
  {
    int i = 1, j = 2;
    Console.WriteLine(UnAmbig(i,j));
  }
  static bool UnAmbig(float x, float y)
    { return x < y; }
  static bool UnAmbig(double x, double y)
    { return x < y; }
}
```

The output from this program is

```
True
```

Although the call could be converted, using widening primitive conversions to match either of the methods, the method that takes two float values is more specific and hence is the one called.

4.13   PROGRAMMING STYLE

Breaking a problem into small subproblems that are then coded as methods is crucial to good programming style. To be easily readable, a method should be at most a page of code. Except for a few cases where the purpose of a method is trivially obvious from the choice of identifier names, methods should begin with an opening comment. In this book, however, we generally omit such comments because they would be redundant with the surrounding expository text. The opening comment should include a description of the input parameters and the return value. The parameter names should be chosen to identify clearly the purpose of the parameter. In some cases, well-chosen parameter names can eliminate the need for any further explanation.

Another stylistic choice is the order in which method definitions occur in a class. It is usually a matter of taste whether a programmer writes `Main()` followed by the other method definitions, or vice versa. If a programmer is doing top-down development, however, it is natural to start with `Main()`.

It is considered good programming style to have only a few `return` statements in a given method. In fact, the best choice is usually a single return as the last statement in the method. If there are many `return` statements, the logic of the code may be difficult to follow.

Earlier we coded the method `Min()` as:

```
public static int Min(int a, int b)
{
   if (a < b)
     return a;
   else
     return b;
}
```

But this can be recoded with one return as follows:

```
public static int Min(int a, int b)
{
  int temp;
  if (a < b)
    temp = a;
  else
    temp = b;
  return temp;
}
```

The idea is to capture the value to be returned in a temporary local variable. This makes the flow of control clear, but costs an extra assignment and extra `int` variable. Better is the use of the conditional operator:

```
public static int Min(int a, int b)
{
  return (a < b) ? a : b;
}
```

4.14 SOFTWARE ENGINEERING: CORRECTNESS

An *assertion* is a program check for correctness that, if violated, forces an error exit. One point of view is that an assertion is a contractual guarantee among the provider of a piece of code, the code's manufacturer, and the code's client or user. In this model, the client needs to guarantee that the conditions for applying the code exist, and the manufacturer needs to guarantee that the code works correctly under these provisions. In this methodology, assertions provide those guarantees.

Program correctness can be viewed in part as a proof that the computation terminated with correct output dependent on correct input. The user of the computation has the responsibility of providing correct input. This is a *precondition*. The computation, if successful, satisfies a *postcondition*. Such assertions can be monitored at runtime to provide very useful diagnostics. Indeed, the discipline of thinking out appropriate assertions frequently allows the programmer to avoid bugs and pitfalls.

In the C# community, there are standard methods in `System.Diagnostics` to do tracing, debugging, and assertion testing. For instructional reasons we use our own method `AssertMsg()`.

```
static void AssertMsg(bool, string)
```

If the `bool` *expression* evaluates as `false`, `AssertMsg()` produces diagnostic output. The following program provides assertions to demonstrate this. The program finds a minimum of three elements and orders them.

In file MyAssert.cs

```csharp
using System;

class MyAssert {
  public static void AssertMsg(bool condition, string msg)
  {
    if (!condition)                        // condition is false
      Console.WriteLine("Assert Failed:" + msg );
  }

  public static void Order2(ref int p, ref int q)
  {
    int temp = p;
    if (p > q) {
      p = q;
      q = temp;
    }
  }

  public static int Order3(ref int a, ref int b, ref int c)
  // return min
  {
    Order2(ref a, ref b);
    Order2(ref a, ref c);
    Order2(ref b, ref c);
    return a;
  }

  public static void Main()
  {
    int  a = 3, b = 2, c = 6, minimum;

    minimum = Order3(ref a, ref b, ref c);
    AssertMsg(minimum == a, " wrong minimum " );
    AssertMsg(a <= b && b <= c, "  not in order" );
    Console.WriteLine("a = " + a + "  b = " +
      b + "  c = " + c);
    AssertMsg(false, " generate an assert failure ");
  }
}
```

The output from this program is

```
a = 2  b = 3  c = 6
Assert Failed: generate an assert failure
```

Dissection of the *MyAssert* Program

```
■public static void AssertMsg(bool condition,
                              string message)
   {
     if (!condition)                // condition is false
       Console.WriteLine("Assert Failed:" + message );
   }
```

The method tests a `bool` condition. The programmer places a condition at a critical point in the code. If the condition is `true`, then the program continues. If the condition reveals an error, then a message that points to this error is printed.

```
■int  a = 3, b = 2, c = 6, minimum;

minimum = Order3(ref a, ref b, ref c);
AssertMsg(minimum == a, " wrong minimum " );
AssertMsg(a <= b && b <= c, "  not in order" );
```

The method `Order3()` orders the three variables and returns the minimum element that is stored in variable a. The first `AssertMsg()` tests for equality. If this discloses a bug, `"wrong minimum"` is printed. The second `AssertMsg()` tests that the three variables are properly ordered. If this discloses a bug, `"not in order"` is printed.

```
■AssertMsg(false, " generate an assert failure ");
```

This final assertion test is guaranteed to print a message. The system provides a standard assertion class as discussed in Section 10.1, *Using the Assert() Method*, on page 419.

4.15   DR. P'S PRESCRIPTIONS

- Methods should be short.

- Methods should do one job.

- Avoid subtle type conversions in overloading.

- Use explicit conversions to provide an exact match.

- Overload only conceptually coherent method definitions.

A large part of the art of writing code is properly writing methods. Think of methods as the paragraph elements in an essay and statements as sentences. Structured programming is a methodology that decomposes parts of a program into elements that are readily coded as methods. Keeping methods short makes them easier to test for correctness, maintain, and document. Like a paragraph in writing, they are meant to be a basic coherent unit that is easily grasped.

A method should have a readily understood purpose as indicated by the method name; for example, `Max()`, which is clear as to intent. Do not obscure what a method does by giving it unrelated tasks. For example, if you want to average two arrays and find the maximum element, write two different methods. Method names are often verbs that describe their action, such as `Swap()`.

Overloading is frequently overused, making code difficult to follow and debug. In the extreme, by using method `Foo()` with different signatures, one can produce any computation—clearly a poor practice.

4.16   C# COMPARED WITH C++ AND JAVA

C# has a method syntax that follows Java more closely than C++, but it differs from both in its variety of parameter passing mechanisms. In C#, as in Java and C++, a parameter is by default passed by value. In order to effect call-by-reference in C# for value types, the `ref` keyword must be used. The `out` keyword must be used if the variable has not yet been initialized by the calling method. In C++, the ampersand is used for call-by-reference. Java cannot pass primitive native types, such as `int`, by reference.

Below we present the various call-by-value and call-by-reference statements in C#, C++ and Java:

```
// Declaring methods with formal parameters

void Swap(int a, int b)              // C# C++ Java by-value
void Swap(ref int c, ref int d)          // C# by-reference
void Swap(out int e, out int f)          // C# by-reference
void Swap(int& g, int& h)               // C++ by-reference
void Swap(int* i, int* j)                // C++ by pointer

// Calling the respective methods with actual arguments

Swap(a, b)                      // C#, C++, and Java by-value
Swap(ref c, ref d)                   // C# by-reference
Swap(out e, out f)                   // C# by-reference
Swap(g, h)                       // C++ by-reference
Swap(&i, &j)                  // C++ pass a pointer value
```

The following Java program is adapted from the C# *AverageAndSum* program in Section 4.9.1, *The out Parameter*, on page 144.

In file AverageAndSum.java

```
import tio.*;

class AverageAndSum {
  public static void main()
  {
    double a = 4.5, b = 6.7, c = 88.6;
    double s, avg;

    averageAndSum(a, b, c, out s, out avg);

    System.out.println("Sum is " + s + "Average is " + avg);
  }

  public static void averageAndSum(double x, double y,
        double z, out double sum, out double average)
  {
    sum = x + y + z;
    average = sum/3.0;
  }
}
```

The only difference between Java and C# is in the use of the I/O methods, and the use of lowercase to start method names.

The following C++ program illustrates the two ways of implementing the call-by-reference from the *AverageAndSum* program in Section 4.9.1, *The out Parameter*, on page 144. Also notice how in distinction to C# and Java, C++ has file scope functions. In other words, `main()` and other functions need not be inside classes. These functions are roughly equivalent to `static public` methods in C#.

In file averageAndSum.cpp

```cpp
#include <iostream>
using namespace std;

void averageAndSum(double x, double y,
        double z, double& sum, double& average)
{
  sum = x + y + z;
  average = sum/3.0;
}

void averageAndSum2(double x, double y,
        double z, double* sum, double* average)
{
  *sum = x + y + z;
  *average = *sum/3.0;
}

int main()
{
  double a = 4.5, b = 6.7, c = 88.6;
  double s, avg;

  averageAndSum(a, b, c, s, avg);
  cout << "Sum is " << s << " Average is " << avg << endl;
  a += 10.0; b+= 11.0; c += 12.0;
  averageAndSum2(a, b, c, &s, &avg);
  cout << "Sum is " << s << " Average is " << avg << endl;
}
```

SUMMARY

- A simple program is made up of one or more static methods contained in a class, one of them being `Main()`. In these simple cases, program execution begins with `Main()`. When program control encounters a method name followed by parentheses, the method is called, or invoked. This means that program control passes to the method.

- Structured programming is a problem-solving strategy and programming methodology that strives for simple flow of control and involves the use of top-down design. Also referred to as stepwise refinement, top-down design consists of repeatedly decomposing a problem into smaller problems.

- A long program should be written as a collection of methods, each one being, in general, no longer than a page. Each method should cover some small task as part of the overall problem.

- A variable declared in the body of a method is called a local variable. The scope of a variable begins at the point it is declared and continues to the end of the block containing the declaration. The scope of formal parameters is the entire method body. The scope of a variable declared in the initialization expression of a `for` statement is the entire `for` statement.

- A programmer creates a method by writing a method definition, which consists of a header and a block, also known as the method body. The header consists of the type returned by the method, the method name, and a comma-separated list of declarations of parameters enclosed by parentheses. The body consists of a block of statements.

- When a method is called, program control is passed to the method. When a `return` statement is executed or the end of the method is reached, control is passed back to the point of the call. If a `return` statement contains an expression, the value of the expression is also passed back to the point of the call.

- In C#, all arguments of primitive types are by default passed call-by-value. That is, when a variable of primitive type is passed as an argument to a method, even though the formal argument in the method can be changed, the value of the actual argument remains unchanged in the calling environment.

- Call-by-reference arguments of primitive types use the keywords `ref` or `out`. For example, the method `Order2()`, using this mechanism, is declared as

```
void Order2(int ref p, int ref q);
```

- Overloading refers to using the same name for multiple meanings of an operator or a method. The meaning selected depends on the types of the arguments used by the operator or method. In the following code, we overload `Average()`:

```
// Average the values in an input sequence

double Average(int size, int sum);
double Average(int size, double sum);
```

- A method that calls itself directly or indirectly is said to be recursive. Many programming problems can be solved with recursion, although an iterative solution is often more efficient.

REVIEW QUESTIONS

1. Within a class, is the order of method definitions important? Why or why not?

2. True or false? When passing parameters, the name of the actual parameter must match the name of the formal parameter.

3. What is the significance of `void` in the following statement?

```
public static void WriteMessage()
```

4. Give an example of method overloading.

5. A method definition must always specify what important aspect of each formal parameter?

6. Where do you specify the type of expression that must follow the keyword `return`?

7. Does writing a method that has several hundred lines of code in its definition violate top-down programming? Explain.

8. The expression `(int)(n * t.Next()) % 10` generates integers in what range?

9. What method generates a random number between 0 and 1?

10. What should assertions test?

EXERCISES

1. Rewrite the class `Message` in Section 4.1, *Method Invocation*, on page 116, so it prints out a personalized happy birthday greeting.

   ```
   Message for FILLIN:Happy Birthday to you!
               You are XX years old!
               Have a nice year!
   ```

   Be sure that it handles the special case of a one-year-old, printing `You are 1 year old!`

2. Rewrite the class `Message` in the previous exercise to read from the keyboard the value `n` that is passed to the method `WriteMessage()`.

3. What is printed by the following program?

   ```
   using System;
   class Fcn {
     static int Foo(int a, int b) { return (a + b); }
     static int Goo(int x) { return (x * x); }
     public static void Main()
     {
       int i = 2;
       Console.WriteLine("foo = " + Foo(i, 3));
       Console.WriteLine("foo = " + Foo(i, 4));
       Console.WriteLine("goo = " + Goo(i));
       Console.WriteLine("goo = " + Foo(Goo(i), ++i));
     }
   }
   ```

4. What syntax errors are in the following program?

```csharp
using System;
class Scope {
  public static void Main()
  {
    int x = 1;

    {
      int x = 2;
      int y = 3;

      Console.WriteLine("x = " + x);
      Console.WriteLine("y = " + y);
    }
    Console.WriteLine("x = " + x);
    Console.WriteLine("y = " + y);
  }
}
```

5. What is the output of the following program?

```csharp
using System;
class PracticeProblem {
public static void Main ()
{
    int x = 10, y = 5;
    WriteProduct(x, y);
    x = 2;
    WriteProduct(x + y, x);
}

static void WriteProduct(int x,int y)
{
    Console.Write("The Product of " + x);
    Console.Write(" and " + y + " is ");
    Console.WriteLine(x * y);
  }
}
```

6. What is printed by the following program?

```
using System;
class RecursionExercise {
  public static void Main()
  {
    for (int i = 0; i < 10; ++i)
      Console.WriteLine(recurse(i));
  }

  static long recurse(long n)
  {
    if (n <= 0)
      return 1;
    else
      return 2 * recurse(n - 1);
  }
}
```

7. Write a static method Square() that takes an integer and returns its square and a static method Cube() that takes an integer and returns its cube. Use your Square() and Cube() methods to write the methods Quartic() and Quintic() that return the fourth and fifth power of an integer, respectively. Use your methods to write a program that prints a table of powers of integers from 1 to 25. The output of your program should look like

```
A TABLE OF POWERS
-----------------

Integer Square  Cube    Quartic Quintic
------- ------  ----    ------- -------
1       1       1       1       1
2       4       8       16      32
.....
```

8. Write the method static double Max(double x, double y). This method can be defined in the same class as static int Max(int x, int y) because the argument types of the two methods are different. See Section 4.3, *The return Statement*, on page 122 for a similar method, Min().

9. In class `RunningSums` in Section 4.5, *Top-Down Design*, on page 129, the method `ReadAndWriteData()` used a sentinel value -99999 to terminate input. Rewrite the program to ask the user for the number of items and use this positive integer to terminate the input loop.

10. Modify the coin toss simulation in Section 4.7, *Simulation: Probability Calculations*, on page 137, to compute the probability that you get 5 of 10 heads exactly.

11. Modify `IsAllHeads()` in Section 4.7, *Simulation: Probability Calculations*, on page 137, to compute the probability using an unfair coin that comes up heads with probability 0.8. How do fair and unfair coins compare for producing five heads in a row? If you know the probability theory for this case, work it out theoretically. Does the theoretical result agree with your computational experiments?

12. Modify `IsAllHeads()` in Section 4.7, *Simulation: Probability Calculations*, on page 137, to compute `AlmostAllHeads(int n, int k)`, which is true if at least k out of n heads are tossed. Test it by computing the probability that you would toss at least 6 of 10 heads.

13. Write a weather prediction program using the random number generator. Three outcomes should be possible: rain, sun, or clouds. Assume that each outcome occurs one-third of the time.

14. Write a fortune-telling program, using the random number generator to pick 1 of at least 10 fortunes. Use the `switch` statement in the following way.

```
switch((int)(10 * t.NextDouble()) {
   case 0:  ..... break;
   case 1:  ..... break;
   // more cases with fortunes
   case 9:  ..... break;
}
```

15. Write a program to print the values of $f(x) = x^2-2$ for the range $0 < x < 10$. Print the values in this range at a step size of 0.01. Also find the largest and smallest value of $f(x)$ in this interval.

16. Modify `SimpleFindRoot` in Section 4.11, *Problem Solving: Mathematics*, on page 148, to find x, such that $f(x)$ is nearest to zero. You can use the `static` method `Math.abs()` to solve this problem.

17. Modify `FindRoot` to solve for a root of $f(x) = e^x - 10$. (See Section 4.11, *Problem Solving: Mathematics*, on page 150.) Use as your starting interval (0, 5). How do we know this interval works? (The answer can be found in Section 4.11, *Problem Solving: Mathematics*, on page 148.) The method `Math.Pow(double n1, double n2)` computes `n1` raised to the `n2` power. The class also defines the constant `Math.E`.

18. A further method for finding roots employs a Monte Carlo search. A random point in the search interval is chosen. The function is evaluated at this point. If the result is closer to zero than the value of the function for any previous point, then this point is kept as the current candidate solution. The more points evaluated, the greater becomes the confidence in the final solution. This approach is similar to `SimpleFindRoot` and is a brute force, computationally expensive method. (See Section 4.11, *Problem Solving: Mathematics*, on page 148.) It avoids some subtle problems because it chooses its candidate points at random. Write such a method and use 100 points in the interval 0 through 5 to solve for a root of $f(x) = e^{x^2} - 10$. Now try the method with successively 100 and 10,000 points. Observe how slowly the accuracy of the root improves compared to that of the bisection method.

19. Write a program that allows the user to play the game of Craps, which is played with two dice. A simple version of the game between one player and "the house" can be described as follows.

    ### Playing the Game of Craps

    1. The player bets some amount of money.

    2. The player throws the dice.

    3. If the dice total 2 or 12, the player loses the bet and play starts again at step 1.

    4. If the dice total 7 or 11, the player wins the amount of the bet from the house and play starts again at step 1.

    5. If the dice total any other value, this value is called the point.

    6. The player continues to roll the dice until they total either 7 or the point.

    7. If the dice total is 7, the player loses the bet; otherwise, the player has made the point and wins the amount of the bet from the house. In either case, play starts again at step 1.

Play continues until the player indicates that he or she wants to quit or until the player runs out of money. Before you begin to write the code for this program, you should develop a design. Convert the description of play to pseudocode and identify the primary methods that you'll need. You may even need to refine the specification some more first. For example, how much money does the player start with? To simulate the roll of the dice, you can use

```
Random t = new Random();          // declare Random type
(int)(t.NextDouble() * 6) + 1        // get next number
```

to generate a random integer of 1 through 6. You must simulate rolling each die separately. Generating a random number in the range 2 through 12 isn't sufficient.

20. Write and test a method that recursively prints all the characters from *a* through *z*. Remember that each character is one more than the previous.

21. Write and test a method that recursively prints the characters from `first` through `last`:

```
static void WriteRange(char first, char last)
// example if first = 'c' and last = 'g' then
// prints c d e f g
```

(*Hint:* recur on the variable `first`.)

22. *Fibonacci Recursion*: Many algorithms have both iterative and recursive formulations. Typically, recursion is more elegant and requires fewer variables then does iteration to make the same calculation. Recursion takes care of its bookkeeping by stacking arguments and variables for each invocation. This stacking of arguments, although invisible to the user, is still costly in time and space. Let's investigate efficiency with respect to the calculation of the Fibonacci sequence, which is defined recursively by

$$f_0 = 0, \ f_1 = 1,$$
$$f_{i+1} = f_i + f_{i-1} \quad \text{for } i = 1, 2, \ldots$$

Except for f_0 and f_1, every element in the sequence is the sum of the previous two elements. The sequence begins 0, 1, 1, 2, 3, 5, ... Here is a function that computes Fibonacci numbers recursively:

```
static long Fibonacci(int n)
  {
  if (n <= 1)
    return n;
  else
    return (Fibonacci(n - 1) + Fibonacci(n - 2));
}
```

Write a class that tests this recursive calculation. Choose a large enough n, say, $n = 40$, to see the results of the computation on the screen where the calculation visibly slows. On a 400 megahertz Pentium it visibly slows in the range $n > 35$.

Now write an iterative version of this same algorithm and run it up to the same n or larger. It should run instantaneously. Explain why.

ARRAYS

S o far we've been dealing with distinct variables for referring to any particular stored value. However, there are countless collections of similar values in everyday situations—for example, students' test scores, the daily temperature at each city in the country, or the social security numbers of all the students at a university. An array in C# is a data structure that stores and processes such related values. An array is a simple form of *container* that holds a related group of values of the same type. For example, you can use an array of integers to represent student test scores or an array of floating-point values to represent city temperatures or an array of strings to represent the names of students in a class.

5.1   ONE-DIMENSIONAL ARRAYS

C# provides a special syntax for dealing with arrays. In C#, the elements in an array are always numbered 0 through *n*-1, where *n* is the number of individual items or elements in the array. The elements in an array are ordered, and the position of an element in the array is called the element's *index*. This position can result in some awkward or ambiguous statements about arrays. For example, when a person talks about the "first" element in an array, he or she usually means the element at index 0, not the element at index 1. The main reason for starting at 0 instead of 1 is to make C# arrays the same as that of C and C++, both of which use this convention. The reason that those languages start at 0 has to do with how arrays are arranged in the computer's memory and how an individual element is located. Arrays of values are arranged in contiguous memory locations. The name of the array is viewed as referring to the first element in the array. To find the address in memory of a specific element, the computer can add the element's index to the address of the location of the first element. The following shows an integer array of four elements having the values 1, 3, 5, 7 stored in its four elements. The array is named `data`.

```
int [] data = new int[4];

data[0] = 1;
data[1] = 3;
data[2] = 5;
data[3] = 7;
```

The variable `data` tells the computer where the first element in the array is located. To find the value at index 3 in the array the computer locates the first element and then moves down three locations. In this case the element at index 3 contains the integer value 7.

You declare array variables just like any other variable, by specifying a type followed by the name of the variable. For any type `T` in C#, `T[]` is the notation for the type: array of `T`s. Some array variable declarations are

```
int[]    data;              // reference to array of ints
string[] sentence;          // reference to array of strings
```

These are reference declarations. As the preceding figure suggests, the memory location most closely associated with an array variable doesn't contain the array data itself. Rather, it contains a reference or pointer to the actual array data. *Reference variables* are declared with a class type or are declared with an array type. No actual arrays are created by the declarations shown. Arrays are created by using the operator `new`. The general syntax for creating an actual array and assigning an array variable to refer to the newly created array is

someArrayVariable = new *type* [*length*];

Execution of this statement evaluates *length*, an integer expression, and then creates an array with *length* elements of type *type*. The array variable *someArrayVariable* is assigned to reference this newly created array object. For example, assume that we use $v = $ new `int[n]` to allocate an array v. After this statement has been executed, the `int` variables $v[0]$, $v[1], v[2], \cdots, v[n - 1]$ come into existence and can be used by the program. Once an array has been created, its size may not be changed. Here are some more examples.

```
data = new int[7];                           // 7 ints
sentence = new string[2 * n];                // 2n strings
```

Array variables can be declared and assigned initial values in one statement just as other variables are, as in

```
int[]    data = new int[100];
string[] names = new string[1000];
```

5.1.1 INDEXING AN ARRAY ELEMENT

To manipulate each individual element we use *subscripting* or *indexing*. Let's assume the following declarations have been made:

```
int[] someArray = new int [length];
int  i;                      // used to index or subscript array
```

Now we can write someArray[i] to access an element of the array. More generally, to access an element of the array we write someArray[*expr*], where *expr* is an integral expression. We call *expr* a *subscript*, or *index*, of someArray. The value of a subscript should lie in the range 0 through *length* – 1, where *length* is the number of elements in the array.

5.1.2 ARRAY INITIALIZATION

Arrays have their individual elements automatically initialized when allocated. Primitive numeric types are initialized to 0, and the type bool is initialized to false. All other types are reference types and are initialized to the special value null, which signifies that the element doesn't currently refer to anything. Once an array has been created, we can assign specific element values using assignment, as in

```
int[] a = new int[2];           // create a[0] = a[1] = 0
a[0] = 10;                       // a[0] now has integer value 10
a[1] = 20;                       // a[1] now has integer value 20
```

For convenience, C# provides a way to declare, create, and initialize an array in one statement. Arrays can be initialized by a comma-separated list of expressions enclosed in braces

```
int[] a = new int[2] { 10, 20 };              // long form
```

or this can be done succinctly with the new omitted as in:

```
int[] a = { 10, 20 };     // allocates and initializes 2 ints
```

The compiler uses the number of expressions as the size for the array.

5.1.3 ARRAY MEMBER LENGTH

An array is a collection type that has methods and special data members associated with it. The most important extra information is the length of the array. The expression *arrayName*.Length can be used to determine the number of elements allocated to an array. It is an integer value greater than or equal to 0. A common use of the Length member for an array is in a for statement header. Using *arrayVariable*.Length is preferable to coding a particular integer constant or other expression. Technically, Length is a public property of System.Array. This is explained in Section 6.11, *Properties and Data Hiding*, on page 269.

5.2   AN EXAMPLE: SUMMING AN ARRAY

The following simple program initializes an array, prints its values, and computes its sum and average value.

In file ArraySum.cs

```
// Sum the elements in an array and compute their average

using System;
class ArraySum {
  public static void Main()
  {
    int[] data = { 11, 12, 13, 14, 15, 16, 17 };
    int sum = 0;
    double average;
```

```
for (int i = 0; i < data.Length; ++i)
{
  sum = sum + data[i];
  Console.Write(data[i] + ", ");
}

average = sum / (double)(data.Length);
Console.WriteLine("\nsum = " + sum + " average = "
                  + average);
  }
}
```

The output of this program is

```
11, 12, 13, 14, 15, 16, 17,
sum = 98 average = 14
```

Dissection of the *ArraySum* Program

■`int[] data = { 11, 12, 13, 14, 15, 16, 17 };`

The variable `data` is declared to refer to an array of integers. It is allocated seven integer elements, which are initialized to the values 11 through 17.

■`for (int i = 0; i < data.Length; ++i)`

The `for` statement declares the local variable i to be used as an index or subscript variable. This `for` statement is the most common array code idiom. The initial subscript for array objects in C# is 0, so the subscript variable is usually initialized to 0. The array length is kept in the special data member *arrayName*.`Length`, so the terminating condition for this array p is i < data.`Length`. The last part of the `for` statement header is the increment of the index variable, ensuring that each array element gets processed in turn.

```
■sum = sum + data[i];
 Console.Write(data[i] + ", ");
```

The element `data[i]` is selected by computation of the index value. A common error that results is for the index value to be out of range. These subscripted or indexed elements can be used as simple variables of type `int`. In this code, each element's integer value is added to the variable `sum`. Then, in turn, each element's value is printed.

5.3   PASSING ARRAYS TO METHODS

In the previous section, we had code that summed the integer array `data` in `Main()`. This standard action is better packaged as a method so that it can be reused. The following program contains a method `Accumulate()` to compute the sum of the elements in an array of integers.

In file Accumulate.cs

```
// Sum the elements in an array using a method++

using System;

class AccumulateArrays {
  public static void Main( )
  {
    int[] data1 = { 1, 2, 3, 4, 5, 6, 7 };
    int[] data2 = { 16, 18, 77 };

    Console.WriteLine("data1:" + Accumulate(data1));
    Console.WriteLine("data2:" + Accumulate(data2));
  }
```

```
// sum the elements in an array
  static int Accumulate(int[] a)
  {
    int sum = 0;
    for (int i = 0; i < a.Length; ++i)
      sum = sum + a[i];
    return sum;
  }
}
```

The output of this program is

```
data1:28
data2:111
```

The length field of each array allows the `Accumulate()` code to index each array properly. In the first invocation, `Accumulate(data1)`, the seven array elements of `data1` are summed. In the second invocation, `Accumulate(data2)`, the method sums the three elements of `data2`.

C# passes array parameters by reference. Recall that arrays are reference types. Thus, although you may casually think of the value of an array like `data1` as the entire array of values, in fact the "value" of the variable `data1` is simply a reference to the array of values. So think of the array variable as storing the address of the actual array data. This address, not the array data, is passed to a method.

One of the reasons for this style of parameter passing with arrays is that arrays are often very large. Passing references to the array instead of the entire array of values enables programs to execute much faster. Each time an array is passed as a parameter, all the data values in the array need not be copied into the method—only the address of the array is copied.

An important consequence of the fact that array references, not the entire array of values, are passed is that we can pass an array variable to a method and have the method modify the contents of the array. This result is called a *side effect* because a side effect of calling the method is that the array's contents are changed. The following program contains a method for copying the values of one array into another array.

In file MyCopy.cs

```
// Demonstrate that array parameters can be modified

using System;
class MyCopy {
  public static void Main( )
  {
    int[] data1 = {1, 2, 3, 4, 5, 6, 7};
    int[] data2 = {8, 9, 10, 11, 12, 13, 14};
    CopyIt(data1, data2);
    Console.Write("data1:");
    for (int i = 0; i < data1.Length; ++i)
      Console.Write(" " + data1[i]);
    Console.WriteLine();                      // Output data1
    Console.Write("data2:");
    for (int i = 0; i < data2.Length; ++i)
      Console.Write(" " + data2[i]);
    Console.WriteLine();                      // Output data2
  }

  static void CopyIt(int[] from, int[] to)
  {
    for (int i = 0; i < from.Length; ++i)
      to[i] = from[i];
  }
}
```

The output of this program is

```
data1: 1 2 3 4 5 6 7
data2: 1 2 3 4 5 6 7
```

The call to `CopyIt()` changes the integer values stored in the elements of the array `data2`. The elements of the array `to` inside `CopyIt()` are *mutable* or changeable. Recall that a primitive type variable, when passed as a call-by-value parameter, can't be changed by the called method, although the copy in the called method can be changed. In contrast, use of an array reference parameter can lead to changes in array element values in the calling environment. When a parameter, such as the second parameter to `CopyIt()`, is used to pass information back to the calling environment, the parameter is called an *output parameter*. It is so called because the parameter is used to send information from the method. This action is shown graphically in the following illustration. The arrows indicate that the array variables are referring to array objects. Although not shown, each array object contains the length of the array, followed by the elements of the array. When the method CopyIt() is called, the *values* in the boxes labeled data1 and data2 are copied into the boxes labeled from and to. Recall also that the value is the reference to the array, not the array of values. The crossed-out values show how the old element values in data2 or to (both refer to the same array of values) are replaced during the execution of the body of method CopyIt().

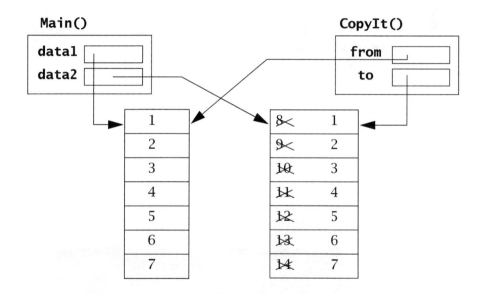

5.3.1   THE System.Array.Copy() METHOD

Just as Length is an available public data member for an array, a Copy() method is publicly available for arrays. The two overloaded definitions are:

```
public static void Copy(T from[], T to[], int howMany);
public static void Copy(T from[], int fromI, T to[],
                        int toI, int howMany);
```

In its first definition the from array is copied from its initial element for howMany elements, over to the to array. In its second definition the from array is copied from its fromT indexed element for howMany elements, over to the to array starting at its toI indexed element.

In file SystemCopy.cs

```
// Demonstrate that array parameters can be modified

using System;
class SystemCopy {
  public static void Main( )
  {
    int[] data1 = {1, 2, 3, 4, 5, 6, 7};
    int[] data2 = {8, 9, 10, 11, 12, 13, 14};

    // We use the standard library method
    System.Array.Copy(data1, data2, data1.Length);
    Console.Write("data1:");
    for (int i = 0; i < data1.Length; ++i)
      Console.Write(" " + data1[i]);
    Console.WriteLine();                          // Output data12
    Console.Write("data2:");
    for (int i = 0; i < data2.Length; ++i)
      Console.Write(" " + data2[i]);
    Console.WriteLine();                          // Output data2
  }
}
```

The output of this program is

```
data1:  1  2  3  4  5  6  7
data2:  1  2  3  4  5  6  7
```

5.4 FINDING ARRAY MINIMUM AND MAXIMUM

We can use the following program to illustrate how to write typical array processing code. Arrays are often used to store large amounts of data that needs to be processed. Here our program reads in an array of values, prints out the values, and finds the minimum and maximum elements.

In file MinMax.cs

```csharp
using System;

class MinMax {
  public static void Main()
  {
    int[] data;
    int n;

    Console.WriteLine("Enter size of data[]:");
    n = ReadInt();
    data = new int[n];
    Console.WriteLine("Enter " + n + " integers,"
                        + " one integer per line:");
    ReadArray(data);
    WriteArray(data, "My Data");
    Console.WriteLine("minimum is " + Minimum(data)
        + "   maximum is " + Maximum(data));
  }

  static int ReadInt()
  {
    string input;
    input = Console.ReadLine();
    return int.Parse(input);
  }

  static void ReadArray(int[] a)
  {
    for (int i = 0; i < a.Length; ++i) {
      a[i] = ReadInt();
    }
  }

    static int Maximum(int[] a)
    {
    int  max = a[0];                        // initial max value
    for (int i = 1; i < a.Length; ++i)
      if (a[i] > max)
        max = a[i];
    return max;
  }
}
```

```
    static int Minimum(int[] a)
  {
   int  min = a[0];                          // initial max value

    for (int i = 1; i < a.Length; ++i)
      if (a[i] < min)
        min = a[i];
    return min;
  }

// print the elements of an array to the console
  static void WriteArray(int[] a, string arrayName)
  {
    Console.WriteLine(arrayName );
    for (int i = 0; i < a.Length; ++i)
      Console.Write(a[i] + "  ");
    Console.WriteLine();
  }
}
```

Sample output for this program is

```
Enter size of data[]:
3
Enter 3 integers, one integer per line:
16
28
4
My Data
16  28  4
minimum is 4    maximum is 28
```

Note that this program contains a series of useful methods, all of which are applicable to the basic container class, integer array. The code also shows the power of the `for` statement as an iterator mechanism for traversing the array container, processing each element in turn.

Dissection of the *MinMax* Program

■
```
int[] data;
int n;
Console.WriteLine("Enter size of data[]:");
n = Console.in.readInt();
data = new int[n];
```

The array reference variable `data` is initially `null`. We dynamically create the array based on user input, namely, the input assigned to `n`.

■
```
readArray(data);
printArray(data, "My Data");
Console.WriteLine("minimum is " + Minimum(data)
      + "   maximum is " + Maximum(data));
```

Once again, we utilize the power of structured programming. We solve the original problem by using a series of method calls. Each method is easily coded as a short block.

■
```
static int Maximum(int[] a)
   {
   int  max = a[0];                    // initial max value

   for (int i = 1; i < a.Length; ++i)
     if (a[i] > max)
       max = a[i];
   return max;
}
```

The maximum value is found by a linear search of the array. One element at a time is tested to determine whether it improves on the maximum value. The term *linear* refers to the fact that computing time is proportional to the size or length of the array. The other methods have similar code, namely, a single `for` statement that processes the entire array.

5.5 ◣ THE foreach STATEMENT

So far we have used `for` statements with specific tests to process arrays. Many of these statements have the form:

for (*indexVar* = 0; *indexVar* < *arrayName.Length*; ++*indexVar*)
  process arrayName[*indexVar*];

This `for` statement can often be replaced by a `foreach` statement.

foreach (*Type variableName* in *arrayName*)
  statement

The `foreach` is an iterator statement that sequences over every element in *arrayName*. The *variableName* is declared to be of a *Type* assignment compatible with the values stored in *arrayName*. Each element of the array is iteratively assigned to *variableName*. Let us rewrite the `WriteArray()` method using the `foreach`.

```
static void WriteArray(int[] a, string arrayName)
{
  Console.WriteLine(arrayName );
  foreach (int element in a)
    Console.Write(element + "   ");
  Console.WriteLine();
}
```

The `foreach` has less machinery and hence is safer. It avoids common indexing errors, such as *off by one* errors. These errors occur when you get the array range wrong and either do not process all the array elements or exceed the array bounds. The `foreach` statement makes it clear what the programmer's intention is—namely, to process all elements in the array. It is important to note that the `foreach` statement cannot be used to modify the array's contents. When you need the array element's values to change, you must use a `for` statement with indexing.

The `foreach` statement is available for any collection that implements the interface `IEnumerable` (see Section 11.5, *Indexers, Iterators, and IEnumerator*, on page 473). In an intuitive sense, such a collection is sequentially indexible. The `foreach` statement always takes each element in turn, for the entire collection; the element cannot, however, be modified by the `foreach` statement.

5.6   ARRAY METHODS AND PROPERTIES

Besides Copy(), other standard methods can be used on any array type. A list of some of these follows with a brief explanation of their use. At this stage in your program you should master the programming idioms to write your own array code. However, reuse is a key to good software development and the standard array methods and properties in Table 5.1 through Table 5.3 should be used unless special needs require that they be replaced by special code for the equivalent operation.

Table 5.1	Array Public Static Methods
BinarySearch()	Searches a one-dimensional sorted Array for a value, using a binary search algorithm.
Clear()	Sets a range of elements in the Array to zero or to a null reference.
Copy()	Copies a section of one Array to another Array, and performs casting as required.
IndexOf()	Returns the index of the first occurrence of a value in a one-dimensional Array or in a portion of the Array.
LastIndexOf	Returns the index of the last occurrence of a value in a one-dimensional Array or in a portion of the Array.
Reverse()	Reverses the order of the elements in a one-dimensional Array or in a portion of the Array.
Sort()	Sorts the elements in one-dimensional Array objects.

Table 5.2	Array Public Instance Properties
Length	Gets the total number of elements in all the dimensions of the Array.
Rank	Gets the rank (number of dimensions) of the Array.

Table 5.3	Array Public Instance Methods
CopyTo()	Copies all elements of the current one-dimensional Array to the specified one-dimensional Array, starting at the specified destination Array index.
GetLength()	Gets the number of elements in the specified dimension of the Array.
GetLowerBound()	Gets the lower bound of the specified dimension in the Array.
GetUpperBound()	Gets the upper bound of the specified dimension in the Array.
Initialize()	Initializes each element of value-type Array by calling the default constructor of the value type.
SetValue()	Sets the specified Array elements to the specified value.

In file ArrayMethods.cs

```csharp
// Use of Array methods
using System;

class ArrayMethods {
  public static void Main()
  {
    string[]  words = {"the", "quick", "brown", "fox",
                       "jumped", "over", "the", "fence"};
    foreach (string s in words)
      Console.Write(s + ", ");
    Console.WriteLine("\nthe is at 1st " +
          Array.IndexOf(words, "the"));
    Console.WriteLine("the is at last " +
          Array.LastIndexOf(words, "the"));
    Array.Reverse(words);
    foreach (string s in words)
      Console.Write(s+ ", ");
    Console.WriteLine("\n\nSorted");
    Array.Sort(words);
    foreach (string s in words)
      Console.WriteLine(s);
  }
}
```

The output for this program is

```
the, quick, brown, fox, jumped, over, the, fence,
the is at 1st 0
the is at last 6
fence, the, over, jumped, fox, brown, quick, the,

Sorted
brown
fence
fox
jumped
over
quick
the
the
```

Dissection of the *ArrayMethods* Program

```
string[] words = {"the", "quick", "brown", "fox",
                    "jumped", "over", "the", "fence"};
foreach (string s in words)
  Console.Write(s + ", ");
```

We use these words to test the methods in the container class System.Array. The foreach statement iterates through the array. It is a basic idiom for processing an array or other indexed container.

```
Console.WriteLine("\nthe is at 1st " +
  Array.IndexOf( words, "the"));
Console.WriteLine("the is at last " +
  Array.LastIndexOf( words, "the"));
```

The first and last instance of the is found in the array. The first instance occurs in element indexed 0. The last instance occurs in element indexed 6.

```
■Array.Reverse(words);
 foreach (string s in words)
   Console.Write(s+ ", ");
 Console.WriteLine("\n\nSorted");
 Array.Sort(words);
 foreach (string s in words)
   Console.WriteLine(s);
```

We first reverse the elements and print them. We then sort the elements and print them.

5.7   A SIMPLE SORTING METHOD

Methods that order information are crucial to searching large databases. Think of a dictionary; it is relatively easy and convenient to use because the information has been sorted and is presented in alphabetic, or lexicographic, order. Sorting is a very useful problem-solving technique. The question of how to sort information efficiently is an important area of computer science theory and practice.

Efficient sorting algorithms typically require approximately $n \log(n)$ comparisons to sort an array with n elements. The selection sort, presented below, is inefficient because it requires n^2 comparisons; nonetheless, for small arrays its performance is usually okay. After presenting the code for `SelectionSort`, we illustrate in detail how the program works on a particular array of integers.

In file SelectionSort.cs

```
// Sort an array of integers

using System;
```

```
class SelectionSort {
  public static void Main( )
  {
    int[] a = { 7, 3, 66, 3, -5, 22, -77, 2 };

    Sort(a);
    foreach (int element in a)
      Console.Write(element + "\t");
  }

  // sort using the selection sort algorithm
  static void Sort(int[] data)
  {
    int next, indexOfNext;

    for (next = 0; next < data.Length - 1; ++next) {
      indexOfNext = Min(data,next,data.Length - 1);
      Swap(data, indexOfNext, next);
    }
  }

  // find the smallest element in a specified range
  static int Min(int[] data, int start, int end)
  {
    int indexOfMin = start;
    for (int i = start + 1; i <= end; ++i)
      if (data[i] < data[indexOfMin])
        indexOfMin = i;                   // found a smaller value
    return indexOfMin;
  }

  static void Swap(int[] data, int first, int second)
  {
    int temp;
    temp = data[first];
    data[first] = data[second];
    data[second] = temp;
  }
}
```

The output of this program is

```
-77    -5    2    3    3    7    22    66
```

Dissection of the *SelectionSort* Program

```
■public static void Main( )
{
    int[] a = {7, 3, 66, 3, -5, 22, -77, 2};

    Sort(a);
    foreach (int element in a)
        Console.Write(element + "\t");
}
```

This program creates a sample array, passes the array to the method Sort(), and then prints the array. Before the call to Sort(), the values in the array are clearly not in increasing numerical order. After the call to Sort() the values in the array are in increasing numerical order. We use the foreach statement to iterate over the entire array.

```
■static void Sort(int[] data)
{
    int next, indexOfNext;
    for (next = 0; next < data.Length - 1; ++next) {
        indexOfNext = Min(data,next,data.Length - 1);
        Swap(data, indexOfNext, next);
    }
}
```

This method does the actual sort. It is called a *selection sort* because the algorithm first finds the smallest value in the array, selects it, and puts it in its proper position. The algorithm then selects the smallest value of those remaining and so on until all values have been selected. Each iteration of the for loop selects the smallest value of the *remaining* values—those with indices between next and data.Length - 1. The first iteration selects the smallest value from the entire array because next is 0. We have written a method, Min(), to do the work of finding the index of the smallest element over a range of indices. The method Swap() moves the selected element, the one with index indexOfNext, into its proper position, next, by swapping it with whichever element is currently next. The operation of Sort() is illustrated for the data in this program, following this dissection of SelectionSort.

```
static int Min(int[] data, int start, int end)
{
   int indexOfMin = start;                  // initial guess

   for (int i = start + 1; i <= end; ++i)
     if (data[i] < data[indexOfMin])
       indexOfMin = i;                // found a smaller value
   return indexOfMin;
}
```

This method finds the index of the smallest value in array `data`, considering only the values with indices between `start` and `end`, inclusive. This method is similar to the `Min()` method discussed earlier; however, the one here doesn't look at the entire array. For the program `SelectionSort`, we didn't need to be able to specify the upper limit for the indices because the method `Sort()` always uses the index of the last element as the upper limit. Writing the method as shown here makes reusing the method easier in other programs where a varying upper limit on the index might be needed.

```
static void Swap(int[] data, int first, int second)
{
   int temp;
   temp = data[first];
   data[first] = data[second];
   data[second] = temp;
}
```

To keep the code for `Sort()` as short and clear as possible, we provide this method to swap the values stored at two different locations in an array.

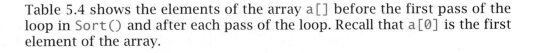

Table 5.4 shows the elements of the array `a[]` before the first pass of the loop in `Sort()` and after each pass of the loop. Recall that `a[0]` is the first element of the array.

| Table 5.4 | Elements of Array a[] After Each Pass | | | | | | | |
Pass	a[0]	a[1]	a[2]	a[3]	a[4]	a[5]	a[6]	a[7]
Unordered	7	3	66	3	–5	22	–77	2
First	–77	3	66	3	–5	22	7	2
Second	–77	–5	66	3	3	22	7	2
Third	–77	–5	2	3	3	22	7	66
Fourth	–77	–5	2	3	3	22	7	66
Fifth	–77	–5	2	3	3	22	7	66
Sixth	–77	–5	2	3	3	7	22	66
Seventh	–77	–5	2	3	3	7	22	66

The first pass finds that the index of the smallest element is 6. The value at index 6 is swapped with the value at index 0 as shown in the row labeled First. In the second pass, only values with indices 1 through 7 are examined. The next smallest element is at index 4. The value at index 4 is then swapped with the value at index 1. The variable second in method Swap() keeps track of where the newly selected element is supposed to be placed. This process continues until the entire array has been sorted. Note that, although the elements are actually in order at the end of the sixth pass, the program continues. In fact, during the last pass the element at index 6 is selected as the smallest and swapped with the element at 6, which of course doesn't actually do anything.

5.8   SEARCHING AN ORDERED ARRAY

Let's assume an array with elements a[0] ≤ a[1] ≤ ... ≤ a[Length - 1]. Now finding the minimum or maximum element in this ordered array can be done in a fixed number of operations, regardless of the size of the array. The minimum is the value a[0], and the maximum is the value a[Length - 1]. Finding the minimum and the maximum requires linear time for an unordered array. That is, the number of operations is directly proportional to the length of the array.

What if we want to find the position of a given value in a sorted array? This problem is common in searching a large database. For example, most people have an identification code, usually their social security number. Their records, such as credit or employment history, can be searched by using this identification code. In general, such an identification code is called a *key* when it is used for searching in a database.

Let's write a routine to look for a particular value in an ordered array and, if the value is found, return its position in the array. If the value isn't found, the routine returns -1.

```
static int LinearSearch(int[] keys, int v)
{
  for (int i = 0; i < keys.Length; ++i)
    if (keys[i] == v)
      return i;
  return -1;
}
```

Note how the loop terminates if the element's position is found. If the element isn't found, the entire array is searched. We call this method `LinearSearch()` because the time required to find the desired element is proportional to the length of the array. We haven't really taken advantage of the fact that the array is ordered. For an ordered array, we can improve on this performance by recognizing that, once we have a value larger than v, we can stop looking.

```
static int BetterLinearSearch(int[] keys, int v)
{
  for (int i = 0; i < keys.Length; ++i)
    if ( keys[i] == v)
      return i;                          // just right
    else if (keys[i] > v)
      return -1;                         // too large
  return -1;                             // not found
}
```

For failed searches, this version should terminate on average in roughly half the time of the method `LinearSearch()`. However, we still haven't taken full advantage of the ordering information.

Consider a number guessing game whereby you try to guess a number within a certain interval, using as few guesses as possible. If asked to guess a number between 1 and 100, inclusive, your optimal strategy is to guess 50. If the other person says that your guess is too big, you should next guess 25; if your guess was too small, your next guess should be 75. After each wrong guess reduce the range of possible guesses by half. Using this strategy, you get the answer in at most seven guesses. The following program uses such an algorithm in the method `MyBinarySearch()`.

In file MyBinarySearch.cs

```csharp
// Use bisection search to find a selected value
// in an ordered array

using System;

class MyBinarySearchArray {
  public static void Main( )
{
    int[] data = {2, 3, 5, 7, 11, 13, 17, 19, 23, 29, 31};
    int index = MyBinarySearch(data, 19);

    Console.WriteLine("index in data is " + index);
  }

  // find the index of element v in array keys
  // return -1 if it is not found
 static int MyBinarySearch(int[] keys, int v)
  {
    int position;
    int begin = 0, end = keys.Length - 1;

    while (begin <= end) {
      position = (begin + end) / 2;
      if (keys[position] == v)
        return position;                        // just right
      else if (keys[position] < v)
        begin = position + 1;                   // too small
      else
        end = position - 1;                     // too big
    }
    return -1;
  }
}
```

The output of this program is

```
index in data is 7
```

Each time through the `while` loop, the search interval is halved—hence the
name `MyBinarySearch()`. Thus the search of an ordered array of keys

makes at most *log(n)* comparisons for an array with *n* elements. A search of roughly one thousand elements is accomplished in no more than 10 iterations (recall that 1024 is 2^{10}), and a search of a million elements takes no more than 20 iterations (1,000,000 is approximately 2^{20}).

5.8.1 RECODING MyBinarySearch() RECURSIVELY

The binary search algorithm has a natural recursive expression. The base cases are either to find the element or to have no more elements to search. Otherwise the general recursion is to look at the middle element of our container and decide to search elements that are less or greater than the element searched for.

In file RBinarySearch.cs

```
// Bisection search finds selected value in an ordered array
using System;

class RBinarySearchArray {
  public static void Main( )
  {
    int[] data = {2, 3, 5, 7, 11, 13, 17, 19, 23, 29, 31};
    int index = RBinarySearch(data, 19, 0, data.Length);

    Console.WriteLine("index in data is " + index);
  }

  // find index of element v in array keys else return -1
  static int RBinarySearch(int[] keys, int v, int b, int e)
  {
    int position = (b + e ) / 2;            // look in middle

    if (b <= e ) {
      if (keys[position] == v)
        return position;                              // found
      else if (keys[position] < v)
        return RBinarySearch(keys, v, position + 1, e);
      else
        return RBinarySearch(keys, v, b, position - 1);
    }
    return -1;                                  // not found
  }
}
```

The output of this program is

```
index in data is 7
```

Dissection of the *RBinarySearch* Program

■`static int RBinarySearch(int[] keys, int v, int b, int e)`

The `keys` are searched for value `v`. The indices `b` and `e` mark the search range.

■
```
int position = (b + e ) / 2;          // look in middle
if (b <= e ) {
```

We look in the middle stored in the variable `position`, and make sure that there is at least one element in this range.

■
```
if (keys[position] == v)
   return position;                            // found
```

Here we have the base case where the element is found.

■
```
else if (keys[position] < v)
   return RBinarySearch(keys, v, position + 1, e);
else
   return RBinarySearch(keys, v, b, position - 1);
```

This is the general recursion. The range that we are looking in is guaranteed to narrow. This guarantees termination. Which half of the range is searched depends on how the comparison of `v` to the midpoint element turns out.

■`return -1;`   `// not found`

The other base case where the test `b <= e` is false, and therefore no elements remain to be tested.

5.9   BIG OH: CHOOSING THE BEST ALGORITHM

Our initial method, `LinearSearch()` from Section 5.8, *Searching an Ordered Array*, on page 193, required as many as $n - 1$ comparisons, and our final version, `RBinarySearch()` from Section 5.8.1, *Recoding MyBinarySearch() Recursively*, on page 195, required at most $log(n)$ commparisons. We say that there are *on the order of n* comparisons in `LinearSearch()` and *on the order of log(n)* comparisons in `RBinarySearch()`. Because this concept is so important in computer science, there is a special notation for it. We say that using `LinearSearch()` to find an element requires $O(n)$ time. Read this expression as "on the order of *n*" or "order *n*" or "big oh of *n*" time. The notation is called *big-oh notation*.

More precisely, $O(n)$ means that as *n* increases the quantity being measured is at most $c \times n$ for some constant *c*. In general, $O(f(n))$ means that the quantity being measured is at most $c \times f(n)$ for some constant *c*. In our example, the quantity is the number of comparisons.

When we convert an expression that involves several terms into big-oh notation, only the fastest-growing term remains. For example, $3n^2 + 20n + 15$ is $O(n^2)$ because $c \times n^2$ is larger than $3n^2 + 20n + 15$ for all values of *n* greater than 3, if $c = 10$. Similarly, $3n + 20\ log(n)$ is $O(n)$ because *n* grows faster than $log(n)$. If an algorithm requires a fixed number of operations, regardless of the size of the problem, it is $O(1)$; it is also known as requiring constant time.

In most cases, an algorithm that requires $O(log(n))$ time is better than an algorithm that requires $O(n)$ time. However, there may be some small values of *n* for which the $O(n)$ algorithm is better. Suppose that the actual number of operations for the $O(log(n))$ algorithm was $512\ log(n)$ and the actual number of operations for the $O(n)$ algorithm was $5n$. Then the $O(n)$ algorithm is faster for all values of *n* less than 1024.

An algorithm that completes in $O(n)$ time is said to be a linear time algorithm because the running time is bounded by a linear function. Similarly, an $O(log(n))$ algorithm is said to be logarithmic and an $O(2^n)$ algorithm is exponential.

Sometimes, big-oh notation isn't enough to help you choose the best algorithm. It can be proved that $n - 1$ comparisons are needed to find either the minimum or the maximum element in an array. Does that mean that `RBinarySearch()` finds the array element using the fewest number of comparisons? The answer is *no*. The following method, `MinMaxOptimal()`, shows how to find the minimum and maximum elements of an array, using approximately 25 percent fewer comparisons involving array elements.

In file FindMinMax.cs

```
// Ira Pohl CACM 1972
using System;

class FindMinMax {
  public static void Main( )
  {
    int[] data = {9, 6, 3, 88, -9, 677};
    int[] mm = MinMaxOptimal(data);
    Console.WriteLine("min is " + mm[0] + "  max is "
                      + mm[1]);
  }

  static int[] MinMaxOptimal(int[] data)
  {
    int[] minMax = new int[2];            // store min and max
    // the length must be even
    int midPoint = data.Length / 2;
    // loop puts the min somewhere in the first half
    // and the max somewhere in the second half
    for (int i = 0; i < midPoint; ++i)
      if (data[i] > data[midPoint + i ])
        Swap(i, midPoint + i, data);
    // loop finds the min which must be in first half
    minMax[0] = data[0];
    for (int i = 1; i < midPoint; ++i)
      if (data[i] < minMax[0])
        minMax[0] = data[i];
    // loop finds the max which must be in second half
    minMax[1] = data[midPoint];
    for (int i = midPoint + 1; i < data.Length; ++i)
      if (data[i] > minMax[1])
        minMax[1] = data[i];
    return minMax;
  }
}
```

```
   static void Swap(int i, int j, int[] data)
   {
     int temp = data[i];
     data[i] = data[j];
     data[j] = temp;
   }
}
```

The output of this program is

```
min is -9  max is 677
```

With `MinMaxOptimal()`, we can find the minimum and the maximum value in an array by using $3(n/2-1)$ comparisons involving array elements. Each loop executes $n/2-1$ comparisons. In the *MinMax* program from Section 5.4, *Finding Array Minimum and Maximum*, on page 182, the two methods used to find the minimum and the maximum use $2(n-1)$ comparisons involving array elements.

Although the `MinMaxOptimal()` solution requires fewer comparisons involving array operations, it is clearly a more complex solution, and for small values of *n* it even takes longer to execute. When you use big-oh notation, the algorithms are considered to have the same complexity: Both are $O(n)$.

5.10 TYPE AND ARRAY

So far, most of our array examples have involved the `int` type. This approach keeps things simple and in most cases allows code to be rewritten to other types. In this section we use one-dimensional arrays of different data types. We also demonstrate techniques and idioms that are common to these different data types.

5.10.1 BOOLEANS: THE SIEVE OF ERATOSTHENES

Let's say that we want to find the prime numbers between 2 and 100. To do so, we write code based on the *sieve of Eratosthenes*. We allocate a boolean array `isPrime` of 100 elements. We set each element to `true`. Starting with element `isPrime[2]` we use its index value 2 and proceed through the remaining array elements `isPrime[4]`, `isPrime[6]`,..., `isPrime[98]`, setting each value to false. Then we go to isPrime[3] and set each element at a spacing of 3 to false. We do this until we reach 10, because 10 is the square root of 100 and is sufficient for checking primality in the range 2 through 100. When we have finished, only those entries that remain true are primes.

In file Primes.cs

```
// Sieve of Eratosthenes for Primes.
using System;

class Primes {
  public static void Main()
  {
    int n;
    Console.WriteLine("Enter n the size of the sieve:");
    string data = Console.ReadLine();
    n = int.Parse(data);
    bool[] sieve = new bool[n];
    int i;
    Console.WriteLine(" Table of primes to " + n);
    for (i = 0; i < sieve.Length; ++i)
      sieve[i] = true;
    for (int j = 2; j < Math.Sqrt(n); ++j)
      if (sieve[j])
        CrossOut(sieve, j, j + j);
    for (i = 2; i < sieve.Length; ++i)         // print primes
      if (sieve[i])                            // 0 and 1 not prime
        Console.Write(" " + i);
  }

  public static
  void CrossOut(bool[] s, int interval, int start)
  {
    for (int i = start; i < s.Length; i += interval)
      s[i] = false;
  }
}
```

Sample output for this program is

```
Enter n the size of the sieve.
25
 Table of primes to 25
 2 3 5 7 11 13 17 19 23
```

5.10.2 char: COUNTING CHARACTERS WITH A BUFFER

Much of character processing is done by sequentially examining a sequence of characters stored in an array called a *buffer*. For example, in a word processing program we might want the capability to count words. To do so we would store a line of text in a buffer and examine the characters in the buffer. A word might be defined as a sequence of alphabetic characters that are adjacent. We write just this program and dissect the parts of it that are idiomatic of character processing.

In file CountChar.cs

```
using System;

public class CountChar {
  public static void Main()
  {
    int[] countCharacters = new int[128];// ascii characters
    Console.WriteLine("type in line");
    string  input = Console.ReadLine();
    Console.WriteLine(input);
    char[] buffer = new char[input.Length];
    for (int i = 0; i < buffer.Length; ++i)
      buffer[i] = input[i];
    Console.WriteLine("character counts are " );
    CharCount(buffer, countCharacters);
    for (int i = 0; i < countCharacters.Length; ++i)
      Console.WriteLine("Char is " + (char)i + "  count is "
                 + countCharacters[i]);
  }
```

```
public static void CharCount(char[] buf, int[] cnt)
{
    for (int i = 0; i < buf.Length; ++i)
     cnt[(int)buf[i]] += 1;
}
}
```

The output of this program shows the input line. It contains some special characters. The output shown is partial, as indicated by ellipses and explanation of what is not shown in parentheses.

```
type in line
This is a sample line. It has some special @#$ chars!
This is a sample line. It has some special @#$ chars!
character counts are
. . . . . (special characters)
Char is   count is 10
Char is !  count is 1
Char is "  count is 0
Char is #  count is 1
Char is $  count is 1
. . . . . (special characters)
Char is .  count is 1
. . . . . (special characters)
Char is @  count is 1
Char is A  count is 0
Char is B  count is 0
. . . . . (uppercase characters)
Char is I  count is 1
. . . . . (uppercase characters)
Char is Z  count is 0
Char is [  count is 0
. . . . . (special characters)
Char is `  count is 0
Char is a  count is 5
Char is b  count is 0
Char is c  count is 2
. . . . . (lowercase characters - many with counts > 0)
Char is s  count is 7
Char is t  count is 1
Char is z  count is 0
Char is {  count is 0
. . . . . (special characters)
```

Dissection of the *CountChar* Program

■ ```
int[] countCharacters = new int[128]; // ascii characters
Console.WriteLine("type in line");
string input = Console.ReadLine();
Console.WriteLine(input);
```

The variable `input` is used to capture an input line typed at the keyboard.

■ ```
char[] buffer = new char[input.Length];
for (int i = 0; i < buffer.Length; ++i)
  buffer[i] = input[i];
```

A `char[]` array is used as a container for the individual characters in the input. Once placed in the buffer, character manipulation is very efficient.

■ ```
public static void CharCount(char[] buf, int[] cnt)
{
   for (int i = 0; i < buf.Length; ++i)
     cnt[(int)buf[i]] += 1;
}
```

We process this character array `buf[]` from the 0th character to the `buf.Length-1` character. We advance through the buffer counting each character. The `cnt[]` array has 128 positions, one for each standard character. The character value serves an index into this array. For example, capital P is integer value 80, and character ( is value 40.

■ ```
CharCount(buffer, countCharacters);
```

Here we call `CharCount()` on the parameter `buffer`.

■ ```
for (int i = 0; i < countCharacters.Length; ++i)
   Console.WriteLine("Char is " + (char)i + " count is "
                   + countCharacters[i]);
```

The counts and their character representation are printed (if printable).
```

5.10.3 OVERLOADING `Accumulate()` FOR `double`

One of our first array examples was `Accumulate()` in Section 5.3, *Passing Arrays to Methods*, on page 176, which worked on an `int` type.

```
// Sum the int elements in an array.
static int Accumulate(int[] a)
{
  int sum = 0;

  for (int i = 0; i < a.Length; ++i)
    sum = sum + a[i];
  return sum;
}
```

This code is also useful for other types. It can be overloaded for the type `double`, as follows.

```
// Sum the double elements in an array.
static double Accumulate(double[] a)
{
  double sum = 0.0;

  foreach (int element in a)
    sum = sum + element;
  return sum;
}
```

Here, we changed the type declaration in three places, namely, the return type, the parameter declaration, and the internal declaration of `sum`. Notice that we also used the `foreach` construct, rather than build our own loop. We can further generalize this code and make it useful for a wider range of computations. We can sum an array over a range from the first element up to, but not including, the last element. We can also accumulate from a starting value that may be different from the value 0. A general algorithm, such as the one below, shows many features of generalizing a basic method by extending its abilities with additional variables.

```
// Accumulate the double elements in an array.
static double Accumulate(double[] a, int first, int last,
                         double sum)
    for (int i = first; i < last; ++i)
      sum += a[i];
  return sum;
}
```

5.11   TWO-DIMENSIONAL ARRAYS

The arrays in the preceding sections are all one-dimensional arrays; that is, the elements are conceptually in a single row or column. C# has arrays of more dimensions. We chiefly discuss two-dimensional arrays. Here are declarations of array variables of different dimension.

```
string[] line;              // one dimension
double[,] matrix;           // two dimensions
int[,,] plane;              // three dimensions
```

We focus on two dimensions because these arrays constitute the most useful and used of the multi-dimensional array types. We can conveniently think of a two-dimensional array as a rectangular collection of elements with rows and columns. To allocate elements we use `new[size1, size2]`. This gets us `size1 * size2` number of elements. For example, if we declare

```
int[,] data = new int[3,5];
```

then we can think of the array elements being arranged as follows.

Table 5.5	Col 1	Col 2	Col 3	Col 4	Col 5
Row 1	a[0,0]	a[0,1]	a[0,2]	a[0,3]	a[0,4]
Row 2	a[1,0]	a[1,1]	a[1,2]	a[1,3]	a[1,4]
Row 3	a[2,0]	a[2,1]	a[2,2]	a[2,3]	a[2,4]

To illustrate these ideas, let's write a program that fills a two-dimensional array with some internally generated values. A one-dimensional array has `Length` as a member that gives its size. For two-dimensional arrays, we instead use `GetLength(0)` and `GetLength(1)` respectively for the length of each dimension.

In file TwoD.cs

```
// Simple two-dimensional array
using System;

class TwoD {
  public static void Main()
  {
    int[,] data = new int[3,5];                    // row x column

    Console.WriteLine("No. of elements = " + data.Length);
    for (int i = 0; i < data.GetLength(0); ++i) {
      Console.Write("Row " + i + ":    ");
      for (int j = 0; j < data.GetLength(1); ++j) {
        data[i,j] = i * j;
        Console.Write(data[i,j] + ", ");
      }
      Console.WriteLine();
    }
  }
}
```

The output of this program is

```
No. of elements = 15
Row 0:    0, 0, 0, 0, 0,
Row 1:    0, 1, 2, 3, 4,
Row 2:    0, 2, 4, 6, 8,
```

Dissection of the *TwoD* Program

```
■int[,] data = new int[3, 5];                    // row x column
```

This declares the variable data to be a reference to a rectangular two-dimensional array of integers. It creates an array with three rows and five columns. Finally, it assigns data to refer to the newly created array. We don't need to create the array in the same statement that declares the variable. However, we must create an array and assign data to refer to that array before we can use data.

```
■Console.WriteLine(("No. of elements = " + data.Length);
  for (int i = 0; i < data.GetLength(0); ++i) {
    Console.Write("Row " + i + ":    ");
    .....
    Console.WriteLine();
  }
```

The `Length` member prints the total number of elements. In this case that is 15 integers. This is the outer loop. For multidimensional arrays, we can write an expression to find the size of each dimension. The expression `data.GetLength(0)` evaluates to the length of the first dimension. Each iteration of this loop prints one row of the array.

```
■for (int j = 0; j < data.GetLength(1); ++j) {
    data[i,j] = i * j;
    Console.Write(data[i,j] + ", ");
  }
```

This loop is the inner loop. A pair of nested loops for accessing a two-dimensional array is an important idiom. The expression `data[i,j]` is of type `int`, one of the elements of the array. The expression `data.GetLength(1)` for the row size is used inside the inner loop to process each `i`th-row element.

5.11.1 TWO-DIMENSIONAL INITIALIZER LISTS

A two-dimensional array can be explicitly initialized with a set of values. The rows are also contained in a set of braces. Each of the following initializations

```
int[,]  a = {{1, 2}, {3, 4}, {5, 6}};
int[,]  b = {{1, 2, 3}, {4, 5, 6}};
int[,]  c = {{1, 2, 3, 4, 5, 6}};
```

creates a two-dimensional array with a total of six elements. But their layout—in other words, their row organization—is completely different. Array a has three rows of two elements each. Array b has two rows of three elements each. Array c has one row of six elements and is a degenerate two-dimensional array.

5.11.2 JAGGED TWO-DIMENSIONAL ARRAYS

We can create a two-dimensional array that is not rectangular. That is, the number of elements in each row can be different. This approach uses a two-dimensional array of integers that is really a one-dimensional array of references to one-dimensional arrays of integers. While C# uses the term *jagged* for these arrays, the more conventional term is *ragged.*

```
int[][]  jaggedData = new int [3][];
jaggedData[0] = new int[1];                    // 1 element
jaggedData[1] = new int[2];                    // 2 elements
jaggedData[2] = new int[3];                    // 3 elements
```

This creates a two-dimensional array of six integer valued elements. But, unlike the previous rectangular array examples, the layout is ragged. This layout also means that there is a different indexing idiom.

In file TwoDJag.cs

```
// Jagged two-dimensional array

using System;
class TwoD {
public static void Main()
{
    int[][]  jaggedData = new int [3][];

    jaggedData[0] = new int[1];                    // 1 element
    jaggedData[1] = new int[2];                    // 2 elements
    jaggedData[2] = new int[3];                    // 3 elements

      Console.WriteLine("Length = " + jaggedData.Length);
                                         // Length here is 3
    for (int i = 0; i < jaggedData.Length; ++i) {
      Console.Write("Row " + i + ":    ");
      for (int j = 0; j < jaggedData[i].Length; ++j) {
        jaggedData[i][j] = i * j;
        Console.Write(jaggedData[i][j] + ", ");
      }
      Console.WriteLine();
    }
  }
}
```

The output of this program is

```
Length = 3
Row 0:    0,
Row 1:    0, 1,
Row 2:    0, 2, 4,
```

Notationally jagged arrays use brackets for each dimension, where rectangular arrays use a comma to separate dimensions.

5.12   SIMULATION: THE GAME OF LIFE

The Game of Life is an archetypal checkerboard simulation. It was invented by the English mathematician John H. Conway for exploring certain formal situations involving reproduction and growth (see *Scientific American,* October 1970, p. 120). The game is a successor to the work of John von Neumann on cellular automata. A checkerboard simulation is a model wherein the world is broken into a rectangular array of cells. Each cell may interact only with its neighboring cells, the interactions occurring once per simulated clock pulse. The rules for a local change are well defined and simple, but predicting global change is impractical without computer simulation. The Game of Life has the following rules.

Game of Life Rules

- A cell is either empty, indicated by a blank, or alive, indicated by an X.

- Each cell is the center of a 3×3 grid of cells, which contains its eight neighbors.

- A empty cell at time t becomes alive at time $t + 1$ if and only if exactly three neighboring cells were alive at time t.

- A cell that is alive at time t remains alive at time $t + 1$ if and only if either two or three neighboring cells were alive at time t. Otherwise, it dies for lack of company (< 2) or overcrowding (> 3).

The simulation is conducted, in principle, on an infinite two-dimensional grid.

A simulation starts with an initial configuration of Xs on the grid. The following example of a simple repeating life form is called a *blinker*, as it repeats every two generations, or time steps.

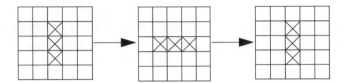

We must first add a few refinements to the specification of the program just described.

- Instead of trying to simulate an infinite two-dimensional grid, simulating a relatively small grid suffices.

- Because the grid isn't infinite, we must decide how to deal with the borders. To keep the program simple, we treat the borders as lifeless zones.

- The initial placement of life forms in the grid is read from the console as a sequence of Xs and dots. The Xs stand for life forms and the dots represent empty cells. If the grid was only 5×5 as shown in the preceding figure, the initial configuration would be specified at the console by typing

  ```
  . . . . .
  . . X . .
  . . X . .
  . . X . .
  . . . . .
  ```

- The user specifies the size of the grid, which is always a square grid, and the number of generations to simulate.

- The program should echo the initial generation and then print each new generation simulated.

5.12.1 THE GAME OF LIFE: DESIGN

We are now ready to begin designing the program. The first—and obvious– decision is that we use a two-dimensional array to represent the grid. We start with pseudocode for the top level.

Top-level Pseudocode for the Game of Life

```
Read in the size of the grid
Read in the initial generation
Read in the number of generations to simulate
Print the current generation
For the specified number of generations
   Advance one generation
   Print the generation
End for loop
```

The most difficult step is "advance one generation" so we need to write some pseudocode for advancing one generation.

Pseudocode for Advancing One Generation

```
For each cell
   Compute the number of neighbors
   Apply the game rules to decide if the cell
      should be alive or dead in the next generation
End for loop
```

Applying the game rules to one cell isn't too hard once we know the number of neighbors. The code is some if-else statement. Either the new cell is dead or it is alive.

Computing the number of neighbors still looks difficult. However, there are several approaches that we can use to solve this problem. A cell and its neighbors can be viewed as a 3×3 subarray. With this in mind, we write the following pseudocode for counting the neighbors.

Pseudocode for Computing the Number of Neighbors

```
Visit each cell in the 3x3 subarray around the cell
Keep a count of how many of those are alive
If the center cell is alive
   Then return one less than the count found
   Else return the count found
```

At this point in the design we need to recognize that we can't simply update the cells in the array as we visit each of them while advancing one generation. A generation is a snapshot of the grid at an instant in time. Changing some of the cells affects the number of neighbors that another cell observes. This type of unsynchronized updating of the cells might be interesting, but it isn't what Conway intended in his Game of Life. We need to not disturb the current generation while creating the next generation. As is often the case, there are several solutions. The one that we have chosen is to use two arrays: one for the current generation and another for the next generation.

Before moving to the implementation stage, we have to refine two of the sections of our pseudocode.

Refined Top-Level Pseudocode for the Game of Life

```
Read in the size of the grid
Create two arrays, currentGen and nextGen
Read the initial generation into currentGen
Read in the number of generations to simulate
Print currentGen
For number of generations
   Update nextGen using currentGen
   Swap currentGen and nextGen
   Print currentGen
End for loop
```

Each iteration of the loop fills the cells of nextGen from the values found in currentGen. Then the arrays referred to by nextGen and currentGen are swapped. Note that after the last iteration currentGen has the data of the most recently computed generation.

Refined Pseudocode for Advancing One Generation

```
Input: currentGen and nextGen
Output: updated nextGen
For each cell in currentGen
   Compute the number of neighbors
   Apply the game rules to decide if the cell
      Should be alive or dead in the next generation
   Store the result, alive or dead, in the
      Corresponding cell in nextGen
End for loop
```

5.12.2 THE GAME OF LIFE: IMPLEMENTATION

The key need for the Game of Life is an appropriate board. We use a square array `bool[,]` that tells if a cell is alive or not. This example shows the power of such arrays to represent complex problems, including ecological simulations.

In file GameOfLife.cs

```csharp
// Conway's Game of Life

using System;

class GameOfLife {
  const int size = 10;
  const  bool ALIVE = true;
  const  bool EMPTY = false;

  public static void Main()
  {
    bool[,]  currentGeneration, nextGeneration;
    currentGeneration = new bool[size, size];
    nextGeneration = new bool[size, size];
    ReadInitialGeneration(currentGeneration);
    // read in the number of generations to simulate
    int cycles = 4;                       // fix at 4 for testing

    WriteState(currentGeneration);
    for (int i = 0; i < cycles; ++i) {
      Console.WriteLine("Cycle = " + i + "\n\n");
      AdvanceOneGen(currentGeneration, nextGeneration);
      WriteState(nextGeneration);
      // swap current and next generations
      bool[,] temp = nextGeneration;
      nextGeneration = currentGeneration;
      currentGeneration = temp;
    }
  }
```

```csharp
// read the initial generation from the input
// a dot means empty and a * means alive
// any other characters are ignored
// the border cells are all set to empty
// the method assumes the array is square

static void ReadInitialGeneration(bool[,] w)
{
  Console.WriteLine("Input * or . for {0} x {0} points ",
                    w.GetLength(0));
  for (int i = 0; i < w.GetLength(0); ++i)
    for (int j = 0; j < w.GetLength(1); ++j) {
      char c = (char)Console.Read();
                                    // skip illegal characters
      while (c != '.' && c != '*')
        c = (char)Console.Read();
      if (c == '.')
        w[i,j] = EMPTY;
      else
        w[i,j] = ALIVE;
    }                           // set border cells to be empty

  for (int i = 0; i < w.GetLength(0); ++i){
    w[i,0] = w[0,i] = EMPTY;
    w[i,w.GetLength(1)-1] = w[w.GetLength(0)-1,i] = EMPTY;
  }
}

static void WriteState(bool[,] w)
  {
    for (int i = 0; i < w.GetLength(0); ++i) {
      System.Console.WriteLine();
      for (int j = 0; j < w.GetLength(1); ++j)
        if (w[i,j] == ALIVE)
          System.Console.Write('X');
        else
          System.Console.Write('.');
    }
    System.Console.WriteLine();
  }
```

```
// compute the number of alive neighbors of a cell
  static int Neighbors(int row, int column, bool[,] w)
  {
    int neighborCount = 0;

    for (int i = -1; i <= 1; ++i)
      for (int j = -1; j <= 1; ++j)
        if (w[row + i,column + j] == ALIVE)
          neighborCount = neighborCount + 1;
    if (w[row,column] == ALIVE)
      neighborCount--;
    return neighborCount;
  }

  static void AdvanceOneGen(bool[,] wOld, bool[,] wNew)
  {
    int neighborCount;
    for (int i = 1; i < wNew.GetLength(0) - 1; ++i)
      for (int j = 1; j < wNew.GetLength(1) - 1; ++j) {
        neighborCount = Neighbors(i, j, wOld);
        if (neighborCount == 3)
          wNew[i,j] = ALIVE;
        else if (wOld[i,j] == ALIVE &&
                 neighborCount == 2)
          wNew[i,j] = ALIVE;
        else
          wNew[i,j] = EMPTY;
      }
  }
}
```

Sample input for this is:

Sample output for Cycle 0 given the above input for this program is

```
. . . . . . . . . .
. . . XXX . . . .
. X . . XX . . X .
. . XX . . XX . .
. . . . . . . . . .
. XXXXXXX .
. XXXXXXX .
. . . . XX . . X .
. XX . . XX . X .
. . . . . . . . . .
Cycle = 0
```

Dissection of the *GameOfLife* Program

```
■class GameOfLife {
    const int size = 10;
```

For testing purposes we have fixed the grid size at 10. In the final version of the program we would replace the assignment of 10 to `size` with a prompt to the user for the desired size and an input statement to read the size from the console.

```
■   const  bool ALIVE = true;
    const  bool EMPTY = false;
```

Because a cell can only be alive or empty, we use the primitive type `bool` for the cells. The value `true` means that the cell is alive. C# initializes all array elements to `false`, which here means *empty*.

```
■ bool[,]  currentGeneration, nextGeneration;
    currentGeneration = new bool[size, size];
    nextGeneration = new bool[size, size];
```

We create two square arrays to represent the cells in the world. Each generation, the cells in `currentGeneration` are used to update the cells in `nextGeneration`.

```
ReadInitialGeneration(currentGeneration);
```

The method `ReadInitialGeneration()` is used to read an initial world from the console. When the method returns, the cells in `currentGeneration` have been modified to correspond to user input.

```
// read in the number of generations to simulate
int cycles = 4;                      // fix at 4 for testing
WriteState(currentGeneration);
```

This comment from the pseudocode reminds us that we haven't finished the implementation. As with the size of the grid, we've fixed the number of generations to simulate. The method `WriteState()` prints the initial generation, which is stored in `currentGeneration`.

```
for (int i = 0; i < cycles; ++i) {
    Console.WriteLine("Cycle = " + i + "\n\n");
    AdvanceOneGen(currentGeneration, nextGeneration);
    WriteState(nextGeneration);
```

This loop is the main simulation loop. Each iteration, the next generation is computed and the state is printed.

```
    // swap current and next generations
    bool[,] temp = nextGeneration;
    nextGeneration = currentGeneration;
    currentGeneration = temp;
}
```

At the end of each iteration, the array variables referring to the two arrays are reversed so that, at the start of the next iteration, the variable `currentGeneration` points to the most recently updated array and the variable `nextGeneration` refers to the array with the older generation, which subsequently is modified to contain the newest generation. Recall that this swapping of the array variables isn't copying the entire array; it is simply changing the variables to refer to different arrays.

```
static void ReadInitialGeneration(bool[,] w)
{
  Console.WriteLine("Input * or . for {0} x {0} points ",
                    + w.GetLength(0));
   for (int i = 0; i < w.GetLength(0); ++i)
      for (int j = 0; j < w.GetLength(1); ++j) {
        char c = (char)Console.Read();
        // skip illegal characters
        while (c != '.' && c != '*')
          c = (char)Console.Read();
        if (c == '.')
          w[i,j] = EMPTY;
        else
          w[i,j] = ALIVE;
      }
```

The first part of this method reads the initial generation in from the console. The call `Console.Read()` reads one character from the input. The return type of `Read()` is `int`, which allows for a return value of −1 to signal that there are no more characters to read. Even if a character were read, the cast to `char` wouldn't lose any information. In this example we haven't checked for the return value of −1. We leave that for you to do as an exercise. The `while` loop is used to skip over any white space or other unexpected characters. To make the code more self-documenting, we have defined constants to encode the fact that true is treated as `ALIVE` and that false is treated as `EMPTY`. The constants are defined at the end.

```
// set border cells to be empty
for (int i = 0; i < w.GetLength(0); ++i) {
  w[i,0] = w[0,i] = EMPTY;
  w[i,w.GetLength(1)-1] = w[w.GetLength(0)-1,i] = EMPTY;
}
```

As discussed in the design section, the border cells require some form of special treatment because they have fewer than eight neighbors. Recall that we decided to treat the border cells as a lifeless zone. To enforce that we set all border cells to `EMPTY`, ignoring border values that were supplied by the user. This code makes the unchecked assumption that the array is actually square.

```
■static void WriteState(bool[,] w)
   {
   for (int i = 0; i < w.GetLength(0); ++i) {
     System.Console.WriteLine();
     for (int j = 0; j < w.GetLength(1); ++j)
       if (w[i,j] == ALIVE)
         System.Console.Write('X');
       else
         System.Console.Write('.');
   }
   System.Console.WriteLine();
}
```

This routine prints the state to the console, with the output format the same as that used for the input. The code doesn't take advantage of the fact that the elements in the array are actually of type bool. At some later time the decision to use a boolean array might be changed. In that case, only the type of the parameter in the method header would need to be changed. In addition, by using the constant ALIVE, the code is self-documenting. It should be clear that X is printed if the cell is ALIVE and that a dot is printed otherwise.

```
■static int Neighbors(int row, int column, bool[,] w)
   {
   int neighborCount = 0;

   for (int i = -1; i <= 1; ++i)
     for (int j = -1; j <= 1; ++j)
       if (w[row + i][column +j] == ALIVE)
         neighborCount = neighborCount + 1;
   if (w[row][column] == ALIVE)
     neighborCount--;
   return neighborCount;
}
```

This routine counts the number of neighboring cells that are alive. It does so by counting the number of alive cells in the 3 × 3 subarray that has the specified cell at its center. Then the center cell is removed from the count if it is alive because a cell isn't a neighbor to itself.

```
■static void AdvanceOneGen(bool[,] wOld, bool[,] wNew)
  {
    int neighborCount;
    for (int i = 1; i < w.GetLength(0) - 1; ++i)
      for (int j = 1; j < w.GetLength(1) - 1; ++j) {
        neighborCount = Neighbors(i, j, wOld);
        if (neighborCount == 3)
          wNew[i,j] = ALIVE;
        else if (wOld[i,j]==ALIVE && neighborCount == 2)
          wNew[i,j] = ALIVE;
        else
          wNew[i,j] = EMPTY;
      }
  }
```

This method implements the rules of the simulation. The array wOld is examined to determine the current number of neighbors for each cell, and then the array wNew is set according to the rules. These loops avoid the borders of the array, implementing our design decision that the borders are lifeless zones.

The GameOfLife program requires enough input that typing the input in each time would be rather tedious. Instead, you can prepare an input file and then use file redirection to cause the program to read from the file instead of from the keyboard with the command GameOfLife < glider. Suppose that the file *glider* contains

```
. . . . . . . . . .
. . . . *. . . . . .
. . . . . *. . . .
. *. . . *. . . .
. . ****. . . .
. . . . . . . . . .
. . . . . . . . . .
. . . . . . . . . .
. . . . . . . . . .
. . . . . . . . . .
```

Execution of this command would be followed immediately by the program output. A portion of the output would be

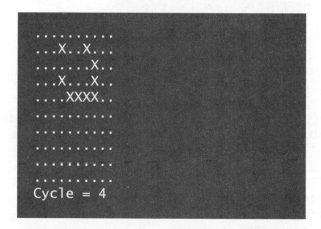

Note that, after four cycles, the initial configuration has reappeared but has moved to the right by one position. This interesting "life form" is one of many that have been discovered. This one is called a *glider* because it sort of glides across the simulated world.

5.13   SOFTWARE ENGINEERING: ARRAYS

Here we look at standard idioms for working with arrays and the common programming problems associated with arrays.

5.13.1 ARRAY LOOP IDIOMS

Stylistically the most common array idiom in C# is

```
for (int i = 0; i < d.Length; ++i)
   computation on d[i]
```

This idiom is preferred to an explicit use of an array upper bound, as in

```
for (int i = 0; i < N; ++i)
   computation on d[i]
```

The use of such an explicit bound, N, is more error-prone and requires more code maintenance than does the preferred idiom. It is a carryover from C programming style, where arrays don't have a length member.

When computing over an array, you should package the computation as a method, as in

```
static Type sumArray(Type[] a)
{
   Type s = 0;
   for (int i = 0; i < a.Length; ++i)
      s += a[i];
   return s;
}
```

If the array loop goes over the full array, and does not modify the array, you can use the foreach statement, as in

```
foreach (int element in a)
  Console.Write(element + "\t");
```

5.13.2 COUNTING FROM ZERO

Much of the syntax for C# is derived from the programming language C. For a number of reasons, C programmers tend to write loops that begin with the loop index at 0. One reason is that in C arrays are represented in such a way that they are always indexed from 0. This C idiom has survived into C# so that even loops that are not indexing an array often start from 0.

```
static void WriteRandomNumbers(int k)
{
  Random r = new Random();

  for (int i = 0; i < k; ++i)
    Console.WriteLine(r.NextDouble());
}
```

However, people more naturally count from 1. Rewriting this code to start from 1 gives

```
static void WriteRandomNumbers(int k)
{
  Random r = new Random();

  for (int i = 1; i <= k; ++i)
    Console.WriteLine(r.NextDouble());
}
```

Either style is reasonable. You need to be able to write and understand code with both counting styles. Many tricky bugs enter code when the end values of loops are *off by one*.

5.13.3 DEBUGGING AND TESTING CODE

An array subscript value outside the range 0 through *length* – 1 causes the program to abort with a System.IndexOutOfRangeException runtime error. When that happens, the condition is called "overrunning the bounds of the array" or "subscript out of bounds." In Chapter 10, *Exceptions and Program Correctness*, we discuss how programs can catch these errors at runtime and attempt to recover. C#, unlike C and C++, is much easier to debug because this common error is caught by the system.

A common error that is more difficult to detect is to begin or end the array computation with the wrong element. It is sometimes called the "off-by-one error." The following code shows this error.

```
for (int i = 1; i < data.Length; ++i)
  sum = sum + data[i];          // forgot to start with i = 0
```

This type of computation is better done using the foreach construct:

```
foreach (int element in a)
  sum += element;
```

When debugging array code it is useful to use *boundary condition testing*. A boundary for a loop is to see that code loops an appropriate number of times. To test this you can try the loop when there are no elements in the array, one element in the array, or a sizable array. This allows you to easily see that the loop works and detects off-by-one errors. It is also important to see that methods work efficiently. To test this you need large data sets. It is convenient to generate data sets using a random number generator.

5.14   DR. P'S PRESCRIPTIONS

- Use the array property Length rather than hard-coded parameters.

- Stay with one increment or decrement style.

- Prefer standard methods to special code.

- Use rectangular arrays in preference to jagged arrays.

- Use the foreach construct when possible.

Always write code that is general when not compromising specific efficiency needs. This makes your code easier to understand and maintain. When you hardcode a for loop with a particular constant that is the size of an array, you are creating a maintenance trap. The use of the property Length avoids this.

In this book we have stayed with the style ++i or --j, for incrementing or decrementing simple variables. This is historically driven by the C++ community preference for prefix operators. While there is no such preference in the C# community, and either pre- or post- operators are suitable, consistency is useful to avoid confusion.

As we saw with the method `System.Array.Sort()`, the standard libraries have a powerful set of methods available for array processing. Using these methods avoids debugging and documentation concerns. There should be a special reason to code similar methods instead of using these.

The C# higher dimensional arrays are lacking in C++ and Java. They are easily used and are typically more efficient than jagged arrays.

The `foreach` idiom is unique to C# and is preferred for its clarity and readily understood meaning.

5.15   C# COMPARED WITH JAVA AND C++

All three languages have an array type. Java and C# support arrays as an object type where allocation is managed by the heap and requires `new`. C++ follows C and sees arrays as a form of pointer with allocation off the stack. C++ also has the STL container class `vector<>`, which improves significantly on the traditional C array code. C# is the only language with a true multidimensional (rectangular) array type.

The following program in C#, C++, and Java initializes an array, prints its values, and computes its sum and average value.

In file SumArray.cs

```csharp
using System;

public class SumArray {
  public static void Main()
  {
    int[]  data = {1, 2, 3, 4, 5, 6, 7};
    int  sum = 0;
    double average;

    foreach (int element in data) {
      sum = sum + element;
      Console.Write(element + ", ");
    }
    average = sum / (double)data.Length;
    Console.WriteLine("\n\nSum = " + sum
        + " average = " + average);
  }
}
```

The output of this program is

```
1, 2, 3, 4, 5, 6, 7,

Sum = 28 average = 4
```

In file sumArray.cpp

```cpp
#include <iostream>
using namespace std;

int main()
{
  const int SIZE = 7;
  int  data[SIZE] = {1, 2, 3, 4, 5, 6, 7};
  int  sum = 0;
  double average;

  for (int i = 0; i < SIZE; ++i) {
    sum = sum + data[i];
    cout << data[i] << ", ";
  }
  average = sum / (double)SIZE;
  cout << "\n\nSum = " << sum
       << " average = " << average <<endl;
}
```

In file SumArray.java

```java
import tio.*;

class SumArray {
  public static void main(string[] args)
  {
    int[]  data = {1, 2, 3, 4, 5, 6, 7};
    int  sum = 0;
    double average;

    for (int i = 0; i < 7; ++i) {
      sum = sum + data[i];
      System.out.print(data[i] + ", ");
    }
```

```
    average = sum / 7.0;
    System.out.println("\n\nSum = " + sum
        + " average = " + average);
  }
}
```

Notice how the three programs are nearly identical. The Java and C# programs differ in their I/O statements. The C# `foreach` statement can be replaced by the Java `for` loop, but the `foreach` is more robust. The C++ program differs from the other two in that the array declaration is done differently, and the array size is not accessible automatically.

In C++ a typical array declaration allocates memory starting from a base address. An array name is, in effect, a pointer constant to this base address. In C++, only one-dimensional arrays are provided, with the first element always indexed as element zero. The C++ array requires enough memory to store seven integer values. Thus, if `a[0]` is stored at location 1000, the remaining array elements on a system needing 4 bytes for an `int` are successively stored at locations 1004, 1008, 1012, . . . , 1024. It is considered good programming practice to define the size of an array as a constant. Since much of the code may depend on this value, it is convenient to be able to change a single `const int SIZE` declaration to process various size arrays. Notice how the various parts of the `for` statement are neatly tailored to provide a terse notation for dealing with array computations.

There are critical differences here from C#. The C++ array is allocated off a stack. The program is not encapsulated in a class. The array does not have a `Length` property, so that an explicit upper bound is needed. At the heart of the program the `for` loop idiom for processing the array can be the same, if a `for` loop instead of the more robust `foreach` is used.

SUMMARY

- An array is a data type used to represent a large number of homogeneous values. It is an elementary form of container.

- Array allocation starts with element 0. The elements of an array are accessed by the use of index expressions. Therefore an array of *size* number of elements is indexed or subscripted from 0 to *size* – 1, inclusive. The array size can be accessed by using the notation *arrayVariable*.`Length`.

- Allocation is often combined with declaration, as in

  ```
  int[] data = new int[100];
  ```

- The expression a[*expr*], where *expr* is an integral expression, accesses an element of the array. We call *expr* a subscript, or index, of a. The value of a subscript should lie in the range 0 to *length* – 1, inclusive. An `IndexOutOfBoundsException` error message is printed when the array subscript value is outside this range.

- Only a reference to an array is passed to a method. That is, the array elements are not copied and passed to the method. Hence the individual elements of an array can be modified by a method passed as an array.

- C# allows arrays of any type, including arrays of arrays. With two bracket pairs, we obtain a jagged two-dimensional array.

  ```
  double[][] upUp;              // jagged two dimensions
  char[][][] andAway;          // jagged three dimensions
  ```

  C# has true rectangular multidimensional arrays as well, where each further dimension is specified by a comma.

  ```
  double[,] matrix;                      // two dimensions
  int[,,] plane;                         // three dimensions
  ```

■ Arrays have their individual elements automatically initialized when allocated. Primitive numeric types are initialized to 0, and the type `bool` is initialized to `false`. All other types are reference types and are initialized to the special value `null`, which signifies that the element doesn't currently refer to anything.

■ Sorting information is a heavily studied subject in computer science. Inefficient sorts such as selection sort take approximately n^2 operations for *n* elements. Efficient sorts take approximately $n \log(n)$ operations. When information is sorted, it can be retrieved efficiently. Methods such as `BinarySearch()` can retrieve keys in $\log(n)$ operations. Unsorted arrays require linear time searches to retrieve keys.

REVIEW QUESTIONS

1. Does the statement `int[] x;` create an array of integers? If you answer *no*, how do you create an array of integers and associate it with the variable x? If you answer *yes*, how many elements are in the array?

2. Can you change the size of an array? Explain.

3. Can an array variable be changed to refer to arrays of different sizes? What about arrays that contain different types of primitive elements?

4. Write a single statement that declares x to be an array of `int` values, creates an array of 10 integers, and assigns x to refer to the newly created array.

5. What is the value of `x[0]` after executing the statement that answers the previous question?

6. What is stored in `s[0]` after executing

   ```
   string[] s = new string[2];                    // s[0] contains ?
   ```

7. In a single statement, create an array of three `string` objects that contains the strings `"one"`, `"two"`, and `"three"`.

8. Assume that x refers to an array of `float` values. Write a loop to print the values in x, one per line. Don't make any assumptions about the length of the array.

9. C# uses call-by-value for parameter passing of an int or a double. That is, a copy of the value of such a variable or expression is passed to the method. When the actual parameter is a variable, the variable in the calling statement can't be changed by the method. However, when passing an array variable, the contents of the array can be changed. What makes this change possible?

10. What does the following code fragment print?

```
int[] y = { 2 };    // create an array of length one
Mystery(y);
Console.WriteLine(y[0]);
```

Assume Mystery() is defined to be

```
static void Mystery(int[] x)  { x[0] = 1; }
```

11. What does the following program print?

```
class Review11 {
  public static void Main()
  {
    int[] data = {1, 3, 5, 7, 9, 11};
    int sum = 0;
      for (int i = 1; i < data.Length; ++i) {
        sum = sum + (data[i] + data[i - 1]);
        Console.WriteLine("sum  = " + sum);
      }
  }
}
```

12. Convert each of the following expressions for running times of an algorithm to big-oh notation.

$$3n + 2$$
$$3n + 2\log n + 15$$
$$256n^2 + 19n + 1024$$

13. How many int values can be stored in the array created with new int[6, 5]? How many in new int[6, 5, 3]?

14. What does the following code fragment print?

```
int[] a1 = { 1, 2 };
int[] a2;
a2 = a1;
a2[0] = 3;
Console.WriteLine(a1[0]);
```

15. Is the following code fragment legal? If so, what does it print?

```
int[] a1 = new int[3];
int[] a2 = new int[10];
a1 = a2;
Console.WriteLine(a1.Length);
```

EXERCISES

1. Allocate an array of integers of length 100. Initialize the array to a series of random numbers. Print the contents of the array.

2. Repeat the preceding, but also find the minimum, maximum, and average value in the array.

3. Repeat the previous exercise, but do not print the contents of the array. Instead use an array of length 10,000 and write out how long each action on the complete array takes if you use the method. You need to investigate how to time your computation. A simple scheme involves methods in the `System.DateTime` class. Try this method for increasingly larger arrays by factors of 10 until your program no longer runs. That happens when you request too large an integer array size from the heap. The *heap* is a place in the computer's memory where these arrays are stored.

4. A palindrome is a sequence of characters that reads the same both forward and backward. Some examples are

```
"otto"      "121"      "i may yam i"
```

Write a method that takes an array of `char` and returns the boolean value true if the string is a palindrome.

5. Modify your palindrome method from the previous exercise so that blanks and capitals are ignored in the matching process. Under these rules, the following are examples of palindromes.

   `"Huh"`   `"A man a plan a canal Panama"`   `"at a"`

6. Write a different version of `ArrayMethods()` from Section 5.6, *Array Methods and Properties*, on page 186, that treats a word as a sequence of characters separated by the white-space characters: `'\t'`, `'\n'`, and `'\b'`.

7. Write a program that inputs a character array and then compiles as an array of strings all the individual words found. Use your instructor's definition of *word*.

8. Write a lexicographic comparison of two character arrays.

   ```
   static bool IsLess(char[] word1, char[] word2) {·····}
   // true if word1 < word2
   ```

   Words should be compared as in the dictionary, so *be, bet, between, bird,* . . . , are in correct order. You first must compare the character in the zeroth position. If two words are of different length and the shorter word is the same as the initial sequence of the longer word, then the longer word is *greater.*

9. Write a routine that sorts character arrays lexicographically. Then modify <Link>Exercise 7 not only to capture the words, but also to print a sorted list of all the words found.

10. Modify the previous exercise to produce a list of unique words independent of case. Turn all the words into lowercase before sorting them. After sorting them print only a single instance of any word. You need a test `IsEqual()` to readily accomplish this task.

11. Write a program to produce the inner product of two arrays of `double`. Each array should be the same length. Write an overloaded form of this method that generalized it as follows.

    ```
    static double InnerProduct(double[] v1, double[] v2,
          int first, int last, double init);
    // v1 and v2 must both have positions first and last
    // but can otherwise be of different lengths
    // init is normally zero.
    ```

12. A real polynomial $p(x)$ of degree n or less is given by

$$p(x) = a_0 + a_1 x + a_2 x^2 + \cdots + a_n x^n$$

with the coefficients $a_0, a_1, ..., a_n$ representing real numbers. If $a_n \mathrel{!}= 0$, the degree of $p(x)$ is n. Polynomials can be represented in code by an array such as

```
public final int N = 5; /* N is the max degree */
double[]  p = new double[N + 1];
```

Write a method

```
static double EvalPoly(double[] p, double x)
  {
    . . . . .
```

that returns the value of the polynomial p evaluated at x. Write two versions of the method. The first version should be a straightforward, naive approach. The second version should incorporate Horner's Rule. For fifth-degree polynomials, Horner's Rule is expressed as

$$p(x) = a_0 + x(a_1 + x(a_2 + x(a_3 + x(a_4 + x(a_5)))))$$

How many additions and multiplications are used in each of your two versions of the EvalPoly() method?

13. Write a method that adds two polynomials as in $f = g + h$:

```
static double[] AddPoly(double[] f, double[] g)
```

14. Write an algorithm to multiply two polynomials. Use your method AddPoly() to sum intermediate results. This approach isn't very efficient, so write a better routine, if you can, to do the same thing.

15. Write a program that reads 10 characters into an array. Then have it print out the letters of the array sorted in alphabetic order.

16. Write a program that reads n letters into an array where n is read in. Then have the program remove adjacent letters that are duplicates.

17. A simple encryption scheme is to interchange letters of the alphabet on a one-to-one basis. This scheme can be accomplished with a translation table for the 52 lowercase and uppercase letters. Write a program that uses such a scheme to encode text. Write another program to decode

text that has been encoded. This isn't a serious encryption scheme. Do you know why? If you're interested, learn about a more secure encryption system and then program it.

18. Recall that simulations involving the repeated use of a random number generator to reproduce a probabilistic event are called *Monte Carlo simulations* (after one of the world's most famous gaming casinos). In this exercise, you are to find the probability that at least two people in a room with n people have birthdays that fall on the same day of the year. Assume that there are 365 days in a year and assume further that the chance of a person being born on each day of the year is the same. A single trial experiment consists of filling an array of size n with integers that are randomly distributed from 1 through 365. If any two elements in the array have the same value, then we say that the trial is true. Thus a true trial corresponds to the case when at least two people in the room were born on the same day of the year. Simulate the probability by running, say, 10,000 trials with n people in the room. Do this for $n = 2, 3, \ldots, 100$. You can use the expression

```
(int)(t.NextDouble() * 365 + 1) // t is Random object
```

to compute the day of birth for each person. The number of true trials divided by 10,000 is the computed simulated probability. What value of n yields the probability of at least 0.5 that there are shared birthdays in the room?

19. Consider again the probability question in the previous exercise, but look for three people in a room of n people sharing the same birthday. By the way, if there are 3 * 365 people in the room, you are guaranteed (forgetting leap day) to have a probability of 1 for this question.

20. Two matrices can be multiplied, provided that the number of columns of the matrix on the left of the multiplication sign equals the number of rows in the matrix on the right of the multiplication sign. If the left matrix, call it L, has m rows and n columns and the right matrix, call it R, has n rows and p columns, then the result, call it X, is a matrix that has m rows and p columns, with each element defined by

$$X_{i,j} = \sum_{k=1}^{n} (R_{i,k} \cdot L_{k,j})$$

Write a method Mult() that takes two two-dimensional arrays of double values representing two matrices and returns the two-dimensional array that results from multiplying the two matrices. The method should return null if the matrices can't be multiplied because the number of columns of the first doesn't equal the number of rows in the second.

21. Write a program to play a number guessing game. The player thinks of a number between 1 and 100 and the computer tries to guess. The program prints out how many guesses the computer used. The player must respond to each guess by typing *correct, too big,* or *too small.* Using top-down design, one possible solution has the following top-level pseudocode.

Pseudocode for Guessing Game

```
Set range to be the initial range of 1-100
Make an intial guess in the range
While the guess is not correct
   Adjust the range based on the feedback
   Make a guess in the revised range
Print the number of guesses
```

Break the problem into smaller problems, each of which can be implemented by using a method. To make reasonable guesses, the computer needs to keep track of the current range of possible values. The pseudocode given suggests the creation of a method AdjustRange() having the following header for the method.

```
static void AdjustRange(string response,
                        int[] range,
                        int currentGuess)
```

This method takes as input the user's response (*too big* or *too small*), the current range of possible values, and the current guess. It updates range to reflect the new information from the user. The parameter range is an input–output parameter and should be an array of length 2. The method modifies the contents of the array to reflect the new information from the user about the current guess.

CHAPTER 6

CLASSES AND ABSTRACT DATA TYPES

A class packages a data type with its associated methods and operators. This in turn can be used to implement abstract data types (ADTs). An *abstract data type*, such as a stack, is a set of values and operations that define the type. The type is abstract in that it is described without its implementation. It is the job of the C# programmer to provide a concrete representation of the ADT, usually with the class construct.

C# classes bundle data declarations with method declarations, thereby coupling data with behavior. The class description also has access modifiers `public` and `private` that allow data hiding. Allowing private and public *visibility* for members gives the programmer control over what parts of the data structure are modifiable. The private parts are hidden from client code, and the public parts are available. It is possible to change the hidden representation, but not to change the public access or functionality. If this is done properly, client code need not change when the hidden representation is modified. A large part of the object-oriented programming (OOP) design process involves thinking up the appropriate ADTs for a problem. Good ADTs not only model key features of the problem but also are frequently reusable in other code.

6.1   TYPE class, DOT OPERATOR, AND new

The class allows the programmer to aggregate components into a single named variable. A class has components, called *members*, that are individually named. Since the members of a class can be of various types, the programmer can create aggregates suitable for describing complicated data.

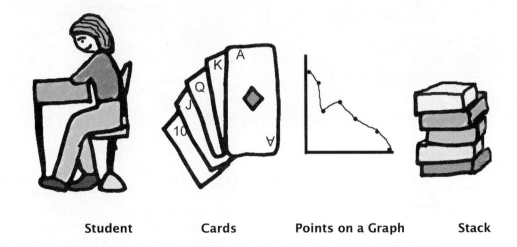

Student   **Cards**   **Points on a Graph**   **Stack**

As a simple example, let us define a class that describes a point. We can declare the class type as follows:

```
class Point {
    public double x, y;
}
```

In C#, the class name is a type. In the preceding declaration, Point is the class name, and the variables x and y are members of the class. The declaration Point can be thought of as a blueprint; it creates the type Point, but no instances are allocated.

The statement

```
Point  pt;
```

declares a reference variable pt. This variable is yet to have a concrete instance of type Point. To create such an instance you need to use new.

```
pt = new Point();                    // create and assign
Point pt2 = new Point();             // declare and create
```

Recall new is an operator of highest precedence. It is an operator that uses system memory to create an instance of a reference type. We have used new in the case of array types to allocate arrays dynamically. The type Point has two data members, each a double. This means new must grab 16 bytes to build an instance of Point.

6.1.1 MEMBER ACCESS OPERATOR

To access the members of pt, we use the member access operator, represented by a period, or dot. Recall dot is also used to access methods in namespaces such as System, as in System.Math.Sqrt(). It is a construct of the form

classVariable . memberName

The construct is used as a variable in the same way that a simple variable or an element of an array is used. Suppose that we want to assign to pt the value (-1, +0.5). To do this, we can write

```
pt.x = -1;
pt.y = 0.5;
```

The member name must be unique within the specified class. Since the member must always be prefaced or accessed through a unique class variable identifier, there is no confusion between two members that have the same name in different classes, as in

```
class Fruit {
  public string  name;
  public int  calories;
}

class Vegetable {
  public string  name;
  public int  calories;
}

Fruit      a = new Fruit();
Vegetable  b = new Vegetable();
```

Having made these declarations, we can access `a.calories` and `b.calories` without ambiguity.

In general, a class is declared with the keyword `class`, followed by an identifier, followed by a brace-enclosed list of member declarations, followed by a semicolon. The class name should be expressive of the ADT concept being modeled.

We use a two-dimensional `Point` example in this chapter. You should see at different places in the text whether you can extend these ideas to a three-dimensional point.

6.2   INSTANCE METHODS

C# requires that methods, or functions, be members of a class. The methods we have been using so far are static methods. Static methods act on arguments that are passed in through the argument or parameter list. The object-oriented idea is that the functionality required by the class should be directly included in the `class` declaration. This construct improves the encapsulation of the ADT `Point` operations by packaging directly with its data representation. An informal idea for designing an object is to think of the object as a *noun*, such as `Point`, and to think of methods as *verbs* that apply to the noun, such as `SetPoint()`. In *instance methods (non-static methods)*, the methods act on an implicit first argument, which is a class variable. To see how this works, let us examine printing and initializing operations to the ADT `Point`:

In file Point1.cs

```
public class Point {
  public double x, y;
  public void SetPoint(double u, double v)
    { x = u; y = v; }
  public void WritePoint()
    { Console.WriteLine("(" + x +", " + y + ")" ); }
}
```

The instance methods, or non-static methods, are written in much the same way that other methods are. One difference is that they can use the data member names directly. Thus, the instance methods in `Point` use `x` and `y` in an unqualified manner. When invoked on a particular object of type `Point`, they act on the specified member in that object.

Let us use these instance methods in an example:

In file Point1.cs

```
using System;

class PointTest {
  public static void Main()
  {
    Point w1 = new Point();

    w1.SetPoint(1.5, 2.5);                    // w1 is implicit
    Console.Write("Point w1 = ");
    w1.WritePoint();                          // w1 is implicit
  }
}
```

This prints

```
Point w1 = (1.5, 2.5)
```

Dissection of the *Point* Program

```
■public class Point {
    public double x, y;
```

Classes are user-defined data types that bundle previously defined data types into a new type. In this case, the new type is Point. Its constituents are two doubles, the coordinates represented by variables x and y.

```
public void SetPoint(double u, double v)
   { x = u; y = v; }
public void WritePoint()
   { Console.WriteLine("(" + x +", " + y + ")" ); }
```

Object-oriented programming requires that methods be bundled with data and become the actions available to the type. Here is a simple `WritePoint()` instance method that prints out a value for a `Point`. The `SetPoint()` instance method is used to change the values of the Point's coordinates. As we shall see in further examples, it is part of the object-oriented programming style to use instance methods to access the data representation of an object type. It is considered poor programming practice to directly manipulate these values in an unrestrained fashion.

```
public static void Main()
{
   Point w1 = new Point();
   Point w2 = new Point();
```

The newly defined type is declared and uses `new` to allocate and initialize concrete instances. Here, two `Point`s are declared and allocated in `Main()`.

```
w1.SetPoint(1.5, 2.5);      // w1 is the implicit argument
w2.SetPoint(-0.5, 1.5);     // w2 is the implicit argument
Console.Write("Point w1 = ");
w1.WritePoint();            // w1 is the implicit argument
```

Notationally, to call methods of type `Point` requires a `Point` variable dotted to the method name. In the first line, the `Point` w1 is set to the coordinates (1.5, 2.5). These coordinates would be printed out by invoking the method w1.WritePoint().

Instance methods within the same `class` can be overloaded. Consider adding to the data type `Point` a print operation that has a string parameter printed as the name of the `Point`. The print operation could be added as the following method within the `class`.

In file Point1.cs

```
public class Point {
  .....
  public void WritePoint(string Pname)
  { Console.WriteLine("Point " +Pname +" = (" +
        x +", " + y + ")" ); }
}
```

The definition that is invoked depends on the arguments :

```
w1.WritePoint();                         // standard print
w1.WritePoint("w1");                      // print with name
```

An instance method is conceptually part of the type. The grouping of operations with data emphasizes their *objectness*. Objects have a description and a behavior. Thinking of an object as a noun and its behavior as the verbs that are most often associated with that noun is key to good object design. OOP is a data-centered design approach. In Section 6.6.1, *The ToString() Method*, on page 254, we show the more typical overloading of the ToString() method for output of user-defined ADTs.

6.3 ACCESS: PRIVATE AND PUBLIC

In C#, classes have public and private members. The keyword private is used to declare members to have private access. The private members can be accessed only by members of that class. The keyword public is used to declare members to have public access. The public members can be used by any code. So far, we have been using public access in our examples. However, an important principle in software engineering is to hide implementation. This data-hiding principle allows implementers to manage access to objects.

We modify Point to hide its data representation, as follows:

In file Point2.cs

```
public class Point {
  public  void SetPoint(double u, double v)
    { x = u; y = v; }
......
  private double x, y;
}
```

Though not desirable, it is possible to have private access by specifying no access modifier to a member as in:

```
public class Point {
  public  void SetPoint(double u, double v)
    { x = u; y = v; }
......
    double x, y;                            // private is implicit
}
```

The public members must have the keyword `public` as part of their declaration. The private members can have the keyword `private` as part of their declaration. If an access keyword is omitted it is `private` by default. As just mentioned, we consider it bad practice to rely on defaults and so always explicitly write `private`.

Restricting access does not affect their use by methods in class `Point`. But, an attempt by a method `Foo()` from another class to access the now private members x and y results in a syntax error:

```
class Test {
  public void Foo(Point w)
  {
    .....
    t = w.x;                               // syntax error
    .....
  }
}
```

Other access protection exists. Most importantly, the keyword `protected` is used to declare members to have protected access. The protected members can be thought of as private members but with special rules when they are used by a derived class. This keyword is not used here but is explained in Section 8.1, *A Derived Class*, on page 329.

For now, we use a method such as `SetPoint()` to modify a data member. In Section 6.11, *Properties and Data Hiding*, on page 269, we show the standard C# way of accessing data members using the `get` and `set` properties.

Hiding data is an important component of object-oriented programming. It allows for more easily debugged and maintained code because errors and modifications are localized. Client programs need be aware only of the type's interface specification. This is also known as the *black box principle*. A good design hides unnecessary implementation detail and presents the simplest possible useful user interface to the client.

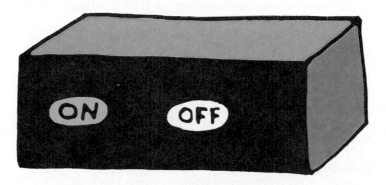

The interface is great, but what does it do?

6.4   AN EXAMPLE: CUSTOMER

As a second example, let us write an ADT for `customer`, which many business applications require.

In file Customer.cs

```csharp
using System;

class Customer {
  public enum Kind { general, wholesale, retail }
  public void SetName(string l, string f)
    { lastName = l; firstName = f; }
  public Kind  GetKind()  { return t; }
  public void SetKind(Kind k) { t = k; }
  public void WriteCustomer()
    { Console.Write(firstName + "  " + lastName); }

  public double PriceDiscount()
  {
    if (t == Kind.wholesale)
      return 0.20;
    else
      return 0.1;
  }
  private   string  lastName, firstName;
  private   Kind  t;
}
```

The class `Customer` is an ADT in which the `enum Kind` distinguishes among three categories of customer so that a different pricing formula can be applied for each category.

Let us write a `Main()` that tests the use of this new type:

```
class CustomerTest {
  public static void Main()
  {
    Customer c = new Customer();

    c.SetName("Pohl", "Ira");
    c.SetKind(Customer.Kind.wholesale);
    c.WriteCustomer();
    Console.WriteLine("\nYour PC costs " +
        900 * (1 - c.PriceDiscount()) + " dollars.");
  }
}
```

Here is the output from this test program:

```
Ira  Pohl
Your PC costs 720 dollars.
```

Dissection of the *Customer* Program

■`enum Kind { general, wholesale, retail };`

Simple ADTs are expressible as an `enum` type. The enumeration can be declared inside or outside the class.

■   `private   string  lastName, firstName;`
    `private   Kind  t;`
`}`

Implementation is almost always hidden in accord with the black box principle.

```
public void SetName(string l, string f)
   { lastName = l; firstName = f; }
public Kind  GetKind() { return t; }
public void SetKind(Kind k) { t = k; }
```

These are typical instance methods. There is usually a `SetField()` and a `GetField()` method for each data member of the internal representation. This is part of the public interface for the ADT. It allows, in a controlled fashion, access to key values for the `Customer` type.

6.5   CLASS SCOPE

Classes provide an encapsulation technique. Conceptually, it makes sense that all names declared within a class be treated within their own scope, as distinct from namespace names, method names, and other class names, creating a need for a *fully qualified name*.

6.5.1   THE DOT OPERATOR, NAMESPACES, AND CLASS NAMES

The dot operator is a highest-precedence operator in the language.

```
System.Console.WriteLine()
```

What is being invoked is a static method `WriteLine()` found in class `Console` within namespace `System`.

6.5.2   NESTED CLASSES

Like blocks and namespaces, classes are scopes and can nest. *Nesting* allows local hiding of names and local allocation of resources. This is often desirable when a class is needed as part of the implementation of a larger construct. The following nested classes illustrate C# rules:

In file Nested.cs

```
namespace MyCode {                          // Outermost name

  using System;                             // A namespace

  public class One {                        // class scope
    public int  c;            // fully qualified MyCode.One.c
  }

  public class Two {               // outer class declaration
    public  int  c;                          // MyCode.Two.c
      public class Three {
                        // inner class declaration Two.Three
        public    int NestIt(int e)
        {
          Two t = new Two();
          One u = new One();
          u.c = 5 + e;
          t.c = c = e;
          return u.c + c;
        }
      private  int  c;                   // MyCode.Two.Three.c
      }
    public Three y;
  }

  public class NestTest {
    public static void Main()
    {
      Two x = new Two();
      x.y = new Two.Three();
      Console.WriteLine("Answer is " + x.y.NestIt(6) );
    }

}
```

The output of this program is

```
Answer is 17
```

There are many Nancies and Jerries in the world. They get told apart by a further name, such as Nancy Lovelace, or Jerry Turing. This still may not be enough context and one might have to add other identification such as Nancy Lovelace of Aptos, CA. The various scopes give one the ability to differentiate among identifiers.

The preceding code has namespace scope, class scope, inner class scope, and method block scope. The several uses of the identifier c in these different scopes leads to the potential ambiguities. You can overcome these ambiguities by using a fully qualified identifier. The qualified identifier MyCode.Two.Three.c clearly discriminates among the various uses of the unqualified identifier c. If you run this code the answer is 17. But it is clearly an artificial example to illustrate how to use qualified names. All three variables named c are accessible using the dot operator.

So which nest is mine?

Avoid unnecessary nesting as it creates hard-to-follow, complex designs. Good choice of distinct names is preferable to distinguishing identifiers by scope.

6.6   THE STANDARD CLASS string

The type string is a standard class that we have used mainly for I/O. String objects are immutable, so when modifying an existing string to produce a new string, the older object is retained, even if it is no longer needed. As we have seen it allows the operator + to provide concatenation. It is useful to study a standard class because much thought has been given to its design. It helps you see what methods are reasonable for a non-trivial class. It also has characteristics of other major classes, especially collection classes, such as class Array and class ArrayList. It is similar to a related class System.Text.StringBuilder, which is used when efficient mutable string creation is important. See Appendix C, *String, String-Builder, and Regex Libraries* for more details.

The three tables below divide the important class members for `String` into three groupings: properties and fields, static methods, and instance methods. First we present properties, fields, and the overloaded operators publicly available for strings in Table 6.1.

Table 6.1	System.String Class Public Properties, Fields, Operators
`Length`	Number of characters in the string.
`Chars`	Character at specified character position
`Empty`	Represents the empty string
`==`	Overloaded operator ==
`!=`	Overloaded operator !=

Some of the important static members of `class System.String` are shown in Table 6.2. Note that most of the methods have multiple overloaded meanings, as represented by the argument list being unspecified.

Table 6.2	System.String Class Static Methods
`int Compare (`*args*`)`	Compares two strings
`string Concat (`*args*`)`	Concatenates the two strings
`string Copy(string)`	Copies a string
`string Format(string, `*args*`)`	Formats a string

Some of the more commonly used instance methods for string are shown in Table 6.3.

Table 6.3 System.String Class Instance Methods	
`bool Equals (args)`	Determines if two strings have the same value
`int CompareTo(string)`	Compares this instance with string
`int IndexOf(args)`	Returns the index of the first occurrence of a string within an instance of string
`string Insert(int, string)`	Returns a new string with a specified value inserted at a specified position in this string
`string Remove(int, int)`	Deletes the specified number of characters from this instance of string, beginning at the specified location
`string Substring(args)`	Returns a substring of this instance of string
`string ToString()`	Returns a string representation as specified by the overridden method. See Section 6.6.1, *The ToString() Method*, on page 254.
`string ToLower(args)`	Returns a copy in lowercase
`string ToUpper(args)`	Returns a copy in uppercase
`string Trim(args)`	Removes leading or trailing white space

A more extensive list of `string` methods is given in Section C.1, *The Standard String Class*, on page 528.

How smart can humans be if strings give them trouble?

In file StringUse.cs

```csharp
// Use string class in a creative way
using System;

public class StringUse {

  public static void Main()
  {
    string lines = "";
    string[] words = {"the", "they", "them", "there"};
    Console.WriteLine("Read 2 lines");
    for (int i = 0; i < 2; ++i)
      lines = string.Concat(lines, Console.ReadLine()
                 + "\n");                // can be used in place of +
    lines = lines.ToLower();
    Console.WriteLine("Read 2 lines");
    Console.WriteLine("Echo 2 lines" + "\n" + lines);

    for (int i = 0; i < words.Length; ++i)
      Console.WriteLine(words[i] + " appears "
                 + CountWords(lines, words[i]) + "  times");
  }

  public static int CountWords(string s, string word)
  {
    string temp = s;
    int i = s.IndexOf(word);
    int count = 0;

    while (i < temp.Length && i != -1) {
      Console.WriteLine("in while " + i);
      ++count;
      temp = temp.Substring(i + word.Length,
                 temp.Length -i - word.Length);
        i = temp.IndexOf(word);
    }
    return count;
  }
}
```

Sample output of this program is

```
Read 2 lines
This is line one
And another line is keyed
Read 2 lines
Echo 2 lines
this is line one
and another line is keyed

in while 24
```

Dissection of the *StringUse* Program

■ for (int i = 0; i < 2; ++i)
    lines = string.Concat(lines, Console.ReadLine()
        + "\n");   // can be used in place of +
  lines = lines.ToLower();

We read in two lines entered from the console. These are concatenated into the variable lines. The instance method ToLower() transforms the string in which all alphabetic characters are in lowercase.

■ for (int i = 0; i < words.Length; ++i)
    Console.WriteLine(words[i] + " appears "
        + CountWords(lines, words[i]) + " times");

We invoke the static method CountWords() to examine how often the second argument, words[i], appears in the first argument, lines.

```
while (i < temp.Length && i != -1) {
   Console.WriteLine("in while " + i);
   ++count;
   temp = temp.Substring(i + word.Length,
                temp.Length -i - word.Length);
      i = temp.IndexOf(word);
}
```

This is the main loop in CountWords(). It searches for an index in temp where the string word appears. If the string appears, its count is incremented and the substring examined moves past the counted word. The two standard methods Substring() and IndexOf() are used to perform these operations. IndexOf() returns with -1 if the searched-for string is not found. Of course we could have written this code without using standard methods, but it would have been much more difficult and error-prone.

6.6.1 THE ToString() METHOD

One very important string method is ToString(). The purpose of ToString() is to provide a string representation of a variable's value, which can then be used by methods such as Write() and WriteLine(). A ToString() method should be included in classes so that class data members can be represented as a single standard string representation. The general form for creating a ToString() method is

```
public override string ToString()
   { return (string-representation) };
```

Until this point, we used WritePoint() and WriteCustomer() to output their respective class data members. ToString() improves on this scheme in that the class object name can be used as a parameter to any method which handles a string. From here on, we implement a ToString() method for classes because it is standard object-oriented methodology and C# style to expect this method.

We take our Point class from Section 6.2, *Instance Methods*, on page 243, and modify it to use data hiding and replace the two WritePoint() methods with a single ToString() method.

In file Point2.cs

```
using System;

public class Point {
  public void SetPoint(double u, double v)
    { x = u; y = v; }
  public override string ToString()
    { return ( " (" + x +", " + y + ") " ); }
  private double x = 0.0, y = 0.0;
}

public class TestPoint {
  public static void Main()
  {
    Point w1 = new Point();

    w1.SetPoint(1.5, 2.5);
    Console.WriteLine("Point w1 = " + w1);
  }
}
```

The output of this program is

```
Point w1 =   (1.5, 2.5)
```

Now, instead of having multiple versions of `WriteX()` that use `Console.Write()` or `Console.WriteLine()`, we have a method that provides a string conversion of a class instance variable that is used by any method which needs a string conversion for this class.

The `ToString()` method is invoked only if the instance variable is not null. This means that there will be no output if you call `Console.Write(x)` when x is null, and you will get only a newline if you call `Console.WriteLine(x)` with x as a null argument.

The `ToString()` method can use the static `String.Format()` method to perform formatting for the output. `String.Format()` takes the same arguments as `Write()` and `WriteLine()` for formatted output—namely, a string containing formatting parameters followed by a list of arguments to be formatted. (See Section 2.2.1, *Formatting the Output*, on page 40.)

In our `Point` example, the return string is difficult to read:

```
return ( " (" + x +", " + y + ") " );
```

By using formatting, we can make the output more readable, and, if we choose, we can limit the number of decimal places to be displayed. The following limits the fractional portion of the output of y to 2 digits while displaying the full value of x:

```
public override string ToString()
  { return  String.Format("({0}, {1:F2})", x, y); }
```

The `ToString()` method requires the use of the keyword `override` which we have not yet discussed. We talk in more detail about overriding and providing a `ToString()` method for classes in Section 8.5, *Everyone's Ancestor `class Object`*, on page 344, and in Section 9.3.1, *ToString() Overriding*, on page 383.

6.7   AN EXAMPLE: FLUSHING

We want to estimate the probability of being dealt a flush in poker. A flush occurs when at least five cards are of the same suit. We simulate shuffling cards by using a random number generator. This is a form of *Monte Carlo* calculation, named after the famous gambling resort. As was already mentioned in Section 4.6, *Problem Solving: Random Numbers*, on page 131, a Monte Carlo calculation is a computer simulation program requiring a probability calculation. The program uses classes to represent the necessary data types and functionality. The key data type is `Card`, which consists of a `Suit` value and a `Pips` value. A `Pips` value is between 1 and 13. On an actual card, these 13 `Pips` values are ace, 2, 3, · · · · ·, 10, jack, queen, and king.

We use a large number of our previous ideas to produce this code. However, the code can still be improved by using more advanced features of the language and we return to this example in Section 9.3.2, *Creating a User-Defined Format*, on page 385.

In file Poker.cs

```csharp
using System;

public class Card {
  public enum Suit { clubs, diamonds, hearts, spades }
  public class Pips
  {                                           // inner class
    public   void SetPips(int n) { p = n % 13 + 1; }
    public   int  GetPips() { return p; }
    private  int  p;                          // values 1 to 13
  }

  public   void SetCard(int n)
    { s = (Suit)(n/13);
      p = new Pips(); p.SetPips(n); }
  public   Suit  GetSuit() { return s; }
  public   Pips  GetPips() { return p; }
  private  Suit  s;
  private  Pips  p;
}                                     // end of Class Card

public class Deck {
  public   void SetDeck()
  {
    d = new Card[52];
    for (int i = 0; i < 52; ++i) {
      d[i] = new Card();
      d[i].SetCard(i);
    }
  }

  public   void Shuffle()
  {
   Random t = new Random();
    for (int i = 0; i < 52; ++i) {
      int k = i + (t.Next() % (52 - i));
      Card  cTemp = d[i];                       // swap cards
      d[i] = d[k];
      d[k] = cTemp;
    }
  }
```

```
public   void Deal(int n, int pos, Card[] hand)
{
   for (int i = pos; i < pos + n; ++i)
      hand[i - pos] = d[i];
}

private   Card[]  d;
}                                            // end of Class Deck
```

Dissection of the *Poker* Program

```
■public class Card {
   public enum Suit { clubs, diamonds, hearts, spades }
   public class Pips
   {                                         // inner class
   .....
     private   int  p;                       // values 1 to 13
   }
   .....
   private  Suit  s;
   private  Pips  p;
}
```

The class Pips and the enum Suit are used to build the Card type. The SetPips() method uses integers 0 to 51 to set an appropriate Pips value for a Card. The clustering of methods and the data members they act on improves modularity. Behavior and description are logically grouped together.

```
■public void SetCard(int n)
   { s = (Suit)(n/13); p =new Pips(); p.SetPips(n); }
```

The SetCard() method uses integer division to generate an enumerator value. It is important to notice that we must allocate a Pips object before initializing it with SetPips().

```
■public class Deck {
.......
   private   Card[]  d;
}
```

The class Deck declares an array of references to Card. A Deck object, as in the real world, has 52 unique cards.

```
■public void SetDeck()
 {
   d = new Card[52];
   for (int i = 0; i < 52; ++i) {
     d[i] = new Card();
     d[i].SetCard(i);
   }
 }
```

The SetDeck() method calls Card.SetCard() to map the integers into card values. Again we notice how each part of the design enables us to segregate method and description into appropriate object types.

```
■public void Shuffle()
 {
   Random t = new Random();
   for (int i = 0; i < 52; ++i) {
     int  k = i + (t.Next() % (52 - i));
     Card  cTemp = d[i];                        // swap cards
     d[i] = d[k];
     d[k] = cTemp;
   }
 }
```

The Shuffle() method uses the library-supplied pseudo-random number generator Random.Next() to exchange two cards for every deck position.

A Bold Bluff

One of a series of
Dogs Playing Poker
by C. M. Coolidge

We now write Main() to test these classes by computing the odds of getting a dealt-out flush in a poker game. We compute this for seven-card stud, where each player gets seven cards. To have a flush you must have five cards of the same suit.

In file Poker.cs

```
class Flush {
  public static void Main()
  {
    Card[] oneHand = new Card[7];
    Deck dk = new Deck();
    int  i, j, k, flushCount = 0;
    int [] sval= new int[4];
    int  ndeal= 1000, nc = 7, nhand = 52/nc;

    dk.SetDeck();
    for (k = 0; k < ndeal; k += nhand) {
      if ((nhand + k) > ndeal)
        nhand = ndeal - k;
      dk.Shuffle();
      for (i = 0; i < nc * nhand; i += nc) {
        for (j = 0; j < 4; ++j)
          sval[j] = 0;
        dk.Deal(nc, i, oneHand);             // deal next hand
        for (j = 0; j < nc; ++j)
          sval[(int)oneHand[j].GetSuit()]++;
        for (j = 0; j < 4; ++j)
          if (sval[j] >= 5)              // 5 or more is flush
            flushCount++;
      }
    }
    Console.WriteLine("In " + ndeal + " " + nc +
    "-card hands there were " + flushCount +
    " flushes");
  }
}
```

The output of this program is

```
In 1000 7-card hands there were 45 flushes
```

Dissection of the *Poker* Program

- ```
  int [] sval= new int[4];
  int  ndeal= 1000, nc = 7, nhand = 52/nc;
  ```

  For a relatively rare hand, such as a flush, we need a high number of hands to get a reasonable estimate of the probability of flushing. We use 1000 seven-card hands.

- ```
  dk.SetDeck();
  for (k = 0; k < ndeal; k += nhand) {
    if ((nhand + k) > ndeal)
      nhand = ndeal - k;
    dk.Shuffle();
  ```

  The deck is initialized and then shuffled using the random number generator. Each time the deck is dealt, the number nhand represents how many poker hands per shuffle can be arranged. If we were dealing six-card hands, this would be 8, as 6*8 is 48, but 7*8 is 56 (too many cards for a 52-card deck).

- ```
  for (j = 0; j < nc; ++j)
    sval[(int)oneHand[j].GetSuit()]++;
  ```

  For each card, we get its Suit value. The Suit value is an enumerator that can be used as an index, after casting to int, into the sval array. Each of the four elements of sval stores how many of each suit is found in a given hand. If one of these values is at least 5, the hand is a flush.

You can test your understanding of the poker program by modifying it to compute the probability of other poker hands. It is straightforward to compute whether a hand has a straight. A straight is a hand that has five cards whose Pips value are in sequence, such as 3, 4, 5, 6, 7.
  ```

6.8　THE this REFERENCE

The keyword `this` denotes an implicitly declared self-reference that can be used in a instance method. A simple illustration of its use extends our Point class from Section 6.3, *Access: Private and Public*, on page 243.

In file Point2.cs

```
// Class illustrating the use of the this reference

public class Point {
  public void SetPoint(double x, double y)
    { this.x = x; this.y = y; }
  public override string ToString()
  { return  String.Format("({0}, {1})", x, y);}
  private double x, y;
}
```

Dissection of the this Reference

■`public void SetPoint(double x, double y)`
　`{ this.x = x; this.y = y; }`

The instance method `SetPoint()` was rewritten with parameter names that are the same as the class member names. The method then uses the built-in self-reference `this` to discriminate between the two. Thus `this.x` refers to the member variable x, whereas x by itself refers to the method parameter.

6.9 static MEMBERS

C# allows static members. Using the modifier `static` when declaring a data member means that the data member is independent of any given class variable. The data member is part of the class but separate from any single class object. Nonstatic data members are created for each instance of the class. Since a static member is independent of a particular instance, it is accessed in the form

class-name`.`*identifier*

Note the use of the dot operator. For example, if we want a counter to keep track of how many `Point`s are declared at any time, we can add to class `Point` as follows:

```
class Point {
public  static int howMany;                      // declaration
  .....
}

Point.howMany = 0;                               // initialization
  .....
++Point.howMany;               // use independent of any instance
```

The static member `Point.howMany` exists independently from `Point` variables.

Syntactically, a `static` method has the modifier `static` precede the return type inside the class declaration. These are the methods we have been using since the beginning of the text, and include the method `Main()`. Now we can more fully appreciate its meaning. It distinguishes static class methods from nonstatic methods that are invoked with an object instance dotted with the method call.

```
class Point {
  .....
  public static void WriteHowMany()
    { Console.WriteLine("How many Points = " + howMany); }
}
```

Like the data member, the method is accessed by invoking it with the class name:

```
Point.HowMany();
```

6.9.1 const MEMBERS

A data member declared with the `const` modifier cannot be modified after initialization. A `const` member is always static.

The following example illustrates these ideas:

In file Salary.cs

```
// Calculate salary using static members
using System;

class Salary {
  public  void SetSalary(int b)
    { bSalary = b; yourBonus = 0; }
  public void CalcBonus(double perc)
    { yourBonus = (int)(bSalary * perc); }
  public int ComputeTotal()
    { return (bSalary + yourBonus + allBonus); }
  private   int        bSalary;
  private   int        yourBonus;
  private   const int   allBonus = 400;
}

public class SalaryTest {
  public static void Main()
  {
    Salary  w1= new Salary(), w2= new Salary();

    w1.SetSalary(1000);
    w2.SetSalary(2000);
    w1.CalcBonus(0.2);
    w2.CalcBonus(0.15);
    Console.WriteLine(" w1 " + w1.ComputeTotal() +
        "   w2 " + w2.ComputeTotal());
  }
}
```

The output of this program is

```
w1 1600    w2 2700
```

Dissection of the *Salary* Program

```
■class Salary {
   .....
   private    int        bSalary;
   private    int        yourBonus;
   private    const int  allBonus = 400;
}
```

There are three private data members. The `const` member `allBonus` is by default `static` and exists independently of any specific variables of type `Salary` being declared.

```
■void SetSalary(int b) { bSalary = b; yourBonus = 0; }
```

This assigns the value of `b` to the member `bSalary`. This instance method initializes the base salary. The variable `yourBonus` is also initialized. Although our small example did not require this, it is a good habit to initialize all member variables. As we see in Section 7.1, *Classes with Constructors*, on page 287, special methods called *constructor*s are used when initialization and object creation are needed.

```
■void CalcBonus(double perc)
   { yourBonus = (int)(bSalary * perc); }
```

The right-hand side of the assignment is a calculation of an `int` times a `double`. This results in a `double`. The assignment requires an `int`. Casting to `int` is a narrowing conversion resulting in the value for `yourBonus`.

6.10   AN EXAMPLE: CharStack CONTAINER

A *container* is a data structure whose main purpose is to store and retrieve a large number of objects. In the C# language, an array acts as such a structure. In this section, we develop code that is used to store character values in a *stack*, which is a *last-in-first-out* (LIFO) container. We code the stack class CharStack that stores characters.

In file CharStack1.cs

```
public class CharStack {
  public  void  SetStack(int maxSize)
  {
    s = new char[maxSize];
    maxLen = maxSize;
    top = EMPTY;
  }

  public void Reset() { top = EMPTY; }
  public void Push(char c) { s[++top] = c; }
  public char  Pop() { return s[top--]; }
  public char  TopOf() { return s[top]; }
  public bool  Empty() { return (top == EMPTY); }
  public bool  Full() { return (top == maxLen - 1); }

  private const int  EMPTY = -1;
  private int  maxLen;
  private char[] s;
  private int  top;
}
```

The basic operations on a stack are *push* and *pop*. The push operation places a value on the top of the stack, and the pop operation removes the value at the top of the stack. We use a char array to implement the stack. The stack isn't actually created until the space is allocated for it using Set-Stack(). Later, in Section 7.1.3, *Constructing a Stack*, on page 294, we talk about other, more flexible implementations.

We now write Main() to test the same operations.

In file CharStack1.cs

```
// Reverse a string with a CharStack

class CharStackTest {
  public static void Main()
  {
    CharStack  s = new CharStack();
    string  str = "My name is Don Knuth!";
    int    i = 0;

    s.SetStack(str.Length);     // stack can accommodate str
    Console.WriteLine(str);
    while ((i < str.Length) && !s.Full())
      s.Push(str[i++]);
    while (!s.Empty())                    // print the reverse
      Console.Write(s.Pop());
    Console.WriteLine();
  }
}
```

The output from this version of the test program is

```
My name is Don Knuth!
!htunK noD si eman yM
```

Every computer scientist should know the name Donald Ervin Knuth, Professor of Computer Science at Stanford University, and author of the three volumes (to date) series *The Art of Computer Programming*. He is also the developer of literate programming, a style of programming that weaves documentation together with code development. For the beginner, it is very desirable to write documentation as you develop your comments. Student programmers often leave this to a last step and only reluctantly comment code, because they are graded on this element.

Dissection of the *CharStack* Program

```
■public void SetStack(int maxSize)
{
    s = new char[maxSize];
    maxLen = maxSize;
    top = EMPTY;
}
```

This method gets the space allocated for the stack and initializes it to empty. It is the responsibility of the caller to initialize the stack size to the largest that is used. This method foreshadows our study in the next chapter of coding constructor methods.

```
■public void Reset() { top = EMPTY; }
 public void Push(char c) { s[++top] = c; }
 public char  Pop() { return s[top--]; }
```

These methods manipulate and change the stack. They are known as *mutator methods*.

```
■public bool Empty() { return (top == EMPTY); }
 public bool Full() { return (top == maxLen - 1); }
```

These methods do not modify the stack and they are known as *accessor methods*. They access information describing the stack without changing the stack.

```
■private const int  EMPTY = -1;
 private int  maxLen;
 private char[] s;
 private int  top;
```

As usual, we hide the implementation details. In this case, we represent the stack of characters with an array. Note that the declaration of the stack s does not actually allocate the space for the stack. That is done by the SetStack() method.

```
s.SetStack(str.Length);        // stack can accommodate str
Console.WriteLine(str);
while ((i < str.Length) && !s.Full())
    s.Push(str[i++]);
while (!s.Empty())                      // print the reverse
    Console.Write(s.Pop());
```

Access to the hidden variables is controlled. The variables can be changed by the instance methods Reset() but cannot be accessed directly. SetStack() is used to allocate the space for the stack. In this example, we allocate only what we need for the String str. The Push() and Pop() methods are then used to put the characters from the string on the stack, then take the characters off in reverse order.

6.11   PROPERTIES AND DATA HIDING

Let us reexamine our early version of implementing Point in Section 6.2, *Instance Methods*, on page 240.

```
public class Point {
    public double x, y;
    public void SetPoint(double x, double y)
        { this.x = x; this.y = y; }
    public override string ToString()
    { return  String.Format("({0}, {1})", x, y); }
}
```

Here we have given everything public access. This violates the software information principle that says data members should be hidden. Notice the method SetPoint() is allowed to change the values of x and y. Such a method is called a mutator method. Appropriately hiding this data, we could redesign Point as follows:

```
public class Point {
  public void SetPoint(double x, double y)
    { this.x = x; this.y = y; }
  public double GetXCoordinate() { return x; }
  public double GetYCoordinate() { return y; }
  public override string ToString()
  { return  String.Format("({0}, {1})", x, y); } }
  private double x, y;
}
```

Now the GetXCoordinate() and GetYCoordinate() methods can access the underlying data. Such a method is often called an *accessor* method. The x and y values are now hidden from users of this class. This access protection makes the software more robust.

C# introduces a uniform scheme called *properties* for providing this style of access. A *property* acts like a method and is used to access and modify private data members, often called *field*s. It uses three special keywords, set, get, and value, within the property declaration. Recoding Point with properties, we have:

In file Point3.cs

```
public class Point {
  public override string ToString()
  { return  String.Format("({0}, {1})", x, y); }

  public double X                 // property for manipulating x
  { get { return x; }  set { x = value; }   }

  public double Y                 // property for manipulating y
  { get { return y; } set { y = value; } }

  private double x, y;
}
```

Notice that the property declaration has two code bodies introduced respectively by the keywords get and set. It is C# style to name the property with the same name as the private data except that its first character is in uppercase. It is also C# style to code the accessor get first, and the mutator set second. Now the properties are public so anyone can use them to access the underlying members as follows:

In file Point3.cs

```
.......
  Point p = new Point();
  p.X = 3;                    // uses set so value = 3 and p.x = 3
  p.Y = 7;                    // uses set so value = 7 and p.y = 7
  Console.WriteLine(" x = " + p.X);        // uses get so p.x
.....
```

This code fragment produces the following output:

```
x = 3
```

6.12   SOFTWARE ENGINEERING: CLASS DESIGN

The style of having `public` class members coded first is the norm in C#. It follows the rule that the widest audience needs to see the public members. More specialized information is placed later in the class declaration. This can be thought of as a *need-to-know* principle or *newspaper* principle. In a newspaper, the first sentence gives the most important and most widely disseminated information. Details are left for later.

Data members should in general be private. This is an important coding heuristic. Generally, data are part of an implementation choice and should be accessed through public methods. Such methods are called accessor methods when they do not change, or mutate, the data and they are called mutator methods when they do change the underlying structure. Notice how much safer such a design is. If the data members were directly accessible, it would be easy for them to be inappropriately changed.

In OOP design, the public members are usually methods and are thought of as the type's *interface.* These are the actions, or behaviors, publicly expected of an object. If we think of the object type as a noun, the behaviors are verbs. In the implementation, data members are generally placed in private access. This is a key data-hiding principle; namely, that implementation is kept inside a black box that cannot be directly exploited by the object's user.

Noun: Ball   Verbs: Bounce   Hit   Throw

Additional data hiding is provided by indirection through the use of a separate class for the underlying data representation. This technique is called the *Cheshire Cat* technique, in honor of Lewis Carroll's cat that disappeared leaving only a smile.

The class `CharStack` can be coded in terms of a class `CharStackRep`. All the data and underlying operations are handled through a `class CharStackRep` reference. The class `CharStack` is therefore known as a *wrapper class.* The relationship between the wrapper class and the underlying representation class is called the *handle* design pattern. We illustrate this relationship when we introduce Unified Modeling Language (UML) diagrams in Section 6.12.2, *Unified Modeling Language (UML) and Design*, on page 273.

6.12.1 TRADEOFFS IN DESIGN

Design is all about tradeoffs. Recall our poker example in Section 6.7, *An Example: Flushing*, on page 257, and our use of enum to describe suit. What if this were recoded as a class?

We change the `suit` declaration from an enumerated type to a class and use the `get` and `set` properties as follows:

```
public class Suit {
  public int S
    { get { return s; } set { s = value / 13; } }
  public override string ToString() { ····· }
  private int s;    //values 0 to 3
}
```

We add the `get` and `set` properties for each class to access the hidden variables. The advantage is that `Suit` and `Pip`s are now treated symmetrically, with both being given class definitions. The disadvantage is that we have added more code and a layer of methods to access what is basically a simple type having four unique values. There is no clear answer as to which choice for `suit` is better. (See Exercise 14 on page 284.) In one sense, the curse of C# is that there are too many opportunities, but this is also its great benefit over simpler languages such as Java.

6.12.2 UNIFIED MODELING LANGUAGE (UML) AND DESIGN

The Unified Modeling Language (UML) is a graphical depiction of class relationships that helps the coder design, document, and maintain object-oriented code. The simplest diagram is a rectangle that represents a class. Generally, the class has three things depicted: its name, placed at the top; its data members, placed in the middle; and its methods, placed at the bottom. The following UML diagram corresponds to the `Customer` class in Section 6.4, *An Example: Customer*, on page 245.

```
┌─────────────────────────────┐
│          Customer           │
├─────────────────────────────┤
│          lastName           │
│          firstName          │
│            Kind             │
├─────────────────────────────┤
│          SetName()          │
│          GetKind()          │
│          SetKind()          │
│        PriceDiscount()      │
│        WriteCustomer()      │
└─────────────────────────────┘
```

UML Diagram for Class Customer

A class diagram describes the types and relationships in the system. It is very useful documentation, and a number of systems, such as Rational Rose, now provide automated tools to develop such documentation along with coding. A relationship that can be depicted by UML includes the part-to-whole, or aggregation, relationship (*HASA*). Notice that `Customer` *has a* `lastname`, `firstName`, and `Kind`.

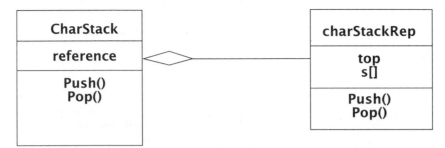

Handle Class in UML

The representation class is used to concretely implement the handle class. This relationship recurs in many object-oriented coding schemes. It is called the *bridge* or *handle design pattern*. A *design pattern* is a recurring software solution to a problem, usually involving several classes collaborating to solve the problem. The book *Design Patterns: Elements of Reusable Object-Oriented Software*, by Gamma, et al. (Addison-Wesley, 1995) popularized this approach by listing over 20 such patterns with catchy names, such as the bridge pattern.

6.13   DR. P'S PRESCRIPTIONS

- Indentation is as follows: `class` and closing brace all line up and are placed on separate lines. Member declarations are indented and line up vertically.

- Access privileges are in order: `public`, `protected`, and `private`.

- Data members should be `private`.

- Provide a uniform set of methods and properties, such as `get` and `set`.

- Provide a `ToString()` method for classes in which output of the class data members has a standard form.

The indentation rules are consistent with industry practice. The idea behind placing more visible members first is based on the same logic used in newspaper articles—namely, what everyone needs to know comes first. What everyone needs to know are the public members. This is the interface available to all users of the class.

In most designs, it is appropriate to make data members `private`. This is the black box principle. The builder (read: programmer) hides the details of the implementation. The client benefits by having to see and understand fewer details and being protected from obvious misapplications.

A client expects to print information about a data type, so almost all data types need write methods in their interface. A client expects to retrieve and change key values of the object. A proper choice of `set` and `get` properties allows the programmer to provide these services. Providing these properties makes it easier to code new types and have clients use them easily.

The `Object` method `ToString()` should be overridden for any type you implement. This is an expectation by users of such a type. It is a great convenience as it makes the type available for use with `Write()` and `Write-Line()` methods.

6.14 C# COMPARED WITH JAVA AND C++

C# classes are based on the Java and C++ aggregate type `class`. A `class` provides the means for implementing a user-defined data type and associated methods. Therefore, a `class` can be used to implement an ADT. Like Java, functions, or methods, as they are called in Java and C#, cannot exist outside a class construct. This differs from C++, in which functions can reside on their own. In addition, Java `class` types are always reference types. The Java primitive types, such as `int` or `char`, are value types. Let us write a `class` called `Person` that is used to store information about people. In this first version of writing `class Person` we will not use properties. Properties are not available in Java and C++. At the end of this section we recode `Person` using properties, standard C# practice.

In file Person1.cs

```
public class Person {
  public void SetName(string name) { this.name = name; }
  public void SetAge(int age) { this.age = age; }
  public void SetGender(char gender) {this.gender = gender;}
  public override string ToString() {return String.Format
    ("Name: {0}  Age: {1}  Gender: {2}",
        name, age, gender);}
  private string name;
  private int age;
  private char gender;                    //male 'M', female 'F'
}
```

Now we show the class in Java. It is very nearly identical to the C# version.

In file Person1.java

```
// An elementary Java implementation of type Person

class Person {
  public void setName(String nm) { name = nm; }
  public void setAge(int a) { age = a; }
  public void setGender(char b) { gender = b; }
  public String ToString()
     { return ("Name: " + name   + " Age: " + age
                     + " Gender: " + gender); }
  private String name;
  private int age;
  private char gender;                    // male 'M', female 'F'
}
```

Java, C++, and C# all have two important additions to the structure concept of traditional C. First, they have members called *class methods* that are methods, such as `setAge()`. Second, they have access specifications, such as `public`, `private`, or `protected`. The keyword `public` indicates the visibility of the member that follows it. Private members are available for use only by other methods of the same class. Public members are available anywhere the class is available. Privacy allows part of the implementation of a class type to be *hidden* and prevents unanticipated modifications to the data structure. Restricted access, or *data hiding*, is a feature of object-oriented programming.

The declaration of methods inside a class allows the ADT to have actions, or behaviors, that can act on its private representation. We can now use this data type `Person` as if it were a basic type of the language. Other code that uses this type is a *client*. The client can use only the public members to act on variables of type `Person`.

Next, we implement the classes which make use of class `Person`.

In file Person1.cs

```
// Uses Person Class

public class Person1 {
  public static void Main (String[] args)
  {
    Console.WriteLine("Person test:");
    Person p1 = new Person();              // create Person
    p1.SetAge(20);
    p1.SetName("Alan Turing");
    p1.SetGender('M');
    Console.WriteLine(p1);
  }
}
```

The output of this example program is

```
Person test:
Name: Alan Turing   Age: 20   Gender: M
```

Next we show the code in Java. Notice how it is nearly identical, with the exception of output `println()` and use of lowercase as standard start of method names.

In file Person1.java

```
// Uses Person

public class PersonTest {
  public static void main (String[] args)
  {
    System.out.println("Person test:");
    Person p1 = new Person();              // create Person
    p1.setAge(20);
    p1.setName("Alan Turing");
    p1.setGender('M');
    System.out.println(p1);
  }
}
```

Notice the use of `new Person()` to create an instance of `Person`. The `new` operator goes off to the heap, as it does in C++, and obtains memory for creating an instance of object `Person`. The value of `p1` is a reference to this object. In effect, this is the address of the object. For a more detailed look at a similar example, and explanation of the nuances of Java classes, read *Java by Dissection* (Addison-Wesley) by Ira Pohl and Charlie McDowell, pages 234 to 242.

C++ has some differences from either Java or C#. This code exhibits some of these differences.

In file person1.cpp

```cpp
#include <iostream>
#include <string>
using namespace std;

class person {
  public:
  void setName(string nm) { name = nm; }
  void setAge(int ag) { age = ag; }
  void setGender(char gen)
    { gender = gen; }
  void writePerson() const
    { cout << "Name: " << name << "  Age: " << age <<
        "  Gender: " << gender << endl; }
private:
  string name;
  int age;
  char gender;                        //male 'M', female 'F'
};

int main ()
{
  cout << "Person test:" << endl;
  person p1;                                // create Person
  p1.setAge(20);
  p1.setName("Alan Turing");
  p1.setGender('M');
  p1.writePerson();
}
```

In C++ access is specified by writing the specifier followed by a colon. For example, writing `public:` makes all members after this specification `public`. Also fully coded methods are inlined. This is an efficiency hack that avoids function call overhead for methods that are uncomplicated. Finally methods can have the keyword `const` come after their parameter list. This designates them as non-mutator methods, or in other words methods that do not modify the contents of instance data members. This use of `const` is unique to C++ and does not have an analogue in Java or C#.

Better C# style would recode class `Person` to use properties.

In file Person2.cs

```
public class Person {
  public string Name
    { set { name = value; } get{ return name; }  }
  public int Age { set { age = value; } get {return age; } }
  public char Gender
    { set { gender = value; } get {return gender;} }
  public override string ToString() {return String.Format
    ("Name: {0}  Age: {1}  Gender: {2}",
        name, age, gender);}

  private string name;
  private int age;
  private char gender;                    //male 'M', female 'F'
}

public class PersonTest {
  public static void Main (String[] args)
  {
    Console.WriteLine("Person test:");
    Person p1 = new Person();                // create Person
    p1.Age = 20;
    p1.Name = "Alan Turing";
    p1.Gender = 'M';
    Console.WriteLine(p1);
  }
}
```

SUMMARY

- A class is a way of implementing a data type and associated methods and operators. It is the mechanism for implementing ADTs, such as complex numbers and stacks.

- The class type allows the programmer to aggregate components into a single named variable. A class has components, called members, that are individually named. Critical to processing structures is the accessing of their members. This is done with the member access operator, also called the dot operator.

- The concept of class allows methods to be members. The method declaration is included in the class declaration and is invoked using access methods for class members.

- Classes have public and private members that provide data hiding. The keyword `private` restricts the access of the members that follow it. The private members are only available to the methods in the class.

- Data members can be declared with the storage class modifier `static`. A data member that is declared `static` is shared by all variables of that class and is stored in one place only. Therefore, the data member can be accessed using the form

  class-name`.`*identifier*

- The keyword `this` denotes an implicitly declared self-reference that can be used in an instance method. Therefore static methods cannot use the `this` reference.

- Classes can be nested. The inner class is inside the scope of the outer class.

REVIEW QUESTIONS

1. A private member (can or cannot) _____ be used by a method of that class.

2. The `static` modifier used in declaring a data member means that the data member is _____.

3. The preferred style is to have members of _____ access given first and members of _____ access declared last in a class declaration.

4. A stack is a LIFO container. A container is a data structure whose main purpose is _____.

5. LIFO means _____.

6. Seeing *this.member* means an _____ is used.

7. Draw the UML diagram for `class Salary`.

8. UML stands for _____ _____ _____.

9. If an access specifier is left off a member, it is implicitly _____.

EXERCISES

1. Design a class to store a dairy product name, portion weight, calories, protein, fat, and carbohydrates. Twenty-five grams of American cheese has 375 calories, 5 grams of protein, 8 grams of fat, and 0 carbohydrates. Show how to assign these values to the member variables of your structure. Write a method that, given a variable of type `class Dairy` and a weight in grams (portion size), returns the number of calories for that weight.

2. Write a class `Point` that has three coordinates x, y, and z. How can you access the individual members?

3. Use the class `Card` defined in the *Poker* program in Section 6.7, *An Example: Flushing*, on page 257, to write a hand-sorting routine. In card games, most players keep their cards sorted by pip value. The routine places aces first, kings next, and so forth, down to twos. A hand is five cards.

4. In this exercise, use the class `CharStack`, defined in Section 6.10, *An Example: CharStack Container*, on page 266. Write the method

   ```
   void Reverse(char s1[], char s2[])
   ```

   The strings `s1` and `s2` must be the same size. String `s2` should become a reversed copy of string `s1`. Internal to `reverse`, use a `CharStack` to perform the reversal.

5. Rewrite the methods `Push()` and `Pop()` discussed in Section 6.10, *An Example: CharStack Container*, on page 266, to test that `Push()` is not acting on a full `CharStack` and that `Pop()` is not acting on an empty `CharStack`. If either condition is detected, print an error message. Contrast this to an approach using asserts.

6. Write `Reverse()` as a instance method for type `CharStack`, discussed in Section 6.10, *An Example: CharStack Container*, on page 267. Test it by printing normally and reversing the string

   Gottfried Leibniz wrote Toward a Universal Characteristic

7. Rewrite the `CountWords()` method in the *TestString* program in Section 6.6, *The Standard Class string*, on page 252 to use recursion.

8. For the `CharStack` type in Section 6.10, *An Example: CharStack Container*, on page 266, write as instance methods

   ```
   // Push n chars from s1 onto the CharStack
   void PushM(int n, const char s1[])

   // Pop n chars from CharStack into char string
   void PopM(int n, char s1[])
   ```

9. Code a class `Deque`, which is a double-ended queue that allows pushing and popping at both ends.

```
public class Deque
{
  public void Reset() {top = bottom = maxLen/2; top--; }
  .....
  private   char  s[];
  private   int   bottom, top, maxLen;
}
```

Declare and implement `PushT()`, `PopT()`, `PushB()`, `PopB()`, `ToString()`, `TopOf()`, `BottomOf()`, `Empty()`, and `Full()`. The method `PushT()` stands for push on top and `PopT()` for pop on top; `PushB()` stands for push on bottom and `PopB()` for pop on bottom. `TopOf()` gets the front of the queue and `BottomOf()` gets the rear of the queue. The `ToString()` method should return a string of blank separated elements of the stack from bottom to top. An empty stack is denoted by having the top fall below the bottom. Test each method. Draw the UML diagram for this class.

10. Extend the data type `Deque` by adding a instance method `Relocate()`. If the `deque` is full, `Relocate()` is called, and the contents of the `deque` are moved to balance empty storage around the center `maxLen/2` of array `s`. Its method declaration header is

```
// Returns true if it succeeds, false if it fails
bool deque::Relocate()
```

11. Recode `deque` to hide the representation in a `class DequeRep`. Draw an appropriate UML diagram for this handle class design.

12. Write a method that swaps the contents of two strings. If you pushed a string of characters onto a `CharStack` found in Section 6.10, *An Example: CharStack Container*, on page 266, and popped them into a second string, they would come out reversed. In a swap of two strings, we want the original ordering. Use a `deque` to do the swap. The strings are stored in character arrays of the same length, but the strings themselves may be of differing lengths. The method prototype is

```
void Swap(char s1[], char s2[]);
```

13. Write `ToString()` methods for `Card` and `Deck` and add them to the *Poker* program found in Section 6.7, *An Example: Flushing*, on page 257. Print the deck after it is initialized.

14. Change the `suit` declaration from the previous exercise from an enumerated type to a class and recode the `Pips`, `Card`, and `Deck` classes to use `get` and `set` properties:

```
public class Suit {
  public int S
    { get { return s; } set { s = value / 13; } }
  private int s;    //values 0 to 3
}
```

15. Using the revised *Poker* program from the previous exercise which has the overloaded `ToString()` method and the `get` and `set` properties, write a method `PrintOneHand()` that prints out card hands. Add it to the *Poker* program and use it to print out each flush.

16. Section 6.7, *An Example: Flushing,* on page 260, `Main()` detects flushes. Write the following methods to return `true` if the condition is met:

```
bool   IsFlush(Card[] hand)
bool   IsStraight(Card[] hand)
bool   IsStraightFlush(Card[] hand)
```

A straight is five cards that have sequential pip values. The lowest straight is ace, 2, 3, 4, 5, and the highest straight is 10, jack, queen, king, ace. Run experiments to estimate the probability that dealt cards result in a straight, and compare the results of five-card hands with results of seven-card hands. *Hint:* You may want to set up an array of 15 integers to correspond to counters for each pip value. Be sure that a pip value of 1 (corresponding to ace) is also counted as the high card corresponding to a pip value of 14.

A straight flush is the rarest poker hand and has the highest value. Note that, in a hand of more than five cards, it is not sufficient to merely check for the presence of both a straight and a flush to determine that the hand is a straight flush. In order to get meaningful statistics, you will need to increase the number of hands from 1000 to perhaps 50,000.

17. Change class `CharStack` in Section 6.10, *An Example: CharStack Container*, on page 266, to `IntStack` by substituting type `int` for type `char` in the class definition as appropriate. Test the code with an appropriate `Main()`.

18. *(Java to C++)* Recode the Java program *PersonTest.java* in Section 6.14, *C# Compared with Java and C++*, on page 276, to run as C#.

CONSTRUCTORS, CONVERSION, AND OVERLOADING

O bjects are class instances. This chapter continues the previous chapter's discussion of how to code ADTs as class types. A key to doing this is the use of special methods called constructors which typically construct and initialize objects.

A class variable is a reference type. Variables of class types declare a reference to an object of that type. The keyword `null` is a reference constant that indicates no object yet exists. Constructing an *object* requires memory and an initial value. We call operator `new` to allocate the object. For example, in

```
static public void Foo()
{
   int     n = 5;
   double[] z = new double[10];
   Point p = new Point();
   .....
}
```

all of the variables are created at block entry when `Foo()` is invoked. A typical implementation uses a runtime system stack. Thus, for the `int` variable n, the system allocates a four-byte integer off the stack and initializes it to the value 5. The array variable z requires 4 bytes to represent a reference to where the allocated array is stored. The array of `double` variable z requires 10 times `sizeof(double)` to store its elements. This is allocated by new dynamically off the system heap memory. In each case, the system provides for the construction and initialization of these variables. On exit from Foo(), deallocation of the stack-allocated variables occurs automatically. The heap-allocated variables are deallocated automatically by a system program called a *garbage collector*.

A *constructor* is a method whose name is the same as the class name; it creates objects of the class type. This process involves *initializing* data members and, frequently, allocating storage from the heap by using new. A *destructor* is a method whose name is the class name preceded by the tilde character, ~. A destructor's usual purpose is *finalizing* objects of the class type. Finalizing objects involves retrieving resources allocated to the object. It is not usual for classes to have destructors, because garbage collection often provides the only needed cleanup.

Whereas constructors can be overloaded and take arguments, destructors can do neither. A constructor is invoked when its associated type is used in a definition, when call-by-value is used to pass a value to a method, or when the return value of a method must create a value of associated type. The destructor is invoked when an object of its type is garbage collected. Constructors and destructors do not have return types and cannot use return *expression* statements.

Hey, you must have the wrong address for demolition. We don't need a destructor yet! We are still constructing this thing!

7.1 CLASSES WITH CONSTRUCTORS

The simplest use of a constructor is for initialization. In this and later sections, we develop some examples that use constructors to initialize the values of the data members of the class. Our first example is an implementation of a data type `Counter` to store numbers that are computed with a modulus of 100. A car's trip odometer is a counter.

In file Counter.cs

```
// Counter and constructor initialization

public class Counter {
  // simple constructor for initialization
  public Counter(int i) { count = i % 100; }
  public int Count
    { get { return count; }  set { count = value % 100; } }
  public override string ToString()
    { return (count + "\t"); }
  public void Click() { count = (count + 1) % 100; }

  private  int  count;                              // 0 to 99
}
```

Dissection of the *Counter* Program

```
■public class Counter {
  public Counter(int i) { count = i % 100; }
```

The `class Counter` is to be used as a simple data type that counts from 0 to 99. It has a constructor that initializes variables to a value between these limits.

```
■public int Count
     { get {return count;}  set { count = value % 100; } }
  public override string ToString()
     { return (count + "\t"); }
 public void Click() { count = (count + 1) % 100; }
```

Here, we have a typical group of methods and properties. The counter's click operation is implemented by adding 1 and using the modulus operator to guarantee that the value of the counter stays inside its limits.

```
■private  int  count;                              // 0 to 99
```

The integer count is restricted in value to 0, 1, 2, . . . , 99. It is the class implementer's responsibility to enforce this restriction by having all methods and properties guarantee this behavior.

Some examples of this are

```
Counter  a = new Counter(0);                      // a.count = 0;
Counter  b = new Counter(1);                      // b.count = 1;
```

but not

```
Counter  a = new Counter();            // illegal: no parameter
```

Since this class has only the one constructor of argument list int, a Counter declaration must have an integral expression passed as an initializing value. Not allowing a Counter variable to be declared without an initializing expression prevents runtime errors due to uninitialized variables. In the next section, we provide a constructor, the *default constructor*, that remedies the preceding illegal declaration. It does not require an initializing value. Such a constructor should perform initialization of a class variable to a default value.

Man, oh, man, I wish I could automate this counting!

7.1.1 THE DEFAULT CONSTRUCTOR

A constructor requiring no arguments is called the default constructor. It is invoked when called as follows:

```
Counter c = new Counter();
```

When the class does not explicitly provide a constructor, the compiler provides such a constructor by default. Hence the term default instead of empty argument constructor.

In our Counter example, the following constructor could serve as a general default constructor:

```
public Counter() { count = 0; }
```

This initializes Counter variable's count to 0 by default. It is also possible to provide default values by initializing member variables.

```
public Counter() { }        // default initialized count is 0
```

The empty argument constructor implicitly creates a Counter instance whose member value is initialized to 0. With this set of constructors, the following code is possible:

In file Counter.cs

```
class CounterTest
{
  static void Main()
  {
    Counter a = new Counter(13);              //a.count = 13
    Counter b = new Counter(1);               // b.count = 1
    Counter c = new Counter();                // c.count == 0
    Counter d = new Counter(102);             // e.count == 2
    Counter e;       // reference is created but not instance
    e = new Counter();                        // f.count == 0

    e.Click();
    Console.WriteLine("a-e are " + a + b + c + d + e);
  }
}
```

The output of this program is

```
a-e are 13   1   0   2   1
```

7.1.2 IMPROVING THE Point CLASS

The class `Point` from Section 6.11, *Properties and Data Hiding*, on page 270, is readily improved by adding constructors. There are usually several constructors per class. Each constructor signature represents a useful way to declare and initialize an object of that type. Notice that the class contains the property `set` which can be used to change the value of a `Point` object but cannot be used to create a `Point` object.

In file PointParabola.cs

```
class Point {
  public Point() { }                                    // default
  public Point(double x) { this.x = x; }  // double to Point
  public Point(double x, double y) {this.x = x; this.y = y;}

  public override string ToString()
   { return String.Format("({0}, {1})", x, y); }
```

```
public double X  { get { return x; } set { x = value;} }
public double Y  { get { return y; } set { y = value;} }
public void Plus(Point c) { x = c.x; y = c.y; }

private double x = 0.0, y = 0.0; // default initialization
}
```

This class has three individually coded constructors. To test this class, we write a program to produce a series of points. Many scientific problems require producing a table of points or a graph by using a function. For example, a parabola can be coded as

```
static double Parabola(double x, double p)
        { return(x * x) / p; }
```

We produce a table of points graphing the parabola from 0 to 2 in increments of 0.1.

In file PointParabola.cs

```
using System;

class ParabolaTest {
  static void Main()
  {
    const int nPoints = 20;
    Console.WriteLine("Parabola Test Program");
    Point [] g = new Point[nPoints];
    GraphParabola(0, 2, 0.1, 5.0, g);
    Console.WriteLine("First 20 samples:" );
    for (int i = 0; i < nPoints; ++i) {
      Console.Write("{0,15:S}", g[i]);
      if (i % 3 == 2)                          //put 3 on a line
        Console.WriteLine();
    }
  }

  static double Parabola(double x, double p)
    { return(x * x) / p; }
```

```
    static void GraphParabola(double a, double b,
                        double incr, double p, Point[] gr)
    {
      double x = a;
      for (int i = 0; x <= b; ++i) {
        gr[i]= new Point(x, Parabola(x, p));
        x += incr;
      }
    }
  }
}
```

The output of this program is

```
Parabola Test Program
First 20 samples:
          (0, 0)       (0.1, 0.002)     (0.2, 0.008)
    (0.3, 0.018)       (0.4, 0.032)      (0.5, 0.05)
    (0.6, 0.072)       (0.7, 0.098)     (0.8, 0.128)
    (0.9, 0.162)          (1, 0.2)      (1.1, 0.242)
    (1.2, 0.288)       (1.3, 0.338)     (1.4, 0.392)
     (1.5, 0.45)       (1.6, 0.512)     (1.7, 0.578)
    (1.8, 0.648)       (1.9, 0.722)
```

Dissection of the *PointParabola* Program

```
■public Point() { }                                  // default
 public Point(double x) { this.x = x; }// double to Point
 public Point(double x, double y){this.x = x; this.y = y;}
 .....
 private  double x = 0.0, y = 0.0;        // default init
 }
```

The default assignments to members x and y are value 0.0. The constructor can overwrite this value.

```
■public override string ToString()
   { return String.Format("({0}, {1})", x, y);
```

Here we used format style inside the `ToString()` method to output `x` and `y`. In this form, `x` and `y` are output with as much precision as they have with no further formatting. We can output the points as 8 character strings with four places of precision with

```
   { return String.Format("({0,8:F4}, {1,8:F4})", x, y); }
```

The $\{n,8:F4\}$ form forces nice alignment and puts limits on the precision size, but may have lots of space or trailing zeroes that seem extraneous.

```
■static void GraphParabola(double a, double b,
                           double incr, double p, Point[] gr)
{
  double x = a;
  for (int i = 0; x <= b; ++i){
    gr[i]= new Point(x, Parabola(x, p));
    x += incr;
  }
}
```

We graph the parabola from `a` to `b`. We graph the parabola at point `x`. The parabola is defined as $f(x) = x^2/p$. It is computed at increments `incr`. Notice how at each value of `x` a new point is allocated and assigned to the array parameter `gr`. It calls the constructor `Point(double, double)`.

7.1.3 CONSTRUCTING A STACK

We modify the `CharStack` type from Section 6.10, *An Example: CharStack Container*, on page 266, so that its maximum length is initialized by a constructor. The length of the stack is a parameter to a constructor. This parameter is used to call the operator `new`, which can allocate storage dynamically.

The design of the object `CharStack` includes hidden implementation detail. Data members are placed in the `private` access region of class `CharStack`. The public interface provides clients with the expected stack abstraction. These are all public methods, such as Push() and Pop(). Some of these methods are accessor methods that do not change the stack object, such as TopOf() and Empty(). Some of these methods are mutator methods that do change the CharStack object, such as Push() and Pop(). The constructor methods have the job of creating and initializing CharStack objects.

In file CharStack2.cs

```csharp
class CharStack {
  public  CharStack()
  {
    top = EMPTY;
    s = new char[maxLen];
  }

  public  CharStack(int size)
  {
    maxLen = size;
    top = EMPTY;
    s = new char[size];
  }

  public override string ToString()
  {
    if (top != EMPTY)
      return new string(s, 0, top + 1););
    else
      return String.Empty;              //Special empty string
  }

  public  void Reset() { top = EMPTY; }
  public  void Push(char c) { s[++top] = c; }
  public  char  Pop() { return s[top--]; }
  public  char  TopOf() { return s[top]; }
  public  bool  Empty() { return (top == EMPTY); }
  public  bool  Full() { return (top == maxLen - 1); }
  public  int  Length() { return s.Length; }

  private const int  EMPTY = -1;
  private int  maxLen = 100;               // default value
  private char[] s;
  private int  top;
}
```

Dissection of *CharStack* Program

■
```
public CharStack()
{
  top = EMPTY;
  s = new char[maxLen];
}

public CharStack(int size)
{
  maxLen = size;
  top = EMPTY;
  s = new char[size];
}
```

The constructors initialize various member variables. Importantly, they also use new to allocate memory off the heap. The empty argument constructor uses the implicit initialization of maxLen to 100. These constructors make the SetStack() member from Section 6.10, *An Example: CharStack Container*, on page 266 unneeded.

■
```
private const int  EMPTY = -1;
private int maxLen = 100;
```

In the CharStack implementation EMPTY is const and therefore is static. EMPTY is always -1, but maxLen depends on which constructor is called and must be assignable.

Constructors are important because they create possibilities for conveniently initializing the abstract data type. For example, we can code a one-parameter constructor whose parameter would be a string to initialize the CharStack as follows:

```
// Copy a string into the CharStack

public CharStack(string str)
{
  maxLen = str.Length;
  top = EMPTY;
  s = new char[maxLen];
  for (int i = 0; i < str.Length; ++i)
    s[++top] = str[i];
}
```

We show the use of these constructors:

In file CharStack2.cs

```
using System;

class CharStackTest {
  static public void Main() {
    CharStack data = new CharStack();          // data.s[100]
    CharStack w = new CharStack("ABCD");            // w.s[4]
    CharStack x = new CharStack(30);        // creates x.s[30]

    data.Push('Z');
    x.Push('Z');
    Console.WriteLine("data=" + data.Length() '\n' + data);
    Console.WriteLine("w=" + w.Length() + '\n' + d2);
    Console.WriteLine("x=" + x.Length() + '\n' + x);
  }
}
```

The output of this program is

```
data=100
Z
w=4
ABCD
x=30
Z
```

7.1.4   THE COPY CONSTRUCTOR

A copy constructor takes an existing object and creates a new object by copying its member values. Unlike C++, the compiler does not automatically provide a copy constructor. The class CharStack can define its own copy constructor, as is appropriate.

In file CharStack2.cs

```
//Copy constructor for CharStack of characters
public CharStack(CharStack stk)
{
  maxLen = stk.maxLen;
  top = EMPTY;
  s = new char[maxLen];
  for (int i = 0; i < stk.maxLen; ++i)
    s[++top] = stk.s[i];
}
```

This is called a *deep copy*. The character arrays are distinct because they refer to different memory locations. If instead the body of this routine were s = stk.s; this would be a *shallow copy*, with CharStack variables sharing the same representation. Any change to one variable would change the other. If w is an existing stack, then the copy constructor is invoked as follows:

```
CharStack  y = w;
```

7.2 ◢ CLASSES WITH DESTRUCTORS

A *destructor* is a method whose name is the class name preceded by a tilde, ~. Destructors cannot have access modifiers. Destructors are called implicitly for an object when it is garbage collected. In most cases, classes do not require destructors, as garbage collection is sufficient for finalization. Let us augment our CharStack example with a destructor:

In file CharStack2.cs

```
//Destructor for CharStack
~CharStack()                              // access is not allowed
{
  Console.WriteLine(" destructor called " + this);
}
```

The addition of the destructor allows the class to provide a runtime trace on when garbage collection is invoked and on what. In C++, where memory off the heap is not returned automatically, proper coding of destructors is vital. The alleviation of this burden by C# enhances the language's productivity and safety when compared to C and C++.

7.3 ◢ MEMBERS THAT ARE CLASS TYPES

In object-oriented programming (OOP) methodology, complicated objects are built from simpler objects. For example, a house is built with a foundation, rooms, and a roof. The house has a roof as a subobject. This part-to-whole relationship is called in OOP the *HASA relationship*. Complicated objects can be designed from simpler ones by incorporating them with the *HASA* relationship. In this section, the type Address is used as a member of the class Person.

In file Person3.cs

```
class Address {
  public Address(string street, string city)
    { cityName = city; streetName = street; }
  public override string ToString()
    { return (streetName + ", " + cityName); }
```

```
  public string CityName
    { get { return cityName; }  set { CityName = value; } }
  public string StreetName
    { get {return streetName;}  set {streetName = value;} }
  private string cityName, streetName;
}

// Person - characteristics common to all people
class Person {
  public Person(string name, Address home)
    { this.name = name; this.home = home; }
  public string Name
    { get { return name; }  set { name = value; } }
  public int Age
    { get { return age; }  set { age = value; } }
  public char Gender
    { get {return gender;}  set { gender = value; } }
  public override string ToString() {  return String.Format
     ("Name: {0:-20}  Age: {1,2}  Gender: {2} \n{3}",
        name, age, gender, home);}

  private Address home;
  private string name;
  private int age;
  private char gender;              // male == 'M', female == 'F'
}
```

We can test this with the following code:

```
public class PersonTest {
  public static void Main() {
    Person p = new Person("Philip Pohl",
                new Address("MainStreet", "Miami"));
    p.Age = 39;
    p.Gender = 'M';
    Console.WriteLine("Test of Person:\n" + p);
  }
}
```

The output of this program is

```
Test of Person:
Name: Philip Pohl    Age: 39   Gender: M
MainStreet, Miami
```

7.4   POLYMORPHISM: METHOD OVERLOADING

In computer science, *polymorphism* is a means of giving different meanings to the same method name or operator, dependent on context. The appropriate meaning is selected on the basis of the type of data being processed. We have encountered one form of polymorphism when writing expressions of mixed type. Depending on the type of the operands, the division operator on native types might be either an integer division or a floating-point division.

Object orientation takes advantage of polymorphism by linking behavior to the object's type. Operators, such as + and *, have distinct meanings overloaded by operand type. For example, the expression `"Test of Person:\n"` + p has the plus operator meaning the string operator concatenate. Overloading of methods gives the same method name different meanings. The name has several interpretations that depend on method selection. This is called *ad hoc polymorphism*. The remainder of this chapter discusses overloading, especially operator overloading, and conversions of data types.

Operators are overloaded and selected based on the signature-matching algorithm. Overloading operators gives them new meanings. For example, the meaning of the expression a + b differs depending on the types of the variables a and b. Overloading the operator + for user-defined types allows them to be used in addition expressions in much the same way native types are used. The expression a + b could mean string concatenation, complex-number addition, or integer addition, depending on whether the variables were `string`, the standard library class `Complex`, or the native type `int`. Mixed-type expressions are also made possible by defining conversion methods.

One principle of OOP is that user-defined types must enjoy the same privileges as native types. Where the library adds the complex number type, the programmer expects the convenience of using it without regard to a native/nonnative distinction. Operator overloading and user-defined conversions let us use complex numbers in much the same way as we can use `int` or `double`.

In Section 8.3, *Virtual Methods*, on page 337, we discuss pure polymorphism using virtual methods.

7.5 ADT CONVERSIONS

Explicit type conversion of an expression is necessary when either the implicit conversions are not desired or the expression is not otherwise legal. One aim of OOP using C# is the integration of user-defined ADTs and built-in types. To achieve this, C# uses the keywords `implicit` and `explicit` to modify single-argument static methods. For example:

```
public static implicit operator Point(double u)
{ return new Point(u); } // note relationship to constructor
```

is automatically a type conversion from `double` to `Point`. The conversion is available both explicitly and implicitly. Explicitly, it is used as a conversion operation in either cast or functional form. Thus

```
Point   s;
double  d = 3.5;

s = (Point)(d);
```

and

```
s = d;                      // implicit invocation of conversion
```

both work.

In the `Point` example in Section 7.1.2, *Improving the Point Class*, on page 290, one may want a conversion from `Point` to `double`. This can be done for the `Point` class, as follows:

```
public static explicit operator double(Point p)
// use distance from origin
   { return Math.Sqrt(p.x * p.x + p.y * p.y); }
```

Notice that we used a specific conversion that is by no means unique or universally understood. Another possibility is to return the x value only. A class having a particular meaning for a conversion should be fully documented and intended for custom use. When such a class is intended for general use, it is best to omit such conversions, as they can readily lead to unintended results.

7.6   SIGNATURE MATCHING

Overloaded methods are an important polymorphic mechanism in C#. The overloaded meaning is selected by matching the argument list of the method call to the argument list of the method declaration. When an overloaded method is invoked, the compiler must have a selection algorithm with which to pick the appropriate method. The algorithm that accomplishes this depends on what type conversions are available and is called the *signature-matching algorithm*. A best match must be unique, must be best on at least one argument, and must be as good as any other match on all other arguments. The following list shows the signature-matching algorithm for each argument.

Basic Signature-matching Algorithm

1. Use an exact match if found.

2. Try standard type promotions.

3. Try user-defined conversions.

An exact match is clearly best. Casts can be used to force such a match. The compiler complains about ambiguous situations. Thus, it is poor programming practice to rely on subtle type distinctions and implicit conversions that obscure the overloaded method. When in doubt, use explicit conversions to provide an exact match.

Let us write an overloaded method `Greater()` and follow our algorithm for various invocations. In this example, the user type `Rational` is available. In class `Rational`, we implement a number type that is of the form p/q, where p and q are integers. The methods `Greater()` are used for finding the greater of two arithmetic types.

In file Rational.cs

```
// Overloading methods
class Rational {
  public Rational(int n ) { a = n; q = 1; }
  public Rational(int i, int j) { a = i; q = j; }
  public Rational(double r) { a =(int) (r * BIG); q = BIG;}
  public override string ToString()
            { return ( a + " / " + q); }

  public static implicit operator double(Rational r)
            { return (double)(r.a) / r.q; }
  public static implicit operator Rational(int n)
            { return new Rational(n); }
  private int  a, q;
  private const int BIG = 100;
}
```

Dissection of the *Rational* Program

■`public Rational(int n ) { a = n; q = 1; }`
 `public Rational(int i, int j) { a = i; q = j; }`
 `public Rational(double r) { a =(int) (r * BIG); q = BIG;}`

There are three overloaded constructors. The most interesting is for
`double`. It uses an approximation since not all real numbers have an
exact conversion to a rational. So a double that represents 0.3333...
would convert to a = 33 and q = 100.

■`public static implicit operator double(Rational r)`
 `            { return (double)(r.a) / r.q; }`
 `public static implicit operator Rational(int n)`
 `            { return new Rational(n); }`

Here are two conversion operators. One provides a conversion from
`int` to `Rational`. Notice how this calls the constructor whose signature is `int`. This is a common idiom for conversion.

In file Rational.cs

```
using System;

class GreaterTest {
  public static int Greater(int i, int j)
    { return (i > j ? i : j); }
  public static double  Greater(double x, double y)
    { return (x > y ? x : y); }
  public static Rational Greater(Rational w, Rational z)
    { return (w > z ? w : z); }

  public static void Main()
  {
    int i = 10, j = 5;
    double x = 7.0, y = 14.5;
    Rational w = new Rational(10);
    Rational z = new Rational(3.5);

    Console.WriteLine("Greater({0}, {1}) = {2}",
      i, j, Greater(i, j));
    Console.WriteLine("Greater({0}, {1}) = {2}",
      x, y, Greater(x, y));
    Console.WriteLine("Greater({0}, {1}) = {2}",
      i, z, Greater((Rational)(i), z) );
    Console.WriteLine("Greater({0}, {1}) = {2}",
      w, z, Greater(w, z) );
  }
}
```

The output from this program is

```
Greater(10, 5) = 10
Greater(7, 14.5) = 14.5
Greater(10, 350 / 100) = 10 / 1
Greater(10 / 1, 350 / 100) = 10 / 1
```

A variety of conversion rules, both implicit and explicit, are being applied.

Dissection of the *Rational* Program

■ ```
public static int Greater(int i, int j)
   { return (i > j ? i : j); }
public static double Greater(double x, double y)
   { return (x > y ? x : y); }
```

Three distinct methods are overloaded for `Greater()`. The first two are standard methods that return the greater of two compared integer or floating-point numbers.

■ ```
public static Rational Greater(Rational w, Rational z)
   { return (w > z ? w : z); }
```

The most interesting of the three overloaded methods has `Rational` type for its argument list variables and its return type. The conversion `operator double()` is required to evaluate `w > z` because the comparison of two `Rational`s requires implicit conversion to two `double`s.

■ ```
Console.WriteLine("Greater({0}, {1}) = {2}",
   i, j, Greater(i, j));
Console.WriteLine("Greater({0}, {1}) = {2}",
   x, y, Greater(x, y));
```

The first statement selects `Greater(int, int)` because of the exact-match rule. The second statement selects `Greater(double, double)`.

■ ```
Console.WriteLine("Greater({0}, {1}) = {2}",
   i, z, Greater((Rational)(i), z) );
```

The third definition of `Greater(Rational, Rational)` is selected. The explicit conversion of `i` to a `Rational` avoids ambiguity.

7.7   OVERLOADING OPERATORS

In the previous example, it would have been desirable to have a definition of the operator > for two `Rational` numbers. This is possible in C#. Many but not all of the unary and binary operators are overloadable. The overloadable unary operators are:

```
+    -    !    ~    ++    --    true    false
```

The overloadable binary operators are:

```
+    -    *    /    %    &    |    ^    <<    >>    ==    !=    >    <    >=    <=
```

This means that we can use ordinary infix expression notation for user-defined types. This is especially important for extending C# libraries for use in scientific computation. For example, rationals, polynomials, and vectors all have well-known algebras that can be implemented in C#.

When a binary operator, such as +, is overloaded then its associated assignment operator, namely +=, is also implicitly overloaded. Note that ordinary assignment cannot be overloaded.

Overloaded operators retain the precedence and associativity of the operator. For example, the divide operator / is always a binary operator, has the same precedence level as it has for `doubles` or `ints`, and is left-associative.

Overloading operators allows infix expressions of both ADTs and built-in types to be written. In many instances, this important notational convenience leads to shorter, more readable programs.

Unary and binary operators can only be overloaded as static methods. Unary operators can be overloaded for a single argument of class type. Binary operators can be overloaded taking one or both arguments of class type. Here, we expand our `Rational` class from Section 7.6, *Signature Matching*, on page 303.

In file Rational.cs

```
// Overloading operators

public static bool operator>(Rational w, Rational z)
  { return ((double)(w.a) / w.q > (double)(z.a) / z.q); }
public static bool operator<(Rational w, Rational z)
  { return !(w > z); }
```

Here we have added meanings for the two comparison operators, but their associativity and precedence remain the same. For certain paired operators, such as the comparison (<, >) or logical equality (==, !=) both operators must be overloaded. This is an improvement that C# has made over C++, which does not have this requirement. This forces the programmer to be consistent about her semantics. Notice in this example that operator<() is coded using a call to operator>(), where the expression is then logically negated. This is an important technique for maintaining consistent semantics between operators that are logically paired.

We can invoke the overloaded operators with the following statements in which parentheses are required because + is higher precedence than >:

```
Console.WriteLine("w > z: " + (w > z));
Console.WriteLine("w < z: " + (w < z));
```

7.8 UNARY OPERATOR OVERLOADING

To continue the discussion of operator overloading, we demonstrate how to overload unary operators, such as !, ++, and ~. For this purpose, we develop the class MyClock, which can be used to store time as days, hours, minutes, and seconds. We develop familiar operations for MyClock.

In file MyClock.cs

```
using System;

class MyClock {
  public MyClock() { }                  // initialize default 0
  public MyClock(uint i) { Reset(i);  }
```

```csharp
public void Reset(uint i)
{
  totSecs = i;
  secs = i % 60;
  mins = (i / 60) % 60;
  hours = (i / 3600) % 24;
  days = i / 86400;
}

public override string ToString()
{
  Reset(totSecs);
  return String.Format(
      "day {0:D2} time:{1:D2}:{2:D2}:{3:D2}",
          days, hours, mins, secs) ;
}

public void Tick() { Reset(++totSecs); }

public static MyClock operator++(MyClock c)
    { c.Tick(); return c; }

private uint  totSecs = 0, secs = 0, mins = 0,
              hours = 0, days = 0;
}
```

Dissection of the *MyClock* Program

```csharp
■public MyClock() { }                    // initialize default 0
 public MyClock( uint i ) { Reset(i); }
```

The no argument constructor uses the default 0 values for initializing all the private data members. The `int` argument constructor converts a total number of seconds into seconds, minutes, hours, and days by calling the `Reset()` method.

```
public MyClock Reset(uint i)
{
  totSecs = i;
  secs = i % 60;
  mins = (i / 60) % 60;
  hours = (i / 3600) % 24;
  days = i / 86400;
}
```

The Reset() method assures that secs, mins, hours, and days are appropriately set for the totSecs value which is passed in.

```
public void Tick() { Reset(++totSecs); }
```

The method advances the MyClock time by 1 second. We use the Reset() method to recompute time.

```
public static MyClock operator++(MyClock c)
  {c.Tick(); return c; }
```

The overloaded operator++() also updates the MyClock variable and returns the updated value as well. Note that operator++() always overloads both the prefix and postfix versions.

Let us test this class to check that everything works:

In file MyClock.cs

```
// MyClock and overloaded operators

class MyClockTest {

  public static void Main()
  {
    MyClock a = new MyClock(59), b = new MyClock(172799);
    Console.WriteLine("Initial times\n" + a + '\n' + b);
    ++a; ++b;
    Console.WriteLine("One second later\n" + a + '\n' + b);
  }
}
```

The output is

```
Initial times
day 00 time:00:00:59
day 01 time:23:59:59
One second later
day 00 time:00:01:00
day 02 time:00:00:00
```

7.9   BINARY OPERATOR OVERLOADING

We continue with MyClock and show how to overload binary operators. Let us create an addition operation for type MyClock that adds two values:

In file MyClock.cs

```
public static MyClock operator+(MyClock c1, MyClock c2)
  { return new MyClock(c1.totSecs + c2.totSecs); }
```

The return expression is a MyClock object. The constructor returns the appropriate conversion of the sum of the total seconds.

We define a multiplication operation as a binary operation, with one argument an uint and the second a MyClock variable.

```
public static MyClock operator*(uint m, MyClock c)
  { return new MyClock(m * c.totSecs); }
```

This requirement forces the multiplication to have a fixed ordering that is type-dependent. In order to avoid this, it is common practice to write a second overloaded method. The second method is defined in terms of the first, as follows:

```
public static MyClock operator*(MyClock c, uint m)
  { return (m * c); }
```

Defining the second implementation in terms of the first implementation reduces code redundancy and maintains consistency. It is the coder's responsibility to make sure that the related sets of operators are overloaded consistently.

7.10   STATIC CONSTRUCTORS

Specialized constructors are prefaced by the keyword `static`. These `static` constructors are used to initialize `static` data members and to perform startup or prologue code that precedes any single class instance being created. These constructors have no access keyword and cannot be explicitly called. Instead the system runs this code before any given instance of the class type is created.

A typical use of statics is to track the number of instances created for a given class. We could add a static field to count how many in our `Point` class from Section 7.1.2, *Improving the Point Class*, on page 290.

In file Point4.cs

```
class Point {
  static Point()                            // static constructor
  {
     countPoint = 0;
     Console.WriteLine("start up code countPoint = 0");
  }
  public Point() { ++countPoint; }                    // default
  public Point(double x) { ++countPoint; this.x = x; }
  public Point(double x, double y)
    { ++countPoint; this.x = x; this.y = y; }

 public static int HowMany() { return countPoint; }

// code as before·····
  private static int countPoint;
  private double x = 0.0, y = 0.0;// default initialization
}
```

So in using this class the `static` constructor is invoked anonymously before any `Point` instances are created. The static method `HowMany()` reports on the number of currently living `Point`s.

In file Point4.cs

```
// The conversions from double to Point return a new
// Point structure, so count keeps going up

class PointTest
{
  static void Main()
  {
    Point  s = new Point (1.1, 2.2);
    double  d = 3.5;                    //won't ever see 3.5 used

    WritePointAndCount(s);
    d = (double)s;                      //conversion to double
    s = d;                    //implicit conversion from double
    WritePointAndCount(s);
    s = (Point)(d);        //explicit invocation of conversion
    WritePointAndCount(s);
    s = 4.3;              // implicit invocation of conversion
    WritePointAndCount(s);
  }

  public static void WritePointAndCount(Point p)
   {Console.WriteLine("Point is {0,22}  Point Count is {1}",
      p, Point.HowMany()); }
}
```

The output from this program is

```
start up code countPoint = 0
Point is                   (1.1, 2.2)  Point Count is 1
Point is   (2.45967477524977, 0)  Point Count is 2
Point is   (2.45967477524977, 0)  Point Count is 3
Point is                   (4.3, 0)  Point Count is 4
```

Notice that the number of points went up each time we did either explicit or implicit conversion. This is because the conversion method created a new Point each time it was invoked.

7.11   SOFTWARE ENGINEERING: OVERLOADING

Explicitly casting arguments can be both an aid to documentation and a useful way to avoid poorly understood conversion sequences. It is not an admission of ignorance to cast or to parenthesize arguments or expressions that otherwise could be converted or evaluated properly.

Operator overloading is easily misused. Do not overload operators when doing so can lead to misinterpretation. Typically, operator overloading is appropriate when there is a widely used notation that conforms to your overloading, such as complex arithmetic. Also, overload related operators in a manner consistent with C# community expectations. For example, the relational operators <, >, <=, and >= should all be meaningful and provide expected inverse behaviors.

7.12   DR. P'S PRESCRIPTIONS

- Constructors should be public methods.

- Constructors come first followed by other methods.

- Classes with dynamically allocated memory should have a copy constructor.

- Constructors have two uses: allocation and initialization. Avoid other purposes.

- A set of overloaded operators should be developed for scientific types and not for nonstandard purposes.

The idea behind placing more visible members first is the newspaper principle—namely, what everyone needs to know comes first. What everyone needs to know are the public members. This is the interface available to all users of the class. Constructors are needed by anyone using the class, so they go first. Construction or object initialization is needed to use an ordinary type, so it is usual to have a constructor be public.

Constructors are for initialization. In the debugging and prototyping phase of code development, it is also useful to add code that outputs or tests behavior. Other work should not be carried out by a constructor, for this would be unexpected. For example, if in initializing an integer variable the system printed out its square root and whether it was prime, we would be properly upset.

Destructors are for finalization, such as closing files. Deallocation is done automatically by the garbage collection scheme in C#.

Idiosyncratic algebras and personal notations are a bad idea. They lead to dense and obscure code that is hard for others to follow and test. Where community-understood algebras exist, as in the mathematical and scientific disciplines, operator overloading should follow normal definitions and contain no surprises. One guideline is to be complete. For example, if the `operator==()` is defined, then define the corresponding `operator!=()`. Types that might have arithmetic operator overloading might include polynomials, vectors, matrices, and rational numbers.

7.13 C# COMPARED WITH JAVA AND C++

As in C#, Java and C++ have constructors. Because C++ does not have garbage collection, it relies heavily on destructors to deallocate memory using an operator `delete` that is the inverse of the operator `new`.

Let us rewrite our programs for making change from Section 1.8, *C# Compared with Java and C++*, on page 21. Here we present C#, Java, and C++ versions of the program. We can look at change as an object returned when we have a purchase. We have to decide which data members are needed for making change. Generally, objects mimic the real world. In this case, we need members that track the number of coins of each denomination. We also need actions that are useful with these types. For example, what would be the value of a set of coins containing three quarters and two dimes?

Here is the C# version of the program:

In file MakeChange.cs

```
using System;

class Change {
  public Change(int dlrs, int qtr, int dm, int pen)
  {
    dollars = dlrs;
    quarters = qtr;
    dimes = dm;
    pennies = pen;
    total = dlrs + 0.25 * qtr + 0.1 * dm + 0.01 * pen;
  }

  public static Change MakeChange(double paid, double owed)
  {
    double  diff = paid - owed;
    int  dollars, quarters, dimes, pennies;
    dollars = (int)diff;
    pennies = (int)((diff - dollars) * 100);
    quarters = pennies / 25;
    pennies -= 25 * quarters;
    dimes = pennies / 10;
    pennies -= 10 * dimes;
    return new Change(dollars, quarters, dimes, pennies);
  }

  public override string ToString()
  {
    return ("$" + total + "\n"
            + dollars + " dollars\n"
            + quarters + " quarters\n"
            + dimes + " dimes\n"
            + pennies + " pennies\n");
  }

  private int dollars, quarters, dimes, pennies;
  private double total;
}
```

```
public class ChangeTest {
  public static void Main()
  {
    double owed = 12.37;
    double paid = 15.0;
    Console.WriteLine("You owe $" + owed);
    Console.WriteLine("You gave me $" + paid);
    Console.WriteLine("Your change is " +
              Change.MakeChange(paid, owed));
  }
}
```

The output of this program is

```
You owe $12.37
You gave me $15.0
Your change is $2.63
2 dollars
2 quarters
1 dimes
3 pennies
```

Here is the equivalent Java program.

In file MakeChangeTest.java

```
import tio.*;

class Change {
  private int dollars, quarters, dimes, pennies;
  private double total;

  Change(int dlrs, int qtr, int dm, int pen)
  {
    dollars = dlrs;
    quarters = qtr;
    dimes = dm;
    pennies = pen;
    total = dlrs + 0.25 * qtr + 0.1 * dm + 0.01 * pen;
  }
```

```
    static Change MakeChange(double paid, double owed)
    {
      double  diff = paid - owed;
      int  dollars, quarters, dimes, pennies;

      dollars = (int)diff;
      pennies = (int)((diff - dollars) * 100);
      quarters = pennies / 25;
      pennies -= 25 * quarters;
      dimes = pennies / 10;
      pennies -= 10 * dimes;
      return new Change(dollars, quarters, dimes, pennies);
    }

    public String ToString()
    {
      return ("$" + total + "\n"
              + dollars + " dollars\n"
              + quarters + " quarters\n"
              + dimes + " dimes\n"
              + pennies + " pennies\n");
    }
}

public class MakeChangeTest {
  public static void Main(String[] args)
  {
    double owed = 12.37;
    double paid = 15.0;

    System.out.println("You owe $" + owed);
    System.out.println("You gave me $" + paid);
    System.out.println("Your change is " +
              Change.MakeChange(paid, owed));
  }
}
```

Here is the C++ version:

In file makeChange.cpp

```cpp
#include <iostream>
using namespace std;

class change {
public:
  change(int dlrs=0, int qtr=0, int dm=0, int pen=0) :
    dollars(dlrs), quarters(qtr), dimes(dm), pennies(pen)
    { total = dlrs + 0.25 * qtr + 0.1 * dm + 0.01 * pen; }
  friend ostream& operator<<(ostream& out, const change& x);
private:
  int dollars, quarters, dimes, pennies;
  double total;
};

change& makeChange(double paid, double owed)
{
  double  diff = paid - owed;
  int  dollars, quarters, dimes, pennies;
  dollars = diff;
  pennies = (diff - dollars) * 100;
  quarters = pennies / 25;
  pennies -= 25 * quarters;
  dimes = pennies / 10;
  pennies -= 10 * dimes;
  return *(new change(dollars, quarters, dimes, pennies));
}

ostream& operator<<(ostream& out, const change& x)
{
    return (out << "$" << x.total << "\n"
            << x.dollars << " dollars\n"
            << x.quarters << " quarters\n"
            << x.dimes << " dimes\n"
            << x.pennies << " pennies\n");
}
```

```
int main()
{
  double owed = 12.37;
  double paid = 15.0;

  cout << "You owe $" << owed << endl;
  cout << "You gave me $" << paid << endl;
  cout << "Your change is " << makeChange(paid, owed)
       << endl;
}
```

As defined, the only way to construct a Change object is by specifying the number of each type of coin. We chose not to use nickels or half-dollars, just to keep the code shorter.

Because there is not a no-argument constructor (in C# terminology, the default constructor) in this class, we can't create a Change object by using the expression new Change(). We intentionally left the no-argument constructor out because, as currently implemented, there is no use for it. Java, like C#, does not have initializing syntax for its constructors. In the C++ version, we used the initializing syntax with default values of 0.

The C# and Java return type syntax is identical, but the comparable C++ method needs to use the token ampersand in its return type declaration.

The C# version is identical to the Java version, with the addition of the keyword override. In Java and C#, all classes should include a method ToString(), which returns a string representation of the class. The ToString() method gives slightly nonstandard output for values when no pennies are involved. For example, the total for $1.50 prints out as $1.5, with no trailing 0. The ToString() method is a polymorphic conversion method.

As with C# and C++, Java methods and constructors are typically overloaded.

```
// Constructor to be placed in Java class Person

public Person() { name = "Unknown"; }
public Person(String nm) { name =nm; }
public Person(String nm, int a, char b)
                { name = nm; age =a; gender = b; }
```

These constructors would be invoked when new is used to associate a created instance with the appropriate type reference variable. For example:

```
p1 = new Person();
// make Unknown 0 M
p1 = new Person("Laura Pohl");
// make Laura Pohl 0 M
p1 = new Person("Laura Pohl", 12, 'F');
// make Laura Pohl 12 F
```

The overloaded constructor is selected by the set of arguments that match the constructor's parameter list.

A copy constructor takes an existing object and creates a new object by copying its member values. Unlike in C++, the compiler does not automatically provide a copy constructor.

In both Java and C#, destruction is done automatically by the system, using automatic garbage collection. This differs from C++, in which the programmer must provide the destructor. When the object can no longer be referenced—for example, when the existing reference is given a new object—the now inaccessible object is called garbage. Periodically, the system sweeps through memory and retrieves these *dead* objects. The C# programmer need not be concerned with such apparent memory leaks.

Unlike C++ and C#, Java does not have operator overloading. Unlike C++, C# has a more restricted set of overloadable operators. Most notably absent in C# is the ability to overload the assignment operator =. Unlike C++, C# operator overloading for both ++ and -- always overloads both the prefix and postfix versions. Also C# overloading is always via static methods. C++ allows instance method and non-class function overloading of operators. As a consequence C++ overloading is more nuanced and more error-prone.

SUMMARY

■ A constructor, a method whose name is the class name, constructs objects of its class type. This can involve initializing data members and allocating the heap, using the operator new. A constructor is invoked when its associated type is used in a definition.

```
TYPEFoo y(3);          // invoke TYPEFoo::TYPEFoo(int)
extern TYPEFoo x;      // declaration but not definition
```

Again, not all declarations are definitions. In those cases, no constructor is invoked.

■ A destructor is a method whose name is the class name preceded by the tilde character, ~. Its usual purpose is to do finalization for the class (for example, close files and print end messages). Garbage collection is automatically done by the C# system.

■ A constructor requiring no arguments is called the default constructor. It can be a constructor with an empty argument list or one whose arguments all have default values. It has the special purpose of initializing arrays of objects of its class.

■ Overloading operators gives them new meanings. For example, the meaning of the expression a + b depends on the types of the variables a and b. The expression could mean string concatenation, complex number addition, or integer addition, depending on whether the variables were the ADT CharStack, the ADT Complex, or the built-in type int, respectively.

REVIEW QUESTIONS

1. What operation does new perform?

2. Outline the signature-matching algorithm.

3. What is a member of the form *ClassName*() called?

4. Constructors and destructors do not have _____ types and cannot use _____ statements.

5. The constructor `public Counter(int i) { count = i % 100; }` is called with new as follows: _____

6. The method

   ```
   public static implicit operator Point(double u)
     { return new Point(u); }
   ```

   is automatically a type conversion from _____ to _____. The conversion is available both _____ and _____.

7. List three operators that are not overloadable.

8. True or false: Operators are overloadable with instance methods.

9. Static constructors have no _____ keyword and cannot be called. Instead the system runs this code _____ any given instance of the class type is created.

10. A set of overloaded operators should be developed for _____ types and not for nonstandard purposes. An example would be _____.

EXERCISES

1. For the type `Rational` in Section 7.6, *Signature Matching*, on page 303, explain why the conversions of integer 7 and double 7.0 lead to different internal representations.

2. The following line of code is from the *Rational.cpp* program in Section 7.6, *Signature Matching*, on page 303.

```
Console.WriteLine("Greater({0}, {1}) = {2}",
    i, z, Greater((Rational)(i), z) );
```

If the preceding statement is replaced by

```
Console.WriteLine("Greater({0}, {1}) = {2}",
    i, z, Greater(i, z) );
```

what goes wrong?

To test your understanding, write a `Rational` constructor that, given two integers as dividend and quotient, uses a greatest common divisor algorithm to reduce the internal representation to its smallest a and q value.

3. Overload the `++` and `!=` comparison operators for `Rational`. Notice that two `Rationals` are equal in the form given by the previous exercise if and only if their dividends and quotients are equal. (See Section 7.6, *Signature Matching*, on page 303.)

4. Define class `Complex` as

```
public class Complex {
  public Complex(double r)
    { real = r; }

  public Complex(double r, double i)
    { real = r; imag = i; }

  public Complex(Complex a)
    { real = a.real;  imag = a.imag; }
```

```
public override string ToString()
  { return (real + " + " + imag + "i "); }

// if we make this implicit, complex number will always
// be printed as a double
public static explicit operator double(Complex u)
  { return (Math.Sqrt(u.real*u.real + u.imag*u.imag));}
private double real, imag;
}
```

We wish to augment the class by overloading a variety of operators. Code and test a unary minus operator. It should return a `Complex` whose value in each part is negated.

5. For the type `Complex`, write the binary operator methods add, multiply, and subtract. Each should return `Complex`.

6. Write the methods

```
public static Complex  operator+(Complex, double);
public static Complex  operator+(double, Complex);
```

In the absence of a conversion from type `double` to type `Complex`, both types are needed to allow completely mixed expressions of `Complex` and `double`. Explain why writing one with an `int` parameter is unnecessary when these methods are available.

7. Program a class `VecComplex` that is a type whose element values are `Complex`. Overload operators + and * to mean, respectively, element-by-element `Complex` addition and dot-product of two `Complex` vectors.

8. Redo the `CharStack` ADT by using operator overloading. (See Section 7.11, *Software Engineering: Overloading*, on page 313.) Overload `operator*` to return the `i`th character in the `CharStack`. If there is no such character, the value –1 is to be returned. So if `cstk` is a `CharStack` then `cstk * 2` returns the second character in the stack. Note, this use of operator overloading is not recommended as it leads to obfuscated code, that is code that is hard to understand and maintain. A better scheme for indexing into container classes will be explained in Chapter 11 using the construct `this[`*argument*`]`.

9. Test your understanding of `CharStack` by implementing additional members of `CharStack`.

```
// StrCmp is negative if s < s1,
//         is 0 if s == s1,
//         and is positive if s > s1
//         where s is the implicit argument
int Strcmp( CharStack s1);

// strrev  reverses the CharStack
void StrRev();
```

10. Write a substring method for the `CharStack` class. The substring operation should search a string for a given character sequence and return `true` if the subsequence is found. To further test your understanding, recode this method to test that the positions are within the actual string. This means that they cannot have negative values and they cannot go outside the null character terminator of the string.

11. Code a `class IntStack`. Use this to write out integer subsequences in increasing order by value. In the sequence (7, 9, 3, 2, 6, 8, 9, 2), the subsequences are (7, 9), (3), (2, 6, 8, 9), (2). Use a stack to store increasing values. Pop the stack when a next sequence value is no longer increasing. Keep in mind that the stack pops values in reverse order. Redo this exercise using a queue, thus avoiding this reversal problem.

12. Rewrite the *MakeChange* program in Section 7.13, *C# Compared with Java and C++*, on page 315, to take input from the user for the amounts owed and paid. Also add nickels and half-dollars to the change, and ensure that the output for sums such as $1.50 are printed with the ending zeroes.

13. *(Project)* Write code that fleshes out the `Rational` type of Section 7.7, *Overloading Operators*, on page 307. Have the code work appropriately for all major operators. Allow it to properly mix with other number types, including integers, floats, and complex numbers. There are several ways to improve the `Rational` implementation. You can try to improve the precision of going from `double` to `Rational`. Also, many algorithms are more convenient when the `Rational` is in a canonical form in which the quotient and divisor are relatively prime. This can be accomplished by adding a greatest common division algorithm to reduce the representation to the canonical form. (See Exercise 2 on page 323.)

14. *(Java)* Rewrite in Java the class `Rational` in Section 7.6, *Signature Matching*, on page 303. You must substitute ordinary methods for any operator overloading.

INHERITANCE

nheritance is the powerful code-reuse mechanism of deriving a new class from an old one. That is, the existing class can be added to or altered to create the derived class. Through inheritance, a hierarchy of related types that share code and interfaces can be created.

Many useful types are variants of one another, and it is frequently tedious to produce the same code for each. A derived class inherits the description of the *base* class, which can then be altered by adding members and modifying existing instance methods and access privileges. The usefulness of inheritance can be seen by examining how taxonomic classification compactly summarizes large bodies of knowledge.

For example, knowing the concept *mammal* and knowing that an elephant and a mouse are both mammals allows our descriptions of them to be considerably more succinct than they are otherwise. The root concept contains the information that mammals are warm-blooded higher vertebrates and that they nourish their young through mammary glands. This information is inherited by the concept of both *mouse* and *elephant*, but it is expressed only once: in the root concept. In C# terms, both elephant and mouse are derived from the base class mammal.

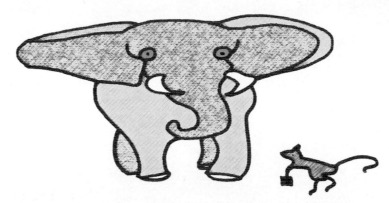

Hey! Don't flatten me, I'm your cousin from Chicago!

C# supports *virtual methods*: methods declared in the base class and over-ridden in a derived class. A class hierarchy that is defined by public inheritance creates a related set of user types, all of whose objects may be pointed at by a base-class reference. By accessing the virtual method through this reference, C# selects the appropriate method definition at runtime. The object being referenced must carry around type information so that this distinction can be made dynamically, a feature typical of object-oriented code. Each object knows how it is to be acted on. This is a form of polymorphism called *pure polymorphism*.

Inheritance should be designed into software to maximize reuse and to allow a natural modeling of the problem domain. With inheritance, the key elements of the OOP design methodology are as follows:

OOP Design Methodology

1. Decide on an appropriate set of types.

2. Design in relationships among types and use inheritance to share code.

3. Use virtual methods to polymorphically process like objects.

8.1   A DERIVED CLASS

A class can be derived from an existing class by using the form

class *class-name* : *base-name*
{
    member declarations
}

The keyword `protected` is introduced to allow data hiding for members that must be available in derived classes but that otherwise act like private members. It is an intermediate form of access between `public` and `private`.

Consider developing software to track everyone at a college or university. First, everyone is a person. Then some people are employees and some people are students. Each of these two major categories has further subcategories: undergraduate and graduate students, staff and faculty employees. Understanding a university leads to a natural hierarchy of the groups that participate at the university.

We start with our `Person` class from Section 6.14, *C# Compared with Java and C++,* on page 279, which has members that describe a person, such as name and gender. We modify it to have protected members instead of private members.

In file Person3.cs

```
// Characteristics common to all people
class Person {
  public Person(string name, int age, char gender)
    { this.name = name; this.age = age;
      this.gender = gender; }
  public string Name
    { set { name = value; } get { return name; }  }
  public int Age { set { age = value; } get {return age; } }
  public char Gender
    { set { gender = value; } get {return gender;} }
  public override string ToString() { return String.Format
      ("Name: {0:-20}  Age: {1,2}  Gender: {2}",
        name, age, gender);}
```

```
  public static Person Older(Person a, Person b)
  {
    if (a.Age >= b.Age)
      return a;
    else
      return b;
  }

  protected string name;
  protected int age;
  protected char gender;        // male == 'M', female == 'F'
}
```

The class `Person` has the access keyword `protected`, which makes its members inaccessible to nonclass methods. We could use `Person` in a code fragment, as follows:

```
// Declare and initialize

Person abe = new Person("Abe Pohl", 92, 'M');
Console.WriteLine(abe);                // Abe info printed out
```

The output from these statements is

```
Name: Abe Pohl   Age: 92   Gender: M
```

We can now create a new class for representing students that is derived from class `Person`. The idea is that a student is a type of person, and this idea is expressed by `Student` inheriting `Person`'s code.

In file Student.cs

```
using System;

class Student: Person {
  public Student(string nm, int a, char g, double gp,
              Year yr)
      : base(nm, a, g) { gpa = gp; y = yr; }
```

```
public static string YearName(Year y)
{ switch (y) {
  case Year.fresh:  return "freshman";
  case Year.soph:   return "sophomore";
  case Year.junior: return "junior";
  case Year.senior: return "senior";
  default: return "unknown";
  }
}

public override string ToString()
{ return String.Format("{0}, {1}, GPA: {2}",
           base.ToString(), YearName(y), gpa); }

public enum Year { fresh, soph, junior, senior };
protected  double gpa;
protected  Year y;
}
```

Dissection of the *Student* Program

■`public enum Year { fresh, soph, junior, senior };`

An enumerated type is used to describe a student's year at college. The corresponding string entries are used in the output.

■`class Student: Person {`

Student inherits the members of Person and keeps their access at the same visibility level. So if in Person, the member gender is protected, it remains protected in Student. But it also means that Student is a subtype of Person. This is important in that it allows code that is written to operate on Person to also operate on Student.

■`public  Student(string nm, int a, char g, double gp,`
`                 Year yr)`
`       : base(nm, a, g) { gpa = gp; y = yr; }`

Here, we have the constructor for Student. Inside the constructor's initializer list is the keyword base called with three arguments. This calls the Person constructor to initialize the part of Student that consists of Person's members.

```
■   public override string ToString()
    { return String.Format("{0}, {1}, GPA: {2}",
                 base.ToString(), YearName(y), gpa); }
```

The method declared here is our standard override of `ToString()`. We also have a `ToString()` method in the base class. We want to output both the `Person` information and `Student` information, so we output via reference to `base.ToString()`. This notion of overriding is very important to inherited methods and is explained in Section 8.3, *Virtual Methods*, on page 337.

We could use `Student` in a code fragment as follows:

```
Person a = new Student("Abe Pohl", 92, 'M', 3,
                       Student.Year.soph);
Console.WriteLine(a);
```

The output from this `Write()` statement is

```
Name: Abe Pohl   Age: 92   Gender: M, sophomore, GPA: 3
```

Here, `Student` is the derived class and `Person` is the base class. Inheritance means that the derived class `Student` *is a* subtype of `Person`. Thus, a student *is a* person, but a person does not have to be a student. This subtyping relationship is called the *ISA* relationship, or *type inheritance*.

A derived class is a modification of the base class, inheriting the public and protected members of the base class. Thus, in the example of `Student`, the `Person` members `name`, `age`, `gender`, `ToString()` and `Older()` are inherited. Frequently, a derived class adds new members to the existing class members. This is the case with `Student`, which has two new data members and a redefined instance method `ToString()`, which is *overridden*. The method definitions of `Person.ToString()` and `Student.ToString()` are distinct. Implementation of the method in the derived class is different from that of the base class. This is different from overloading, in which the same method name has different meanings for each unique signature.

Benefits of Using a Derived Class

- Code is reused: Student uses existing, tested code from Person.

- The hierarchy reflects a relationship found in the problem domain. When speaking of persons, the special grouping *student* is an outgrowth of the real world and its treatment of this group.

- Various polymorphic mechanisms allow client code to treat Student as a subtype of Person, simplifying client code while granting it the benefits of maintaining these distinctions among subtypes.

8.1.1 MORE UNIFIED MODELING LANGUAGE (UML)

A standard relationship between two classes is the inheritance relation. It is usual to have the base class at the top of the diagram and the derived class underneath, with an arrow pointing from the derived class to the base class.

A key inheritance relationship between classes is the *ISA* or subtype relationship. In the following basic UML diagram, we show the Person-Student class diagram, which shows data members, methods, and properties:

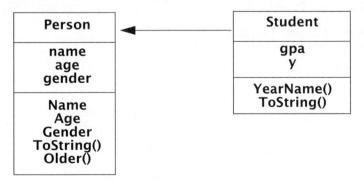

Basic Inheritance in UML

8.2   A STUDENT ISA PERSON

The first thing to understand about C# inheritance logic is that inheritance is used to generate subtypes, so in the first example, a Student is a Person. This implies that wherever Person is allowed, so is Student. We code a test for our previous example:

In file Student.cs

```
public class StudentTest {
  public static void Main()
  {
    // declare and initialize
    Person abe = new Person("Abe Pohl", 92,'M');
    Person sam = new Person("Sam Pohl", 66, 'M');
    Student phil = new Student("Philip Pohl", 68, 'M', 3.8,
                      Student.Year.junior);
    Student laura = new Student("Laura Pohl", 12, 'F', 3.9,
                    Student.Year.fresh);

    Console.WriteLine("{0}\n{1}\n{2}\n{3}",
                    abe, sam, phil, laura);
    Person p;
    p = sam;
    Console.WriteLine(p);
    p = laura;
    Console.WriteLine(p);

    Console.WriteLine("Older of {0} and {1} is\n{2}",
      laura.Name, phil.Name, Person.Older(laura, phil) );
    Console.WriteLine("Older of {0} and {1} is\n{2}",
      phil.Name, sam.Name, Person.Older(phil, sam) );
  }
}
```

The output from this program is

```
Name: Abe Pohl   Age: 92   Gender: M
Name: Sam Pohl   Age: 66   Gender: M
Name: Philip Pohl   Age: 68   Gender: M, junior, GPA: 3.8
Name: Laura Pohl   Age: 12   Gender: F, freshman, GPA: 3.9
Name: Philip Pohl   Age: 68   Gender: M, junior, GPA: 3.8
Name: Sam Pohl   Age: 66   Gender: M
Older of Laura Pohl and Philip Pohl is
Name: Philip Pohl   Age: 68   Gender: M, junior, GPA: 3.8
Older of Philip Pohl and Sam Pohl is
Name: Philip Pohl   Age: 68   Gender: M, junior, GPA: 3.8
```

Dissection of the *Student* Program

■`Console.WriteLine("{0}\n{1}\n{2}\n{3}",`
                `abe, sam, phil, laura);`

When we go to print `abe` or `philip`, they print as `Person`s: name, age, and gender. When we print `sam` or `laura`, they print as `Student`s, so their college years and GPAs are printed. The `WriteLine()` method invokes the correct version of `ToString()` depending on the variable type.

■`Person p;`
`p = phil;`
`Console.WriteLine(p);`

Here, the method `Person.ToString()` is called because `phil` is of type `Person`.

■`p = laura;`
`Console.WriteLine(p);`

Here, the method `Student.ToString()` is called. This is because the `laura` object referenced is a `Student`. Nevertheless, the variable type is `Person`. In this situation, when a method is overridden the object referenced determines the method called. This is known as runtime invocation or pure polymorphism.

```
Console.WriteLine("Older of {0} and {1} is\n{2}",
    laura.Name, phil.Name, Person.Older(laura, phil) );
Console.WriteLine("Older of {0} and {1} is\n{2}",
    phil.Name, sam.Name, Person.Older(phil, sam) );
```

In the first case, `laura` and `phil` are type `Student`, so there is an exact match with the parameter types. The second case is mixed, with `phil` being of type `Student` and `sam` being of type `Person`. The method `Older(Person, Person)` works regardless. The key point here is that a derived class from `Person`, namely `Student`, can be used for this method's arguments. It is also possible to invoke the `Older()` method by using `Student.Person()`. There is no difference in the output.

A student is a type of person, a person is a type of ape—they all derive from DNA/GENOME.

8.3   VIRTUAL METHODS

Overloaded methods are invoked by a type-matching algorithm that includes having the implicit argument matched to an object of that class type. All this is known at compile time, and it allows the compiler to select the appropriate member directly. As becomes apparent, it is important to dynamically select at runtime the appropriate method from among base- and derived-class methods. The keyword `virtual`, a method specifier that provides such a mechanism, may be used only to modify instance method declarations. The *overridden* derived method is declared with the keyword `override`. The combination of *virtual methods* with inheritance is our most general and flexible way to build a piece of software. This is known as pure polymorphism.

An ordinary virtual method must be executable code. When invoked, its semantics are the same as those of other methods. In a derived class, it can be overridden; the derived method must have a matching signature and return type. The selection of which method definition to invoke for a virtual method is dynamic. A base class has a virtual method, and derived classes have their versions of this method. A reference variable for a base class can have as its value a base-class object or a derived-class object. The instance method selected depends on the class of the object being referenced, not on the variable type. In the absence of a derived type member, the base-class virtual method is used by default.

Note the difference in selection of the appropriate overridden virtual method from an overloaded method. The overloaded method is selected at compile time based on its signature, and it can have distinct return types. A virtual method is selected at runtime based on the object's type. Also, once it is declared `virtual`, it is necessary in the derived class to use the method modifier `override`.

This note says to take my medicine at 8 o'clock, but which one?

Facilities that allow the implementation of ADTs, inheritance, and dynamic objects are the essentials of OOP. Consider the following *VirtualSelect.cs* program example:

In file VirtualSelect.cs

```csharp
// Virtual method selection
using System;
class Base {
  public virtual void Status()
    { Console.WriteLine("inside Base"); }
}

class Derived : Base {
  public override void Status()
    { Console.WriteLine("inside Derived"); }
}

class VirtualSelectTest {
  public static void Main()
  {
    Base    b = new Base();
    Derived    f = new Derived();

    b.Status();                              // Base.Status()
    f.Status();                              // Derived.Status()
    b = f;              // Derived object is also of type Base
    b.Status();                              // Derived.Status()
  }
}
```

The output of this program is

```
inside Base
inside Derived
inside Derived
```

Dissection of the *VirtualSelect* Program

```
class Base {
   public  virtual void Status()
     { Console.WriteLine("inside Base"); }
}
```

The base class `Base` has the virtual method `Status()`. We know when it executes by its output " inside Base".

```
class Derived :  Base {
   public override void Status()
     { Console.WriteLine("inside Derived"); }
}
```

The derived class `Derived` has the overridden method `Status()`. We know when it executes by its output, `"inside Derived"`. Now an object of type `Derived` is also an object of type `Base` because of the inheritance ISA relationship.

```
public static void Main()
{
   Base  b = new Base();
   Derived  f = new Derived();
```

We test what gets called by using both class types. A base class variable, such as b, can refer to any object derived from its class.

```
b.Status();                              // Base.Status()
f.Status();                              // Derived.Status()
b = f;           // Derived object is also of type Base
b.Status();                              // Derived.Status()
```

After the base class variable b is assigned the derived class object f, it calls `Derived.Status()`. In OOP terminology, the object is *sent the message* `Status()`, and it selects its own version of the corresponding method. Thus, the variable's base type is not what determines method selection. Different class objects are processed by different methods, determined at runtime.

8.3.1   OVERLOADING AND OVERRIDING CONFUSION

Virtual methods and method overloading cause confusion:

In file VirtualConfused.cs

```
using System;

class Base {
  public  virtual void ShowBase(int i)
    { Console.WriteLine("Base i = " + i ); }
  public  virtual void ShowBase(double x)
    { Console.WriteLine("Base x = " + x ); }
}

class Derived : Base {
  public override  void ShowBase(int i)
    { Console.WriteLine("Derived i = " + i ); }
}

class Derived2 : Derived {
  public override  void ShowBase(int i)
    { Console.WriteLine("Derived2 i = " + i); }
  public override  void ShowBase(double d)
    { Console.WriteLine("Derived2 d = " + d); }
}

class ConfusedTest {
  public static void Main()
  {
    Derived  d = new Derived();
    Derived2  d2 = new Derived2();
    Base  b = new Base(), b2 = d;
    b.ShowBase(9);              // selects Base.ShowBase(int)
    b.ShowBase(9.5);         // selects Base.ShowBase(double)
    d.ShowBase(9);           // selects Derived.ShowBase(int)
    d.ShowBase(9.5);         // selects Base.ShowBase(double)
    b2.ShowBase(9);          // selects Derived.ShowBase(int)
    b2.ShowBase(9.5);        // selects Base.ShowBase(double)
    b2 = d2;
    b2.ShowBase(9);         // selects Derived2.ShowBase(int)
    b2.ShowBase(9.5);    // selects Derived2.ShowBase(double)
  }
}
```

The output of this program is

```
Base i = 9
Base x = 9.5
Derived i = 9
Base x = 9.5
Derived i = 9
Base x = 9.5
Derived2 i = 9
Derived2 d = 9.5
```

Dissection of the *Confused* Program

```
■class Base {
    public  virtual void ShowBase(int i)
      { Console.WriteLine("Base i = " + i ); }
    public  virtual void ShowBase(double x)
      { Console.WriteLine("Base x = " + x ); }
}
```

Here, we have a classic case of signature overloading. In overloading, the compiler at compile time statically selects which method to call.

```
■class Derived :  Base {
    public override  void ShowBase(int i)
      { Console.WriteLine("Derived i = " + i ); }
}
```

The base-class method `Base.ShowBase(int)` is overridden. So far, this is not confusing. However, the base-class method `Base.Show-Base(double)` is inherited in the derived class, but is not overridden.

```
■b.ShowBase(9);              // selects Base.ShowBase(int)
 b.ShowBase(9.5);           // selects Base.ShowBase(double)
 d.ShowBase(9);             // selects Derived.ShowBase(int)
 d.ShowBase(9.5);           // selects Base.ShowBase(double)
```

Here is the cause of the confusion. Obviously, this situation should be avoided. When overriding base-class virtual methods that are overloaded, be sure to overload all of their definitions. This is what was done in `Derived2`, which does not suffer the same confusion.

8.3.2   AN EXAMPLE: CLASS Shape

Virtual methods allow runtime decisions. Consider a computer-aided design application in which the area of the shapes in a design has to be computed. The various shapes are derived from the Shape base class.

In file Shape.cs

```csharp
using System;

class Shape {
  public virtual double  Area() { return 0; }     // default
}

class Rectangle : Shape {
  public  Rectangle(double h, double w)
    { height = h; width = w; }
  public override double  Area() { return(height * width); }
  private  double  height, width;
}

class Circle : Shape {
  public Circle(double r) { radius = r; }
  public override double Area()
    { return (Math.PI * radius * radius); }
private   double   radius;
}
```

In such a class hierarchy, the derived classes correspond to important, well-understood types of shapes. The system is readily expanded by deriving further classes. The area calculation is a local responsibility of a derived class.

Client code that uses the polymorphic area calculation looks like this:

```csharp
class ShapeTest {
  public static void Main()
  {
    Shape[] p = new Shape[3];
    p[0] = new Rectangle(2, 3);
    p[1] = new Rectangle(2.5, 2.001);
    p[2] = new Circle(1.5);
    double tot_area = 0.0;
    for (int i = 0; i < 3; ++i)
       tot_area += p[i].Area();
    Console.WriteLine("{0:F4} is total area", tot_area );
  }
}
```

The output of this program is

```
18.0711 is total area
```

A major advantage here is that the client code does not need to change if new shapes are added to the system. Change is managed locally and propagated automatically by the polymorphic character of the client code.

8.4 ABSTRACT BASE CLASSES

A type hierarchy begins with a base class that contains a number of virtual methods. They provide for dynamic typing. In the base class, virtual methods are often dummy methods and have an empty body. In the derived classes, however, virtual methods are given specific meanings. In C#, the *abstract class* is introduced for this purpose of having abstract methods that have no definition, and are purely intended to be overridden in a derived class. An abstract method is one whose body is undefined. Notationally, such a method is declared inside the abstract class, as follows:

abstract *method header*;

The abstract method declaration is used to defer the implementation decision of the method. In OOP terminology, it is called a *deferred method*.

A class that has at least one abstract method is an *abstract class*. It also needs to be prefaced by the keyword `abstract`. In a type hierarchy, it is useful for the base class to be an abstract class. This base class has the basic common properties of its derived classes but cannot itself be used to declare objects. Instead, it is used to declare references that can access subtype objects derived from the abstract class.

We can readily rewrite the Shape class as `abstract`.

```
abstract class Shape {
   abstract public double  Area();
}
```

8.5   EVERYONE'S ANCESTOR class Object

All types inherit from class `System.Object`. This includes simple native types, such as the native value types `bool` or `int`. The methods of `Object` include the method `ToString()`. Here we have one of the chicken-egg violations in this book, where we have already been using overriding because it is very important for output.

For example, in the class Person:

```
class Person {
   .....
   public override string ToString() {  return String.Format
      ("Name: {0:-20}  Age: {1,2}  Gender: {2}",
         name, age, gender);}

   protected string name;
   protected int age;
   protected char gender;          // male == 'M', female == 'F'
}
```

The purpose of `ToString()` is to provide a string representation of a variable's value. We can now give a more complete explanation of what goes on when `Console.Write()` is invoked on a `string` expression of the form *expression*. The method needs a string to output to the console. If the expression is a string, then the string is output. But if the expression is another type, it must be converted to a string by the method `ToString()`. This is done implicitly. The following code fragment works as expected.

```
Person abe = new Person("Abe Pohl", 92,'M');
Console.Write(abe);
```

Here we see the power of overriding. We can uniformly expect the `ToString()` method to work regardless of type. It is an expectation that any newly coded type has an appropriate `ToString()` definition. The public and protected methods that are defined for `Object` are shown in Table 8.1.

Table 8.1	Object Methods
`bool Equals(object a)`	Returns `true` if two objects are equivalent, else returns `false`
`void Finalize()`	Equivalent to writing a destructor
`int GetHashCode()`	Provides a unique integer for an object's value
`Type GetType()`	Allows type to be dynamically ascertained
`object MemberwiseClone()`	Provides for manufacturing a clone
`bool ReferenceEquals (object a, object b)`	Returns `true` if the objects are the same instance
`string ToString()`	Returns a string that represents the current object

When overriding these methods, you should seek to be consistent with C# community expectations. For example, the distinction between using `==` and the method `Equals()` is usually the distinction between reference equality and contents equality. For example, a library may have two copies of *C# by Dissection*. If `book1` and `book2` are references to two books held by the library and `book1` is *C# by Dissection*, then asking if `book1.Equals(book2)` is asking if both are copies of *C# by Dissection*. But asking if `book1 == book2` is asking if they are the same copy of *C# by Dissection*.

8.5.1 METHODS AND BOXING/UNBOXING

Native simple types, such as `int`, `bool`, and `double` are value types. User-defined class types are reference types. A `string` is a reference type. Reference types such as `Person` call a constructor to build instances of these types. Otherwise they have the special value `null` also known as the *empty reference value*. A key innovation in C# is to treat native simple types as being derived from object. This means that methods or operations that work on objects can be made to work on simple type values. This technique is called boxing. Boxing is the implicit conversion of a simple value type to a reference type `object`. Unboxing is the explicit conversion of the boxed type to a value type.

```
bool flag = true, answer;
double x = 3.5;
object any = flag;          // boxing value to reference type
answer = (bool)flag                              // unboxing
any = x;                           // boxing a double value
```

When a method defined for `Object` such as `ToString()` is called on a value type such as an `int`, the `int` value is boxed. This is the mechanism behind the scene that works with value types as arguments to `Write()` and `WriteLine()`.

Let us write a simple example of boxing and unboxing that uses an object variable and assign it different value types.

In file Boxing.cs

```
// Boxing and Unboxing
using System;

class Boxing {
  public static void Main( )
  {
    object a = 1;                              // box an int value

    Console.WriteLine("a = {0}", a);
    int i = (int)a;                              // unbox
    a = 1.5;                             // box a double
    Console.WriteLine("a = {0}, i = {1}", a, i);
  }
}
```

The output of this program is

```
a = 1
a = 1.5, i = 1
```

The variable a is a generic variable in that it accepts a value of any type.

8.6   GENERIC METHODS

Let us write a method that prints the value of an arbitrary array. A method that works regardless of type is called a *generic method*. To write method this we make use of the boxing/unboxing and Object ideas of the previous sections.

We write a program that prints an arbitrary array of elements of any type. We use a class StringBuilder that is more efficient than string. The reason for this is that string is an unmodifiable string-type. When modifying a string, for example by calling the method ToLower(), we end up with both the old string and the new string. When manipulating an equivalent StringBuilder value, we can mutate the individual characters and thus only have one object.

In file StringBuilderUse.cs

```
using System;
using System.Text;

class StringBuilderUse {
  public static void Main( )
  {
    object[] data1 = {1, 2, 3, 4, 5, 6, 7};
    object[] data2 = {16.5, 18.8, 77.99};
    object[] data3 = {"The", "Cat", "HAD", "A", "CODE"};

    Console.WriteLine("data1:" + Format(data1, ","));
    Console.WriteLine("data2:" + Format(data2, ","));
    Console.WriteLine("data3:" + Format(data3, ","));
}
```

```
  public static StringBuilder Format(object[] t,
                                        string separate)
  {
    StringBuilder s = new StringBuilder("");
    for (int i =0; i < t.Length; ++i)
      s = s.Append(t[i].ToString() + separate);
    return s;
  }
}
```

The output of this program is

```
data1:1,2,3,4,5,6,7,
data2:16.5,18.8,77.99,
data3:The,Cat,HAD,A,CODE,
```

Dissection of *StringBuilderUse* Program

■object[] data1 = {1, 2, 3, 4, 5, 6, 7};
 object[] data2 = {16.5, 18.8, 77.99};
 object[] data3 = {"The", "Cat", "HAD", "A", "CODE"};

We demonstrate how we can work with any data type. Each of the three object arrays is used to box different types.

■public static StringBuilder Format(object[] t,
                                       string separate)

The method works on an object array.

■StringBuilder s = new StringBuilder("");
 for (int i =0; i < t.Length; ++i)
   s = s.Append(t[i].ToString() + separate);
 return s;

The StringBuilder class requires using System.Text; and has the method Append() that concatenates StringBuilder strings.

```
Console.WriteLine("data1:" + Format(data1, ","));
Console.WriteLine("data2:" + Format(data2, ","));
Console.WriteLine("data3:" + Format(data3, ","));
```

Inside Main() we can call the generic routine on any stored values.

8.7   SIMULATION: PREDATOR-PREY

Object-oriented programming was originally developed as a simulation methodology, using the programming language Simula 67. Many of the ideas underlying OOP are therefore best understood in terms of modeling a particular reality. In this section we use a set of classes and inheritance to simulate an artificial ecology.

The world in our example has different forms of life that interact. We derive classes for modeling the life forms from a single abstract class Living. Our simulation includes foxes as an archetypal predator; rabbits are prey. The rabbits eat grass.

If the rabbit is eating grass, can the fox be far behind?

During each cycle of the simulation, certain rules are applied to determine which life form occupies a cell in the next cycle. The rules are based on the populations in the neighborhood of a given cell. This approach is similar to Conway's Game of Life simulation.

The following pseudocode is for the top level of the simulation.

Pseudocode for Predator–Prey Simulation

```
Create two worlds, current and next
Initialize one with some life forms
Print the initial world
For each step of the simulation
   Update next based on current
   Print the next world
   Wwitch the roles of current and next
End of for loop
```

A key element of the rules used to compute which life form occupies a cell in the next cycle is the number of various life forms in adjacent or neighbor cells. To handle this, each class that implements a life form must contain a static count to store the count of that particular life form. Using these counts in the various life form classes, we can use the following pseudocode to describe how we compute the count of neighbors for a single cell.

Pseudocode for Counting Neighbors

```
Set the count for all life form types to 0
For each of current cell's 8 immediate neighbors
   If the neighbor is type LifeType
      Then increment the count for LifeType
```

We are now ready to look at the actual implementation of the classes. We begin at the top, with the class `Predator`, which has the method `Main()` for the program, and key constants needed for the simulation.

In file Predator.cs

```
// Top level class
public class Predator {

   // various constants used in the simulation
   public const int EMPTY = 0, GRASS = 1, RABBIT = 2,
                    FOX = 3, STATES= 4;
   public const int DRAB = 7, DFOX = 6, TMFOX = 5,
                    CYCLES = 15, N = 30;

   // DRAB rabbits die at 7, DFOX foxes at 6,
   // TMFOX too many foxes, CYCLES of simulation,
   // N size of square for simulations
```

```
public static void Main()
{
  Living[,]  odd  = new Living[N,N],
            even = new Living[N,N];

  InitializeWorld(odd);
  InitializeWorld(even);
  Eden(even);
  WriteWorld(even);
  string data = Console.ReadLine();
  for (int i = 0; i < CYCLES; ++i) {
    if (i % 2 == 1) {
        Update(even, odd);
        WriteWorld(even);
    }
    else {
      Update(odd, even);
      WriteWorld(odd);
    }
  }
}
}
```

In our implementation we have two square arrays of Living, namely even and odd. The code indicates that the class Predator must contain the methods Eden(), Update(), InitializeWorld(), and WriteWorld().

In file Predator.cs

```
public static void InitializeWorld(Living[,] w)
{
  for (int i = 0; i < N; ++i)
    for (int j = 0; j < N; ++j)
      w[i,j] = new Empty(i,j);
}

public static void Update(Living[,] w_new,
                          Living[,] w_old)
{
  for (int i = 1; i < N - 1; ++i)      // borders are taboo
    for (int j = 1; j < N - 1; ++j)
    w_new[i,j] = w_old[i,j].Next(w_old);
}
```

```
public static void Eden(Living[,] w)
{
  Random t = new Random();
  int    lifeNo;

  for (int i = 2; i < N - 2; ++i)
    for (int j = 2; j < N - 2; ++j) {
      lifeNo = t.Next() % 3;
      if ( lifeNo == 1)
        w[i,j] = new Rabbit(i, j, 0);
      else
        if ( lifeNo == 2)
          w[i,j] = new Fox(i, j, 0);
        else
          w[i,j] = new Grass(i, j);
    }
}

public static void WriteWorld(Living[,] w)
{
  for (int i = 0; i < N; ++i) {
    Console.WriteLine();
    for (int j = 0; j < N; ++j)
      Console.Write(w[i,j].Who());
  }
  Console.WriteLine();
}
```

The method `Update()` visits each cell in the previous world passed as a parameter to `Update()`, invoking the `Next()` operation on the cell. The result of `Next()` is stored as the state of the cell in the new world, which is the one upon which `Update()` was invoked. Note that `Update()` doesn't visit any of the cells on the outer border. This omission avoids an index out-of-bounds error when the neighbors are counted. Note that border cells are missing some neighbors. As a result, the state of a border cell never changes.

All life form classes are derived from an abstract class `Living`.

In file Living.cs

```
public abstract class Living {
  abstract public int  Who() ;        // state identification
  abstract public Living Next(Living[,] w) ;
  protected   int  row, column;                    // location
```

```
protected  void Sums(Living[,] w, int[] sm)
{
  sm[Predator.EMPTY] = sm[Predator.GRASS] = 0;
  sm[Predator.FOX] = sm[Predator.RABBIT] = 0;
  for (int i = -1; i <= 1; ++i)
    for (int j = -1; j <= 1; ++j)
      sm[w[row + i, column + j].Who()]++;
}
}
```

In this simulation, a life form "knows" its location, as represented by the two integer instance variables `row` and `column`. For each new life form, implementations for `Next()` and `Who()` must be provided. We discuss these methods in the dissection of the class `Fox`.

The method `Sums()` is used by each of the classes derived from `Living`. The double `for` loop increments the count for the current cell, as well as the counts for each of the neighbors. We don't want to count the current cell as a neighbor, so we set the count for the current cell's type to `-1` initially.

We are now ready to present the implementation of the actual life form classes. In addition to the three life forms fox, rabbit, and grass, we need to provide a class that extends `Living` to represent an empty cell, which becomes the class `Empty`. The rules of the simulation are contained in the `Next()` methods of these classes. Each implementation of `Next()` begins by computing the counts of neighbors, using the method `Sums()` inherited from `Living`. Then each life form class can query the various other life form classes to determine how many neighbors of a particular type exist. Most life forms care only about some of the other life forms. For example, in our rules, the `Fox` class only cares about how many foxes and how many rabbits are nearby. The `Fox` class doesn't care about how much grass is nearby.

In file Living.cs

```
// Prey class
class Fox : Living {
  public  Fox(int r, int c, int a )
     { row = r; column = c; age = a; }
  public override  int  Who() { return Predator.FOX; }
```

```
public override   Living Next(Living[,] w)
{
  int[]  sum = new int[Predator.STATES];
  Sums(w, sum);
  if (sum[Predator.FOX] > Predator.TMFOX)// too many foxes
    return (new Empty(row, column));
  else if (age > Predator.DFOX)                // fox too old
    return (new Empty(row, column));
  else
    return (new Fox(row, column, age + 1));
}

  protected   int  age;                        // decide on dying
}
```

Dissection of the *Living* Program

■class Fox : Living {
```
  public   Fox(int r, int c, int a )
    { row = r; column = c; age = a; }
```

Each life form "knows" where it is located. We create a Fox by specifying the coordinates of the cell in which it is placed and giving it an initial age.

■public override Living Next(Living[,] w)
```
{
  int[]  sum = new int[Predator.STATES];

  Sums(w, sum);
  if (sum[Predator.FOX] > Predator.TMFOX)//too many foxes
    return (new Empty(row, column));
  else if (age > Predator.DFOX)            // fox too old
      return (new Empty(row, column));
  else
    return (new Fox(row, column, age + 1));
}
```

The method Next() contains the rules for what happens in the next cycle to a cell that currently contains a fox. In our simple rules the fox dies if there are too many foxes nearby, or if the fox is too old.

■ `public override   int  Who() { return Predator.FOX; }`

We use the method Who() in the method Sums() to find out who lives in a given cell of Living[,].

■ `private int age;`

This field, along with the row and column fields inherited from Living, constitute the state of a particular Fox object. In our simulation all foxes die after DFOX = 6. To alter the simulation, we could easily change this parameter to some random value over a range of values.

The classes Rabbit, Grass, and Empty are essentially the same as Fox, except that the rules in Next() are different.

In file Living.cs

```
class Rabbit :  Living {
  public     Rabbit(int r, int c, int a )
   { row = r; column = c; age = a;}
  public override  int  Who() { return Predator.RABBIT; }
  public override  Living Next(Living[,] w)
  {
    int[]  sum = new int[Predator.STATES];
    Sums(w, sum);
    if (sum[Predator.FOX] >= sum[Predator.RABBIT])
      return (new Empty(row, column));        // eat rabbits
    else if (age > Predator.DRAB)          // rabbit too old
      return (new Empty(row, column));
    else
      return (new Rabbit(row, column, age + 1));
  }
  protected   int  age;
}
```

```
class Grass : Living {
  public Grass(int r, int c) { row = r; column = c; }
  public override   int Who() { return Predator.GRASS; }
  public override   Living Next(Living[,] w)
  {
    int[]  sum = new int[Predator.STATES];

    Sums(w, sum);
    if (sum[Predator.GRASS] > sum[Predator.RABBIT])
      return (new Grass(row, column));
    else
      return (new Rabbit(row, column, 0));
  }
}

class Empty : Living {
  public Empty(int r, int c) { row = r; column = c; }
  public override   int  Who() { return Predator.EMPTY; }
  public override   Living  Next(Living[,] w)
  {
    int[]  sum =new int[Predator.STATES];

    Sums(w, sum);
    if (sum[Predator.FOX] > 1)
      return (new Fox(row, column, 0));
    else if (sum[Predator.RABBIT] > 1)
      return (new Rabbit(row, column, 0));
    else if (sum[Predator.GRASS] > 0)
      return (new Grass(row, column));
    else
      return (new Empty(row, column));
  }
}
```

Note that Living is completely independent of the specific life form classes. Hence we can easily add new life forms without changing the existing life-form classes. Here the only change required is to add a line for each new life form to the method Sums(). We also need to provide some way to get the new life forms into the world. We could do so either via Eden() or via the rules in one or more of the existing life-form classes. For example, we might add a new class Clover and modify the rules in class Empty to create Clover if there is nothing nearby.

If we run the *Predator* program with the classes in `Living`, the first set of data generated is

```
000000000000000000000000000000
000000000000000000000000000000
001211233121331222232222313200
002322111111212113311213112100
001233112131121332222223311100
002333121221222313313322112300
001233311131211321331213331300
002312132221332322122112223200
002212323213231133232232131300
001231233132322312111323221100
002331223213312112222221223200
003231232322212332131232113100
002133232132122113132223122300
003333322223212132123131312200
003213122311223211123133111300
001321232322333233112132132200
003312311321321312113212323100
001113311221113112132323133200
001122133321333333313221313100
002213232211111231313223231100
002222331233131132331222322300
002233133231212211112221111300
003211312231113223332121133100
001233231312212232122131232300
001121332112323222313121312300
002122212131221333333311323200
001332321223112121332321213100
002333323113332133311331322200
000000000000000000000000000000
000000000000000000000000000000
```

8.8   INTERFACES

C# has a classlike form called an *interface* that can be used to encapsulate only abstract methods or properties. Think of an interface as a blueprint. A class that uses this blueprint is a class that *implements* the interface. An interface is an alternative to an abstract class, wherein all implementation details are deferred.

Let's consider a simulation like the one in the previous section. Suppose that not all life forms have the same notion of what it means to be a neighbor. For example, the neighborhood for a fox is probably different than that for a rabbit. If that's the case, our superclass `Living` wouldn't be able to implement `Sums()` for all derived classes. In this case we could use an interface instead of an abstract class. The interface for `ILiving` might be

In file ILiving.cs

```
public interface ILiving {          // style starts name with I
  int  Who() ;                       // state identification
  ILiving Next(ILiving[,] w) ;
  void Sums(ILiving[,] w, int[] sm);
  int  row { get; set; }            // properties are allowed
  int  column { get; set; }
}
```

An interface is allowed to have only public methods, and by convention the keyword `public` is omitted from the member declarations. It is C# community style to start an interface name with a capital "I", hence the name `ILiving`. Because all methods in an interface are abstract, the keyword `abstract` is also omitted. Implementing an interface is like implementing an abstract class. The class that implements the interface must provide an implementation for all methods in the interface. We leave an exercise recoding our predator-prey simulation by changing our abstract `class Living` to an `interface ILiving`. (See Exercise 12 on page 375.)

In the next section we present a brief example in which abstract classes can't be used but interfaces can.

8.9   INTERFACE AND MULTIPLE INHERITANCE

Classes can inherit from only a single parent class. This is known as single inheritance. This restriction does not apply to interfaces. Classes can implement an arbitrary number of interfaces. This is the basis for a useful form of multiple inheritance allowed in C#.

Let us design the tracking system for a university that contains records for students, faculty, and staff. Some parts of the system operate only on student records, others only on faculty records, and so on; some parts operate on the records for any type of person. As described so far, the system might be modeled with a UML diagram like the one shown in the following:

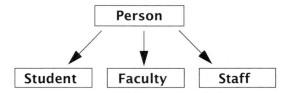

What happens when a student is also a staff member? We could create two records for the person—a student record and a staff record—but that could cause problems. Parts of the system dealing with person records might treat the staff record and the student record as two different people.

We need the ability to create a single record that sometimes can be treated as a student, sometimes as a person, and sometimes as a staff member. We can use interfaces to create such a record. Our university record system then might include the following interfaces.

In file StudentEmployee.cs

```
interface IPerson
{
  char Gender { get; set; }
  string Name { get; set; }
  int Age { get; set; }
}
```

```
interface IStudent : IPerson
{
  double Gpa { get; set; }
  int Year { get; set; }
  string YearName(int y);
}

interface IStaff : IPerson
{
  double Salary { get; set; }
  string Ssn { get; set; }
}
```

An interface can extend another interface; however, an interface can't include data members. When we use interfaces, we do not inherit method implementations, only their specification. We can now create classes that implement these various interfaces. The following class can be used to store student employee records.

In file StudentEmployee.cs

```
class StudentEmployee : IPerson, IStudent, IStaff
{
  // methods and properties required by IPerson
  public string Name
    { get { return name; } set { name = value; } }
  public int Age
    { get {return age; } set { age = value; } }
  public char Gender
    { get {return gender;} set { gender = value; } }

  // methods and properties required by IStudent
  public double Gpa
    { get {return gpa;} set { gpa = value; } }
  public int Year
    { get { return year; }  set { year = value; } }
  public string YearName(int y)
    { switch (y)
      { case 0:  return "freshman";
        case 1:  return "sophomore";
        case 2:  return "junior";
        case 3:  return "senior";
        default: return "unknown";
      }
    }
```

```csharp
    // methods and properties required by IStaff
    public double Salary
      { get { return salary; }  set { salary = value; }   }
    public string Ssn
      { get { return ssn; }  set  { ssn = value; } }

    // constructors for student employee
    public StudentEmployee (string nm, int a, char g,
      double gp, int yr, string socsec, double sal)
      { name = nm; age = a; gender =  g;
        gpa = gp; year = yr;
        ssn = socsec; salary = sal; }

    // implement other constructors and methods
    .....

  public override string ToString()
    {
      return String.Format
        ("Name: {0:-20}  Age: {1,2}  Gender: {2}" +
         "\nSocial Security: {3}   Salary: {4:C}" +
         "\nGpa: {5}  Year:  {6}",
        name, age, gender, ssn, salary, gpa, YearName(year));
    }

    private string name;
    private int age;
    private char gender;
    private int year;
    private double gpa;
    private double salary;
    private string ssn;
}

class StudentEmployeeTest {
  public static void Main()
    {
      StudentEmployee tanya =
          new StudentEmployee("Tanya Pohl", 18,
          'F', 3.9, 0, "522-30-2572", 9285.60);
    Console.WriteLine(tanya);
    }
}
```

The output of this program is

```
Name: Tanya Pohl   Age: 18   Gender: F
Social Security: 522-30-2572    Salary: $9,285.60
Gpa: 3.9   Year:   freshman
```

The preceding example shows how multiple interfaces are implemented. In this case, all the interface methods are implemented in the StudentEmployee class. Using multiple interfaces is different from deriving a class because only a single class can be derived from. An alternate design would be to implement a concrete base class Person, and let StudentEmployee inherit from Person, while still implementing the interfaces Student and Staff. StudentEmployee would inherit the Person methods, properties, and data members, and would not need to reimplement them.

Some OOP languages, such as C++, permit multiple inheritance of classes, but various subtle complexities arise when code is inherited directly from several different classes. However, many of the programming problems that might otherwise be solved with multiple inheritance of classes can be solved by using C#'s multiple inheritance of interfaces. Note that we are talking about multiple inheritance from more than one immediate parent class. But multiple inheritance means more than simply having multiple parent classes. For example, if Student extends Person and Person extends Object, that isn't multiple inheritance. Only when a class *directly* extends two or more classes is it called multiple inheritance, and only then do the problems that we've alluded to arise.

8.10   ODDS AND ENDS

This section looks at some of the less-used features of C#. These include the new keywords sealed, is, and as, internal access, and another use for new.

8.10.1   SEALED CLASSES

Inheritance from a class can be disallowed by use of the new keyword sealed. A sealed class can be handled more efficiently by the compiler. Since its methods cannot be overridden, these method calls are compiled as nonvirtual.

8.10.2 is AND as

The operator `is` can be applied to an object to determine if it supports an interface. Its form is

> *expression* `is` *type*

The operator returns `true` if the expression can be cast to *type*. An example is

```
if (x is Shape)
  // x is a Shape
else
  // x is not a Shape
```

The `is` operator is used when ordinary polymorphism with overridden methods is inappropriate. An example is

```
if (x is Point)
  Console.WriteLine("Point has no area" + x);
else
  Console.WriteLine("Area is " + x.area());
```

Here we have two behaviors: a polymorphic behavior for shapes, which involves computing their area, and the special case of `Point` not having an area calculation.

The `as` operator provides a cast as well as a test for type. The `as` operator is used in the form:

> *expression* `as` *type*

The operator returns the expression converted to the *type* or, if the conversion is disallowed, it returns a null reference. An example is

```
AShape t = x as AShape; // AShape has an area calculation
if (t == null)
  Console.WriteLine("Point has no area" + t);
else
  Console.WriteLine("Area is " + t.area());
```

8.10.3 INTERNAL ACCESS

So far we have discussed `public`, `private`, and `protected` access. Two less common access modifiers are `internal` and `internal protected`. The `internal` modifier is somewhat like `private`, but extends access to other classes being assembled at the same time. The `internal protected` modifier is equivalent to either `protected` or `internal`. So members labeled with this form of access can be visible in derived classes or alternatively are visible within classes assembled at the same time.

8.10.4 LABELING DERIVED METHODS NEW

Normally in object-oriented code you override a base class method, for example:

```
public override void Draw() {·····}      // Draw a rectangle
```

but when you do not want to override a virtual base class method, you write:

```
public new virtual void Draw() {·····}      // new version
```

8.11   SOFTWARE ENGINEERING: INHERITANCE

At one level, inheritance is a code-sharing technique. At another level, it reflects an understanding of the problem and relationships between parts of the problem space. Much of inheritance is the expression of an *ISA* relationship between the base and derived classes. The rectangle is a shape. This is the conceptual underpinning for making `shape` a superclass and allowing the behavior described by its public instance methods to be interpretable on objects within its type hierarchy. In other words, subclasses derived from the superclass share its interface.

A design cannot be specified in a completely optimal way. Design involves tradeoffs between the various objectives one wishes to achieve. For example, generality is frequently at odds with efficiency. Using a class hierarchy that expresses *ISA* relationships increases our effort to understand how to compartmentalize coding relationships and potentially introduces coding inefficiencies by having various layers of access to the (hidden) state description of an object. However, a reasonable *ISA* decomposition can simplify the overall coding process. For example, a shape-drawing package need not anticipate shapes that might be added in the future. Through inheritance, the class developer imports the base-class shape interface and provides code that implements operations, such as *draw*. What is primitive or shared remains unchanged. Also unchanged is the client's use of the package.

An undue amount of decomposition imposes its own complexity and ends up being self-defeating. There is a granularity decision whereby highly specialized classes do not provide enough benefit and are better folded into a larger concept.

Single inheritance (SI) conforms to a hierarchical decomposition of the key objects in the domain of discourse. Multiple inheritance (MI) is more troubling as a modeling or problem-solving concept. In MI, the new object is composed of several pre-existing objects and is usefully thought of as a form of each. The term *mixin* is used to mean a class composed using MI, with each base class orthogonal. Much of the time, there is an alternative *HASA* formulation. For example, is a vampire bat a mammal that happens to fly, a flying machine that happens to be a mammal, or both a flying machine and a mammal? Depending on what code is available, developing a proper class for vampire bat might involve an MI derivation or an SI with appropriate *HASA* members.

Interfaces generally take the form of mixins providing a *HASA* relationship. None of this diminishes the attraction of MI as a code-reuse technique as in our example of `StudentEmployee`.

8.12   DR. P'S PRESCRIPTIONS

- Use *ISA* inheritance.

- Usually, a base class is abstract.

- Minimize interactions between classes.

- Avoid deep hierarchies.

Public inheritance creates a class hierarchy in which a derived class object is a form of base-class object. This is called *ISA* inheritance. In the classic example, an abstract base class `Shape` describes the properties and behaviors of all `Shape` types using virtual and abstract virtual member functions. The derived classes such as `Circle` implement the specifics. The `Circle` *ISA* `Shape`. A base-class reference can be assigned a derived-class object or address. Manipulation by such a reference can be polymorphic—namely, by using virtual functions, the properly overridden function defined in the derived class is called dynamically. Usually, such a base class is abstract. This identifies the class as an important type to be used polymorphically. It guarantees that the compiler insists on overridden member function definitions where concrete behavior for derived types is needed.

Class dependencies lead to extra difficulty in software maintenance. Classes that depend on many other relationships, including inheritance, add linkages across boundaries.

Overdoing complexity by using deep hierarchies leads to code that can be inefficient and difficult to maintain and modify.

8.13 C# COMPARED WITH JAVA AND C++

C#, C++, and Java all have the inheritance mechanism, which extends a new class from an existing one. Java uses different terminology with respect to inheritance. The Java base class is called the *superclass*. The extended class adds to or alters the inherited superclass methods and is used to share an interface and to create a hierarchy of related types. In Java, ordinary class inheritance is single inheritance. Java also has interface inheritance, which can be used for a restricted form of multiple inheritance. Java uses the keyword `extends` rather than the colon for inheritance.

Let us compare Java inheritance by looking at the C# `Person` class in Section 8.1, *A Derived Class*, on page 329. This class could be used in a database for a college in which the registrar tracks various types of students. We start with the superclass `Person1`. This class is similar to `Person` in Section 6.14, *C# Compared with Java and C++*, on page 276. Note that the `private` instance variables are changed to have access `protected`. This access allows their use in the subclass but otherwise acts like `private`.

In file Person1.java

```
import tio.*;

public class Person1 {
  Person1() { };
  Person1(String nm, int a, char g)
    { this.name = name; this.age = a; this.gender = g; }
  void setAge(int a) { this.age = a; }
  void setGender(char b) { this.gender = b; }
```

```
   void setName(String nm) { this.name = nm; }
   int getAge() { return age; }
   char getGender() { return gender; }
   String getName() { return name; }

   public String ToString()
      { return ("Name: " + name   + " Age: " + age
                       + " Gender: " + gender); }

   protected String name;
   protected int age;
   protected char gender;          // male == 'M', female == 'F'
}
```

Now we derive `Student` from `Person1`, according the model we used in Section 8.1, *A Derived Class*, on page 330.

In file StudentTest.java

```
class Student extends Person1 {
   Student() { super(); }
   Student(String nm, int a, char g, byte y, double gp)
      { super(nm, a, g); this.gpa = gp; this.year = y; }
   void setYear(byte y) { year = y; }
   void setGpa(double g) { gpa = g; }

   String YearName(byte y)
   { switch (y) {
     case FRESHMAN:  return "freshman";
     case SOPHOMORE:   return "sophomore";
     case JUNIOR: return "junior";
     case SENIOR: return "senior";
     default: return "unknown";
     }
   }

   public String toString() { return(super.toString()
      + " Year: " + YearName(year) + "  GPA: " + gpa); }
   static final byte FRESHMAN = 1;
   static final byte SOPHOMORE = 2;
   static final byte JUNIOR = 3;
   static final byte SENIOR = 4;
   private byte year;                   // 1=fr, 2=so, 3=jr, 4=sr
   private double gpa;                          // 0.0 to 4.0
}
```

In this example, Student is the subclass, and Person1 is the superclass. Notice the use of the keyword super, which provides a means of accessing the instance variables or methods found in the superclass.

Java does not have enumerated types, so we provide constants so that code that sets the field Year is self-documenting. The Java primitive type byte can represent small integers and requires only 1 byte of memory, so we use this over int, which would require 4 bytes.

The inheritance structure provides a design for the overall system. The superclass Person1 leads to a design whereby the subclass Student is derived from it. Other subclasses, such as GradStudent or Employee, could be added to this inheritance hierarchy.

In Java, polymorphism comes from both method overloading and method overriding. Overriding occurs when a method is redefined in the subclass. The toString() method is in Person1 and is redefined in Student extended from Person1.

```java
// Overriding the toString() method

class Person1 {
    .....
  public String toString()
     { return ("Name: " + name    + "  Age: " + age
                     + " Gender: " + gender); }
   .....
}

class Student extends Person1 {
   .....
   public toString() { return(super.toString()
      + "  Year: " + YearName(year) + "  GPA: " + gpa); }
   .....
}
```

The overridden method toString() has the same name and signature in both the superclass Person1 and the subclass Student. Which one gets selected depends on what is being referenced at runtime. For example:

In file StudentTest.java

```
// Uses Student which uses Person1

public class StudentTest {
  public static void main (String[] args)
  {
    Student q1, q2;
    q1 = new Student();
    q2 = new Student("Buzz Dolsberry", 18, 'M',
                    (byte)2, 3.4);
    q1.setName("Betty Holmstrom");
    q1.setAge(17);
    q1.setGender('F');
    q1.setYear((byte)3);
    q1.setGpa(3.2);
    System.out.println(q1.toString());
    System.out.println(q2.toString());
  }
}
```

The variable q1 can refer to either the Person1 object or the subtype Student object. At runtime, the correct toString() is selected. The setName() method is known at compile time, since it is the superclass Person1 method.

C++ does not have interfaces and has a different scheme for declaring abstract methods and classes. It also has more complicated inheritance schemes which allow very confusing multiple inheritance that is controversial in its details and use.

Here is the student example written out in C++.

In file student.cpp

```
#include <iostream>
#include <string>
using namespace std;
```

```
class person {
public:
  person() {}
  person(const string& nm, int a, char g) :
       name(nm), age(a), gender (g) {}
  void setAge(int a) { age = a; }
  void setGender(char b) { gender = b; }
  void setName(string nm) { name = nm; }
  int  getAge() { return age; }
  char getGender() { return gender; }
  string getName() { return name; }
  friend ostream& operator<<(ostream& out, const person& p);
protected:
  string name;
  int age;
  char gender;                    // male == 'M', female == 'F'
};

ostream& operator<<(ostream& out, const person& p)
{
  return (out << "Name: " << p.name <<  Age: "  <<
         p.age <<    "  Gender: " << p.gender);
}

enum undergrad {freshman, sophomore, junior, senior };

class student : public person {
public:
  student() : person() { }
  student(const string& nm, int a, char g, double gp,
         undergrad y)
    : person(nm, a, g), gpa(gp), year(y) { }
  void setYear(undergrad y) { year = y; }
  void setGpa(double g) { gpa = g; }
  string yearName(undergrad y);
  friend ostream& operator<<(ostream& out,
                             const student& s);
private:
  undergrad year;                 // 1=fr, 2=so, 3=jr, 4=sr
  double gpa;                     // 0.0 to 4.0
};
```

```
string student::yearName(undergrad y)
{
   switch (y) {
    case freshman:  return "freshman";
    case sophomore:   return "sophomore";
    case junior: return "junior";
    case senior: return "senior";
    default: return "unknown";
    }
}

ostream& operator<<(ostream& out, const student& s)
{
  return (out << static_cast<person>(s) << "  Year: " <<
          s.yearName(s.year) << "GPA: " << s.gpa);
}

int main ()
{
  student q1;
  student q2 (string("Buzz Dolsberry"), 18, 'M', 3.4,
              undergrad(2));
  q1.setName("Betty Holmstrom");
  q1.setAge(17);
  q1.setGender('F');
  q1.setGpa(3.2);
  q1.setYear(freshman);
  cout << q1 << endl;
  cout << q2 << endl;
}
```

In C++, the `override` keyword is not used. Inheritance in C++ can be `public`, `private`, or `protected`, where only public inheritance is allowed in C#. C++ allows multiple inheritance, but does not have interface inheritance. The overloading of I/O is also significantly different for C++ than for Java and C#. The allocation of the instances of classes also differ: both C# and Java use `new`. In contrast, C++ uses implicit invocation of a constructor when declaring class variables. Not shown here, abstract methods in C++ are denoted by $= 0$; used instead of a compound statement for their body. Once declared virtual, all derived methods of the same name and signature are implicitly virtual.

SUMMARY

■ Inheritance provides the ability to create new derived classes by adding to or altering existing classes. Through inheritance, a hierarchy of related, code-sharing types is created.

■ A class can be derived from an existing class using the form

class *class-name* : *base-name*
{
    member declarations
}

■ The keywords public, private, and protected are available as visibility modifiers for class members. A public member is visible throughout its scope. A private member is visible to other member functions within its own class. A protected member is visible to other member functions within its class, and within any class immediately derived from it.

■ The derived class has its own constructors, which invoke the base-class constructor. A special syntax is used to pass arguments from the derived-class constructor back to the base-class constructor:

constructor header : base (*argument list*)

■ A derived class is a subtype of its base class. A variable of the derived class can in many ways be treated as if it were the base-class type. A reference whose type is the base class can reference objects of the derived-class type.

■ The keyword virtual is a function specifier that provides a mechanism to dynamically select at runtime the appropriate member function from among base- and derived-class functions. This specifier may be used only to modify nonstatic method declarations. This is called overriding. This ability to dynamically select a routine appropriate to an object's type is a form of polymorphism. The keyword override is needed as a modifier declaring the derived class method.

■ Inheritance provides for code reuse. The derived class inherits the base-class code and typically modifies and extends the base class. Inheritance also creates a type hierarchy, allowing further generality by providing additional implicit type conversions. Also, at a runtime cost, it allows for runtime selection of overridden virtual functions. Facilities that allow the implementation of inheritance and the ability to process objects dynamically are the essentials of OOP.

■ An *abstract class* is introduced for the purpose of having abstract methods that have no definition, and are purely intended to be overridden in a derived class. An abstract method is one whose body is undefined. Notationally, such a method is declared inside the abstract class, as follows:

abstract *method header;*

The abstract method declaration is used to defer the implementation decision of the method. In OOP terminology, it is called a *deferred method.*

■ C# has a classlike form called an *interface* that can be used to encapsulate only abstract methods or properties. Think of an interface as a blueprint. A class that uses this blueprint is a class that *implements* the interface. An interface is an alternative to an abstract class, wherein all implementation details are deferred.

REVIEW QUESTIONS

1. In class X : Y { ····· }, X is a _____ class and Y is a _____ class.

2. True or false: If D inherits from B, D is a subtype of B.

3. The term overriding refers to _____ methods.

4. An abstract base class contains a _____.

5. The subtyping relationship is called the _____.

6. True or false: Interfaces can inherit from other interfaces, but not from classes.

7. What is wrong with the following?

```
class A:B {·····}
class B:C {·····}
class C:A {·····}
```

8. In multiple inheritance, why is interface inheritance used?

9. The operator is provides a test _____.

10. True or false: An abstract class can have only abstract methods.

EXERCISES

1. Derive a class from `Person` that is `class Employee`. An `Employee` should have a `salary` and a `departmentNumber`.

2. Create an array of `Employees` and assign appropriate information to each array element. Write a method that looks for all `Employees` who have a salary greater than a parameter `salaryLevel`. Then print those out.

3. Recode the `Format()` method in Section 8.6, *Generic Methods*, on page 348, so as to print the last element of an array without a separator.

4. Further enhance the `Format()` method in the preceding exercise to take a parameter that decides how many values to print on a line and to add a message that precedes the printing of the array.

5. Create an abstract class `Counter`. It should have only abstract virtual functions. It should have a method `Click()` that advances the counter. It should have properties using `get()` and `set()` for accessing and mutating the counter's value.

6. Create a concrete class `Timer` derived from the abstract class `Counter`. This class should simulate a timer that has seconds and minutes as readout. Write a program that tests this implementation.

7. Develop a class `Clock` based on `Timer`. It should have the same functionality as an ordinary house clock or watch. Write a program that tests this implementation.

8. Write a `class Pair` that hold two `doubles`. Derive a `class TwoPair` from `class Pair` that is capable of handling two pairs. Contrast this to developing the same class by having an array of `Pair` as a member of `TwoPair`. Which design makes better sense?

9. Write a `class Point` derived from `Pair` that has the same functionality as `class Point` from Section 7.1.2, *Improving the Point Class*, on page 290. Is this an improvement? Sometimes using an advanced feature of language makes the code more complex without providing a significant benefit.

10. Write a `class Stack` that stores values that are `object`. This is a form of generic stack. Now derive a form of this stack that stores `ints`. Write some code testing this. One such standard test would be to use the stack for reversing a set of values.

11. Add a new life form to the predator-prey simulation found in Section 8.7, *Simulation: Predator-Prey*, on page 351.

12. Recode our predator-prey simulation in Section 8.7, *Simulation: Predator-Prey*, on page 350, by changing our abstract `class Living` to an `interface ILiving`. (See Section 8.8, *Interfaces*, on page 358.)

13. Recode the predator-prey simulation to not use a `Who()` method. You may want to use the `typeof` operator.

14. *(Project)* Design and implement a graphical user interface (GUI) for the predator-prey simulation of Section 8.7, *Simulation: Predator-Prey*, on page 351. It is beyond the scope of this book to describe various available GUI toolkits. The program should draw each iteration of the simulation on the screen. You should be able to directly input a *Garden of Eden* starting position. You should also be able to provide other settings for the simulation, such as the size of the simulation. Can you allow the user to define other life forms and their rules for existing, eating, and reproducing? Make the graphical interface as elegant as possible. The user should be able to position it on the screen, resize it, and select icons for the various available life forms.

15. Recode `class StudentEmployee : IPerson, IStudent, IStaff` to be based on a concrete `class Person`. Have this class implement `IPerson`.

INPUT/OUTPUT

This chapter describes input/output in C#, using its libraries. We begin by describing in more detail how to use `Console` I/O and explain in more detail how to use format characters. C# I/O makes heavy use of streams. A *stream* is a sequence of data that can be read or written. In C#, the abstract class `Stream` provides basic methods for reading and writing.

Stream I/O is described as a set of classes used by C#. Streams can be associated with files, and examples of file processing using streams are discussed in this chapter. A lot of file processing requires character handling, which is also discussed here.

In OOP, objects should know how to print themselves. Notationally, it is important to override `ToString()` for user-defined ADTs. In this section, we develop output methods for the types `Card` and `Deck` to illustrate these techniques.

9.1   CONSOLE OUTPUT

Two standard console output objects are `Console.Out` and `Console.Error`. We have ignored `Console.Error` and instead relied for simplicity on `Console.Out` throughout this text. Both can be used in much the same way. The chief use of `Console.Error` is to continue to print to console when `Console.Out` is redirected to a file.

The methods `Console.Out.WriteLine()` and `Console.Out.Write()` are also usually invoked in a shorter form as `Console.WriteLine()` and `Console.Write()`. The distinction between the two methods is that `WriteLine()` flushes its buffer and moves the screen cursor to the next line. The statement

```
Console.Out.WriteLine("x = " + x );
```

prints to the screen a string of four characters, followed by an appropriate representation for the output of x, followed by a new line. The representation depends on the type of variable x and how it is converted to a `string`. This form of `WriteLine()` takes a single expression, converts it to a `string` if necessary, and displays it on the screen. It is often the case that the expression is formed from a concatenated number of subexpressions converted to strings.

```
Console.Out.WriteLine("Temp = " + (x * 1.8 + 32) + "F");
```

Here the string `"Temp = "` is concatenated with the subexpression (x * 1.8 + 32), which is a `double`. The `double` expression is evaluated and then is implicitly converted to a string and concatenated. Finally the string literal `"F"` is concatenated and the entire resulting string printed to the console.

9.2   FORMATTED OUTPUT

As we discussed in Section 2.2.1, *Formatting the Output*, on page 40, the `Write()` and `WriteLine()` methods are overloaded to take a format string followed by a list of arguments. We reiterate some of that information here.

First, a list of arguments of arbitrary length can be printed and second, the printing is controlled by simple conversion specifications, or formats. Both methods deliver the resulting string to the standard output file Out, which is normally connected to the screen. The argument list has two parts:

control_string and *other_arguments*

In the example

```
Console.Write("she sells {0} peas for {1:C}", 99, 3.77);
```

we have

control_string: `"she sells {0} peas for {1:C}"`
other_arguments: `99, 3.77`

The screen prints:

```
she sells 99 peas for $3.77
```

The expressions in *other_arguments* are evaluated and converted according to the formats in the control string and are then placed in the output stream. Characters in the control string that are not part of a format are placed directly in the output stream. The {} symbol introduces an argument number followed by a colon, followed by a conversion specification, or format. If only an argument number is used then the conversion is implicit and printing is based on the ToString() method for that type. A simple conversion specification is a conversion character.

If we change the above to:

```
Console.Write("she sells {0} peas for {1:C} or " +
              "{2} carrots for {1:C}", 99, 3.77, 49);
```

We print the argument {1:C} twice and so what prints is

```
she sells 99 peas for $3.77 or 49 carrots for $3.77
```

Table 9.1 shows some of the more frequently used conversion characters.

Table 9.1	Some Standard Formatting Codes
Conversion character	How the corresponding argument is printed
C, c	As currency
D, d	As a decimal integer
X, x	As an unsigned hexadecimal integer
E, e	As a floating-point number
F, f	As a fixed-point number
G, g	In the e-format or f-format, whichever is shorter
S, s	As a string
N, n	A numerical fixed point format with embedded commas

"Boy-oh-boy, have you noticed how snooty Melvyn has gotten since he converted to a double?"

It is also possible to specify a field width for the formats by writing a digit after the conversion character. The next example uses both numerical formats and widths.

In file CircleArea.cs

```
// pi to 21 places
// Write with numerical formats and widths
using System;

class CircleArea {
  public static double area(double rad)
    { const  double pi = 3.14159265358979323846;
         return (pi * rad * rad); }
  public static void Main()
  {
    double  r; string data;

    Console.Write("Enter radius: ");
    data = Console.ReadLine(); r = double.Parse(data);
    Console.WriteLine("Area is {0:F5}", area(r));
    Console.WriteLine("Area is {0:F9}", area(r));
    Console.WriteLine("Area is {0:F20}", area(r));
    Console.WriteLine("Area is {0:e5}", area(r));
    Console.WriteLine("Area is {0:g5}", area(r));
  }
}
```

The output from this program when 1.0 is entered for r is

```
Enter radius: 1.0
Area is 3.14159
Area is 3.141592654
Area is 3.14159265358979000000
Area is 3.14159e+000
Area is 3.1416
```

Dissection of the *CircleArea* Program

■`const double pi = 3.14159265358979323846;`

We want to display a large number of digits in this test program.

```
■Console.WriteLine("Area is {0:F5}", area(r));
```

The number of decimal places for printing the `area(r)` for the format code `F5` is 5, therefore it prints as `3.1415`

```
■Console.WriteLine("Area is {0:F9}", area(r));
 Console.WriteLine("Area is {0:F20}", area(r));
```

This prints `3.141592654` and `3.14159265358979000000`. Notice how these change the number of significant digits printed. The first result has 9 significant figures in its fraction. The second result has 20 significant figures, but the last 4 are meaningless because they exceed the precision of type `double`.

```
■Console.WriteLine("Area is {0:e5}", area(r));
 Console.WriteLine("Area is {0:g5}", area(r));
```

This prints `3.14159e+000` and `3.1416`. The first notation specified by the format code `e` is scientific with an exponent expression. The fraction part is five significant figures. The second notation specified by the format code `g` is printed as fixed point because it is shorter in this form than scientific would be. It prints as exactly five digits of fraction.

9.3   USER-DEFINED TYPES FOR OUTPUT

User-defined types have typically been printed by creating a method `ToString()` in each class as discussed in Section 6.6.1, *The ToString() Method*, on page 254. Remember that the `ToString()` method is invoked only if the instance variable is not null. This means that there will be no output if you call `Console.Write(x)` when `x` is null, and you will get only a newline if you call `Console.WriteLine(x)` with `x` as a null argument.

After learning about overriding the method `ToString()`, we were able to implement the standard C# idiom for output of these types. We reiterate some of that information here.

9.3.1 ToString() OVERRIDING

Here we show a more complex example demonstrating the use of formatting, the ToString() method, and inheritance for the types Card and Deck as an example of a simple user-defined type. We modify our *Poker* program from Section 6.7, *An Example: Flushing*, on page 257, and write out a set of output routines for displaying cards. We also update the class to use get and set properties and appropriate constructors:

In file PrintDeck.cs

```
using System;

public class Suit
{
  public Suit(int n) { s = n / 13; }
  public int S
  { get { return s; } set { s = value / 13; } }
  public static char[]  suitSymbol =
    new char[4] {'c', 'd', 'h', 's'};
  public override string ToString()
    {return suitSymbol[s].ToString(); }
  private int s;    //values 0 to 3
}

public class Pips
{
  public Pips (int n) { p = n % 13 + 1; }
  public int P { get {return p;} set {p = value % 13 + 1;} }

  public static char[]  pipsSymbol = new char[14]
  {'?','A','2','3','4','5','6','7','8','9','T','J','Q','K'};

  public override string ToString()
    { return pipsSymbol[p].ToString(); }

  private   int  p;                         // values 1 to 13
}
```

```
public class Card
{
  public Card(int n) { s = new Suit(n); p = new Pips(n);   }
  public override string ToString()
    { return String.Format("{0}{1} ", s, p); }
  public int S {get { return s.S; } set { s.S = value/13;} }
  public int P {get {return p.P;} set {p.P = value%13 + 1;}}
  private  Suit  s;
  private  Pips  p;
}

public class Deck
{
  public Deck()
  {
    d = new Card[52];
    for (int i = 0; i < 52; ++i)
      d[i] = new Card(i);
  }

  public override string ToString()
  {
    string temp = "";
    for (int i = 0; i < 52; ++i)
    {
      if (i % 13 == 0)                    // 13 cards to a line
        temp = temp + "\n";
      temp = temp + d[i].ToString() + "   ";
    }
    return temp;
  }

  private   Card[]  d;
}

class DeckTest
{
  public static void Main()
  {
    Deck d = new Deck();
    Console.WriteLine(d);
  }
}
```

The output of this program is

```
Ac  2c  3c  4c  5c  6c  7c  8c  9c  Tc  Jc  Qc  Kc
Ad  2d  3d  4d  5d  6d  7d  8d  9d  Td  Jd  Qd  Kd
Ah  2h  3h  4h  5h  6h  7h  8h  9h  Th  Jh  Qh  Kh
As  2s  3s  4s  5s  6s  7s  8s  9s  Ts  Js  Qs  Ks
```

Each Card is printed out in two characters. If d is a variable of type Deck, then Console.WriteLine(d); prints out the entire deck, 13 cards to a line.

Notice that we can also output a Deck using the format string overloaded version of the Console.WriteLine() method.

```
Console.WriteLine("Before shuffling {0}\nis the order", d);
```

Here {0} refers to the 0th argument in the associate argument list, which is d.

9.3.2 CREATING A USER-DEFINED FORMAT

There is no format specification for Deck, but we can invent a format specification for displaying a deck. To do this we make Deck inherit from the interface IFormattable, we add a method Format to the Deck class, and we include an additional using statement.

In file PrintDeck.cs

```
// Output with ToString() only if not format {n:DK}
class Deck: IFormattable {
.....
  public string ToString(string format, IFormatProvider fp)
  {
    if (format == null)  return this.ToString();
    if (format.Equals("DK"))
      { return "The Deck is " + this.ToString(); }
    else
      { return this.ToString(); }
  }
  private   Card[] d;
}
```

```
class DeckTest
{
  public static void Main()
  {
    Deck d = new Deck();
    Console.WriteLine("{0:DK}", d);
  }
}
```

The output of this program is

```
The Deck is
Ac  2c  3c  4c  5c  6c  7c  8c  9c  Tc  Jc  Qc  Kc
Ad  2d  3d  4d  5d  6d  7d  8d  9d  Td  Jd  Qd  Kd
Ah  2h  3h  4h  5h  6h  7h  8h  9h  Th  Jh  Qh  Kh
As  2s  3s  4s  5s  6s  7s  8s  9s  Ts  Js  Qs  Ks
```

As seen in this example, to produce a `Format()` method we need to inherit from the interface `IFormattable`. The method signature is `Format(string format, IFormatProvider fp)`. The field width parameter still works in that it will pad this resulting string with blanks to the left or right, but it doesn't make much sense to use a field width in this context. In this case the field is the entire string "The Deck . . . Ks".

Dr. P says using Format( ) is a character builder!

9.4 CONSOLE INPUT

So far we have largely used `Console.ReadLine()` for input. This reads a line at a time into a string. We have parsed the string to obtain an appropriate input value. We can use the method `Console.Read()` to get a single character value. If no character is available, it returns -1 indicating end-of-file. This is useful when we want to do character-by-character text manipulation.

This method does not return until the read operation is terminated; for example, by the user pressing the Enter key. Upon hitting the Enter key, the carriage return and newline character are also returned.

In file MyEcho.cs

```
// Echo characters-print int value with character value
using System;

class MyEcho {
  public static void Main()
  {
    int i;

    Console.WriteLine("Type characters - followed by " +
              "cntrl-Z on a new line for EOF");
    while ((i = Console.Read()) != -1) {
      Console.WriteLine ("Echo: int {0}  char {1}",
          i, (char)i);
    }
    Console.WriteLine ("EOF");
  }
}
```

If we type "Day One" then Ctrl-z on its own line, we get the following output

```
Type characters - followed by cntrl-Z on a new line
for EOF
day one
Echo: int 100  char d
Echo: int 97  char a
Echo: int 121  char y
Echo: int 32  char
Echo: int 111  char o
Echo: int 110  char n
Echo: int 101  char e
Echo: int 13  char
Echo: int 10  char

^Z
EOF
```

Dissection of the *MyEcho* program

▪ `Console.WriteLine("Type characters - followed by " + "cntrl-Z on a new line for EOF");`

The special value -1 is the value meaning end-of-file or no more characters available. On a Windows console this happens when Ctrl-z is typed. On a Unix system this happens when Ctrl-d is typed.

▪ `while ((i = Console.Read()) != -1) {`
  `Console.WriteLine ("Echo: int {0}  char {1}",`
          `i, (char)i);`

The `while` loop reads one character at a time from the `Console` stream `In`. This is echoed to the terminal `Console` stream `Out` in two ways: its Unicode integer value and its printing character. A nonprinting character such as the integer value 7 representing the bell does not print, but rings.

```
Console.WriteLine ("EOF");
```

Upon exiting the `while` loop, the string `"EOF"` is printed. Test this on your system to make sure you know how to produce an end-of-file.

9.5   STANDARD METHODS FOR CHARACTERS

The system provides a standard set of methods used to test characters and a set of methods used to convert characters, as shown in Table 9.2. All the methods here return boolean `true` or `false` depending on whether the character is of the type being tested. This is mentioned here because of its usefulness in C# input/output. These methods are in `struct Char`.

Table 9.2	Some Char Static Methods
`bool IsLetter(c)`	A letter
`bool IsUpper(c)`	An uppercase letter
`bool IsLower(c)`	A lowercase letter
`bool IsDigit(c)`	A digit
`bool IsLetterOrDigit(c)`	A letter or digit
`bool IsWhiteSpace(c)`	A white space character
`bool IsPunctuation(c)`	A punctuation character
`bool IsControl (c)`	A control character

Table 9.3 shows methods that provide for the appropriate conversion of a character value while leaving unchanged the value of `c` stored in memory.

Table 9.3	Char Conversion Methods
`char ToUpper(c)`	Returns uppercase `c`
`char ToLower(c)`	Returns lowercase `c`
`string ToString(c)`	Returns `c` as a string

Let us use these to write a method that takes an input string and count the number of characters that are alphabetic. It also outputs the line with all the alphabetic characters in uppercase.

In file UpperCount.cs

```
// Output the line in uppercase and count letters
using System;

class UpperCount {
  public static void Main()
  {
    string data;
    Console.WriteLine("Enter Lines until cntrl-z:");
    while ((data = Console.ReadLine()) != null) {
      Console.WriteLine(ToUpperString(data));
      Console.WriteLine("alphabetic characters = {0}",
                    CountLetters(data));
    }
  }

  public static string ToUpperString(string s)
  {
    string upper = "";

    for (int i = 0; i < s.Length; ++i)
      upper = upper + Char.ToUpper(s[i]);
    return upper;
  }

  public static uint CountLetters(string s)
  {
    uint count = 0;

    for (int i = 0; i < s.Length; ++i)
      if ( Char.IsLetter(s[i]) )
        ++count;
    return count;
  }
}
```

Sample output of this program is

```
Enter Lines until cntrl-z
This is my test
THIS IS MY TEST
alphabetic characters = 12
Of two lines
OF TWO LINES
alphabetic characters = 10
^Z
Press any key to continue
```

Dissection of the *UpperCount* Program

```
■public static uint CountLetters(string s)
   {
     uint count = 0;
     for (int i = 0; i < s.Length; ++i)
       if ( Char.IsLetter(s[i]) )
         ++count;
     return count;
   }
```

The idiom treats each character in the string. We iterate over the entire length of the string and test whether or not a character is a letter.

```
■public static string ToUpperString(string s)
   {
     string upper = "";
     for (int i = 0; i < s.Length; ++i)
       upper = upper + Char.ToUpper(s[i]);
     return upper;
   }
```

Similarly, here we convert each character as necessary to uppercase. We build up a resulting output string through repeated concatenation.

```
Console.WriteLine("Enter Lines until cntrl-z:");
while ((data = Console.ReadLine()) != null) {
   Console.WriteLine(ToUpperString(data));
   Console.WriteLine("alphabetic characters = {0}",
                     CountLetters(data));
}
```

By typing Ctrl-z on a new line and hitting Enter, ReadLine() returns
null. We could also end the program with Ctrl-c. Otherwise each line is
processed as a string.

9.6   CONSOLE INPUT FOR AN ARRAY

It is cumbersome to constantly request arguments for array processing
from the console. Thus far, we have used one new line per argument. It is
more convenient to allow multiple arguments in one line. We accomplish
this using some additional methods taken from class String.

In file ReadArray.cs

```
// Use string and get multiple arguments

using System;

class ReadArray {
   public static void Main()
   {
      int[] idata = new int[10];
      int i = 0;

      char[] separate = new char[]{','};
      Console.WriteLine("Enter up to 10 " +
                        "comma-separated integers:");

      string data = Console.ReadLine();
```

```
        foreach (string arg in data.Trim().Split(separate )) {
          idata[i] = int.Parse(arg);
          Console.WriteLine(idata[i]);
          ++i;
        }
      }
}
```

Sample output of this program is

```
Enter upto 10 comma separated
ints
1,3,5,7,9
1
3
5
7
9
```

Dissection of the *ReadArray* Program

■ `int[] idata = new int[10];`

  A 10-element `int` array is created.

■ `char[] separate = new char[]{','};`
  `Console.WriteLine("Enter up to 10 " +`
  `              "comma-separated integers:");`

  The input is to be separated by the character comma. Notice that we create an array of the characters to be used to separate input values.

```
string data = Console.ReadLine();
foreach (string arg in data.Trim().Split(separate )) {
  idata[i] = int.Parse(arg);
  Console.WriteLine(idata[i]);
  ++i;
}
```

The line of values entered at the console is placed in the string `data`. We use the class `String` method `Split()` to break up the string into substrings. The break occurs after each comma. We use the class `String` method `Trim()` to squeeze out white space.

9.7   FILES

File I/O is handled by a variety of `Stream` classes. Here is a very simple example where a file is opened for reading and is copied. This example relies on two standard types, `File` and `Stream`. Both files reside in the current directory. Nothing is displayed during program execution.

In file OutToFile.cs

```
// Read and write text files in current directory
using System;
using System.IO;

class OutToFile {
  public static void Main()
  {
    Stream inF = File.OpenRead("test.txt");
    Stream outF = File.OpenWrite("result.txt");
    int bytesRead = 0;
    byte [] buffer = new byte[1024];
    while ((bytesRead = inF.Read(buffer, 0, 1024)) > 0 )
      outF.Write(buffer, 0, bytesRead);
    inF.Close();
    outF.Close();
  }
}
```

This program copies the *test.txt* file into a file named *result.txt*. If result.txt does not exist, it is created; If it does exist, it is overwritten. This program reads a file as a series of bytes. Such a file is known as a binary file.

Dissection of the *OutToFile* Program

■`using System.IO;`

This statement is needed to access the `Stream` and `File` classes.

■`Stream inF = File.OpenRead("test.txt");`

The `Stream inF` is constructed to have read access to the file `test.txt`. The file needs to be available on the local directory. Otherwise, you should use a full file path name such as: `C:\PrC#\test.txt`. The file must exist and be readable, or else `OpenRead()` fails. It then throws an appropriate exception. This is explained in the next chapter.

■`Stream outF = File.OpenWrite("result.txt");`

The `Stream outF` is constructed to have write access to the file `result.txt`. The file is written to the local directory. Otherwise, you should use a full file path name such as: `C:\PrC#\result.txt`. If the file exists and is not writable, `OpenWrite()` fails. It then throws an appropriate exception. If the file does not exist, it is created.

■`while ((bytesRead = inF.Read(buffer, 0, 1024)) > 0 )`
   `outF.Write(buffer, 0, bytesRead);`

This `Stream Read()` method has three arguments. The first is an array of bytes that are read into. This is called a *buffer*. The second is the position in the file to start reading from. The third is the buffer size. The number of bytes actually read is returned to the `int` variable `bytesRead`. Each buffer is output to the `Stream outF`. This continues until an end-of-file is encountered.

■`inF.Close();`
`outF.Close();`

It is good programming to close both `Stream`s. On many operating systems this is a critical resource.

Important properties found in `Stream` are shown in Table 9.4 and `Stream` instance methods are shown in Table 9.5.

Table 9.4	Public Stream Properties
`Null`	Redirect output to a dummy stream: subsequent stream operations return without doing anything
`CanRead`	Indicates if read supported
`CanSeek`	Indicates if seek supported
`CanWrite`	Indicates if write supported
`Length`	Stream length in bytes
`Position`	Gets or sets position within stream

Table 9.5	Stream Instance Methods
`Flush()`	Clears the buffer or if no buffer exists, does nothing
`Read()`	Reads bytes from the stream and advances the position by the number of bytes read
`ReadByte()`	Reads a byte from the stream or -1 if at the end of the stream
`Seek()`	Sets the position within stream
`SetLength()`	Sets the length of stream
`ToString()`	Returns a string that represents the current `Object`
`Write()`	Writes bytes to the stream and advances the position by the number of bytes written
`WriteByte()`	Writes a byte to the current position in the stream

Some methods and properties in `File` are shown in Table 9.6. Note that the `File` methods are all `static`, and thus use `File.`*methodname*`()` instead of using the stream name as do the instance methods found in `Stream`.

Table 9.6	Some File Static Methods
`Open()`	Returns a `FileStream` for reading and writing, depending on permissions
`OpenRead()`	Returns a `FileStream` for reading
`OpenWrite()`	Returns a `FileStream` for reading and writing
`Delete()`	Deletes the named file
`Copy()`	Copies the named file
`Create()`	Creates a file and returns a `FileStream`
`CreateText()`	Creates a text file and returns a `StreamWriter`
`OpenText()`	Returns an associated `StreamReader`
`OpenWrite()`	Returns an associated `FileStream`
`Move()`	Moves and renames the file

9.8   TEXT FILES

Much of file I/O is working with text. This is especially easy to do with the derived `Stream` classes `StreamReader` and `StreamWriter`. Here is an idiomatic example where a file is copied and double-spaced.

This program expects command-line arguments. Command-line arguments can be passed as `string` arguments to `Main()`.

In file DoubleSpaceFile.cs

```
// A program to double-space a file.
// Usage: executable f1 f2
// f1 must be present and readable
// f2 must be writable if it exists

using System;
using System.IO;
```

```
class DoubleSpaceFile {
  public static
  void DoubleSpace(StreamReader f, StreamWriter t)
  {
    int  c;

    while ((c = f.Read()) != -1) {
      t.Write((char)c);
      if ((char)c == '\n')
        t.Write((char)c);
    }
  }

  public static void Main(string[] args)
  {
    if (args.Length != 2) {
      Console.Error.WriteLine("\nUsage:" +
          " prog.exe infile outfile");
      return;
    }
    StreamReader strIn = new StreamReader(args[0]);
    StreamWriter strOut = new StreamWriter(args[1]);

    DoubleSpace(strIn, strOut);
    strIn.Close();
    strOut.Close();
  }
}
```

Nothing is output to the screen, and the input file is duplicated to the output file with each line of the original file being followed by an additional blank line. Note that this program takes its file names from the command-line arguments. If you are using an integrated development environment (IDE), you will need to set the command-line arguments by selecting options within the IDE. The instructions for Visual Studio for this are given in Section D.10, *Compile and Command-Line Options*, on page 556.

Dissection of the *DoubleSpaceFile* Program

■`public static`
`void DoubleSpace(StreamReader f, StreamWriter t)`

This method is a typical file manipulation method idiomatic of much of file processing. In this case, the input stream is processed with the results going to an output stream. The streams are tied to files.

■`while ((c = f.Read()) != -1) {`

Much of file processing is handled one character at a time. The expression `f.Read()` returns as -1 when the stream can no longer be read. Otherwise, it returns with a nonzero value and reads into `c` the character value, including white space characters.

■`t.Write((char)c);`
`  if ((char)c == '\n')`
`    t.Write((char)c);`

The loop places each character into the output file. It tests each character for being a newline. Where a newline is found, it outputs a second newline, thus double-spacing the file.

■`public static void Main(string[] args)`
`  {`
`    if (args.Length != 2) {`
`      Console.Error.WriteLine("\nUsage:"" +`
`          " prog.exe infile outfile");`
`      return;`
`  }`

This is idiomatic for generating an executable that utilizes command-line arguments. The resulting code would be something like

 doublespacefile myInput myOutput

Here, the expectation is that there are three strings on the command line: the name of the executable, followed by the input and output file names. The string *doublespacefile* is discarded under Windows and the argument *myInput* is placed in `args[0]` and the argument *myOutput* is placed in `args[1]`. This correct usage is tested by `Main()`.

```
StreamReader strIn = new StreamReader(args[0]);
StreamWriter strOut = new StreamWriter(args[1]);
```

The declarations of the two streams cause constructor invocation to properly open these files.

```
DoubleSpace(strIn, strOut);
strIn.Close();
strOut.Close();
```

Now the DoubleSpace() method is invoked. After it processes the streams, it closes them.

9.9   AN EXAMPLE: COUNTING WORDS

The following program counts the number of words coming from an existing file. This is a nice example of several themes emphasized in our text. First there is the use of structured programming. We use a problem decomposition that allows us to code each task as a small method. We make heavy use of library methods and library objects. Good software engineering practice is to use standard libraries whenever possible.

The program illustrates ideas discussed in this and the previous sections. Remember that this program expects a command-line argument for the input file. (See Section D.10, *Compile and Command-Line Options*, on page 556.)

In file WordCount.cs

```
// A program to count words in a file.
// Usage: executable f1
// f1 must be present and readable

using System;
using System.IO;
```

```
class WordCount {
  public static int FoundNextWord(StreamReader strIn)
  {
    int  c;
    int   wordSize = 0;

    while ((c = strIn.Read()) != -1)
      if (!char.IsWhiteSpace((char)c))
        break;
      if (c == -1)
        return 0;
      else ++wordSize;

    while (((c = strIn.Read()) != -1)  &&
           (char.IsLetterOrDigit((char)c)))
        ++wordSize;
    return wordSize;
  }

  public static int CharCount(StreamReader strIn)
  {
    int  c;
    int   fileSize = 0;

    while ((c = strIn.Read()) != -1)
      ++fileSize;
    return fileSize;
  }

  public static void Main(string[] args)
  {
    if (args.Length != 1) {
      Console.Error.WriteLine("\nUsage:  prog.exe infile ");
      return;
    }
    StreamReader strIn = new StreamReader(args[0]);

    int  wordCnt = 0;

    while (FoundNextWord(strIn) > 0)
      ++wordCnt;
```

```
    Console.WriteLine("word count is " + wordCnt);
    strIn = new StreamReader(args[0]);

    Console.WriteLine("char count is " + CharCount( strIn));
    strIn.Close();
  }
}
```

We used a preliminary version of the first three paragraphs of this chapter as the input file. The output is

```
word count is 152
char count is 869
```

Dissection of the CharCount() and WordCount() Methods

■
```
public static int CharCount(StreamReader strIn)
{
   int   c;
   int    fileSize = 0;

   while ((c = strIn.Read()) != -1)
     ++fileSize;
   return fileSize;
}
```

The Read() method is available for most forms of Stream types. Here is the standard idiom of iterating up to the guard, or sentinel, value -1.

■
```
strIn = new StreamReader(args[0]);

Console.WriteLine("char count is " + CharCount( strIn));
strIn.Close();
```

We use a command-line string, expected to be the name of a file opened for reading. It is a good practice to close such streams after they are used. Here it is unnecessary in that the program would terminate and the system would close the file.

```
■public static int FoundNextWord(StreamReader strIn)
```

The argument type `StreamReader` and the name `strIn` show that this method is expected to read from an input stream.

```
■while ((c = strIn.Read()) != -1)
    if (!char.IsWhiteSpace((char)c))
      break;
   if (c == -1)
      return 0;
   else ++wordSize;
```

This method looks for and computes the length of the next word. If there are no more words, the word length is returned as zero. The `struct Char` method `IsWhiteSpace()` is used to determine that you are at the end of a word.

```
■while (((c = strIn.Read()) != -1)  &&
        (char.IsLetterOrDigit((char)c)))
     ++wordSize;
   return wordSize;
```

Contiguous characters that are letters or digits are defined to be allowed in words. Notice the `while` expression is a short-circuited "logical and" that first tests if the end-of-file is read.

9.10   NETWORK I/O

This is an advanced section and might be omitted on first reading. It uses exception handling that is discussed in the next chapter. Sockets can be used for communication across different machines. Like files, they can be attached to streams. Sockets make sophisticated communication protocols relatively simple once you know how to make the connection.

The `System.Net.Sockets` namespace provides the Windows Sockets interface for access to the network. `NetworkStream` provides the underlying stream of data for network access. `Socket` uses the Berkeley sockets interface.

In writing a network I/O program, we need two pieces: a server-side program that distributes the information and a client-side program that receives the information.

Here we show the server program.

In file SocketsUse.cs

```csharp
// A server program to use sockets to copy over the net
using System;
using System.IO;
using System.Net.Sockets;

class SocketsUse {
  public static void Main(string[] args)
  {
    SocketsUse app = new SocketsUse();
    app.Run();
  }

  private void Run()
  {
    TcpListener myListener = new TcpListener(65010);
    // must synch
    myListener.Start();

    while (true) {
      Socket client = myListener.AcceptSocket();
      if (client.Connected)   {
        Console.WriteLine("Client is on ");
        SendFile(client);
        Console.WriteLine("Client is off ");
        client.Close();
        break;
      }
    }
  }
```

```
private void SendFile(Socket client)
{
  string data = null;
  NetworkStream strIn = new NetworkStream(client);
  StreamWriter strOut = new StreamWriter(strIn);
  StreamReader stxt = new StreamReader("test.txt");
  do { data = stxt.ReadLine();
    if (data != null) {
      Console.WriteLine("Sending " + data);
      strOut.WriteLine(data);
      strOut.Flush();
    }
  } while (data != null);
  stxt.Close();

  strIn.Close();
  strOut.Close();
}
}
```

We have a file, *test.txt*, which is echoed in the output on the MyClient side.

```
Client is on
first line to send
second line to send
third and final line to send
Client is off
```

Dissection of the *SocketsUse* Server-Side Program

■TcpListener myListener = new TcpListener(65010);

Here, the client and server use a port 65010 as their transmission vehicle. A port number is a way to identify a specific process to which a network message is to be forwarded when it arrives at a server. It is a 16-bit integer that is put in the header of the message. Using a Socket is similar to using a file. It is a source of text to read or write.

```
myListener.Start();
```

Start() initializes a Socket and starts listening for a connection request.

```
while (true) {
   Socket client = myListener.Accept();
   if (client.Connected)    {
      Console.WriteLine("Client is on ");
      SendFile(client);
      Console.WriteLine("Client is off ");
      client.Close();
      break;
   }
}
```

An apparent infinite loop. It keeps waiting for the Socket client to accept a request. Once client.Connected is set true, the client can send the file "test.txt" across the network. As with files, we also should perform a Close() on a Socket. The break gets us out of the "infinite loop".

```
private void SendFile(Socket client)
{
   string data = null;
   NetworkStream strIn = new NetworkStream(client);
   StreamWriter strOut = new StreamWriter(strIn);
   StreamReader stxt = new StreamReader("test.txt");
```

NetWorkStream is another class derived from Stream. As with files we have the ability to read and write.

```
do { data = stxt.ReadLine();
   if (data != null) {
      Console.WriteLine("Sending " + data);
      strOut.WriteLine(data);
      strOut.Flush();
   }
} while (data != null);
```

Here, each line of text is read line by line into data.

Here is the client side program:

In file MyClient.cs

```
// Client to use sockets to copy over the net
using System;
using System.IO;
using System.Net.Sockets;

class MyClient {

  public static void Main(string[] args)
  {
    TcpClient myServer = null;
    try {
      myServer = new TcpClient("Sparepc", 65010);
      //"ip-address ok"
    }
    catch  {
      Console.Error.WriteLine("Failed connect to Sparepc");
    }
    Console.WriteLine(myServer);

    NetworkStream netStream = myServer.GetStream();
    StreamReader strin = new StreamReader(netStream);

    try {
      string data;
      do {
        data = strin.ReadLine();
        Console.WriteLine(data);
      } while (data != null);
    }
    catch  {
      Console.Error.WriteLine("Read exception: myServer");
    }
    netStream.Close();
  }
}
```

The *SocketsUse* program is sending text to the client. There are several advanced concepts here that are left for the more advanced reader to test.

The output of this program on the MyClient side is

```
System.Net.Sockets.TcpClient
first line to send
second line to send
third and final line to send
```

Dissection of the *MyClient* Program

```
■TcpClient myServer = null;          // need here for scope
 try {
   myServer = new TcpClient("Sparepc", 65010);
   //"ip-address ok"
 }
 catch  {
   Console.Error.WriteLine("Failed connect to Sparepc");
 }
 Console.WriteLine(myServer);
```

The client is the machine named Sparepc. This is assumed to be available over a LAN (local area net) to the server.

```
■NetworkStream netStream = myServer.GetStream();
 StreamReader strin = new StreamReader(netStream);

 try {
   string data;
   do {
     data = strin.ReadLine();
     Console.WriteLine(data);
   } while (data != null);
 }
```

The server retrieves text from the client using the method ReadLine() and prints it as a string to its console.

9.11 SOFTWARE ENGINEERING: I/O

Well-written I/O involves prompting and testing and echoing the data. When writing code you must assume that the user knows only what is being asked at the console. We have already seen one common form of I/O prompt by `Main()`:

```
if (args.Length != 1) {
  Console.Error.WriteLine("\nUsage: prog.exe infile ");
  return;
}
```

Here we exit the program if the user gives an inappropriate list of arguments and we inform the user of the correct usage. The user can now re-execute the program with correct command-line arguments.

Frequently when inputting data we use the wrong format. Try inputting text when an integer or a double is expected. The system aborts with an error message mentioning an appropriate exception. In Chapter 10, *Exceptions and Program Correctness*, we show you how to write your own exception handlers that can make I/O more forgiving for the naive user.

9.12 DR. P'S PRESCRIPTIONS

- Remember GIGO—garbage in, garbage out.

- Input should be prompted for and checked by echoing.

- Output should be easily readable by a user of the program who does not have source code available.

- Provide overridden `ToString()` methods in classes.

Garbage in, garbage out is one of the prime axioms of computation. This implies that the program must check input as rigorously as possible. I/O is critical to the user of your program. Without meaningful I/O, the program is useless. In this text, we have kept many of the examples simple, and the text programs assume that a user enters meaningful data. In real-world programs, the user interface has to be robust. This implies that the user is prompted for appropriate data. The program tests that the input is what the user intended by asking the user to confirm that the data is correct. In the case of incorrect data, the user is allowed to re-enter new data.

Output needs to be formatted in a readable manner. Think in terms of the naive user being able to read the output without having to understand any detail of the program or algorithm.

There is an expectation in the C# community that any user-defined type has overridden the ToString() method. This design consistency is a trait of a good object-oriented programmer.

9.13   C# COMPARED WITH JAVA AND C++

In C++, file I/O is handled by including *fstream*, which contains the classes ofstream and ifstream for output and input file-stream creation and manipulation. The following program is the C++ version of the *DoubleSpaceFile* program found in Section 9.8, *Text Files*, on page 397, and it uses both the *fstream* and the *cstdlib* C++ libraries:

In file doubleSpaceFile.cpp

```cpp
// A program to double-space a file.
// Usage: executable f1 f2
// f1 must be present and readable
// f2 must be writable if it exists

#include <fstream>
#include <cstdlib>
using namespace std;

void double_space(ifstream& f, ofstream& t)
{
  char   c;

  while (f.get(c)) {
    t.put(c);
    if (c == '\n')
      t.put(c);
  }
}
```

```
int main(int argc, char** argv)
{
  if (argc != 3) {
    cout << "\nUsage: " << argv[0]
         <<  "  infile  outfile" << endl;
    exit(1);
  }

  ifstream  f_in(argv[1]);
  ofstream  f_out(argv[2]);

  if (!f_in) {
    cerr << "cannot open " << argv[1] << endl;
    exit(1);
  }
  if (!f_out) {
    cerr << "cannot open " << argv[2] << endl;
    exit(1);
  }
  double_space(f_in, f_out);
}
```

Notice how C++ uses the overloaded shift operators << and >> to perform I/O. These are overloaded for class types to provide correct type-safe behavior.

Now we present the *DoubleSpaceFile* program in Java.

In file DoubleSpaceFile.java

```
// Double-spacing a Java file

import java.io.*;

class DoubleSpaceFile {
  public static void Main(String[] args)
    throws java.io.IOException
  {
    if (args.length != 2) {
      System.out.println("\nUsage: DoubleSpaceFile " +
                         "infile outfile");
      System.exit(0);
    }
    BufferedReader input =
      new BufferedReader(new FileReader(args[0]));
```

```
PrintWriter out =
  new PrintWriter(new FileWriter(args[1]));

String line = input.readLine();
while (line != null) {
  out.println(line);
  out.println();
  line = input.readLine();
  }
 }
}
```

Java has type-safe I/O but does not have operator overloading. In Java, most output to the terminal is done using `println()`, as we discussed in Section 2.9, *C# Compared with Java and C++*, on page 70. Java also has the GUI library *Swing*, which is discussed extensively in *Java by Dissection* by Ira Pohl and Charlie McDowell (Addison-Wesley 1999), Chapters 7 and 8.

The simplest way to write text to a file requires the use of two different classes—`PrintWriter` and `FileWriter`—both from the standard package `java.io`. The class `PrintWriter` has the familiar methods `Print()` and `println()` that we've been using to write to the console. To create a `PrintWriter` object that is associated with a particular file, we must first create a `FileWriter` object for that file.

Why do we need the two classes `PrintWriter` and `FileWriter`? The reason is that the Java I/O package is designed to support many different types of input/output processing. Think of the classes in the package as building blocks. By assembling the correct set of building blocks, you can meet many different I/O processing needs. You can use the class `File-Writer` to write a stream of text characters into a file, but the methods in `FileWriter` are fairly primitive and support only the writing of text from `string`, `char`, and `char[]` values. The class `PrintWriter` from the same package can generate a stream of text characters from any value. The primary methods in class `PrintWriter` are the familiar `print()` and `println()` used for writing to the console. By passing a `FileWriter` object to the constructor of a `PrintWriter`, you are logically creating a sequence or pipeline of processing steps.

You can use the class `PrintWriter` to create text streams that go somewhere other than to a file. For example, you can also use a `PrintWriter` to write over a network or to write to a character array. The output of the `PrintWriter` is sent to the stream specified in the constructor. In this case, it is a `FileWriter`.

SUMMARY

■ Two standard console output objects are `Console.Out` and `Console.Error`. Both can be used in much the same way. The chief use of `Console.Error` is to continue to print to console when `Console.Out` is redirected to a file.

■ The `Write()` and `WriteLine()` methods are overloaded to take a format string followed by a list of arguments. First, a list of arguments of arbitrary length can be printed, and second, the printing is controlled by simple conversion specifications, or formats. The methods deliver the character stream to the standard output file `Out`, which is normally connected to the screen. The argument list has two parts:

control_string and *other_arguments*

■ To produce a `Format()` method we need to inherit from the interface `IFormattable`. The method signature is `Format(string format, IServiceObjectProvider sop)`.

■ File I/O is handled by using `Stream`, which is a class for output and input file-stream creation and manipulation. You can open a file with `File.Open("filename")`. Much of file I/O is working with text. This is especially easy to do with the derived `Stream` classes `StreamReader` and `StreamWriter`.

REVIEW QUESTIONS

1. List three format characters and their uses.

2. How is file redirection accomplished on the command line?

3. In the example

   ```
   Console.Write("He sells {0} peas for {1:C}", 3, 1.47);
   ```

   What gets printed?

4. To open a file for reading call the method _____.

5. The class `String` method `Split()` has an array of `char` as a parameter, which is used to _____.

6. Sockets can be used for communication across _____.

7. In `Main(string[] args)`, the parameter `args` is gotten from _____.

8. The term GIGO stands for _____.

EXERCISES

1. Read an array of up to 10 integers from the console and compute the median.

2. Read an array of 100 integers with 10 per line from the console and compute the median. For more credit make the program flexible as to how many values are read from a single line and how many overall values are requested.

3. Read an array of doubles from the console and compute the maximum and minimum.

4. Read a line and split it into an array of strings where the separator is a comma. Use this array of inputted arguments to be parsed to different expected and typed variables. So `"Enter an int, followed by two doubles and a bool:"` could be the prompt and the system would internally assign them to variables `i`, `x`, `y` and `flag` and print each value.

5. Write an array of strings to a file named *strings.txt*. Initialize the array with the four strings `"I am"`, `"a text"`, `"file written"`, and `"to strings.txt"`.

6. Create an array of strings that receive their input from the file *save.txt*. Specify the number of strings by asking the user to enter the number of lines to be read. Echo the strings read to the console.

7. Redo the preceding exercise to end when the input is a special sentinel string. For example, you may use ### as the sentinel.

8. Write a program that prints 1,000 random numbers to a file.

9. Write a program to read 1,000 random numbers in the range 0 to 1 from a file and plot their distribution, writing it to the file *stats.txt*. Divide the interval from 0 to 1 into tenths and count the numbers that fall into each tenth. A fairly even distribution gives you some confidence in their randomness.

10. Modify the preceding two exercises to allow the user to specify the number of random numbers and the name of the file on the command line. Store the number of generated numbers as the first entry in the file.

11. Read a text file and write it to a target text file, changing all lowercase to uppercase and double-spacing the output text.

12. Modify the program in the previous exercise to number each nonblank line.

13. Write a class `Dollar`. Have its `ToString()` method print a number such as 12345.67 as $12,345.67.

14. Write a program that reads a text file and computes the relative frequency of each of the letters of the alphabet. You can use an array of length 26 to store the number of occurrences of each letter. You can use `ToLower()` to convert uppercase letters. Subtracting "a" then gives you a value in the range 0 to 25, inclusive, which you can use to index into the array of counts.

15. Run the program from the previous exercise on several large text files and compare the results. This information can be used to break a simple substitution code. Such a code replaces one letter with a second letter, such as replacing all "A"s by "F"s.

16. Write a program to number the lines in a file. The input file name should be passed to the program as a command-line argument. The program should write to the console. Each line in the input file should be written to the output file with the line number and a space prepended. The program should write the line numbers as right-adjusted. The following output is *not* acceptable:

```
. . . . .
9 This is line nine.
10 This is line ten.
```

17. Our *DoubleSpaceFile* program in Section 9.8, *Text Files*, on page 397, can be invoked with the command

    DoubleSpaceFile infile outfile

    But if *outfile* exists, it is overwritten; this is potentially dangerous. Rewrite the program so that it writes to the console instead. Then the program can be invoked with the command

    DoubleSpaceFile infile > outfile

    This program design is safer. Of all the system commands, only a few are designed to overwrite a file. After all, nobody likes to lose a file by accident.

18. Rewrite the *DoubleSpaceFile* program from Section 9.8, *Text Files*, on page 397, to prompt the user for input and output file names if they are not present on the command line. Additionally, if the output file name already exists, prompt to ask for an alternate file name or permission to overwrite the current file.

19. Write the method `Getwords(in, k, words)` so that it reads k words from a file using the input stream `in` and places them in the string `words`, separated by newlines. The method should return the number of words successfully read and stored in `words`. Write a program to test your method.

20. Write a program that displays a file on the screen 20 lines at a time. The input file should be given as a command-line argument. The program should display the next 20 lines after a carriage return has been typed. (This is an elementary version of the Unix *more* utility.)

21. Modify the program you wrote in the previous exercise. Your program should display one or more files given as command-line arguments. Also, allow for a command-line option of the form -*n*, where *n* is a positive integer specifying the number of lines that are to be displayed at one time.

22. Write a program called *Search* that searches for patterns. If the command

    Search hello myFile

    is given, then the string pattern *hello* is searched for in the file *myFile*. Any line that contains the pattern is printed. (This program is an elementary version of the Unix *grep* utility.)

23. (*Java*) In the following Java example, we demonstrate how to detect an EOF with the standard Java class `BufferedReader`. The program opens the file specified on the command line and echoes its contents to the console. Rewrite this code as C#.

```
// Echo file contents to the screen
// Java by Dissection page 365.

import java.io.*;
class MyEcho {
  public static void main(string[] args)
                    throws IOException
  {
    if (args.length < 1) {
      System.out.println("Usage: " +
                    "java Echo filename");
      System.exit(0);
    }

    BufferedReader input =
      new BufferedReader(new FileReader(args[0]));
    string line = input.readLine();
    while (line != null) {
      System.out.println(line);
      line = input.readLine();
    }
  }
}
```

EXCEPTIONS AND PROGRAM CORRECTNESS

This chapter describes exception handling in C#. *Exceptions* are generally unexpected error conditions. Normally, these conditions terminate the user program with a system-provided error message. An example is floating-point divide-by-zero. Usually, the system aborts the running program. C# allows the programmer to attempt to recover from these conditions and to continue program execution.

Assertions are program checks that force error exits when correctness is violated. One point of view is that an exception is based on a breakdown of a contractual guarantee between the provider of the code and the user of the code. (See Section 12.2, *ADTs: Encapsulation and Data Hiding*, on page 496.) In this model, the user needs to guarantee that the conditions for applying the code exist, and the provider needs to guarantee that the code works correctly under these conditions. In this methodology, assertions enforce the various guarantees.

10.1　USING THE Assert() METHOD

Program correctness can be viewed in part as a proof that the computation terminated with correct output, dependent on correct input. The user of the computation had the responsibility of providing correct input. This was a *precondition*. The computation, if successful, satisfied a *postcondition*. Providing a fully formal proof of correctness is ideal but is not usually done. Nevertheless, such assertions can be monitored at runtime to provide very useful diagnostics. Indeed, the discipline of thinking out appropriate assertions frequently causes the programmer to avoid bugs and pitfalls.

The standard library class `Debug` provides a method `Assert()`, which is invoked as

Assert(boolean expression, message string);

If the *expression* evaluates as `false`, execution contains a diagnostic output. The assertions are enabled if the preprocessor variable `DEBUG` is defined.

To access these diagnostics, it is customary to provide a listener. The following example shows how all this is done.

In file AssertSqRoot.cs

```
#define DEBUG
// Simple assertion   compile with csc /r:system.dll
using System;
using System.Diagnostics;

class AssertSqRoot {
  public static void Main()
  {
    Debug.Listeners.Clear();
    Debug.Listeners.Add(new
                TextWriterTraceListener(Console.Out));

    double x;
    string data;

    Console.WriteLine("Enter a positive Double:");
    data = Console.ReadLine();
    x = double.Parse(data);
    Console.WriteLine(x);
    Debug.Assert(x > 0, "Non-positive value");
    Console.WriteLine("square root is " + Math.Sqrt(x));
  }
}
```

If we enter –2.0 instead of a positive integer, the output of this program is

```
Enter a positive Double:
-2.0
-2
Fail: Non-positive value
square root is NaN
```

Dissection of the *AssertSqRoot* Program

■ #define DEBUG

A standard preprocessing directive that defines an identifier. These are stylistically written as all capitals. For debugging to be activated, this identifier must be defined.

■ ```
// Simple assertion compile with csc /r:system.dll
using System;
using System.Diagnostics;
```

Need to load in the *system.dll* to have working diagnostics. The Debug class is in the System.Diagnostics namespace.

■ ```
Debug.Listeners.Clear();
Debug.Listeners.Add(new
      TextWriterTraceListener(Console.Out));
```

The Listeners object gets these debugging messages and prints them to the console. Other possibilities could be placing them in an error text file or printing to a GUI.

■ Debug.Assert(x > 0, "Non-positive value");

This assert tests a boolean condition and if false places the string as a message to be heard by the Listeners object. Unlike in C and C++, an assert does not automatically abort the program.

The use of assertions replaces the ad hoc use of conditional tests with a more uniform methodology. The downside is that the assertion methodology does not provide a retry or other repair strategy to continue program execution.

10.2   C# EXCEPTIONS

C# has a standard class `System.Exception`. This is the object or the base class of an object that is thrown by the system or user when an error happens at runtime. C# has a context-sensitive exception-handling mechanism. The context for handling an exception is a `try` block. The handlers are declared at the end of a `try` block, using the keyword `catch`.

C# code can raise an exception in a `try` block by using the `throw` expression. The exception is handled by invoking an appropriate handler selected from a list found at the end of the handler's `try` block. An example of this follows.

In file SimpleThrow.cs

```
// Simple exception handling
using System;

class SimpleThrow {
  public static void Main()
  {
    try {
      double x;
      string data;
      Console.WriteLine("Enter Double:");
      data = Console.ReadLine();
      x = double.Parse(data);
      Console.WriteLine(x);
      if (x < 0)
        throw(new System.Exception());
      else Console.WriteLine("square root is "
                                  + Math.Sqrt(x));
    }
    catch(Exception e)
      { Console.WriteLine( "base class exception thrown "
        + e); }
  }
}
```

If we enter data that is not a `double`, the output of this program is

```
Enter Double:
-34,24
-3424
base class exception thrown System.Exception:
Exception of type System.Exception was thrown.
    at SimpleThrow.Main() in
c:\c#bd programs\ch10-except\simplethrow.cs:line 17
```

Dissection of the *SimpleThrow* Program

■`try {`
    `double x;`
    `string data;`

The `try` block is a scope in which an exception is thrown and caught.

■`if (x < 0)`
    `throw(new System.Exception());`
`else Console.WriteLine("square root is "`
                        `+ Math.Sqrt(x));`

Exceptions are frequently thrown when a value is out of range. Here a non-negative value is expected by the `method Sqrt()`. This exception is handled at the end of the enclosing `try` block.

■`}`
`catch(Exception e)`
    `{ Console.WriteLine( "base class exception thrown "`
        `+ e); }`

This `catch` is of the base class type `Exception` and so can handle an arbitrary exception. It is a minimal handler, in that it just prints a message. The `throw()` has an `Exception` argument and matches the `catch(Exception e)` signature. The `catch()` is called an exception handler.

10.3   THROWING EXCEPTIONS

Syntactically, *throw expressions* come in two forms:

```
throw expression
throw
```

The throw *expression* raises an exception. This expression must be an object of type Exception. The innermost try block in which an exception is raised is used to select the catch statement that processes the exception. The throw with no argument can be used inside a catch to *rethrow* the current exception. This throw is typically used when you want a second handler called from the first handler to further process the exception.

The expression thrown is a temporary object that persists until exception handling is completed. The throw causes the flow of control to exit the try block. This is called termination semantics. The expression is caught by a handler that may use this value, as follows:

In file ThrowAlways.cs

```
// Simple exception handling
using System;

class ThrowAlways {

  public static int ThrowMinus()
  {
    int  i = -1;                        // -1 forces exception
    if (i < 0)
      throw new Exception("i < 0 ");
    return i;
  }

  public static void Main()
  {
    try
      { ThrowMinus(); }
    catch(Exception e)
      { Console.WriteLine("exception caught " + e); }
  }
}
```

The `Exception` object created by `new Exception("i < 0")` persists until the handler with the integer signature `catch(Exception e)` exits and is available for use within the handler as its argument.

When executed with a computation that throws the exception, the output is as follows:

```
exception caught System.Exception: i < 0
at ThrowAlways.ThrowMinus() in
c:\c#bd programs\ch10-except\throwalways.cs:line 12
at ThrowAlways.Main() in
c:\c#bd programs\ch10-except\throwalways.cs:line 19
```

Dissection of the *ThrowAlways* Program

■`public static int ThrowMinus()`
```
{
  int  i = -1;                          // -1 forces exception
  if (i < 0)
    throw new Exception("i < 0 ");
  return i;
}
```

The `throw` expression has a simple syntax. It throws some `Exception` object. In this case the object contains a message. The idea is that `ThrowMinus()`, to be correct, must return an integer value greater or equal to zero. The `if` test, like an assertion, detects an incorrect computation and throws an exception that interrupts the normal flow of control for `ThrowMinus()`. Normal execution would have been to return a value `i` to the point in `Main()` where `ThrowMinus()` is called.

■`public static void Main()`
```
{
  try { ThrowMinus(); }
```

The `try` block is a scope within which an exception is caught. An exception, such as the `throw` inside `ThrowMinus()`, is caught at the end of the `try` block.

```
■catch(Exception e)
    { Console.WriteLine("exception caught " +e); }
```

A list of handlers, namely catch(*signature*) { *catch executable* },
comes at the end of the try block. The throw expression has a type,
which must match the catch signature. The output traces where the
exception happened. Also the message includes the text i < 0 that
was used to initialize the Exception object.

```
exception caught System.Exception: i < 0
at ThrowAlways.ThrowMinus() in
c:\c#bd programs\ch10-except\throwalways.cs:line 12
at ThrowAlways.Main() in
c:\c#bd programs\ch10-except\throwalways.cs:line 19
```

When a nested method throws an exception, the process stack is *unwound*
until an exception handler is found. This means that block exit from each
terminated local process causes automatic objects to be destroyed.

In file ThrowUnwind.cs

```
using System;

class ThrowUnwind {

  static int Throwi()
  {
    int  i = 0, j = 0;
    //.....
    throw new Exception("i = " + i.ToString());
    // Throwi() terminates with Exception object persisting
    // i and j are destroyed
    //.....
    return i;
  }
```

```
static void CallThrowi()
  {
    int  k = 0;
    //.....
    Throwi();
    // when Throwi() throws new Exception("i = " + i);
    // CallThrowi() exits
    // exception object from Throwi() persists
    // k is destroyed
    //.....
  }

  public static void Main()
  {
    try {
      CallThrowi();
    }
    catch(Exception e)
      { Console.WriteLine("exception caught " +e); }
  }
}
```

The output of this program is

```
exception caught System.Exception: i = 0
at ThrowUnwind.Throwi() in
c:\c#bd programs\ch10-except\throwunwind.cs:line 10
at ThrowUnwind.CallThrowi() in
c:\c#bd programs\ch10-except\throwunwind.cs:line 21
at ThrowUnwind.Main() in
c:\c#bd programs\ch10-except\throwunwind.cs:line 32
Press any key to continue
```

10.3.1   RETHROWN EXCEPTIONS

Using throw without an expression rethrows a caught exception. The catch that rethrows the exception cannot complete the handling of the existing exception. This catch passes control to the nearest surrounding try block, where a handler capable of catching the still-existing exception is invoked. The exception expression exists until all handling is completed. Control resumes after the outermost try block that last handled the rethrown expression.

An example of rethrowing of an exception follows.

In file Rethrow.cs

```csharp
// Rethrowing an exception
using System;

  class Rethrow {
  public static void ThrowMsg()
  {
    try {
    //·····
    throw new Exception("Thrown in ThrowMsg");;
    }
    catch(Exception e)
    {
    //····· do some work here
    Console.WriteLine("First caught " + e);
    throw;                                    // rethrown
    }
  }

  public static void Main()
  {
    try {
    //····· more code
    ThrowMsg();
    //·····
    }
    catch(Exception e)
      { Console.WriteLine("Exception recaught " + e); }
  }
}
```

The output from the two handlers is as follows:

```
First caught System.Exception: Thrown in ThrowMsg
    at Rethrow.ThrowMsg() in
c:\c#bd programs\ch10-except\rethrow.cs:line 11
Exception recaught System.Exception: Thrown in ThrowMsg
    at Rethrow.ThrowMsg() in
c:\c#bd programs\ch10-except\rethrow.cs:line 17
    at Rethrow.Main() in
c:\c#bd programs\ch10-except\rethrow.cs:line 25
```

The rethrown exception is the same persistent object that is handled by the nearest handler suitable for that type.

I don't understand why I have to put in this error detection code: My code is always perfect, the machine has infinite resources, and I'm quite sure the interface code is every bit as perfect as my own!

10.3.2 EXCEPTION EXPRESSIONS

Conceptually, the thrown expression *passes* information to the handlers. Frequently, the handlers do not need this information. For example, a handler that prints a message and aborts needs no information from its environment. However, the user might want additional information printed to select or to help decide the handler's action. In this case, it can be appropriate to package the information as an object derived from a preexisting Exception class.

```
class StackError : Exception {
public StackError(Stack s, string message)
.....
}
```

Now, throwing an expression using an object of type StackError can be more informative to a handler than just throwing expressions of simple types.

```
.....
throw StackError(stk, "out of bounds");
.....
```

Let us use these ideas to write a complete example.

In file StackError.cs

```
// Example of using an StackError object

using System;

class Stack {                          // extremely simple stack
  public  char[]  s = new char[100];
}

class StackError: Exception {
  public   StackError(Stack  s,  string message)
    { st = s; msg = message; }
  public   char TopEntry()  { return  st.s[99]; }
  public string Msg
    { set { msg = value; } get { return msg; } }
  private  Stack st;
  private  string msg;
}
```

```
class StackErrorTest {
  public static void  Main()
  {
    Stack stk = new Stack();
    stk.s[99] = 'z';                         //set for message
    try {
      throw new StackError(stk,"out of bounds");
    }
    catch(StackError se)
    {
      Console.WriteLine(se.Msg + " with last char "
            + se.TopEntry());
    }
  }
}
```

The output of this program is

```
out of bounds with last char
```

Dissection of the *StackError* Program

```
■class StackError: Exception {
 public   StackError(Stack  s,  string message)
   { st = s; msg = message; }
 public   char TopEntry()  { return  st.s[99]; }
 public string Msg
   { set { msg = value; } get { return msg; } }
```

We create a specialized object that is used in conjunction with stack errors. It bundles information within a single object. It allows us to have methods that can provide different pieces of information. It can be used as the base class for a hierarchy of exception objects.

```
■   private  Stack st;
   private  string msg;
}
```

The hidden-away data members are used for diagnostic purposes.

```
■throw StackError(stk,"out of bounds");
```

In `Main()` we throw our exception.

```
■ catch(StackError se)
    {
      Console.WriteLine(se.Msg + " with last char "
              + se.TopEntry());
    }
```

The `catch` uses the different `StackError` methods to provide diagnostic information.

10.3.3 Exception OBJECT STANDARD METHODS

Table 10.1 contains standard properties that every exception object has. We leave to the exercises the use of these properties.

Table 10.1	Exception Properties
HelpLink	Gets or sets link to associated help file
InnerException	Gets Exception instance that caused exception
Message	Text that describes the meaning of the exception
StackTrace	Tracks where the exception was called
Source	Application or object that generated exception
TargetSite	The method that threw this exception

10.4   try BLOCKS

Syntactically, a `try` block has the form

try
compound statement
handler list

The `try` block is the context for deciding which handlers are invoked on a raised exception. The order in which handlers are defined determines the order in which a handler for a raised exception of matching type is tried.

```
try {
  .....
  throw ("SOS");
  .....
  io_condition eof(argv[i]);
  throw (eof);
  .....
}
catch(MyException e) {.....}
catch(Exception e) {.....}
```

The following lists the conditions under which throw expressions match the catch handler type:

Throw Expression Matches Catch Handler Type

- If there is an exact match
- If there is a derived type of the public base-class handler type

It is an error to list handlers in an order that prevents them from being called. For example:

```
catch(BaseTypeError e)          // always on DerivedTypeError
catch(DerivedTypeError e)            // before BaseTypeError
```

A `try` block can be nested. If no matching handler is available in the immediate `try` block, a handler is selected from its immediately surrounding `try` block. If no handler that matches can be found, the default behavior is to print an exception message and terminate the program.

10.5   HANDLERS

Syntactically, a handler has the form

catch (*formal argument*)
compound statement

The catch looks like a method declaration of one argument without a return type. There is also a catch without any argument, which is a catch of last resort and handles any exception that is not handled by catches with signatures.

```
catch(MyException e)
{
  Console.WriteLine("Message from MyException" + e);
}

catch                              // default action to be taken
{
  Console.WriteLine("THAT'S ALL FOLKS.");
}
```

The handler is invoked by an appropriate throw expression. At that point, the try block is exited. The system calls clean-up methods that include destructors for any objects that were local to the try block. A partially constructed object has destructors invoked on any parts of it that are constructed subobjects. The program resumes at the statement after the try block.

10.5.1 finally CODE

The keyword finally after a try block introduces a block that is executed upon termination of the try block. It is executed even when an exception occurs. For example, you might want to close an open file regardless of whether a method has aborted or not. The finally clause lets you do this.

```
try { ..... }
finally {
//.....code to always be executed regardless of how
//.....the try block was executed
}
```

For all our listeners out there who may be unfamiliar with the new expansion team, the Silicon Valley Exceptions, we have to say that they don't have a running game at all. But they sure can catch and throw exceptionally well!

10.6 CONVERTING ASSERTIONS TO EXCEPTIONS

We revisit class Assert and use exceptions instead of assertions. Here we can see that the exception logic is more dynamic because the handlers can be more informed than with asserts. The asserts print an assertion failure message. Exception handlers can print arbitrary information and either abort the program or attempt to continue the program.

In file ExceptionSqRoot.cs

```
// Precondition assertions

public class ExAssert {
  public static void MyAssert(bool cond,
                              string message, Exception e)
  {
    if (!cond) {
      Console.Error.WriteLine(message);
      throw e;
    }
  }
}
```

This method provides an assertion test using the exception mechanism. If the boolean expression passed in for the parameter `cond` is `false`, a message is printed, and an exception is thrown. Let us write a `Main()` that tests these assertions.

In file ExceptionSqRoots.cs

```csharp
using System;

class ExceptionUse {
  public static void ConsoleSqrt()
  {
    double x;
    string data;
    Console.WriteLine("Enter a positive Double:");
    data = Console.ReadLine();
    x = double.Parse(data);
    Console.WriteLine(x);
    try {
      ExAssert.MyAssert(x > 0, "Non-positive value: x = "
                        + x.ToString(), new Exception());
     Console.WriteLine("square root is " + Math.Sqrt(x));
    }
    catch(Exception e){
      Console.WriteLine(e);
      ExceptionUse.ConsoleSqrt();
    }
  }

  public static void Main()
  {
    Console.WriteLine("Testing Square Roots ");
    ConsoleSqrt();
  }
}
```

The output of this program is

```
Testing Square Roots
Enter a positive Double:
23.55
23.55
square root is 4.85283422342037
```

In this version of our program for doing square roots, the program uses the exception mechanism to recursively call itself until the user enters an acceptable positive value at the terminal. Here we see how the exception-handling mechanism is used to retry the method and is preferable to an assertion mechanism that would require termination.

10.7 STANDARD EXCEPTIONS

C# provides a large number of standard exceptions, which derive from the base class Exception. An important derived class is System.Exception. For example, the exception type DivideByZeroException is thrown if there is a division by zero.

Here is a program that lets you test this behavior.

In file DivideByZero.cs

```
using System;

class DivideByZero {
  public static void Main()
  {
    int p = 1, q = 2;

    try {
      Console.WriteLine("p/q = " + p/q);
      q = 0;
      Console.WriteLine("p/q = " + p/q);
    }
    catch(Exception e) { Console.WriteLine(e); }
  }
}
```

This program prints:

```
p/q = 0
System.DivideByZeroException: Attempted to divide by zero.
    at DivideByZero.Main() in
c:\c#bd programs\ch10-except\dividebyzero.cs: line 13
```

The standard exceptions are derived from the base class `Exception`. Table 10.2 provides a partial list of standard exceptions and their uses.

Table 10.2	Standard Exception Classes
`SystemException`	Base class for the non-0 system exceptions
`ApplicationException`	Base class for users to provide application errors
`ArgumentException`	One or more method arguments are invalid
`ArgumentNullException`	Null passed but is disallowed
`ArgumentOutOfRangeException`	Not within allowed values
`ArithmeticException`	Unrepresentable or infinite value
`DivideByZeroException`	Self-explanatory
`IndexOutofRangeException`	Index outside of array bounds
`InvalidCastException`	Cast is disallowed
`IOException`	Base class in System.IO namespace for I/O exceptions
`NullReferenceException`	Attempt to dereference a null
`OutOfMemoryException`	Running out of system heap

When ordering catches, you must be sure to have a derived class exception occur earlier than its base class exception. For example, `OutOfMemoryException` is derived from `SystemException`.

10.8   SOFTWARE ENGINEERING: EXCEPTIONS

Paradoxically, error recovery is concerned chiefly with writing correct programs. Exception handling is about error recovery. Exception handling is also a transfer-of-control mechanism. The client/manufacturer model gives the manufacturer the responsibility of making software that produces correct output, given acceptable input. The question for the manufacturer is how much error detection and, conceivably, correction should be built in. The client is better served by fault-detecting libraries, which can be used in deciding whether to attempt to continue the computation.

If we throw an uncaught exception, it might blow up part of Moscow.

Error recovery is based on the transfer of control. Undisciplined transfer of control leads to chaos. In error recovery, one assumes that a condition has corrupted the computation, making it dangerous to continue—like driving a car after realizing that the steering mechanism is damaged. Useful exception handling is the disciplined recovery when damage occurs.

In most cases, programming that raises exceptions should print a diagnostic message and gracefully terminate. Special forms of processing, such as real-time processing and fault-tolerant computing, require that the system not go down. In these cases, heroic attempts at repair are legitimate.

What can be agreed on is that classes can usefully be provided with error conditions. In many of these conditions, the object has member values in illegal states—values it is not allowed to have. The system raises an exception for these cases, with the default action being program termination.

But what kind of intervention is reasonable to keep the program running? And where should the flow of control be returned? C# uses a termination model that forces the current `try` block to terminate. Under this regime, one retries the code, ignores the result, or substitutes a default result and continues. Retrying the code seems most likely to give a correct result.

Code is usually too thinly commented. It is difficult to imagine a program that would be too rich in assertions. Assertions and simple throws and catches that terminate the computation are parallel techniques. A well-thought-out set of error conditions detectable by the user of an ADT is an important part of a good design. An over-reliance on exception handling in normal programming, beyond error detection and termination, is a sign that a program was ill-conceived, with too many holes, in its original form.

When designing classes, an object's constructor can look like the following:

```
Object(arguments)
{
  if (illegal argument1)
    throw exception1;
  if (illegal argument2)
    throw exception2;
  .....                              // attempt to construct failed
}
```

The `Object` constructor now provides a set of thrown exceptions for an illegal state. The `try` block can now use the information to repair or to abort the incorrect operation.

```
try {
  // ..... fault-tolerant code
}
  catch(exception1) { /* fixup this case */ }
  catch(exception2) { /* fixup this case */ }
  .....
  catch(exceptionK) { /* fixup this case */ }
  // correct or repaired - state values are now legal
```

When many distinct error conditions are useful for the state of a given object, a class hierarchy can be used to create a selection of related types to be used as throw expressions.

```
class ObjectError: Exception {
  public ObjectError(arguments);       // capture useful info
  members that contain thrown expression state
  public  virtual void Repair()
    { Console.Error.WriteLine("Repair failed in Object"); }
}

ObjectErrorS1 : ObjectError {
  public ObjectErrorS1(arguments);
  added members that contain thrown expression state
  public override void Repair(); // override provides repair
}
.....                              // other derived error classes as needed
```

These hierarchies allow an appropriately ordered set of catches to handle exceptions in a logical sequence. Recall that a base-class type should come after a derived-class type in the list of `catch` declarations.

10.9   DR. P'S PRESCRIPTIONS

- Avoid the use of exceptions as a sophisticated transfer of control.

- Avoid using exceptions for continuing computations that have undiagnosed errors.

- Use exceptions and assertions to check both preconditions and postconditions.

- Program by contract, where exceptions guarantee the terms.

- Use exceptions to test if system resources are exhausted, unavailable, or corrupted.

- Use exceptions to provide soft, informative termination.

- Use exceptions to restart corrected computations.

Exceptions are often misused when they are used as a patch to fix code, much in the way the `goto` was used to hack changes to poorly designed programs. Exceptions are meant to detect errors; therefore, they should be used mostly to provide informed termination and soft failure.

Programming by contract is the ability of one part of the code to rely on guarantees from another part of the code. For example, to properly merge two lists, the merge code must rely on the input lists being ordered. Checking that the list is indeed in sort order is often done with assertions. The assertion methodology can be mimicked by exceptions that abort when guarantees are not met.

Exceptions should be thrown when requested resources are unavailable. The `OutOfMemoryException` exception thrown by `new` when it fails is an example of this approach. In such cases, there may be ways to add to the system resources, allowing the program to continue.

Unless program termination is unacceptable, as in mission-critical real-time systems, ad hoc error correction and program resumption should be avoided. Such unexpected conditions should be diagnosed and the code redone. Special techniques exist for mission-critical code.

10.10   C# COMPARED WITH JAVA AND C++

Java and C++ have exception-handling mechanisms that are integral to the language and are heavily used for error detection at runtime. The mechanisms are similar to that found in C#. An exception is thrown by a method when it detects an error condition. The following code robustly reads one positive integer from the console. If the user doesn't type an integer, he or she is prompted to try again.

In file ExceptionExample.cs

```
using System;
public class ExceptionExample {
  public static void Main()
  {
    int aNumber = 0;
    bool success = false;
    string data;

    Console.WriteLine("Type a positive integer.");
    while (!success) {
      try {
        data = Console.ReadLine();
        aNumber = int.Parse(data);
        if (aNumber <= 0)
          throw(new System.Exception());
        else
          success = true;
      }
      catch (Exception e) {
          Console.WriteLine(aNumber +
            " is not a positive integer. " );
          Console.WriteLine(e);
          Console.WriteLine ("Try again!" );
      }
    }
    Console.WriteLine("You typed " + aNumber);
                    // continue with code to process aNumber
  }
}
```

The output of this program is

```
Type a positive integer.
-5
-5 is not a positive integer.
System.Exception: Exception of type System.Exception was
thrown.
at ExceptionExample.Main() in
c:\c#bd programs\ch10-except\exceptionexample.cs:line 18
```

Here is the same program in C++.

In file exceptionExample.cpp

```cpp
#include <iostream>
using namespace std;

int main()
{
  int aNumber = 0;
  bool success = false;

  cout << "Type a positive integer." << endl;
  while (!success) {
    try {
      cin >> aNumber;
      if (aNumber <= 0)
        throw(aNumber);
      else
        success = true;
    }
    catch (...) {
      cout << aNumber << " is not a positive integer. "
           << endl;
      cout << "Try again!" << endl;
    }
  }
  cout << "You typed " << aNumber << endl;
}
```

This is similar to our previous C# program. Unlike C#, any expression type can be thrown, not just ones derived from `Exception`. C++ allows the signature `...` to mean accept any argument type. In most regards, C++ shares the logic and syntax of C# exception handling, though C++ does not allow a `finally` clause.

In file ExceptionExample.java

```java
import tio.*;

public class ExceptionExample {
  public static void Main(String[] args)
  {
    int aNumber = 0;
    boolean success = false;
    String inputString = "";

    System.out.println("Type an integer.");
    while (!success) {
      try {
        aNumber = Console.in.readInt();
        success = true;
      }
      catch (NumberFormatException e) {
        inputString = Console.in.readWord();
        System.out.println(inputString +
            " is not an integer. Try again!");
      }
    }
    System.out.println("You typed " + aNumber);
                    // continue with code to process aNumber
  }
}
```

In Java, an uncaught exception is handled by a default Java handler that issues a message and terminates the program. An exception is itself an object, which must be derived from the superclass `Throwable`.

In all three languages, exceptions are handled by invoking an appropriate *handler* picked from a list of handlers, or catches. These explicit catches occur at the end of an enclosing `try` block.

Incorrectly entered input is a common programming error. In robust programs, input should be tested to determine whether it is both syntactically and semantically correct. Frequently, good practice is to ask the user to confirm the value entered. The following Java loop does just that.

```java
while (confirm != 'Y') {
                             //   ..... ask for data in dollars
   System.out.println("Did you mean " + dollars);
   System.out.println("Please Enter Y or N:");
   confirm = Console.in.readChar();
}
```

This technique can be combined with the exception-handling methodology of the preceding examples.

SUMMARY

- Exceptions are generally unexpected error conditions. Normally, these conditions terminate the user program with a system-provided error message. An example is divide-by-zero.

- The standard library class `Debug` provides a method `Assert()`, which is invoked as

  `Assert(`*boolean expression, message string*`)`;

  If the *expression* is `false`, execution contains a diagnostic output. The assertions are enabled if the preprocessor variable `DEBUG` is defined.

- C# has a standard class `System.Exception`. This is the object or the base class of an object that is thrown by the system or user when an error happens at runtime.

- C# code can raise an exception by using the `throw` expression. The exception is handled by invoking an appropriate handler selected from a list of handlers found at the end of the handler's `try` block.

- The `throw` *expression* raises an exception in a `try` block. The `throw` with no argument may be used in a `catch` to rethrow the current exception. Syntactically, throws come in two forms:

  ```
  throw
  throw exception
  ```

■ Using `throw` without an expression rethrows a caught exception. The `catch` that rethrows the exception cannot complete the handling of the existing exception. This `catch` passes control to the nearest surrounding `try` block, where a handler capable of catching the still-existing exception is invoked. The exception expression exists until all handling is completed. Control resumes after the outermost `try` block that last handled the rethrown expression.

■ The `try` block is the context for deciding which handlers are invoked on a raised exception. The order in which handlers are defined determines the order in which a handler for a raised exception of matching type is tried. Syntactically, a `try` block has the form

```
try
```
compound statement
handler list

■ The `catch` looks like a method declaration of one argument without a return type. Syntactically, a handler has the form

```
catch  (formal argument)
```
compound statement

REVIEW QUESTIONS

1. True or false: In C#, `new` cannot throw an exception.

2. The context for handling an exception is a _____ block.

3. A standard exception class is _____ and is used for _____.

4. Handlers are declared at the end of a `try` block, using the keyword _____.

5. Name three standard exceptions provided by C# libraries.

6. What two actions should most handlers perform?

7. In the following example, what exception is thrown and why?

```
using System;
class DivideByZero {
  public static void Main()
  {
    int p = 1, q = 0;

    try {
      Console.WriteLine("p/q = " + p/q);
      q = 2;
      Console.WriteLine("p/q = " + p/q);
    }
    catch(Exception e) { Console.WriteLine(e);}
  }
}
```

8. In the code from the previous question, what is printed and why?

9. What does the expression `throw;` do?

10. What system exception is likely to happen for the following:
    `double []x = new double[HumongousNumber]; ?`

EXERCISES

1. The following bubble sort does not work correctly:

```
// Incorrect bubble sort

using System;
class BubbleSort {
  public static void Swap(int a, int b)
  {
    int  temp = a;

    a = b;
    b = temp;
  }
```

```
public static void Bubble(int []a, int size)
{
  int  i, j;

  for (i = 0; i != size; ++i)
    for (j = i ; j != size; ++j)
      if (a[j] < a [j + 1])
        Swap (a[j], a[j + 1]);
}

public static void  Main()
{
  int[] t = { 9, 4, 6, 4, 5, 9, -3, 1, 0, 12};

  Bubble(t, 10);
  for (int i = 0; i < t.Length; ++i)
    Console.Write( t[i] + '\t');
}
}
```

Place assertions in this code to test that it is working properly. Besides detecting errors, placing assertions in code as a discipline helps you to write a correct program. Correct the program.

2. Replace the assertions you wrote in the previous exercise with an equivalent version using exceptions.

3. Write a program that asks the user to enter a positive integer. Have it throw an exception when the user fails to enter a correct value. Have the handler write out the incorrect value and abort.

4. Rewrite the previous program to require the handler to ask the user for a correct value. The program should terminate after printing the correct value. Many programs try to ensure that input is failure-proof. This is an aspect of good software engineering.

5. The following code calls `Main()` recursively from the handler. Run it and explain its behavior when you enter several incorrect values first.

```
using System;
public class ExAssert {
  public static void Assert(bool cond, string message,
                              Exception e)
  {
    if (!cond) {
      Console.Error.WriteLine(message);
      throw e;
    }
  }
}

class ExAssertTest {
  public static void Main()
  {
    double x;
    string data;
    Console.WriteLine("Enter a positive Double:");
    data = Console.ReadLine();
    x = double.Parse(data);
    Console.WriteLine(x);
    try {
      ExAssert.Assert(x > 0, "Non-positive value: x = "
                        + x.ToString(), new Exception());
      Console.WriteLine("sqrt is " + Math.Sqrt(x));
    }
    catch(Exception e) { ExAssertTest.Main(); }
    Console.WriteLine("sqrt is " + Math.Sqrt(x));
  }
}
```

6. The following code segment reads a text file, one line at a time, into a string. Write code to avoid the exception that is thrown after the Read-Line() method sees an end-of-file.

```
while( true ){
   line = strIn.ReadLine();
   // Streamreader strIn connected to input file
   string[] word = line.Split(delims);
   // Split() is a method in class String
   foreach(string w in word){
      if (w == "")        // Split can produce empty strings
         continue;

      // process each subtring
      //.....
   }
}
```

Use this code in a try block to read a file of text, converted to words, into a Dictionary collection class.

7. Write a program that finds the roots of a quadratic $ax^2 + bx + c$. You need to compute b*b - 4*a*c and make sure it is non-negative. If not, throw an exception and compute its complex number roots. Discuss whether or not this is an appropriate scheme. How would you write the same code without exceptions? Why is that better?

8. Can you write a piece of code that throws the system exception for having run out of memory? What was the size of memory in bytes you needed to allocate to achieve this on your system?

9. Write a simple recursive function such as one that sums the elements of an integer array recursively. Try it on increasingly larger arrays until it throws an exception. What type exception do you expect it to throw?

10. Rewrite the class Person in Section 8.1, *A Derived Class*, on page 329, to have exceptions in any method that mutates the underlying data describing a person. It should make sure that the values used in a constructor are appropriate, and that properties and methods such as Age use appropriate values. For example, no person can have a negative age or be older than 123 years old. Discuss using exceptions versus assertions for these precondition and postcondition tests.

CONTAINER CLASSES

C ontainer classes are used to store and retrieve large amounts of data. We have made heavy use of the array container class. Many container classes are dynamic data structures, such as lists or stacks, which are able to expand and contract during a computation. In this chapter, we show how to implement a dynamic list and similar data structures. We also discuss the standard C# `ArrayList` class, which is an expandable container class.

The single most important difference between arrays and the list implementations we describe in this chapter is that the capacity of an array is fixed. If you need to change the size of a list implemented as an array, you have to create a new array, larger or smaller, and then copy the items from the old array to the new, resized array.

The list data structures we describe are called dynamic data structures because they can be resized readily. A second important characteristic of such data structures is that at least part of the data structure is implemented by a class that contains, as a member, a reference variable of the same type as the class itself. For this reason, these data structures are frequently called *self-referential*, or *recursive*, data structures.

11.1   SELF-REFERENTIAL STRUCTURES

A simple type of self-referential list structure is a sequence of elements. Each element contains some data and a reference to the next element in the list. In the following example, we create an arbitrarily long list of integer values.

In file IntStack.cs

```
// A self-referential class
using System;

public class IntListElement {
  public IntListElement(int val) { data = val; }

  public IntListElement Next     // property-accessor method
    { get { return next; }  set { next = value; } }

  public int Data                // property-accessor method
    { get { return data; }  set { data = value; } }

  private  IntListElement next;    // self-referential field
  private  int data;
}
```

Dissection of the *IntStack* Program

```
■private  IntListElement next;  // self-referential field
 private  int data;
```

The declaration of `IntListElement` has two fields. The field `data` stores the data member for this element. The reference variable `next` is called a *link*. Each element is linked to a succeeding element by way of the member `next`.

```
■public IntListElement(int val) { data = val; }
```

For convenience, we also include a constructor that fills in the data field. We use `val` for the variable name instead of `value`. Either could be used, but `value` has a special meaning in `get` and `set` property-accessor methods, so we chose `val` to distinguish the two uses.

```
■public IntListElement Next     // property-accessor method
    { get { return next; }  set { next = value; } }
public int Data                 // property-accessor method
    { get { return data; }  set { data = value; } }
```

For convenience and good software engineering practice, we create two properties to be the surrogates for the private fields `next` and `data`. The property names `Next` and `Data` are the capitalized versions of the private field names. This is customary C# style.

A list implemented with this structure can be conveniently displayed pictorially with links shown as arrows. In the following figure, the field `data` contains the value 2. The field `next` is pointing to some other, unspecified element.

If there is no succeeding element because we are at the end of the list, the field `next` contains the special value `null`. We can create two elements with

```
IntListElement first = new IntListElement(1);
IntListElement second = new IntListElement(2);
```

The `next` field defaults to `null`. Pictorially, the result of this code is

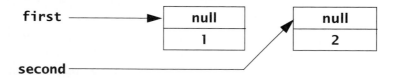

To make these two elements into a list, with `first` as the first element in the list, we link them.

`first.Next = second;`

The diagram now looks like this.

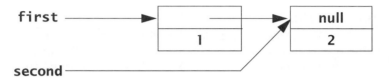

The links allow us to retrieve data from successive elements, beginning with the first element. Thus

`first.Next.Data`

has the value 2.

A common mistake is to attempt to access a field or method for an object with a reference value that is `null`. Doing so generates an exception. For example, given the short list that we just created, attempting to reference `first.Next.Next.Data` would generate a `System.NullReferenceException` error. The expression `first.Next.Next` refers to the reference value stored in the field `next` of the second element in the list. This field is `null`, so `first.Next.Next.Data` is asking for the field `data` of the `null` value.

In some cases letting the program abort with the exception is acceptable. In other cases using the mechanism for handling exceptions may be appropriate—to catch the exception and take some corrective action. Yet another approach is to test for a null reference before accessing any fields. Better still is to design the program so that such null references do not occur.

11.2   LINKED LIST IMPLEMENTATION OF A STACK

A common container used in computers is a stack. A *stack*, like an array, stores a sequence of similar objects. The difference between stacks and arrays lies in how you put values in the container. In an array, you create the container with a fixed size and then store and retrieve values at any index in the array. In contrast, a stack is like a stack of plates. You can add a plate to the top of the stack, you can look at the plate on the top of the stack, and you can remove a plate from the top of the stack. You can't look at, add, or remove plates from the middle. Because of this insertion/removal discipline, a stack is a last-in-first-out (LIFO) data structure.

A stack class for storing integers should have the following methods.

```
class IntStack {
  public int Top() { ····· }
  public void Push(int val) { ····· }
  public int Pop() { ····· }
  public bool Empty() { ····· }
}
```

The method `Top()` returns the value of the integer on the top of the stack without changing the stack's contents. If the stack is empty, `Top()` throws an exception. The method `Push()` pushes an integer value onto the top of the stack, increasing the number of integers contained in the stack. The method `Pop()` returns the same thing as `Top()`, but it also removes the top value from the stack, reducing the number of integers contained in the stack by 1. If the stack is empty, `Pop()` throws an exception. The method `Empty()` returns `true` if the stack is empty and `false` otherwise. The following figure shows the integers 1, 2, and 3 being pushed onto a stack and then popped back off.

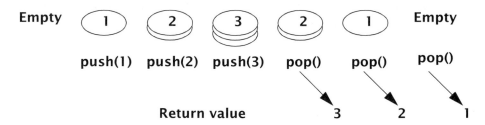

There are many ways to implement the operations of the class `IntStack`. An important aspect of object-oriented programming is the ability to hide and change the implementation without affecting other parts of a program that use the class. Here we implement the class `IntStack`, using the class `IntListElement` introduced in Section 11.1, *Self-Referential Structures*, on page 452.

In file IntStack.cs

```csharp
using System;

// A stack implemented with a list

public class IntStack {

  public int Top()
  {
    if (top != null)
      return top.Data;
    else
      throw new Exception("stack null");
  }

  public void Push(int val)
  {
    if (top == null) {
      top = new IntListElement(val);
    }
    else {
      IntListElement temp = new IntListElement(val);
      temp.Next = top;
      top = temp;
    }
  }

  public int Pop()
  {
    int result = Top();
    if (top != null)
      top = top.Next;
    return result;
  }

  public  bool Empty() { return top == null; }
  private IntListElement top = null;
}
```

Dissection of the *IntStack* Program

```
public int Top()
{
  if (top != null)
    return top.Data;
  else
    throw new Exception("stack null");
}
```

The private instance variable `top` is a reference to the `IntListEle-`
`ment` at the top of the stack. If the stack is empty, `top` equals `null` and
the result is an exception. Otherwise, the result of `Top()` is the `Data`
property for the element referred to by `top`.

```
void Push(int val)
{
  if (top == null) {
    top = new IntListElement(val);
  }
  else {
    IntListElement temp = new IntListElement(val);
    temp.Next = top;
    top = temp;
  }
}
```

We must check for the special case of pushing onto an empty list, in
which case we set `top` to be a new element. If the stack isn't empty, we
create a new element, set its link to point to the current top of the
stack, and then move `top` to point to the new element. In both cases,
we then store the new `val` in the `data` field of the new top element.

```
■int Pop() {
   int result = Top();
   if (top != null)
     top = top.Next;
   return result;
}
```

We reuse the method Top() to find the value that should be returned from Pop(). By reusing our code in this way, we reduce the chances of making a mistake. If the stack isn't already empty, we move top to point to the next element in the list, thus removing what was the top element from the stack. We need to save the result before moving top; otherwise, we wouldn't be able to find the value to return.

The next figure shows the sequence of inserting an element into a nonempty stack. Here, 1 and 2 were previously pushed onto the stack, and we are now executing Push(3).

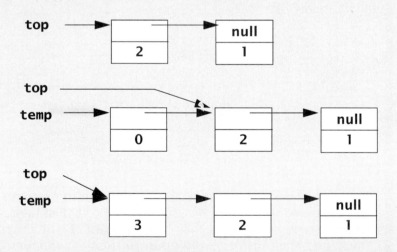

```
■bool Empty() { return top == null; }
 private IntListElement top = null;
```

The method Empty() is straightforward, returning true if the stack is empty. The only instance variable is the pointer to the top element. Note the absence of any specification of how large the stack is.

Let us write a test program using the IntStack.

In file IntStack.cs

```csharp
public class IntStackTest {
  public static void Main()
  {
    IntStack s1 = new IntStack(), s2 = new IntStack();

    s1.Push(3);
    s1.Push(2);
    s1.Push(1);
    s2.Push(s1.Pop());
    s2.Push(s1.Pop());
    s2.Push(s1.Pop());
    Console.WriteLine("Pop s2 " + s2.Pop());
    Console.WriteLine("Pop s2 " + s2.Pop());
    Console.WriteLine("Pop s2 " + s2.Pop());
  }
}
```

The output of this program is

```
Pop s2 3
Pop s2 2
Pop s2 1
```

Here two stacks are in use. Before you go on, try to follow what is printed. We push onto stack s1 the values 3, 2, and 1. They get popped off stack s1 in reverse order as 1, 2, and 3. These values are pushed onto s2. When popped off s2, they print as 3, 2, and 1.

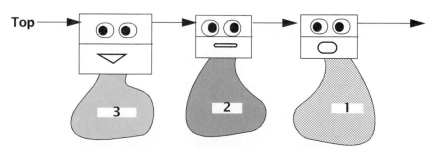

Top

"Just because he's first, he got a swelled head."

11.3   A DOUBLY LINKED LIST

A stack is a specialized list because it permits insertion and removal of elements from only one end of the list, the top. In this section we consider a more general list class that implements a linked list. This class allows for insertion, removal, and examination of elements at any point in the list. We could just use the class `IntListElement` in each program that uses lists. Doing so, however, would require us to recode repeatedly the error-prone operations of connecting and disconnecting links. Instead, we create a class that does all of the work for us.

We create an `IntDList` that hooks together doubly linked elements of `class IntDListElement`. In a list, we want to navigate both in a forward and a backward direction. This makes insertion and deletion into the list far easier.

Here is the code for an element.

In file IntDList.cs

```
public class IntDListElement {
  public IntDListElement(int val) { data = val; }
  public IntDListElement(int val, IntDListElement d)
  {
    data = val;
    next = d;
    d.previous = this;
  }

  public IntDListElement Next
  { get { return next; }  set { next = value; } }

  public IntDListElement Previous
  { get { return previous; }  set { previous = value; } }

  public int Data
  { get { return data; }  set { data = value; } }

  private  IntDListElement next, previous;
  private  int data;
}
```

Dissection of the *IntDList* Program

■private   IntDListElement next, previous;
 private   int data;

The two links are next and previous. The field data stores each element's value. This means that each element has one extra field than in a single linked list. There is no free lunch—this extra space and the associated update cost are the tradeoffs with the increased ease of use in comparison to a single linked list.

■public IntDListElement(int val) { data = val; }
 public IntDListElement(int val, IntDListElement d)
 {
    data = val;
    next = d;
    d.previous = this;
 }

The constructors are very basic. One builds a stand-alone element. The other constructs an element linked to the next element in a chain of elements.

■public IntDListElement Next
    { get { return next; }   set { next = value; } }
 public IntDListElement Previous
    { get { return previous; }   set { previous = value; } }
 public int Data
    { get { return data; }   set { data = value; } }

Here are three properties that give access to the underlying private data fields.

The basic operations for a list include constructing an empty list, constructing a list of one element, adding to the front of a list, finding an element in a list, and deleting an element from a list. We show code for these operations and leave other operations as exercises.

In file IntDList.cs

```csharp
public class IntDList {
  public IntDList() { head = null; }
  public IntDList(int val)
  {
    head = new IntDListElement(val);
    head.Next = head.Previous = null;
  }

  public bool IsEmpty() { return head == null; }

  public void Add(int val)                        // add to front
  {
    if (IsEmpty()) {
      head = new IntDListElement(val);
      head.Next = head.Previous = null;
    }
    else {
      IntDListElement h = new IntDListElement(val, head);
      head.Previous = h;
      head = h;
    }
  }

  public int Front()
  {
    if (IsEmpty())
      throw new System.Exception("Empty IntDList");
    return head.Data;
  }
  private IntDListElement head;
}
```

We start by examining a minimum set of methods for building a doubly linked list.

Dissection of the *IntDList* Program

```
■public IntDList() { head = null; }
 public IntDList(int val)
    {
      head = new IntDListElement(val);
      head.Next = head.Previous = null;
    }
```

The no-argument constructor sets the head to the null reference representing the empty list. The one-argument constructor sets up a list with one element.

```
■public bool IsEmpty() { return head == null; }
```

The method IsEmpty() tests for the empty list. There are functions that must handle an empty list differently than an already established list. There are also functions that expect to find an established list and may not work on an empty list.

```
■public void Add(int val)                         // add to front
 {
   if (IsEmpty()) {
     head = new IntDListElement(val);
     head.Next = head.Previous = null;
   }
   else {
     IntDListElement h = new IntDListElement(val, head);
     head.Previous = h;
     head = h;
   }
 }
```

The method Add() adds to the front of the list. A doubly linked element is created with val in its data field and inserted at the front of the list. This new element becomes the head of the list. We must also update the previous link.

Now let us add a method that can find an element containing a given value and then use this in turn to delete selected elements.

```
public IntDListElement Find(int val)
{
  IntDListElement h = head;

  while (h != null) {
    if (val == h.Data)
      break;
      h = h.Next;
  }
  return h;
}
```

Dissection of `IntDListElement Find()` Method

■ `IntDListElement h = head;`

As with most linked-list operations, we start at the head of the list.

■
```
while (h != null){
   if (val == h.Data)
     break;
   h = h.Next;
}
```

This is idiomatic for both single-list and doubly linked list operations. We traverse the list until we hit the sentinel value `null`. On each iteration we advance the *cursor* reference `h`. On each list element we perform the necessary operation, in this case, the test to see if we have the searched-for `val` stored in the data field.

■ `return h;`

We return with the reference to the element that had `val` stored in its data field. If this value is not found, the `null` reference is returned.

Now we can write `Delete()` methods. The first `Delete()` method is given a link reference to delete. We have to check for various cases, including whether the element is `null`. The element can be at the front of a list, in the middle of the list, or at the end of the list.

```
public IntDListElement Delete(IntDListElement h )
{
  if (h == null) return null;                //if nothing in list
  IntDListElement np = h.Next, pp = h.Previous;

  if (np != null)
     np.Previous = pp;
  else
     head = null;                            // one element deletion
  if (pp != null)
     pp.Next = np;
  return h.Next;
}

public IntDListElement Delete(int v )
  { return  Delete(Find(v)); }
```

11.3.1 MORE OPERATIONS ON LISTS

In the previous section, we introduced and described a class `IntDList` that supported arbitrary insertion and removal but implemented only a minimal set of operations. Many more common operations can be used on lists, and implementing them once in our list class allows us to use them in other programs. Table 11.1 contains a list of typical operations; for completeness we included those already implemented.

Table 11.1	Linear List Operations

Create an empty list.

Insert after the current position.

Insert before the current position.

Insert at position *n* in the list. Zero means insert before the first element.

Remove the element at the current position.

Find an element in the list.

Append the elements of one list to the elements of another list.

Count the elements in a list.

Print a list.

11.3.2 IMPLEMENTING ToString() FOR CLASS IntDList

Some list operations are easier to implement than others. A simple but useful operation is printing a list, which we did in our examples. However, by creating a method to print the list, our programming task becomes simpler. The preferred approach in C# is to create a method ToString(), which returns a string representation that can then be printed. This can then be used to output an arbitrary IntDList. It traverses the list and converts each value into a string for output. Here is a simple implementation of ToString().

```
public override string ToString()           // write recursion
{
  string temp = "";                         // not most efficient
  IntDListElement h = head;

  while (h != null) {
    temp = temp + h.Data + "\n";
    h   = h.Next;
  }
  return temp;
}
```

The class string is implicitly derived from the class Object, as are all classes except the class Object itself. Because the method ToString() is defined as a public method in `Object`, the method, when redefined in other classes, must also be public—hence the keyword `public` in the definition. (See the discussion in Section 6.3, *Access: Private and Public*, on page 243.)

Often, a convenient way of working with lists is to write recursive methods. We can easily write a method that recursively calls itself to generate a string representation of a list when given a reference to the first element in the list.

```
static string ToStringRecursive(IntDListElement first)
{
  if (first == null)
    return "";
  else
    return (first.Data + "\n")
            + ToStringRecursive(first.Next);
}
```

Using this method, `ToString()` in the class `IntDList` can be implemented as

```
public override string ToString()
  { return ToStringRecursive(head); }
```

Note that there are no local variables in either of these last two methods. The result is built in the stack of method calls. Suppose that the list contains the elements `10`, `20`, and `30`, in that order. Then a call to `ToString()` would result in the following sequence of calls.

```
ToString()
  ToStringRecursive(first.Data is 10)
    ToStringRecursive(first.Data is 20)
      ToStringRecursive(first.Data is 30)
        return "30\n"
      return "20\n30\n"
    return "10\n20\n30\n"
  return "10\n20\n30\n"
```

Note how the result is built in reverse order as the method calls return. We can test the `IntDList` code:

In file IntDList.cs

```
public class IntDListTest
{
  public static void Main ()
  {
    IntDList a = new IntDList(1);
    a.Add(5);
    a.Add(10);
    Console.WriteLine(a);
    a.Delete(5);
    Console.WriteLine(a);
  }
}
```

The output generated by the recursive version of ToString() is

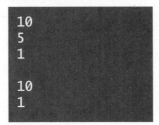

```
10
5
1

10
1
```

11.4   A GENERIC LIST

The list and stack classes that we implemented in the preceding sections work only with integers. What if we wanted to store strings or other objects in a doubly linked list? One solution would be to create different classes for each type, which is cumbersome and unnecessary. Recall that C# supports polymorphism, which means that we can create one class to handle many different types. The changes to our previous classes from the IntDList classes are minor. Let's start with a generic list element.

In file DListElement.cs

```
public class DListELement {
  public DListELement(object val) { data = val; }
  public DListELement previous, next;
  public object data;
}
```

We replace the `IntD` with `D` and `int` with `object`, wherever the `int` is used for the type `data`, which is now an object. The class `Object` is a standard C# class, and a reference of type `object` can refer to any type. So,

```
DListElement elem1 = new DListElement(3);
```

places an integer value in the `data` field. Similarly, we could create `DListElement` containing the `double` value 1.25 with

```
DListElement elem2 = new DListElement(1.25);
```

Next, a `DListElement` containing a `String`.

```
DListElement elem3 = new DListElement("element 3");
```

To retrieve the data from the elements, the program using the data has to know what type of value is really there. Provided that we know the true type, we can use a cast to convert from type `object` back to the true type, also known in C# as unboxing. For example, if the list element contains an `int` value, we can use the following expression to retrieve it.

```
int x = (int)elem1.data;
```

If you don't know what type of value is stored in a `DListElement`, C# provides the operators `is` and `typeof` that you can use to test the type.

We also need to make sure that comparison works for any variables of type `object` in the new type. Instead of using the comparison operators `==` and `!=`, we use the inherited `Object.Equals()` method when comparing the value of a referenced object.

Now that we have a generic list element, we can use it to create a generic list or a generic stack. Here, we make the change for the list and leave the changes for the stack for you to do as an exercise. We start with our *IntDList* program from Section 11.3, *A Doubly Linked List*, on page 462 and follow the same general procedure as we did for the `IntDListElement` change to `DListElement`: we replace all `IntD` with `D` and `int` with `object` where `int` is used for data reference, and change data comparison to use the `Equals()` method.

In file DList.cs

```csharp
using System;
public class DListElement
{
  public DListElement(object val) { data = val; }

  public DListElement(object val, DListElement d)
  {
    data = val;
    next = d;
    d.previous = this;
  }

  public DListElement Next
  { get { return next; } set { next = value; } }

  public DListElement Previous
  { get { return previous; } set { previous = value; } }

  public object Data
  { get { return data; } set { data = value; } }

  public  DListElement next, previous;
  public  object data;
}

public class DList
{
  public DList() { head = null; }
  public DList(object val)
  {
    head = new DListElement(val);
    head.Next = head.Previous = null;
  }

  public bool IsEmpty() { return head == null; }
```

```
public void Add(object val)                    // add to front
{
  if (IsEmpty())
  {
    head = new DListElement(val);
    head.Next = head.Previous = null;
  }
  else
  {
    DListElement h = new DListElement(val, head);
    head.Previous = h;
    head = h;
  }
}

public object Front()
{
  if (IsEmpty())
    throw new System.Exception("Empty DList");
  return head.Data;
}

public DListElement Find(object val)
{
  DListElement h = head;

  while (h != null)
  {
    if (val.Equals(h.Data))         //== won't work on h.Data
      break;
    h = h.Next;
  }
  return h;
}
```

```
public DListElement Delete(DListElement h )
{
  if (h == null) return null;        //if nothing in element

  DListElement np = h.Next, pp = h.Previous;

  if (np != null)
    np.Previous = pp;
  else
    head = null;                     // one element deletion
  if (pp != null)
    pp.Next = np;
  return h.Next;
}

public DListElement Delete(object v )
{ return  Delete(Find(v)); }

public override string ToString()
{ return ToStringRecursive(head); }

static string ToStringRecursive(DListElement first)
{
  if (first == null)
    return "";
  else
    return (first.Data + "\n")
      + ToStringRecursive(first.Next);
}
private DListElement head;
}
```

In the following program we use the new list to store both floating-point
and integer values.

In file DList.cs

```
public class DListTest
{
  public static void Main ()
  {
    DList a = new DList(1.3563);
    a.Add(5);
    a.Add(10.66);
    Console.WriteLine(a);
    a.Delete(5);
    Console.WriteLine(a);
  }
}
```

The output of this program is

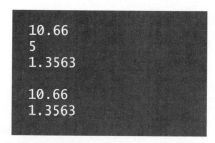

```
10.66
5
1.3563

10.66
1.3563
```

11.5   INDEXERS, ITERATORS, AND IEnumerator

Classes, such as `DList`, and data structures, such as arrays, are called *collection classes*. They store a large number of elements and have an access methodology for their retrieval. In the case of arrays, the usual access is through an index. Classes that can be accessed through indexing are called sequential collections or sequential container classes. It is possible to create such a class by providing a class with an indexer property. This is done with the following construction:

```
returnType this [argument] { get; set; }
```

The *returnType* is usually the value type of the objects stored in the container. The argument is usually an integer type, but can be a string type as well.

Let us add indexing to our DList.

In file DList.cs

```csharp
public object this[int index]
{
  get {
    DListElement temp = head;
    if (temp == null)
      throw new System.Exception(index +
                                 " index out of range");
    for (int i = 0; i < index; ++i) {
      if (temp.Next == null)
        throw new System.Exception(index +
                                   " index out of range");
      temp = temp.Next;
    }
    return temp.Data;
  }

  set {
    DListElement temp = head;
    if (temp == null)
      throw new System.Exception(index +
                                 " index out of range");

    for (int i = 0; i < index; ++i) {
      if (temp.Next == null)
        throw new System.Exception(index +
                                   " index out of range");
      temp = temp.Next;
    }
    temp.Data = value;
  }
}
```

```
public int Length()
{
  int listLength = 0;
  DListElement temp = head;
  while (temp != null) {
    temp = temp.Next;
    ++listLength;
  }
  return listLength;
}
```

It is important to notice that indexing in a list can be an expensive operation. It takes order *n* operations where *n* is the index value. An array takes constant time to access any element through its index.

An *iterator* is a construct that allows you to iterate over a collection of objects such as a list or an array. Any integer variable can be used as an iterator for an array. It is often useful to be able to maintain more than one iterator simultaneously for a single collection of objects. For example, using one forward iterator and one backward iterator, you can reverse the elements in a list, implemented as an array, as shown in the following example.

In file DList.cs

```
public static void Reverse(DList list)
{
  int forward = 0, backward = (list.Length() - 1);
  while (forward < backward) {
    object temp = list[forward];
    list[forward] = list[backward];
    list[backward] = temp;
    forward++;
    backward--;
  }
}
```

There are two iterators in this example: `forward` and `backward`. Because arrays are a fundamental type in C# and many other programming languages, there is a built-in syntax for iterators that iterate over arrays. The `for` and `foreach` statements both provide convenient iterator schemes. Note that method `Reverse()` is static. We test our new methods with the following program:

In file DList.cs

```
public class DListTest
{
  public static void Main ()
  {
    DList a = new DList(1.3563);
    a.Add(10.66);
    a.Add(56.78);
    a.Add(6);
    Console.WriteLine(a);
    DList.Reverse(a);
    a[3] = 2.1;                              //test set and index
    Console.WriteLine(a);
  }
}
```

The output from this program is

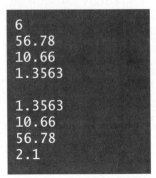

```
6
56.78
10.66
1.3563

1.3563
10.66
56.78
2.1
```

Two things are required of an iterator. You need some way to advance the iterator and fetch the next value. You also need some way to determine when you've iterated over the entire collection. For an array, you can increment or decrement the index variable and then test it to determine whether you've reached the end or the beginning of the array.

The `IEnumerable` interface provides a collection class with the means to use the `foreach` statement as an iterator mechanism. It declares the single method `IEnumerator GetEnumerator()`. To provide a concrete implementation we must write methods `MoveNext()` and `Reset()`. Also we must provide the property `Current` that gets the value at the current iterator position. The `Reset()` method places the iterator at the beginning of the collection. The `MoveNext()` increments the iterator.

We must also be able to manufacture an appropriate iterator using the method GetEnumerator(). We briefly show how this can be done for a simple collection class ArrayOdd. The class contains a fixed-length array that is 100 elements long. We provide an iterator that indexes only its odd elements.

In file ArrayOdd.cs

```
// A program to test odd enumerator
using System;
using System.Collections;

class ArrayOdd : IEnumerable {
  public int [] d = new int[100];
  public IEnumerator GetEnumerator()
    { return (IEnumerator) new ArrayOddEnumerator(this); }

  public int this [int index]
    { get { return d[index]; }  set { d[index] = value; } }
}
```

So far we have a simple container and have added to it an indexer property. Now we add the enumerator class as an inner private class. This hides the details of the iterator logic. These methods are needed to make the foreach iterator statement work on ArrayOdd.

```
// Nested class inside ArrayOdd
private class ArrayOddEnumerator: IEnumerator
{
  public ArrayOddEnumerator(ArrayOdd d)
  {
    this.d = d;
    index = -1;                              // start here
  }

  public void Reset() { index = -1; }

  public bool MoveNext()
  {
   index += 2;
    if (index >99)
      return false;
    else
      return true;
  }
```

```
    public object Current { get { return(d[index]); } }

    private int index;
    private ArrayOdd d;                    // refers to collection
}
```

Now we have all the methods required to implement the `IEnumerator` interface. We can test it in `Main()`.

```
class ArrayOddTest {
  public static void Main()
  {
    ArrayOdd t = new ArrayOdd();
    for (int i = 0; i < 100; ++i)
     t.d[i] = 2 * i +1;
    for (int i = 0; i < 100; ++i)
      Console.Write(" " + t.d[i]);
    foreach (int element in t)
      Console.Write(" " + element);
  }
}
```

The output of this program is

```
 1 3 5 7 9 11 13 15 17 19 21 23 25 27 29 31 33 35
37 39 41 43 45 47 49 ...(odd numbers)... 197 199 3
7 11 15 19 23 27 31 35 39 43 47 51 55 59 63 67 71
75 9 83 87 91 95 99 103 107 111 115 119 123 127 131
135 139 143 147 151 155 159 163 167 171 175 179 183
187 191 195 199
```

11.6   ARRAY LISTS

The C# library contains an `ArrayList` class. This has properties of both arrays and lists. It can be dynamically resized and it is indexable. It is generic in that it stores objects. A subset of the publicly available properties is given in Table 11.2.

Table 11.2	ArrayList Public Properties
Capacity	Gets or sets the number of elements the ArrayList can contain
Count	Gets the number of elements actually in the ArrayList
IsFixedSize	Indicates whether the ArrayList is fixed size
Item	Gets or sets the element at the specified index

Table 11.3 gives a subset of the instance methods available in ArrayList.

Table 11.3	Some ArrayList Instance Methods
Add()	Adds an object
AddRange()	Adds a sequence of elements to the end
BinarySearch()	Search a sorted ArrayList
Insert()	Inserts an element
Remove()	Deletes the first occurrence of the element
RemoveAt()	Deletes the element at the specified position
Sort()	Sorts the elements
IndexOf()	Returns position of the element's first occurrence

We give a small example and a few operations that show its use. In this example, we convert an array to an ArrayList and remove all elements of a given value.

In file ArrayListUse.cs

```
// Use of standard ArrayList
using System;
using System.Collections;  // collections classes found here

class ArrayListUse {
  public static void Main()
  {
    ArrayList scores = new ArrayList();     // or (capacity)
    int [] data = { 23, 44, 16, 17, 23, 19, 50 };
```

```
      scores.AddRange(data);                    // adds ICollection
      scores.Add(data[0]);
      scores.Add(data[1]);
      scores.Add(data[0]);
      for (int i = 0; i < scores.Count; ++i)
        Console.WriteLine("scores: " + scores[i]);
      RemoveAll(23, scores);
      Console.WriteLine("");
      for (int i = 0; i < scores.Count; ++i)
        Console.WriteLine("scores : " + scores[i]);
    }

  public static void RemoveAll(object v, ArrayList list)
  {
    while (list.Contains(v) == true)
      list.Remove(v);
  }
}
```

The output of this program is

```
scores: 23
scores: 44
scores: 16
scores: 17
scores: 23
scores: 19
scores: 50
scores: 44
scores: 23

scores : 44
scores : 16
scores : 17
scores : 19
scores : 50
scores : 44
```

Dissection of the *ArrayListUse* Program

■
```
ArrayList scores = new ArrayList();      // or (capacity)
int [] data = { 23, 44, 16, 17, 23, 19, 50 };
scores.AddRange(data);                    // adds ICollection
```

The container `scores` is an expandable `ArrayList`. The `AddRange()` method takes elements in the ordinary array `data` and places them in `scores`.

■
```
scores.Add(data[0]);
scores.Add(data[1]);
scores.Add(data[0]);
```

`Add()` appends each passed-in value to the end of `ArrayList scores`.

■
```
for (int i = 0; i < scores.Count; ++i)
    Console.WriteLine("scores: " + scores[i]);
RemoveAll(23, scores);
```

`ArrayList scores` is indexable as if it were an ordinary array. We must use the property `Count` rather than `Length` to track the current number of elements in the collection.

■
```
public static void RemoveAll(object v, ArrayList list)
{
  while (list.Contains(v) == true)
    list.Remove(v);
}
```

This method removes all elements of a given value v from the `ArrayList`. It uses the standard methods `Contains()` and `Remove()`.

■
```
RemoveAll(23, scores);
Console.WriteLine("");
  for (int i = 0; i < scores.Count; ++i)
    Console.WriteLine("scores : " + scores[i]);
```

All elements of value 23 are removed. The `ArrayList scores` contracts. You should run the program and verify this behavior.

11.7   SOFTWARE ENGINEERING: CODE REUSE

Code reuse is the practice of reusing existing code in new programs. It has been an important part of programming from the beginning, but the amount of reuse is increasing. The complexity of current applications requires code reuse because it reduces development time and improves reliability. Increased reliability, in general, is the result of thorough testing of the reused components.

There are two aspects of code reuse: creation of reusable components and use of those components. One of the strengths of C# is the large and growing collection of reusable components called classes. In this chapter we introduced some basic data structures. When building real applications, you should, in general, not reimplement these basic data structures. Instead, you should select some appropriate class that provides the functionality that your application needs.

If you determine that the performance of a standard class is inadequate for your application, you should be able to replace that class with an implementation of your own.

The standard C# classes include several useful containers, such as `Array-List`, `Stack`, and `Queue` in `System.Collections`.

11.8   DR. P'S PRESCRIPTIONS

- For sequence containers, think array first and `ArrayList` second.

- Use the most efficient container for a computation.

- Remember that `foreach` provides an iterator construct.

- Use iterator parameters rather than container variables.

- Use the most efficient algorithm for a computation.

The array is generally the easiest container to use. It is very efficient because it is geared to random access. It is also the most familiar to programmers. It is also often the most efficient over a large class of operations. It should be your default container choice. The `ArrayList` is the next most useful. Its ability to add and remove elements dynamically in linear time is its greatest strength. It also supports random access. Other more specialized collections are available in System.Collections. Again, be guided by the most frequent operations required by your problem in making these choices.

There is relative ease in switching among containers. One container can be constructed by passing it a range from another container. Do not be afraid of using multiple representations for some problems that dictate a combination of space-operation cost tradeoffs. The point of Collections is to use a more efficient algorithm. Usually, this involves selecting the appropriate container.

Iterator sequences are not tied to a particular type of container. Container types are a narrower style of representation than iterator ranges. Ergo, using iterator sequences leaves algorithms more general and hence more reusable.

11.9   C# COMPARED WITH JAVA AND C++

In this section we show the use of library classes in C#, Java, and C++ to allocate a list, sort the elements, sum the elements, and print the list. Here is the C# code, which uses ArrayList found in System.Collections.

In file SortPrintSum.cs

```csharp
using System;
using System.Collections;  // collections classes found here

class SortPrintSum {
  public static void Print(ArrayList z)
  {
    foreach (object element in z)
      Console.Write(element + "\t");
    Console.WriteLine();
  }

  public static double Accumulate(ArrayList z)
  {
    double sum = 0.0;
    foreach (object element in z)
      sum += (double)element;
    return sum;
  }
```

```
  public static void Main()
  {
    ArrayList z = new ArrayList();          // or (capacity)
    double [] w = { 0.9, 0.8, 88, -99.99 };

    z.AddRange(w);                          // adds ICollection
    Print(z);
    z.Sort();
    Print(z);
    Console.WriteLine("sum is " + Accumulate(z));
  }
}
```

The output of this program is

```
    0.9      0.8      88       -99.99
    -99.99   0.8      0.9      88
    sum is -10.29
```

Note that the `object` type must be cast to `double` for the `Accumulate()` method to work properly, since operator + is not overloaded in `ArrayList`. ArrayList does not provide a `ToString()` method nor does it have accumulation or summation methods.

C++ has used templates to implement generic collection classes. They are highly efficient and very powerful. Templates are proposed for Java and C#, but are only in experimental use. The C++ implementation of the *Sort-SumPrint* program uses the STL list container, an iterator, and the generic algorithm `accumulate()`. The *list* and *numeric* libraries are required.

In file sortPrintSum.cpp

```
#include <iostream>
#include <list>                            // list container
#include <numeric>                         // for accumulate
using namespace std;
```

```
// Using the list container

void print(list<double> &lst)
{
   list<double>::iterator p;                // traverse iterator

   for (p = lst.begin(); p != lst.end(); ++p)
      cout << *p << '\t';
   cout << endl;
}

int main()
{
   double w[4] = { 0.9, 0.8, 88, -99.99 };
   list<double> z;

   for (int i = 0; i < 4; ++i)
      z.push_front(w[i]);
   print(z);
   z.sort();
   print(z);
   cout << "sum is "
        << accumulate(z.begin(), z.end(), 0.0) << endl;
}
```

In this example, a list container is instantiated to hold `doubles`. An array of `doubles` is pushed into the list. The `print()` function uses an iterator to print each element of the list in turn. The `accumulate()` function is a generic function in the *numeric* package that uses `0.0` as an initial value and computes the sum of the list container elements by going from the starting location `z.begin()` to the ending guard location `z.end()`.

Java collection classes are similar to C# classes. Java has the interface `java.util.AbstractCollection`. Derived from this is `AbstractList` and from this the concrete class `ArrayList`. There are the usual such collection classes in the Java library.

In file SortPrintSum.java

```java
import tio.*;
import java.util.*;

public class SortPrintSum {
  public static void print(ArrayList z)
  {
    for (int i = 0;  i < z.size(); i++)
      System.out.print(z.get(i) + "\t");
    System.out.println();
  }

  public static double accumulate(ArrayList z)
  {
    double sum = 0.0;
    for (int i = 0;  i < z.size(); i++)
      sum +=   ((Double)(z.get(i))).doubleValue();
    return sum;
  }

  public static void addRange(double  w[], ArrayList z)
  {
    for (int i = 0;  i < w.length; i++)
      z.add(new Double(w[i]));
  }

  public static void main(String[] args)
  {
    ArrayList z = new ArrayList();
    double [] w = { 0.9, 0.8, 88, -99.99 };

    addRange(w, z);
    print(z);
    Collections.sort(z);
    print(z);

    System.out.println("sum is " + accumulate(z));
  }
}
```

We must use the Java wrapper class Double because, unlike C#, Java does not treat native types as derived from class Object. In this regard C# is the clearly superior language.

SUMMARY

- Self-referential structures use references to link items.

- The simplest self-referential structure is the linear or singly linked list. Each element points to the next element, with the last element having a link value of `null`.

- Many list processing algorithms are naturally implemented recursively. Frequently, the base case is when the end of the list is reached. The general case recurs by moving to the "next" element.

- The abstract data type (ADT) stack is implementable as a linked list, with access restricted to its first element, called the top. The stack has a last-in-first-out (LIFO) discipline implemented by the routines `Push()` and `Pop()`.

- A doubly linked list has a link to the next and preceding elements. Having both forward and backward links facilitates some list operations.

- Generic list structures can be created by having the list elements store a reference to an `object`. Any type can be stored directly in such an element.

- Classes that can be accessed through indexing are called sequential collections or sequential container classes. It is possible to create such a class by providing a class with an indexer property. This is done with the following construction:

  returnType `this` [*argument*] `{ get; set; }`

- An *iterator* construct allows you to iterate over a collection of objects such as a list or an array. The `IEnumerable` interface provides a collection class with the means to use the `foreach` statement as an iterator mechanism. It declares the method `IEnumerator GetEnumerator()`.

- The C# library contains an `ArrayList` class. This has properties of both arrays and lists. It can be dynamically resized and it is indexable. It is generic in that it stores objects. The standard C# classes include several useful containers, such as `ArrayList`, `Stack`, and `Queue`, in `System.Collections`.

REVIEW QUESTIONS

1. Name two methods that are standard for a stack.

2. Draw a picture of a singly linked list containing the values 10, 20, and 30, in that order.

3. Draw a picture of a doubly linked list containing the values 10, 20, and 30, in that order.

4. A stack is used to process data in which order, LIFO or FIFO?

5. What methods or properties are needed for defining an indexer?

6. What methods or properties are needed for implementing `foreach` semantics for a collection class?

7. Name one operation that would be much faster on a doubly linked list than on a singly linked list.

8. Name and describe two methods available on an `ArrayList`.

9. Name three collection classes found in the C# library `System.Collections`.

10. Why might you use an `ArrayList` instead of an array?

EXERCISES

1. Write an `IntList` list. This should have an `IntListElement` as each element. You need a slightly different logic from the `IntDList` in Section 11.3, *A Doubly Linked List*, on page 460.

2. Write an insertion method that inserts an element after the last element of an `IntList` list. Why is this easier for an `IntDList`?

3. Write an insertion method that inserts an element at the first position in an `IntList` list following an element storing a particular `data` value. If there is no such element, insert the element after the last element.

4. Generalize the previous three exercises. Write an insertion method that inserts an element in the *n*th position in a list, where 0 means that the element is placed at the head of the list. If *n* is larger than the length of the list, insert the element at the tail of the list.

5. Write `class PairListElement` that holds a pair of `int`s referred to as first and second. Now implement a `PairList` and write a method that sorts the pair list based on the value of the `second int`.

6. in Section 11.3, *A Doubly Linked List*, on page 462, modify the property `Next` in the class `IntDListElement` to throw an `Exception` if there is no next element.

7. Add a constructor to the class `IntDList` in Section 11.3, *A Doubly Linked List*, on page 462, that takes an array of integers and uses the array to build an initial list. The elements in the list should be in the same order as the elements in the array.

8. Add a method `ToIntArray()` to the class `IntDList` that returns a new array of integers containing the same elements as the list, in the same order.

9. Write a class `OStack` that can store a list of any nonprimitive type values. Start with `IntDStack` in Section 11.2, *Linked List Implementation of a Stack*, on page 459, and make the same sorts of changes that were made to create the generic class `DList` in Section 11.4, *A Generic List*, on page 473.

10. Write a program that uses the class `OStack` from the previous exercise to reverse the words in a sentence. The sentence to be reversed should be read in.

11. Create a class `Data` that contains two integer fields—one for age and one for weight—and one string field for a name. Build a list of `Data` objects, using `DList` from Section 11.4, *A Generic List*, on page 470. Then write a method to count the number of objects in the list that have age and weight fields above a given value.

12. Add a method `RemoveDups()` to class `DList` Section 11.4, *A Generic List*, on page 470, that removes from the list elements having duplicate values.

13. Design and code the class `MyQueue`. It should have a constructor that builds a queue from an array of objects. Queues are first-in-first-out collections (FIFO). You add to the front and remove from the rear.

14. Add a method `ToArray()` to the class `MyQueue` that returns an array containing the same elements as the `MyQueue`. Did you copy the elements into the new array or just the references to the elements? Discuss the two alternatives.

15. Use a general linked list structure to program sparse matrix addition. In a *sparse matrix* most of the values are zero. A nonzero element of a sparse matrix is represented by the triple (*i*, *j*, *value*). For each row *i*, the triples are linked as a linear list. There is an array with as many entries as there are rows in the matrix. Each array entry is the list for the corresponding row. To add matrix A to matrix B, we take each row in the two matrices and merge them into a matrix C. For each row index, if only one matrix contains elements for that row, that row is duplicated in C. If both matrices contain elements for a given row, the rows are merged. If both rows have a triple with the same column value, in the output row $c_{i,j}$ is the sum $a_{i,j} + b_{i,j}$. Otherwise, the element with smallest column number becomes the next element of the output row.

16. Although sparse matrix addition can be performed with just row-linked lists, for multiplication both row- and column-linked lists are required. You won't be able to use the list classes developed in this chapter. Each element can potentially have both a row successor and a column successor. If the elements are implemented by the class `SMElement`, there are two `SMElement` arrays—one for the rows and one for the columns. Each nonnull array entry in the row array is a link to the first nonzero row entry. The columns are handled similarly. Program sparse matrix multiplication.

17. Implement a sparse polynomial class. Use a linked list of elements to represent the nonzero terms of the polynomial. A *term* is a real coefficient and a power. Write a complete polynomial manipulation package. Your package should be able to input and output polynomials, and it should be able to add, subtract, multiply, and copy polynomials.

18. A hash function is a function that uses a key value to compute an index into a hash table. For example you can write a hash function for strings by using the Unicode values of each character as the basis for producing an index. One such hash function is

```
public static uint MyHash(string s)
{
  char[] a = new char[s.Length];
  uint hNumber = 0;

  s.CopyTo(0,a, 0, s.Length);
  foreach (char t in a)
    hNumber =  (hNumber * 31 + t);
  return hNumber % M;
}
```

The variable M is an integer chosen to be the size of the table. When two strings give an identical hash value, it is called a collision. This means more than one string is hashed into the same index. We use a single linked list element to store each string that produces a given hash value. To look up whether a string has been stored in our hash table, we compute its hash. We then search for that hash index in the chained list elements and see if our string is already stored in the hash table. Write a program that reads in a text file of words and computes a hash for each individual word, storing it in the hash table. Use a text file that contains at least 5000 words. Use as M the values 101, 501, 1001, and 5001. What can you say about the length of the collisions lists for the different choices for M? Did this hash perform well?

19. Use a hash table technique on a large text file to produce a count of the individual number of distinct words found in the file. Write the code so that capitalization does not matter.

20. Use the C# collection class Dictionary to solve the previous exercise. Discuss why this is considered a better software engineering approach than writing your own hash table code.

OOP USING C#

C# is a further refinement of C++ and Java. All three are object-oriented languages derived from the kernel language C, which is classically used as a system-implementation language. The class-based additions to the C language support the full range of object-oriented programming requirements. Therefore, C# is suitable for writing reusable libraries, and it supports an object-oriented coding style.

In the 1960s and 1970s, the dominant programming methodology was structured programming that relied on breaking large programs into a series of method or procedure calls. Until the mid-1980s, procedural encapsulation was the dominant academic and professional programming paradigm. In the 1970s, SmallTalk, developed at Xerox Parc, pioneered a new paradigm: object-oriented programming (OOP). It ran on special hardware developed at Parc and was relatively expensive and inefficient in comparison with contemporary procedural languages, such as C and Pascal. C++ added objects to C. It allowed efficient compilation and execution of OOP on most platforms. Starting in 1985, C++ was very quickly embraced by industry. As a hybrid OOP language, C++ allows a multiparadigmatic approach to coding. The advantages of C as an efficient, powerful, procedural language are not lost. The key new ingredients in C++ are inheritance and polymorphism—that is, its capability to assume many forms.

Java corrected many of C++'s deficiencies as an overly complex language. It is a purer object-oriented language than C++ and was released in 1995 by Sun Microsystems. Its great attraction was cross-platform portability and automatic garbage collection features. It had several deficiencies, however, such as slow runtime executables and an inability to write system-level routines.

C#, released officially in 2002 by Microsoft, corrected and improved on Java. It allows Java-style full OOP, but also has unsafe code that can use pointers for writing more low-level system routines. Unlike Java, which precludes operator overloading, it has a well-thought-out operator overloading strategy that is very much simpler than C++. It treats all types as objects. It has a very nice iterator construct, the `foreach` statement, and a very general rectangular array scheme unavailable in its main competitors. Moreover, it supports a common language runtime under .NET that allows different languages to be used seamlessly from C#.

12.1   OOP LANGUAGE REQUIREMENTS

The following list presents four major OOP language characteristics. These features cannot substitute for programmer discipline and community-observed convention, but they can be used to promote such behavior.

OOP Language Characteristics

- Encapsulation with data hiding: the ability to distinguish an object's internal state and behavior from its external state and behavior

- Type extensibility: the ability to add user-defined types to augment the native types

- Inheritance: the ability to create new types by importing or reusing the description of existing types

- Polymorphism with dynamic binding: the ability of objects to be responsible for interpreting method invocation

Typical procedural languages, such as FORTRAN and C, have limited forms of type extensibility and encapsulation. These languages have pointer and record types that provide these features. C also has a scheme of file-oriented privacy, in its `static` file-scope declarations. Such languages as Modula-2 and Ada have more complete forms of encapsulation—namely, `module` and `package`, respectively. These languages readily allow users to build abstract data types (ADTs) and provide significant library support for many application areas. A language such as pure LISP supports dynamic binding. The elements in OOP have been available in various languages since the late 1960s.

LISP, Simula, and SmallTalk have long been in widespread use in both the academic and research communities. However, not until OOP elements were added to C was there any significant movement to use OOP in industry. Indeed, the late 1980s saw a bandwagon effect in adopting C++ that cut across companies, product lines, and application areas; industry needed to couple OOP with the ability to program effectively at a low level.

Also crucial was the ease of migration from C to C++. PL/1, by contrast, is rooted in FORTRAN and COBOL; Ada is rooted in Pascal. But C++ had C as a nearly proper subset. As such, the installed base of C code need not be abandoned. These other languages required a nontrivial conversion process to modify existing code from their ancestor languages.

In 1995, Sun Microsystems introduced Java. Its advantages over C++ were that it was simpler and safer. It also promised to be universal under the rubric "write once, run everywhere" accomplished by having a fully defined semantics that does not allow for distinct platform variation. It was enforced by using the Java Virtual Machine (JVM) as the runtime architecture for compiled Java code. In contrast, C and C++ leave some of their semantics, such as word size of native types, up to the compiler implementer, allowing local variation that can take better advantage of underlying machine architecture.

Java also developed libraries, such as Swing, that embodied modern GUI design. Sun has continued to develop Java by incorporating libraries for practically any major computing activity, including client-server applications, distributed system computing, and database computing.

C# can be seen as Microsoft's attempt to improve on the Sun Java strategy in at least two important ways. First, it is arguably a better programming language. It stays basically with Java's simplification of C++ by incorporating garbage collection and a standard semantics. But it introduces improvements, such as a careful implementation of operator overloading and true higher dimensional arrays. Second, it has programming language interoperability. Its Common Language Runtime (CLR) and Common Type System (CTS) support multiple programming languages. Visual Basic, Eiffel, C++, Java, to name just a few, are compilable for the CLR. The CLR generates Microsoft Intermediate Language (MSIL) instructions, a managed machine code with runtime validations, such as checked index ranges. The managed MSIL instructions are just-in-time (JIT) compiled to the native architecture to enhance efficiency. It is beyond the scope of this book to explore this feature.

12.2   ADTS: ENCAPSULATION AND DATA HIDING

To fully appreciate the OOP paradigm, we must view the overall coding process as an exercise in shared and distributed responsibilities. This book has used the term *client* to mean a user of a class and *manufacturer* to mean the provider of the class.

A client of a class expects an approximation to an abstraction. A stack, to be useful, has to be of reasonable size. A complex number must be of reasonable precision. A deck of cards must be shufflable, with random outcome in dealing hands. The internals of how these behaviors are computed is not a direct concern of the client. The client is concerned with cost, effectiveness, and ease of operation, not with implementation. This is the *black box* principle, and it has two components.

Black Box for the Client

- Simple to use, easy to understand, and familiar

- In a component relationship within the system

- Cheap, efficient, and powerful

Black Box for the Manufacturer

- Easy to reuse and modify; difficult to misuse and reproduce

- Profitable to produce with a large client base

- Cheap, efficient, and powerful

The manufacturer competes for clients by implementing an ADT product that is reasonably priced and efficient. It is in the manufacturer's interest to hide implementation details. This simplifies what the manufacturer needs to explain to the client, and it frees the manufacturer to allow internal repairs or improvements that do not affect the client's use. It restrains the client from dangerous or inadvertent tampering with the product.

A data-hiding scheme that restricts access of implementation detail to manufacturers guarantees client conformance to the ADT abstraction. The private parts are hidden from client code, and the public parts are available. It is possible to change the hidden representation without changing the public access or functionality. If done properly, client code need not change when the hidden representation is modified. The two keys to fulfilling these conditions are inheritance and polymorphism.

12.2.1 REUSE AND INHERITANCE

Library creation and reuse are crucial indicators of successful language strategies. Inheritance, or deriving a new class from an old one, is used for code sharing and reuse, as well as for developing type hierarchies. Inheritance can be used to create a hierarchy of related ADTs that share both code and a common interface, a feature critical to the ability to reuse code.

Inheritance influences overall software design by providing a framework that captures conceptual elements that become the focus for system building and reuse. For example, `System.Collections` supports building generic algorithms. It is based on each collection class implementing `Collections.IEnumerable`.

OOP Design Methodology

1. Decide on an appropriate set of ADTs.
2. Design in their relatedness and use inheritance to share code and interface.
3. Use virtual methods to process related objects dynamically.

Inheritance also facilitates the black box principle and is an important mechanism for suppressing detail. It is hierarchical, and each level provides functionality to the next level that is built on it. In retrospect, structured programming methodology, with its process-centered view, relied on stepwise refinement to nest routines but did not adequately appreciate the need for a corresponding view of data.

12.2.2 POLYMORPHISM

Polymorphism is the genie in OOP, taking instruction from a client and properly interpreting its wishes. A polymorphic method has many forms. Following the categorization developed by the programming theorists L. Cardelli and P. Wegner of Brown University, we make the following distinctions:

Types of Polymorphism

1. Coercion (ad hoc polymorphism): A method or operator works on several types by converting their values to the expected type. An example is conversion of arithmetic types in expressions.

```
// x and d double, i int
x = d + i;          // int i is coerced to double
```

2. Overloading (ad hoc polymorphism): A method is called based on its signature, defined as the list of argument types in its parameter list. The integer-divide operator and float-divide operator are distinguished, based on their argument list.

```
// type of division depends on type of a and b
x = a / b;
```

3. Inclusion (pure polymorphism): A type is a subtype of another type. Methods available for the base type work on the subtype. Such a method can have various implementations that are invoked by a runtime determination of subtype.

```
p.Draw()                    // Draw is overridden
```

4. Parametric polymorphism (pure polymorphism): The type is left unspecified and is later instantiated. Templates provide this in C++. This is in experimental form in C#.

```
template <class T> bool Greater(T a, T b)
  { return (a > b); }
```

Polymorphism localizes responsibility for behavior. The client code frequently requires no revision when functionality is added to the system through manufacturer-provided code additions.

Polymorphism contributes directly to the black box principle. The virtual methods specified for the base class are the interface used by the client throughout. The client knows that an overridden method takes responsibility for a specific implementation of a given action relevant to the object. The client need not know different routines for each calculation or different forms of specification. These details are suppressed.

Which form did you want, master?

12.3 OOP: PROGRAMMING METHODOLOGY

OOP using C++ gained dazzling acceptance in industry from 1986 on, despite acknowledged flaws and unfamiliarity with OOP strategies. The reason for this is that C++ brought OOP technology to industry in an acceptable way. C# piggybacks on the widespread use and success of C++ and later Java. C# allows tight, efficient, portable code to be written. C# coexists with standard languages and requires only an implemented CLR.

C was designed as a system-implementation language and as such allows coding that is readily translated to efficiently use machine resources. Software products gain competitive advantage from such efficiency. Hence, despite complaints that traditional C was not a safe or robust language to code in, C grew in its range of application. The C community, by convention and discipline, used structured programming and ADT extensions. OOP made inroads into this professional community only when it was wed to C within a conceptual framework that maintained its traditional point of view and advantages. Key to the bandwagon move to C++ has been the understanding that inheritance and polymorphism gain additional important advantages over traditional coding practice. The success of C# is that it is carefully implemented and supported by the largest software company in the world—Microsoft. It is easily used by any programmer experienced with modern C++, Java, or Visual Basic.

Polymorphism allows a client to use an ADT as a black box. Success in OOP is characterized by the extent to which a user-defined type can be made indistinguishable from a native type. Polymorphism allows coercions to be specified that integrate the ADT with the native types. Objects from sub-type hierarchies respond dynamically to method invocation, the messaging principle in OOP. Polymorphism also simplifies client protocols, and name proliferation is controlled by method and operator overloading. The availability of polymorphism encourages the programmer to design with encapsulation and data hiding in mind. OOP is many things to many people. Attempts to define it are like blind men's attempts to describe an elephant. Here is a simple equation describing object orientation:

$$OOP = type\text{-}extensibility + polymorphism$$

In many languages and systems, the cost of detail suppression was run-time inefficiency or undue rigidity in the interface. C# has a range of choices that allow both efficiency and flexibility. Also, the success of C++ was a precondition for the introduction of C# in 2002. Together, C#, C++, and Java have established OOP as the dominant contemporary programming methodology.

The following example is a demonstration of the power of type hierarchies and polymorphism. It is used to do expression evaluation.

An expression such as 2 * x + y can be represented as a tree, with each subexpression being a node. The following code uses an expression tree to evaluate an expression and print out its fully parenthesized form:

In file Tree.cs

```
// OOP = type-extensibility + polymorphism
// See also Andrew Koenig JOOP  August 1988

public abstract class Node {
  public abstract int Eval();
}

class IntNode : Node {
  public override int Eval() { return n; }
  public override string ToString() { return n.ToString(); }
  private int n;
  public IntNode(int k) { n = k; }
}
```

Dissection of the *Tree* Program

■`public abstract class Node {`
```
   public abstract int Eval();
}
```

`Node` is an abstract base class for a hierarchy of `Node` subtypes. There is an abstract method `Eval()`. This must be overridden and defined for every concrete subclass.

■`class IntNode : Node {`
```
   public override int Eval() { return n; }
   public override string ToString(){return n.ToString();}
   private int n;
   public IntNode(int k) {n = k;}
}
```

The `IntNode` class inherits from `Node`. We override the abstract method `Eval()`. We also override the `ToString()` method to properly print out our tree types.

```
class IdNode : Node {
  public override int Eval() { return val; }
  private char name;
  private int val;

  public override string ToString()
    { return name.ToString(); }

  public static int ReadInt()
  {
    Console.Write("Enter variable value:");
    string data = Console.ReadLine();
    return int.Parse(data);
  }
}
```

```
      public IdNode(char id)
      {
        name = id;
        val = ReadInt();
      }
    }

    class BinaryNode : Node {
      public override int Eval()
      {
        int ans = 0;
        switch (op) {
          case '-': ans = (left.Eval() - right.Eval()); break;
          case '+': ans = (left.Eval() + right.Eval()); break;
          case '*': ans = (left.Eval() * right.Eval()); break;
          default: throw new Exception();
        }
        return ans;
      }
      private  char op;
      private  Tree left;
      private  Tree right;

      public override string ToString()
        { return "(" + left.ToString() + op.ToString()
              + right.ToString() + ")" ; }

      public BinaryNode(char a, Tree b, Tree c)
        { op = a; left = b; right = c; }
    }
```

The various node types store different types of subexpressions. These are used to build the full expression tree.

Oh, yeah, next to my orange tree is an exotic C++ expression tree. It takes a lot of maintenance because it is prone to bug infestations.

Dissection of the *Tree* Program

```
■class IdNode : Node {
   public override int Eval() { return val; }
   private char name;
   private int val;
   .....
   public static int ReadInt()
   {
     Console.Write("Enter variable value:");
     string data = Console.ReadLine();
     return int.Parse(data);
   }

   public IdNode(char id)
   {
     name = id;
     val = ReadInt();
   }
}
```

The `IdNode` represents a variable. Its `name` can only be a single character. Its value is read in by the method `ReadInt()`. This is done by the class constructor.

```
class BinaryNode : Node {
   private  char op;
   private  Tree left;
   private  Tree right;
   public override string ToString()
     { return "(" + left.ToString() + op.ToString()
            + right.ToString() + ")" ; }
   public BinaryNode(char a, Tree b, Tree c)
     { op = a; left = b; right = c; }
}
```

Here, we see the power of this representation. The tree is a self-referential data structure, such that a tree is made up of a left and right subtree. The `ToString()` method is polymorphic. It parenthesizes the expression and calls the `ToString()` methods to properly turn the subexpressions into strings.

```
public override int Eval()
{
   int ans = 0;
   switch (op) {
     case '-': ans = (left.Eval() - right.Eval()); break;
     case '+': ans = (left.Eval() + right.Eval()); break;
     case '*': ans = (left.Eval() * right.Eval()); break;
     default: throw new Exception();
   }
   return ans;
}
```

The `Eval()` method is both recursive and polymorphic. It calls itself on the two subtrees and then determines from the node type which overridden `Eval()` method to call. Notice how convenient it is to extend the design by adding further operators as `cases`.

The next major piece is the expression tree. By adding further node types, such as a unary `Node` type and tree constructors, we can readily extend this code to more expression types.

In file Tree.cs

```
public class Tree {
  public Tree(int n) { p = new IntNode(n); }
  public Tree(char id) { p = new IdNode(id); }
  public Tree(char op, Tree left, Tree right)
    { p = new BinaryNode(op, left, right); }
  public override string ToString() { return p.ToString(); }
  public int Eval() { return p.Eval(); }
  private Node p;                        // polymorphic hierarchy
}
```

Dissection of the *Tree* Program

■ ```
public class Tree {
   public Tree(int n) { p = new IntNode(n); }
   public Tree(char id) { p = new IdNode(id); }
   public Tree(char op, Tree left, Tree right)
     { p = new BinaryNode(op, left, right); }
```

Each of these constructors works with a different node type calling new to construct them.

■ ```public int Eval() { return p.Eval(); }```

The code for evaluation uses the base class Node variable p to polymorphically call the correct overridden definition of Eval().

■ ```public override string ToString() { return p.ToString();}```

We use p polymorphically to produce a properly parenthesized string expression.
```

Finally, here is code to test our Tree expression class:

In file Tree.cs

```
using System;

class TreeTest {
  public static void Main()
  {
    Tree t1 = new Tree('*', new Tree(5),
              new Tree('+', new Tree('A'), new Tree(4)));
    Tree t2 = new Tree('+',
              new Tree('-',new Tree('A'),new Tree( 1)),
              new Tree('+', t1, new Tree('B')));
    Console.WriteLine(" t1 = " + t1.Eval() +
                      " ;  t2 = " + t2.Eval());
    Console.WriteLine("tree 1 " + t1);
    Console.WriteLine("tree 2 " + t2);
  }
}
```

The output of this program is

```
Enter variable value:10
Enter variable value:20
Enter variable value:55
 t1 = 70 ;  t2 = 144
tree 1 (5*(A+4))
tree 2 ((A-1)+((5*(A+4))+B))
```

Presume that when prompted for variable A in the first Tree t1, we enter 3. Then the first tree evaluates to 35. It prints, fully parenthesized, as tree 1 = (5 * (A + 4)). In Exercise 1 on page 517, you are asked to test this code and enter your own values for the variables.

12.4 DESIGNING WITH OOP IN MIND

Most programming should involve the use of existing designs. For example, the mathematical and scientific communities have standard definitions of complex numbers, rationals, matrices, and polynomials. Each of these can be readily coded as an ADT. The expected public behavior of these types is widely agreed on.

The programming community has widespread experience with standard container classes. Reasonable agreement exists as to the behavior of stack, associative array, binary tree, and queue. Also, the programming community has many examples of specialized programming language oriented to a particular domain. For example, SNOBOL and its successor language, ICON, have powerful string-processing features that can be captured as ADTs in C#.

OOP attempts to emphasize reuse, which is possible on several scales. The grandest scale is the development of libraries that are effective for an entire problem domain. The upside is that reuse contributes in the long run to more easily maintained code. The downside is that a particular application does not need costly library development.

OOP requires programmer sophistication. More sophisticated programmers are better programmers. The downside is high training cost and the potential misuse of sophisticated tools.

OOP makes client code simpler and more readily extensible. Polymorphism can be used to incorporate local changes into a large-scale system without global modification. The downside can be runtime overhead.

C# provides programming encapsulations through classes, inheritance, and namespaces. Encapsulations hide and localize. As systems get bigger and more complex, there is an increasing need for such encapsulations. Simple block structure and functional encapsulation of such languages as Pascal are not enough. The 1970s taught us the need for the module as a programming unit. The 1980s taught us that modules need to have a logical coherence supported in the language and that they must be derivable from one another. When supported by a programming language, encapsulations and relationships lead to increased programmer discipline. The art of programming is to blend rigor and discipline with creativity.

Occam's Razor is a useful design principle: Entities should not be multiplied beyond necessity—or beyond completeness, invertibility, orthogonality, consistency, simplicity, efficiency, or expressiveness. Such ideals can be in conflict and frequently involve tradeoffs in arriving at a design.

This is a little more complex than it needs to be just to hit a key.

Invertibility means that the program should have methods that are inverses. In the mathematical types, addition and subtraction are inverses. In a text editor, add and delete are inverses. Some commands, such as negation, are their own inverses. The importance of invertibility in a non-mathematical context can be seen by the brilliant success of the *undo* command in text editing and the *recover* commands in file maintenance.

Completeness is best seen in Boolean algebra, in which the nand operation suffices to generate all possible Boolean expressions. But Boolean algebra is usually taught with negation, conjunction, and disjunction as the basic operations. Completeness by itself is not enough to judge a design by. A large set of operators is frequently more expressive.

Orthogonality means that each element of a design should integrate and work with all other elements without overlapping or being redundant. For example, on a system that manipulates shapes, one should have a horizontal move, a vertical move, and a rotate operation. In effect, these operations would be adequate to position the shape at any point on the screen.

Hierarchy is captured through inheritance. Design should be hierarchical. It is a reflection of two principles—decomposition and localization. Both principles are methods of suppressing detail, a key idea in coping with complexity. However, there is a scale problem in such a design. How much detail is enough to make a concept useful as its own class? It is important to avoid a proliferation of specialized concepts. Too much detail renders the class design difficult to master.

12.5   CLASS RESPONSIBILITY COLLABORATOR

Designs can be aided by a diagramming process. Several object-oriented design (OOD) notations exist, and a number have been incorporated in CASE (computer-assisted software engineering) tools. The most comprehensive of these are based on Universal Modeling Language (UML), pioneered by Rational Software. Another useful, related low-tech scheme: the Class Responsibility Collaborator (CRC) notecard scheme.

A responsibility is an obligation the class must keep. For example, complex number objects must provide an implementation of complex arithmetic. A collaborator is another object that cooperates with this object providing an overall set of behaviors. For example, integers and reals collaborate with complex numbers to provide a complete set of mathematical behaviors.

12.5.1   CRC CARDS

A CRC notecard is used to design a given class. The responsibilities of the class and the collaborators for that class are initially described. The back of the card is used to describe implementation detail. The front of the card corresponds to public behavior.

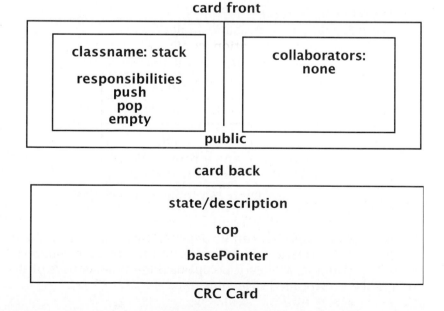

CRC Card

As the design process proceeds, the cards are rewritten and refined. They become more detailed and closer to a set of method headers. The back of the card can be used to show implementation details, including *ISA*, *LIKEA*, and *HASA* relationships.

The attractiveness of this scheme is its flexibility. In effect, it represents a pseudocode refinement process that can reflect local tastes. The number of revisions and the level of detail and rigor are a matter of taste. (See the site at http://c2.com/doc/oopsla89/paper.html for a good description.)

A more formal system for documenting class architectures is Unified Modeling Language (UML), which we already discussed in Section 6.12.2, *Unified Modeling Language (UML) and Design*, on page 273. (See the UML site at http://www.rational.com/uml/ for a full description.) A class diagram describes the types and relationships in the system. It is very useful documentation, and a number of systems, such as Rational Rose, now provide automated tools to develop such documentation along with coding. A key relationship is the *ISA* or subtype relationship. In the following basic UML diagram, we show the Node-IdNode class diagram:

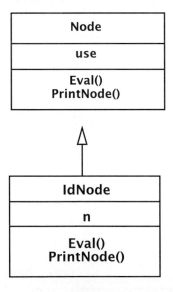

Basic ISA Inheritance in UML

Other relationships that can be depicted by UML include the part-to-whole or *aggregation* relationship (*HASA*), and the *uses* or *collaborates* relationship. For example, a Tree type uses a Node type as part of its representation. This is also called *delegation*.

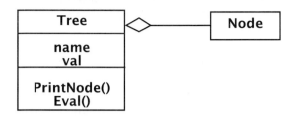

Basic HASA Relationship in UML

12.6 DESIGN PATTERNS

Reuse is a primary theme in modern programming. In early times, reuse was limited to simple libraries of methods, such as the math functions found in `System.Math`. In OOP, the class or interface becomes a key construct for reuse. Classes and interfaces encapsulate code that conforms to certain designs. Thus, the classes that allow the use of the iterator statement `foreach` conform to a *design pattern*. Recently, the concept of design pattern has proved very popular in defining medium-scale reuse. A design pattern has four elements.

Elements of a Design Pattern

1. The pattern terminology: for example, *iterator*

2. The problem and conditions: for example, *visitation* over a container

3. The solution: for example, pointerlike objects with a common interface

4. The evaluation: for example, the tradeoff between defining an iterator on a vector and using a native array

A design pattern is an abstraction that suggests a useful solution to a particular programming problem.

Design Patterns

1. *Iterator*, such as `IEnumerable`; organizes visitation on a container

2. *Composite*, such as `class GradStudent`; composes complex objects out of simpler ones

OOP has stimulated reuse through design patterns. A design pattern is a software solution in search of a problem. Consider how the iterator logic of the `foreach` statement decouples visitation of container elements from specific details of the container. This idea is independent of computer language and is useful in C++ and Java, though implemented differently in these languages. This idea can be summarized as the *iterator* pattern.

The name is of great importance, as it increases the programmer's technical vocabulary. A name should be memorable and illuminate a key characteristic of the method. The problem identifies circumstances under which the pattern provides a solution. The solution shows how the pattern solves the problem. The consequences are a discussion of the cost-benefit tradeoff in using the pattern.

When the pattern is discussed in a specific language context, it is often called a *programming idiom*. This is also sometimes used for smaller coding ideas. For example, in C# or C, `EOF` is frequently used as a guard value to terminate file processing.

When the pattern is used in a wider context to provide a library of routines and components, it is called a *framework*. `System.Collections` can be considered a framework that makes heavy use of the iterator pattern, among others. In Java, the Java Foundation Classes, also known as *Swing*, support Window development. They are implemented with the model-view-controller pattern.

12.7   A FURTHER ASSESSMENT OF C#

C# is the newest of the four languages: C, C++, Java, and C#. It thus benefits from the experience gained in using and implementing compilers and programs in the three older languages.

We are leaving out of the main text certain topics such as threading because they are relatively advanced. Some of these ideas are briefly covered in Appendix E, *Advanced Topics*.

12.7.1 WHY C# IS BETTER THAN JAVA

C# is very close to Java. It normally garbage collects objects automatically. Everything is a class derived from object. It has a machine-independent semantics. It compiles to managed code.

In C#, everything is an object. Native types such as `int` can be treated as an object. This is not the case in Java where native types are strictly value types. C# allows native types to be passed by reference. It has the concept of boxing and unboxing values. This simplifies the treatment of generic routines.

C# has the `foreach` statement coupled with the `IEnumerator` interface. This allows a built-in form of iterator. C# has true multidimensional arrays. C# has `unsafe` code. This allows pointer and `struct` constructs that are low-level and do not permit garbage collection.

C# has retained, though in a more logical and simpler form, C++'s ability to do operator overloading. C# has the concept of properties. This provides `get` and `set` as access methods for retrieving and changing data member's values.

The C# programmer can readily convert Java code to C#, but not vice versa. C# is in effect a conceptual superset of Java. Finally, C# is part of a suite of interoperable languages that are targeted to the Common Language Runtime.

12.7.2 WHY C# IS BETTER THAN C++

C++ is too complex and unsafe. It gives the programmer many opportunities to mismanage pointers in the name of efficiency. It is very hard to master. Many books teach you constrained C++, avoiding the use of multiple inheritance, whereas Java and C# directly restrain the language prohibiting these errors and abuses.

C++ is too large and complex. C++ is system-dependent. C++ is not Web-ready. C++ does not manage memory. When teaching students programming, it is desirable to minimize complexity by teaching a very restricted set of C++, but invariably issues such as signature matching, conversions, and memory management require sophisticated explanations. The mere fact that core C# does not have the pointer type greatly simplifies the teaching of C#.

12.8   SOFTWARE ENGINEERING: LAST THOUGHTS

Let us revisit our *Tree* program in Section 12.3, *OOP: Programming Methodology*, on page 500, and examine software engineering lessons learned from this example. Imagine writing this code in a procedural programming style such as that needed by C or Pascal. Invariably, it would be designed around a big `switch` statement, such as

```
switch (nodetype) {
case 1: ····· break;                    // unary operator
case 2: ····· break;                    // binary operator
·····
}
```

What is required when we write a new version, possibly incorporating the evaluation of additional operators? We have to search out each such `switch` and update with the new case. In the case of our object-oriented code using a related hierarchy of `Node` types, we need only add a new subclass. We do not have to do any global searches.

Notice that we did use a `switch` for evaluating a `BinaryNode`. This can be avoided by having further subclasses. In Exercise 4 on page 517, you are asked to provide this switchless alternative and discuss its design tradeoffs.

Part of the tradeoff comes from value returned by having subclasses of finer granularity. When you have software based on many little classes, you have fine granularity; with software based on very few large classes, you have coarse granularity. Fine granularity has the overhead of writing and maintaining many small classes of limited usefulness. Coarse granularity has the overhead of a relatively rigid design and the need for more revision and testing within these large classes.

12.9   DR. P'S PRESCRIPTIONS

- KISS—"Keep it simple, stupid".

- Use standard libraries.

C# has many complex features. For example, inheritance hierarchies tend to be overused. Remember, code needs to be understood, maintained, and extended by others not as clever as yourself. Sticking to essentials and idiomatic use promotes understanding of your code.

Do not reinvent the wheel—trite but true. `System.Collections` is the culmination of much experience and practice and should be used extensively. It has excellent performance characteristics. Historically, starting with the FORTRAN scientific library package and continuing with the various UNIX libraries, libraries have been the most successful software reuse tool.

SUMMARY

- Object-oriented programming (OOP) has been embraced by industry overwhelmingly. The key ingredient is polymorphism, or the ability to assume many forms. C# builds on Java and C++ in supporting object-oriented concepts.

- A black box for the client should be simple to use, easy to understand, and familiar; cheap, efficient, and powerful; and in a component relationship within the system. A black box for the manufacturer should be easy to reuse and modify and difficult to misuse and reproduce; cheap, efficient, and powerful; and profitable to produce for a large client base.

- Polymorphism contributes directly to the black box principle. The overridden methods specified for the base class are the interface used by the client throughout. The client knows that an overridden method takes responsibility for a specific implementation of a given action relevant to the object.

- The OOP design methodology involves deciding on an appropriate set of ADTs, designing in their relatedness and, using inheritance to share code and interface, using virtual methods to process related objects dynamically.

- Occam's Razor states that entities should not be multiplied beyond necessity—or beyond completeness, invertibility, orthogonality, consistency, simplicity, efficiency, or expressiveness. These principles can be in conflict and frequently involve tradeoffs in arriving at a design.

- The Class Responsibility Collaborator (CRC) notecard scheme is used in OOD. A responsibility is an obligation the class must keep. A collaborator is another object that cooperates with this object to provide an overall set of behaviors. The responsibilities of the class and the collaborators for that class are initially described.

- OOP has stimulated reuse of *design patterns*. A design pattern is a software solution in search of a problem. Consider how the iterator logic of the `foreach` decouples visitation of container elements from specific details of the container. This idea can be summarized as the *iterator* pattern. The pattern name is of great importance, as it increases the programmer's technical vocabulary. The name should be clever and illuminate a key characteristic of the method. The problem identifies circumstances under which the pattern provides a solution. The solution shows how the pattern solves the problem. The consequences are a discussion of the cost-benefit tradeoff in using the pattern.

REVIEW QUESTIONS

1. Name the typical characteristics of an object-oriented programming language.

2. True or false: Conventional academic wisdom is that excessive concern with efficiency is detrimental to good coding practice.

3. Through _____, a hierarchy of related ADTs can be created that share code and a common interface.

4. Name three properties of a black box for the client.

5. Name three properties of a black box for the manufacturer.

6. _____ methodology has a process-centered view and relies on stepwise refinement to nest routines but does not adequately appreciate the need for a corresponding view of data.

7. _____ is the genie in OOP, taking instruction from a client and properly interpreting its wishes.

8. Give an example of ad hoc polymorphism.

9. Describe at least two separate concepts for the keyword `abstract` as used in C#. Does this cause conceptual confusion?

EXERCISES

1. Test the code for the *Tree* program in Section 12.3, *OOP: Programming Methodology*, on page 506, and enter your own values for the variables in the expressions.

2. Add a `UnaryNode` class to our *Tree* program from Section 12.3, *OOP: Programming Methodology*, on page 506. It should deal with unary minus and unary plus. Unary plus is a no-op, meaning nothing is done. Test using the expressions +a - 3 * b and -a + b * -3.

3. Redo the previous exercise by including the increment and decrement operators. Write and run appropriate test cases.

4. (Uwe F. Mayer) Redo the *Tree* program in Section 12.3, *OOP: Programming Methodology*, on page 502, to avoid the `switch` statements. Do this by writing further subclasses for the different binary operators. Discuss the benefits and drawbacks of this approach.

5. *(Java)* C#, Java, and C++ have different casting rules. Investigate the differences. C++ allows a wider range of casting opportunities. Is this desirable?

6. List anything that you would drop from the C# language. Argue why it would not be missed. For example, it is possible to drop the `goto`?

7. List anything that you would add to the C# language. Argue why it would be a major improvement. For example, it might be possible to add C++ templates.

UNICODE AND ASCII CHARACTER CODES

C# uses the Unicode standard UTF-16 as its default character set. This means that C# uses a default size of 16 bits for each character, making it possible to represent 64,536 unique characters. Unicode provides a unique number for every character, no matter what the platform, no matter what the program, no matter what the language. Many other computer languages support the 7-bit 128 ASCII character set with Unicode as an extension.

The Unicode standard is discussed at length at the Web site www.unicode.org. Basically, the Unicode standard assigns values in a given hexadecimal range for character sets. For example, math symbols are in the range 2200 to 22FF. Generally, only a small subset of the Unicode set is installed on any given computer. Generally, you have to purchase and install segments of the Unicode set.

The following program prints out several groupings of Unicode characters that are present on many computers. Unprintable characters are represented with a question mark on output.

In file UnicodeUse.cs

```
using System;

// use www.unicode.org as reference website

// 0000 is Latin Set (basic ascii)
// 0300 is Greek and Diacritical Marks
// 2200 is Math set
// 2500 is Geometrics start

public class UnicodeUse {
  public static void Main()
  {
    int []startPoints = { 0X0, 0X300, 0X2200, 0X2500 };

    foreach (int hexStart in startPoints) {
    Console.WriteLine("Unicode for 256 entries " +
                      "starting at {0:X}", hexStart);
      for (int i = 0; i < 16; i++) {
        Console.Write("{0:X}x  ", (hexStart + (i * 16)));
        for (int j = 0; j < 16; ++j)
          Console.Write(Convert.ToChar(hexStart +
                        ((i * 10) + j)) + "  ");
        Console.WriteLine(" ");
      }
      Console.WriteLine("");        // separator between sets
    }
  }
}
```

The output for the first set of printed values of this program is

```
Unicode for 256 entries starting at 0
0x        ?  ?  ?  ?  ?  ?
   ?  ¤
10x
   ?  ¤  ?  ?  ?  ?  ¶  §  ?  ?  ?  ?
20x  ¶  §  ?  ?  ?  ?  ?  ?  ?  ?  ?  ?        !  "  #
30x  ?  ?        !  "  #  $  %  &  '  (  )  *  +  ,  -
40x  (  )  *  +  ,  -  .  /  0  1  2  3  4  5  6  7
50x  2  3  4  5  6  7  8  9  :  ;  <  =  >  ?  @  A
60x  <  =  >  ?  @  A  B  C  D  E  F  G  H  I  J  K
70x  F  G  H  I  J  K  L  M  N  O  P  Q  R  S  T  U
80x  P  Q  R  S  T  U  V  W  X  Y  Z  [  \  ]  ^
90x  Z  [  \  ]  ^  _  `  a  b  c  d  e  f  g  h  i
A0x  d  e  f  g  h  i  j  k  l  m  n  o  p  q  r  s
B0x  n  o  p  q  r  s  t  u  v  w  x  y  z  {  |  }
C0x  x  y  z  {  |  }  ~  ¡  ?  ?  ?  ?  ?  ?  ?  ?
D0x  ?  ?  ?  ?  ?  ?  ?  ?  ?  ?  ?  ?  ?  ?  ?  ?
E0x  ?  ?  ?  ?  ?  ?  ?  ?  ?  ?  ?  ?  ?  ?  ?  ?
F0x  ?  ?  ?  ?  ?  ?  ?  ?  ?        ¡  ¢  £  ¤  ¥
```

You can print out the entire Unicode set by replacing

```
int []startPoints = { 0X0, 0X300, 0X2200, 0X2500 };
foreach (int hexStart in startPoints) {
```

with the following code

```
int hexStart;
for (int hS = 0; hS < 256; ++hS) {
  hexStart = hS * 256;
```

Unicode incorporates the 128-character ASCII set as its first 128 elements.

Table A.1		American Standard Code for Information Interchange							
	0	1	2	3	4	5	6	7	8	9
0	nul	soh	stx	etx	eot	enq	ack	bel	bs	ht
1	nl	vt	np	cr	so	si	dle	dc1	dc2	dc3
2	dc4	nak	syn	etb	can	em	sub	esc	fs	gs
3	rs	us	sp	!	"	#	$	%	&	'
4	(	)	*	+	,	-	.	/	0	1
5	2	3	4	5	6	7	8	9	:	;
6	<	=	>	?	@	A	B	C	D	E
7	F	G	H	I	J	K	L	M	N	O
8	P	Q	R	S	T	U	V	W	X	Y
9	Z	[	\	]	^	_	'	a	b	c
10	d	e	f	g	h	i	j	k	l	m
11	n	o	p	q	r	s	t	u	v	w
12	x	y	z	{	|	}	~	del		

Some observations:

- Character codes 0 through 31 and 127 are nonprinting.
- Character code 32 prints a single space.
- Character codes for digits 0 through 9e are contiguous.
- Character codes for letters A through Z are contiguous.
- Character codes for letters a through z are contiguous.
- The difference between a capital letter and the corresponding lowercase letter is 32.

Table A.2	The Meaning of Some of the Abbreviations		
bel	audible bell	ht	horizontal tab
bs	backspace	nl	newline
cr	carriage return	nul	null
esc	escape	vt	vertical tab

Table A.3 presents the escape sequences for characters.

Table A.3	Escape Sequence Characters	
Escape Sequence	Meaning	Unicode
\a	Bell (alarm)	\u0007
\b	Backspace	\u0008
	in a [] character class; The escaped character \b is a special case. In a regular expression, \b denotes a word boundary (between \w and \W characters) except within a [] character class, where \b refers to the backspace character. In a replacement pattern, \b always denotes a backspace.	
\t	Tab	\u0009
\r	Carriage return	\u000D
\v	Vertical tab	\u000B
\f	Form feed	\u000C
\n	New line	\u000A
\e	Escape	\u001B
\nnn	ASCII character as octal (up to three digits).	
\xnn	ASCII character using hexadecimal representation (exactly two digits).	
\c	ASCII control character; for example, \cC is Ctrl-c.	
\unnnn	Unicode character using hexadecimal representation (exactly four digits).	
\	When followed by a character that is not recognized as an escaped character, matches that character.	

OPERATOR PRECEDENCE AND ASSOCIATIVITY

All operators in a given table entry, such as ++, new, and &, have equal precedence with respect to one another but have higher precedence than all the operators in the entries below them. The associativity rule for all the operators in a given entry appears on the right side of Table B.1.

Recall that the logical operators: && and || are short circuit evaluated.

Unsafe code allows pointer operations. The pointer operations are

-> pointer—highest precedence which is equivalent to new or []

& address of— second highest precedence: equivalent to unary +

* dereferencing or indirection—also of precedence unary +

Also the operator sizeof() is to be used only in unsafe code. This operator derives from C where types were system-dependent and could be stored and represented differently on different systems. In the C# managed environment, types are the same across all systems.

Table B.1	Operator Precedence and Associativity			
Operators				**Associativity**
func() [] typeof(*e*) checked	(*postfix*)++ sizeof(*e*) unchecked	(*postfix*)-- *name.name* (*e*) new		left to right
++ (*prefix*) + (*unary*)	-- (*prefix*) - (*unary*)	! (*type*)(*e*)	~	right to left
* / %				left to right
+ -				left to right
<< >>				left to right
< <= > >= is as				left to right
== !=				left to right
&				left to right
^				left to right
|				left to right
&&				left to right
||				left to right
?:				right to left
= += -= *= /= %= >>= <<= &= ^= |=				right to left

STRING, STRINGBUILDER, AND REGEX LIBRARIES

The `string` type as defined by the `String` class provides methods and operators that perform string manipulations, such as concatenation, assignment, and replacement. The `StringBuilder` class provides much of the same functionality as `string`, but allows objects to be mutated. This is a very important efficiency consideration. `String` objects are immutable, so when an existing string is modified to produce a new string, the older object is retained, even if no longer needed. The `Regex` class is a powerful class for searching and manipulating text as regular expressions. These three classes allow extensive and convenient functionality for processing text.

This appendix presents only a subset of the more commonly used members of the three classes. C# integrated environments generally have help files, which describe fully the system libraries. In addition, the following Web sites give more information about C# and its libraries:

http://msdn.microsoft.com/vstudio/techinfo/articles/upgrade/Csharpintro.asp

http://www.csharptoday.com/

C.1   THE STANDARD String CLASS

The type `string` as defined by the standard class `String` has been used extensively in the text and is described in detail in Section 6.6, *The Standard Class* `string`, on page 249. For the sake of convenience, we include much of that description here.

The C# IDE that you use most likely has an extensive reference available on line in the Help command. Here is the Visual Studio screenshot showing what you get when you request a search on "String class."

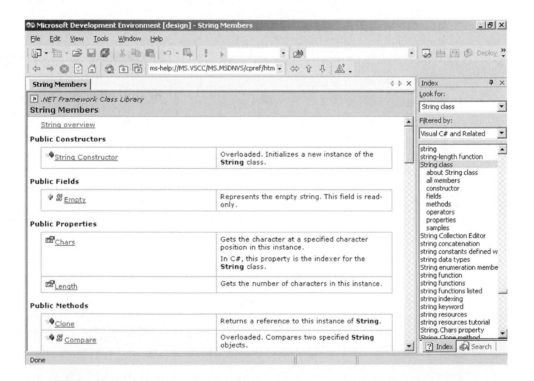

Scrolling down the help page on the left reveals more methods, and clicking on any of the underlined item's members gives you more information about the interface.

The following tables divide the important class members for `String` into five groupings: properties and fields, constructors, overloaded operators, static methods, and instance methods. First we present properties and fields in Table C.1.

Table C.1	System.String Class Public Properties and Fields
Length	Number of characters in the string
Chars	Character at specified character position
Empty	Represents the empty string

The safe constructors shown in Table C.2 make it quite easy to use the string type initialized from `char[]` arrays. Many computations are readily handled as an array of characters. The `string` interface also handles arrays of characters. There are also unsafe constructors, which allow you to initialize `string` from pointers to characters. These are not listed here as unsafe code in C# should be avoided.

Table C.2	Safe String Constructor Members
`String(char[]);`	Initializes to the value indicated by an array of Unicode characters
`String(char, int);`	Initializes to the value indicated by a specified Unicode character repeated a specified number of times.
`String(char[], int, int);`	Initializes to the value indicated by an array of Unicode characters, a starting character position within that array, and a length.

Strings have equality and inequality operators overloaded, as shown in Table C.3.

Table C.3	String Overloaded Operator Members
==	Overloaded operator ==
!=	Overloaded operator !=

Some of the important static members of `class System.String` are shown in Table C.4. Some of these methods have multiple overloaded argument lists, indicated by the use of (*args*) as the parameter list.

Table C.4 System.String Class Static Methods	
`int Compare (`*args*`)`	Compares two strings
`string Concat (`*args*`)`	Concatenates two strings
`string Copy(string)`	Copies a string
`string Format (`*args*`)`	Replaces each format specification in a format string with the textual equivalent of a corresponding object's value. (See Section 9.2, *Formatted Output*, on page 378)

Public instance methods for string are shown in Table C.5.

Table C.5 System.String Class Instance Methods	
`bool Equals (`*args*`)`	Determines if two strings have the same value
`string Clone()`	Returns this string
`CompareTo(string)`	Compares this instance with string
`bool Equals(`*args*`)`	Determines if two strings have the same value
`int IndexOf(`*args*`)`	Returns the index of the first occurrence of a string s within an instance of `String`
`string Insert(int, string)`	Returns a new string with a specified value inserted at a specified position in this string
`int LastIndexOf(`*args*`)`	Gets the position of the last occurrence of the specified character in this string
`string Remove(int, int)`	Deletes the specified number of characters from this instance of `String`, beginning at the specified location
`string Replace(`*args*`)`	Replaces all instances of a specified character or string with a new one

Table C.5	System.String Class Instance Methods
string[] Split(*args*)	Creates an array of strings by splitting this string
string Substring(*args*)	Returns a substring of this instance of String
string ToLower(*args*)	Returns a copy in lowercase
string ToUpper(*args*)	Returns a copy in uppercase
string Trim(*args*)	Removes leading or trailing white space

Many of these methods throw exceptions if the specified string position is out of range, or if the specified string is Null.

Here is an example program making use of String. It reads in text line by line and parses the text into words. It uses a hash table to store the words and counts the number of occurrences.

In file MyHash.cs

```
//use    %MyHash.exe filename

using System;
using System.IO;
public class HashUse {
  public static uint MyHash(string s)          // string to key
  {
    char[] a = new char[s.Length];
    uint hNumber = 0;
    s.CopyTo(0, a, 0, s.Length);
    foreach (char t in a)
      hNumber =  (hNumber * 31 + t);
    return hNumber % M;
  }

  public class Bucket
  {
    public BucketItem head;
    public Bucket(BucketItem h) { head = h; }
```

```csharp
    public override string ToString()
    {
      BucketItem  temp = head;
      string total = "";
      while (temp != null)
      {
        total = total + temp.ToString();
        temp = temp.Next;
      }
      return total;
    }
  }

  public class BucketItem  {
    public BucketItem(string w, BucketItem bi, int c)
    {  word = w; next = bi; count = c;}

    public override string ToString()
    { return String.Format("{0,10} {1,-3}",  word, count); }

   public static void Update(uint key, string w, Bucket[] b)
    {
      if (b[key] == null)
        b[key] = new Bucket( new BucketItem(w, null, 1) );
      else
        Update(b[key].head,b[key].head.next, w);
    }

    public static void Update(BucketItem bi, BucketItem n,
                              string w)
    {
      if (bi.word == w)
        bi.count++;
      else if (n == null)
        bi.next = new BucketItem(w, null, 1);
      else  Update(bi.next, n.next, w.ToLower());
    }

    public BucketItem Next { get {return next;} } //property

    private string word;
    private BucketItem next;
    private int count;
  }
```

```csharp
public static void Main(string[] args)
{
  StreamReader strIn = new StreamReader(args[0]);

  char[] delims = {' ', ',', '.', ';', '\t', '\n', '\0',
      '(', ')', '!', '?', '[', ']', '{', '}', ':' };

  uint keyNumber;
  int[] keys = new int[M];
  Bucket[] bucket = new Bucket[M];
  string line;
  try
  {  // catch eof
    while (true)
    {
      line = strIn.ReadLine();
      Console.WriteLine(line);
      line = line.ToLower();      //words same despite case
      string[] word = line.Split(delims);

      foreach (string w in word)
      {
        if (w == "")            //split produces empty strings
          continue;

        keyNumber = MyHash(w);
        BucketItem.Update(keyNumber, w, bucket);
        keys[MyHash(w)] ++;
      }
    }
  }
  catch(NullReferenceException e )
  { /* No more input  */ }

  int itemNumber = 0;
  foreach (Bucket b in bucket)
    Console.WriteLine("bucket {0}: {1}", ++itemNumber, b);
}                   //M is usually prime to avoid collisions
  private const uint M = 11;   //distribute keys into slots
}
```

The output of this program is

```
testfile, for hash program;
for one: two; One; Two.
Three, one! two; Two. More words get output?
Choose M (size of array) as prime number
adjust according to [input file size] and
distribution properties.

bucket 1:        array 1              to 1
bucket 2:        words 1              of 1   distribution 1
bucket 3:         hash 1          choose 1
bucket 4:          for 2
bucket 5:        three 1          adjust 1              and 1
bucket 6:
bucket 7:          one 3           more 1            size 2
prime 1       number 1
       file 1
bucket 8:          two 4           get 1    according 1
bucket 9:    testfile 1          input 1   properties 1
bucket 10:          as 1
bucket 11:     program 1          output 1              m 1
```

The output starts with the echo of the input lines to hash. Notice how we used Split() to parse each line of text into distinct words. We used a low number for M, which determines the size of the array and the distribution so that we could show output with multiple bucket items per bucket more conveniently on a small file. This number should be adjusted to a larger prime number for larger files.

This program also uses the command line to pass in the argument containing the name of the file to use as input. This is described in Section D.10, *Compile and Command-Line Options*, on page 556.

C.2   THE `StringBuilder` CLASS

The `StringBuilder` class contains a string-like object that is mutable. The string length can change in response to methods that append, remove, replace, or insert characters. The namespace `using System.Text` is needed for `StringBuilder` declarations.

A `StringBuilder` can allocate more memory as needed, and the capacity is adjusted accordingly. A default capacity is used if no capacity is specified when an instance of `StringBuilder` is initialized.

`StringBuilder` has four public properties as shown in Table C.6.

Table C.6	StringBuilder Properties
`Capacity`	Gets or sets the maximum number of characters that can be contained in the memory allocated by the current instance
`Chars`	Gets or sets the character at the specified character position in this instance
`Length`	Gets or sets the length of this instance
`MaxCapacity`	Gets the maximum capacity of this instance

The `StringBuilder` constructors allow objects to be created based on an existing string, substring, specified size, or a combination of these as shown in Table C.7.

Table C.7	StringBuilder Constructor Members
`StringBuilder();`	Initializes a new instance
`StringBuilder(int);`	Initializes using the specified capacity
`StringBuilder(string);`	Initializes using the specified string
`StringBuilder(int, int);`	Initializes to start with specified capacity and maximum growth
`StringBuilder(string, int);`	Initializes using the specified string and capacity
`StringBuilder(string, int, int, int)`	Initializes from the specified substring and capacity

Most of the methods that modify a `StringBuilder` object return a reference to that same instance. The more important `StringBuilder` instance methods are presented in Table C.8.

Table C.8	StringBuilder Instance Methods
`StringBuilder Append(`*args*`)`	Appends the string representation of a specified object to the end of this instance.
`StringBuilder AppendFormat(`*args*`)`	Appends a formatted string, which contains zero or more format specifications, to this instance. Each format specification is replaced by the string representation of a corresponding object argument.
`int EnsureCapacity(`*args*`)`	Ensures that the capacity of this instance is at least the specified value.
`bool Equals(StringBuilder)`	Returns a value indicating whether this instance is equal to a specified object.
`StringBuilder Insert(`*args*`)`	Inserts the string representation of a specified object into this instance at a specified character position.
`StringBuilder Remove(int, int)`	Removes the specified range of characters from this instance.
`StringBuilder Replace(`*args*`)`	Replaces all occurrences of a specified character or string in this instance with another specified character or string.

Here is an example program making use of `StringBuilder`. It takes different arrays of words and arranges them into a rudimentary poem. It should be easy to improve on our scheme by increasing the vocabulary and having the construction process be more sophisticated.

In file Poem.cs

```csharp
// Program produces a poem
using System;
using System.Text;

public class Poem {
  public static string ChooseWord(string[] words, Random r)
    { return words[(int)(r.NextDouble() * words.Length)]; }

  public static void Main(string[] args)
  {
    StringBuilder poem = new StringBuilder(M);
    Random t = new Random();
    string[] nouns = { "roses", "violets", "cars",
                       "tigers" };
    string[] verbs = {"are", "ate", "ran", "walk", "love"};
    string[] rhymes = { "red", "blue", "you", "too" };

    for (int lines = 0; lines < 4; ++lines) {
      poem.Append(ChooseWord(nouns, t));
      poem.Append(' ');
      poem.Append(ChooseWord(verbs, t));
      poem.Append(' ');
      poem.Append(ChooseWord(rhymes, t));
      poem.Append('\n');
    }
    Console.WriteLine(poem);
  }
  private const int M = 1024;
}
```

The output of this program is

```
violets ate you
tigers ate you
tigers ran red
roses walk too
```

This program could be written using only the `string` type. Using the
`StringBuilder` class is more efficient use of memory because `Append()`
does not constantly create new objects.

C.3   THE Regex CLASS

The Regex class represents an immutable regular expression. The namespace using System.Text.RegularExpressions is needed for Regex declarations.

A regular expression is a pattern that is used in matching text. For example the string "the" is a regular expression. This pattern matches the explicit three characters *t, h, e*, if they appear contiguously in a string. So the string "then and there" would have two matches. A regular expression can have metacharacters that have special meaning for matching. For example, "^(Ira|Laura)" means match any line beginning with either the string "Ira" or the string "Laura" because the bar character '|' is used for choice in regular expressions and the up-arrow character '^' is used to indicate that a string must start on a new line.

There are three constructors available for Regex as shown in Table C.9.

Table C.9 The Regex Constructors	
Regex();	Initializes a new instance with no parameters
Regex(string);	Initializes and compiles an instance for the specified regular expression
Regex(string, Options);	Initializes and compiles an instance for the specified regular expression, with options that modify the pattern

There are two public properties as shown in Table C.10.

Table C.10 Regex Properties	
Options	Returns the options passed into the Regex constructor
RightToLeft	Gets a value indicating whether the regular expression searches from right to left

The more commonly used instance methods are shown in Table C.11.

Table C.11	Some Regex Instance Methods
`bool Equals (obj)` `bool Equals (obj, obj)`	Determines whether two `Object` instances are equal
`bool IsMatch(`*args*`)`	Indicates whether the regular expression finds a match in the input string
`Match Match(`*args*`)`	Searches an input string for an occurrence of a regular expression and returns the precise result as a single `Match` object
`MatchCollection Matches (`*args*`)`	Searches an input string for all occurrences of a regular expression and returns all the successful matches as if `Match` were called numerous times
`string Replace(`*args*`)`	Replaces all occurrences of a character pattern defined by a regular expression with a specified replacement character string
`string[] Split(`*args*`)`	Splits an input string into an array of substrings at the positions defined by a regular expression match

Here is an example program making use of `Regex`. It takes a regular expression and uses it to split a string into substrings.

In file RegexUse.cs

```
using System;
using System.Text;
using System.Text.RegularExpressions;

public class RegexUse {
  public static void Main()
  {
    Regex r = new Regex(",");
    string sentence = "i,am,using,as,a,split,character";
    Console.WriteLine("testing Rgex");
```

```
      string[] words = r.Split(sentence);
      foreach (string w in words)
        Console.WriteLine(w);
    }
}
```

The output of this program is

```
testing Rgex
i
am
using
as
a
split
character
```

One way to use regular expressions is to find and replace text. This technique is at the heart of a spell checking program. Write a program that finds all occurrences of the string "thier" and replaces them with the string "their" as an exercise.

VISUAL STUDIO .NET FOR C#

I n this appendix, we explain the basics of using Microsoft's Visual Studio .NET. This is a convenient integrated development environment (IDE) for writing, running, and debugging C# programs. It can also be used for other .NET supported languages, such as C++.

We use the *MakeChange* program from Section 1.4, *Implementing Our Algorithm in C#*, on page 13, to illustrate the use of Microsoft's Visual Studio .NET. Tables are used to present ways of performing tasks by selecting Visual Studio .NET menu options, using shortcuts, or clicking on icons. We use screen shot and partial screen shots to illustrate the steps used in compiling, debugging, and executing our example *MakeChange* program.

D.1   THE *Start Window*

When you open Visual Studio, you get a *Start Window* similar to the one shown following.

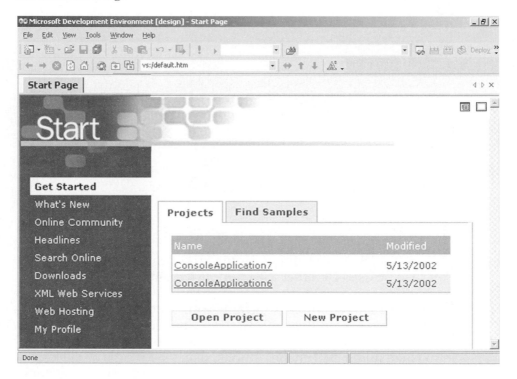

The most recently accessed projects show in the *Projects* tab. Here, *ConsoleApplication6* and *ConsoleApplication7* are shown. If you are using Visual Studio for the first time, there is no table with the name and modification dates shown. In addition to the two main sections on the *Start Window*, other smaller windows may be visible, depending on the Visual Studio settings on your machine.

You can now open an existing project or a new project easily from this *Start Window* by clicking on any of the items in the *Start Window*.

D.2   OPENING A NEW PROJECT

You can always open a new project by either clicking on the *New Project* icon, using the *Ctrl-Shift-N* command, or using the *File* menu. These three ways of opening a new project are always available even when the *Start Window* is not up and are shown in Table D.1.

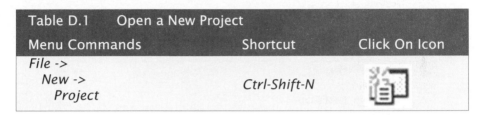

Table D.1 Open a New Project		
Menu Commands	**Shortcut**	**Click On Icon**

File ->
   New ->
      Project
	Ctrl-Shift-N	

Once you have selected *New Project*, you are prompted to select the project type. Note that *MakeChange* has been typed in the name box. If you don't type in a name, one is assigned for you such as *ConsoleApplication5*, which isn't very descriptive and makes it more difficult for you to find your program later. Visual Studio .NET opens a new project and gives you a rudimentary program structure.

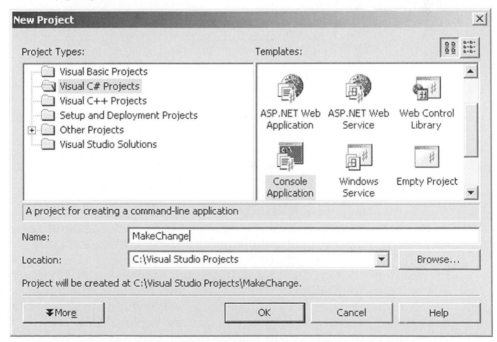

D.3   EDITING YOUR PROGRAM

When you open a new console application, the screen has an *Edit Window* that looks like this:

Notice that the program template has a `namespace`, but not a `using System`. It has suggested comments, the `class Class1`, and the method `Main()`. It is also properly indented. All these entries are typical of many console applications. There is also the attribute `[STAThread]`, which is metadata describing the fact that the method `Main()` is where execution starts. You should directly edit this window, changing the template text to be your specific program. For example, we have not typically been using `namespace`, so we would delete this line and replace it with `using System`. We would change `Class1` to `MakeChange`.

D.4   SYNTAX ERRORS

Once you have entered your program, save it. Visual Studio .NET tries to track simple syntax errors while you are creating the program. These errors show up with a little wavy line at the point of the error. Here, we enter the *MakeChange* program with two introduced syntax errors. First, there is a missing semicolon, noted by the wavy line under a blank area where the semicolon should be. Second, a wavy line appears under the extra close parenthesis.

```
Console.WriteLine("Enter price (0:100): ");
data = Console.ReadLine()
price = int.Parse(data));
change = 100 - price;       // how much change
dimes = change / 10;        // number of dimes
```

If you attempt to compile the *MakeChange* project with these errors, Visual Studio .NET explains the errors in the *Task List Window*, which tells you what it thinks is wrong at the wavy lines:

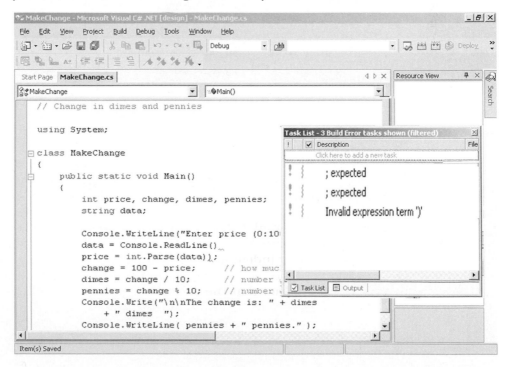

As you correct the errors, they disappear from the *Task List Window*. You can elect to display the *Task List Window* before you attempt to compile to help you with the wavy line error indicators as shown in Table D.2.

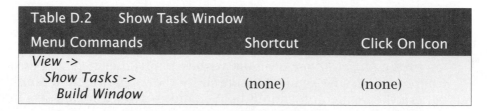

Table D.2 Show Task Window		
Menu Commands	**Shortcut**	**Click On Icon**
View ->
Show Tasks ->
Build Window	(none)	(none)

Here is the screen showing the selection of the *Show Tasks Window*:

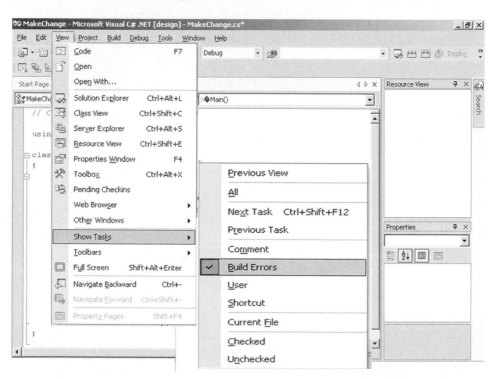

D.5 COMPILING THE PROJECT

If there are no syntax errors, then you can compile the program with the commands shown in Table D.3.

Table D.3 Compile the Program		
Menu Commands	Shortcut	Click On Icon
Build -> *MakeChange*	(none)	
Build -> *Solution*	*Ctrl-Shift B*	

The *Build* procedure accomplishes the compile and load functions that other languages use. The *Build Project* command does the interpretation on all files associated with the current project. The *Build filename* command (in this case *Build MakeChange*) compiles only the file specified. For single-file programs, like the majority in this text, the effect of both commands is the same.

Once the *Build* is complete, an *Output Window* is displayed with information about the *Build*:

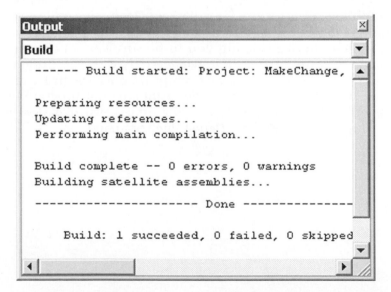

```
Output                                              ×

Build                                               ▼

   ------ Build started: Project: MakeChange,  ▲


   Preparing resources...
   Updating references...
   Performing main compilation...


   Build complete -- 0 errors, 0 warnings
   Building satellite assemblies...

   -------------------- Done ----------------

      Build: 1 succeeded, 0 failed, 0 skipped
                                              ▼
◄                                           ►
```

D.6   TRACING PROGRAM EXECUTION

Now you are ready to test the program by running it. You can either run the program without debugging, or make your program stop at specific points to follow the execution and examine variables. There are four basic ways to start execution of your program, as shown in Table D.4.

Table D.4	Execute the Program		
Menu Commands	Shortcut	Click On Icon	Comment
Debug -> Start Without Debugging	Ctrl-F5		Leaves execution window open at end
Debug -> Start	F5		Stops only if breakpoints are set
Debug -> Step Into	F10		Positions at first executable line
Debug -> Step Over	F11		Positions at first executable line

The advantage of using the *Start Without Debugging* option is that the *Execution Window* is displayed on your screen after termination of the program with a message asking you to hit any key. In contrast, the *Start* command puts up the *Execution Window* only while the program is actually running. The *Execution Window* disappears once the program is complete and you therefore cannot check the results of your program output unless you specifically put in code to wait for some keystroke. Here is the screen after using the *Start Without Debugging* command.

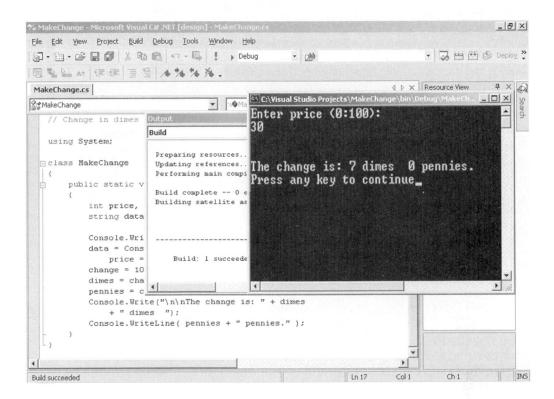

If you want to watch program execution, you must set a *breakpoint*. A breakpoint is a place in the source code where execution stops. Breakpoints are indicated on the screen by a large circle in the far left margin and highlight on the line with a breakpoint. You can easily set or remove a breakpoint just by clicking in the far left margin next to the line where you want the breakpoint to be set or removed. The click acts as a toggle, setting a breakpoint if there is none or removing a breakpoint if there is one. It is set prior to *Start*. Once debugging starts, the debugger executes and stops at each breakpoint.

The following screen shot shows execution stopped just prior to the execution of the calculation of pennies. Note the large arrow in the far left margin, which points at the next line to execute. A breakpoint is set for the line following, and two variables, `change` and `dimes`, are being watched via the *QuickWatch* option of the *Debug* command.

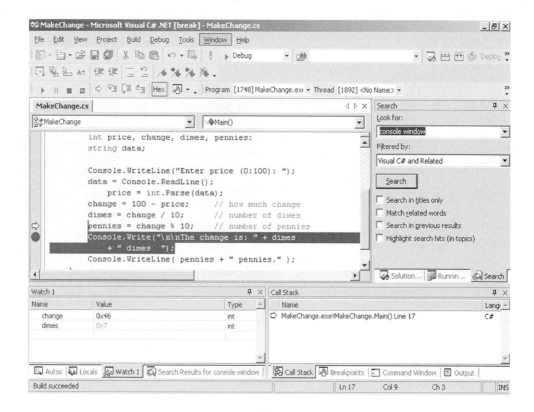

You can also see the stack, which shows the method calls invoked. Since the execution of the program is in the invoking `Main()` method, the stack shows only that the execution is at line 17 in `Main()`.

D.7   WATCHING PROGRAM VARIABLES

While you are debugging, you may want to watch the values of variables to ensure that they are being set according to your plans. This is done via two mechanisms: the *QuickWatch Window* and the *Watch Window*.

The *Watch Window* automatically pops up at the bottom of the screen when execution starts, overlaying the *Output Window* used by the *Build* command. Initially, the window shows an empty table, with columns for name, value, and type. As you add variables, via *AddWatch* or the *Quick-Watch Add* command, the list grows. You can change the display value to hexadecimal or delete entries by right-clicking on any entry in the table.

You must begin execution before you can watch any variables. Before program execution starts, the *Debug* option list is limited:

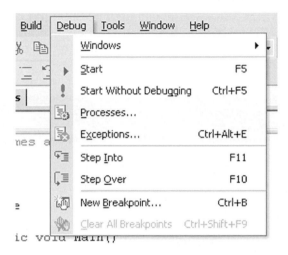

Once you start the debugging process by setting a breakpoint and using *Start*, or by starting execution with *StepOver* or *StepInto*, the *Debug Window* expands the following options: *Continue*, *Stop Debugging*, *Detach All*, *Restart*, *Step Out*, and *QuickWatch*.

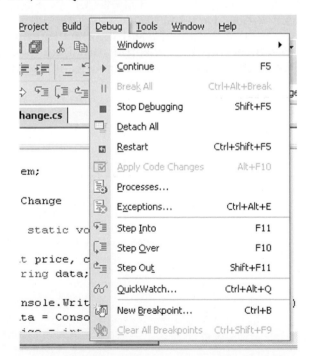

Selecting *QuickWatch* puts up the *QuickWatch Window*, which lets you look at a variable, add the variable to the *Watch Window*, change the variable, or evaluate an expression. The *AddWatch* command puts the variable in the *Watch Window*, where the variable can also be changed. The *Watch Window* is permanent; the *QuickWatch Window* must be closed before you can continue with execution. There are several ways to invoke *QuickWatch* or *AddWatch* as shown in Table D.5.

Table D.5	Watching Variables	
Menu Commands	**Shortcut**	**Comment**

Debug ->
    QuickWatch
        Set variable
	Ctrl-Alt-Q	If a *variable* is assigned at breakpoint, it is the default *variable*

	Right-click on *variable* in program-> *QuickWatch*	*Variable* selected is default in *QuickWatch Window*
	Right-click on *variable* in program-> *AddWatch*	*Variable* name is added to *Watch Window*

The following partial screen shot shows the pop-up menu available when you right-click on a variable name while debugging. The pop-up menu includes a variety of options for editing the program, looking at variables via *QuickWatch* and *AddWatch*, setting breakpoints and tracing execution, and looking at the structure of the program and its substructures and classes.

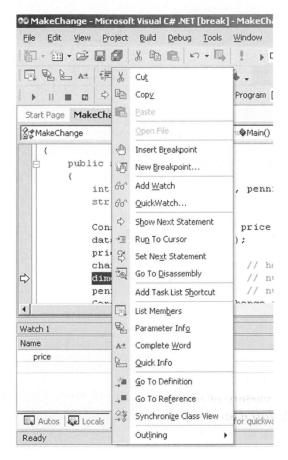

In this example, the variable dimes was selected before right-clicking as indicated by the variable name dimes in white on a black background, hence dimes would be the default variable selected for *QuickWatch* or *AddWatch*.

The *QuickWatch* and *Watch Windows* are shown in the following figure. In this example, the line at the current breakpoint is shown highlighted in a darker gray. Because dimes is the object of an assignment statement at the breakpoint, the *QuickWatch Window* uses dimes as the default value to watch. This can be changed by keying the variable name you want to watch instead into the *QuickWatch Expression* parameter. In addition, the *Add Watch* button in the *QuickWatch Window* was used to put dimes in the *Watch Window*. The *Watch Window* has been set to include two variables: dimes and price. The price variable has already been initialized via keyboard entry to 98, and dimes has not yet been calculated by the statement at the highlighted breakpoint.

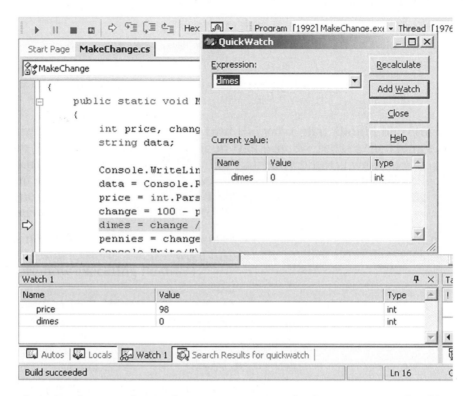

The values in the *Watch Window* are maintained when you save the file so that the next time you want to debug the program, you won't need to reset the items being watched.

D.8   COMPILE ERRORS

The following partial screen shot shows what happens when two compile errors are introduced. `Parse()` is changed to `Farse()` and a division by 0 instead of 10 is requested. The builder complains. You can quickly find the errors in the program by clicking on the error messages. Errors are highlighted for you as you click through the messages.

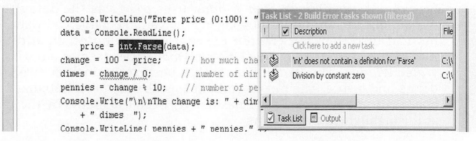

Next, you need to get to the *Property Pages*. There are four ways to do this: by selecting from the *View* menu, by right-click on the solution or project name in the *Solution Explorer*, by Shift-F4 keystroke, and by icon as shown in Table D.7. In order for the *Property Pages* options to be available, you need to have either the solution name or the project name highlighted.

Table D.7	Display Property Pages		
Menu Commands	Shortcut	Click	Click On Icon
View-> *Property Pages*	*Shift-F4*	Right-Click on solution or project name	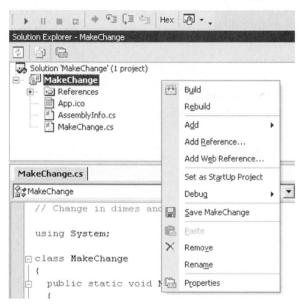

The following screen shot shows the menu that appears when you right-click on the project name.

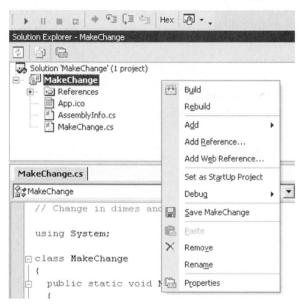

When the *Property Pages* are displayed, you select *Configuration Properties*. You have the option of looking at *Build*, *Debugging*, or *Advanced* properties. Not shown here, the *Allow Unsafe Code Blocks* toggle is on the *Build* page and must be set to *True* in order to compile code with the `unsafe` keyword.

The *Command-line Arguments* are available on the *Debugging* page, as shown below with two command-line arguments:

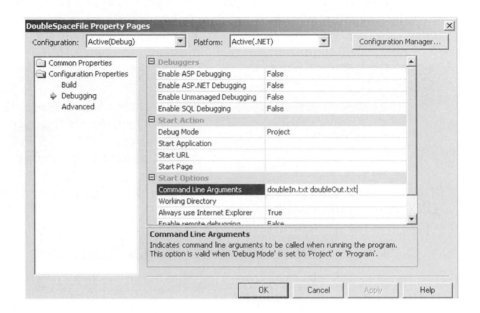

ADVANCED TOPICS

C# has an extensive set of facilities that were not touched on in the main text. In this appendix, we briefly explore some of these topics. The point is to indicate their availability and give some sense of their use. More detailed tutorial material can be found in the Visual Studio help and Microsoft online tutorials.

E.1   PREPROCESSOR DIRECTIVES

C# has preprocessor directives introduced by the special character #. The #define is used to define an identifier that is recognized by the preprocessor and the compiler. This identifier then can be used by other directives and the compiler to alter compilation. The inverse operation #undef is used to undefine an identifier. These preprocessor commands must be on their own line of source code. Unlike C and C++, they cannot be used to also define macros. In reality, they are used by the compiler and not as true preprocessor commands. For example, when using asserts we use #define DEBUG.

We can also test for preprocessor names being defined and compile code conditionally. Here, we need the preprocessor commands: #if, #else, #elif, and #endif. A simple example is

```
#if DEBUG            // if defined the following is compiled
  Console.WriteLine("trace of x : " + x);
#endif
```

A second example that shows the use of various #directives is

```
#define DEBUG
#if DEBUG        // if DEBUG defined the following is compiled
  Console.WriteLine("Debugging x : " + x);
#elif DEBUGMORE          // if DEBUGMORE defined then compile
  Console.WriteLine("Debugging y : " + y);
#else
  Console.WriteLine("No debugging this run");
#endif
```

Other directives are: #warning, #error, #region, #endregion, and #line. The #warning and #error directives tell the compiler to produce warning and error messages, respectively, that are specified by the text after the directive. The #region and #endregion directives specify that the enclosed source code should be hidden when displayed by the Visual Studio editor. Instead Visual Studio displays the text after the #region directive. The #line directive specifies a line number the programmer wishes to give the source text.

E.2   struct: A LIGHTWEIGHT OBJECT

C# has a value type alternative to class, the struct. The struct can be used in place of class when efficiency is a concern and certain features of class are unneeded. A struct is declared and used much as a class type, except it cannot support inheritance and it is a value type. Because it is a value type, it does not have destructors. It must be allocated off the stack.

The following simple example of struct pair illustrates this construct.

In file Pair.cs

```
// Example of the use of struct
// struct is a lightweight object

using System;

public struct Pair {

  public static void Main()
  {
    Console.WriteLine("testing struct");
    Pair p1 = new Pair(2, 3);      // allocate off the stack
    Console.WriteLine(p1);
  }

  public Pair(int first, int second)
  { this.first = first; this.second = second; }

  public int First
    { get { return first; }  set { first = value; } }

  public int Second
    { get { return second; }  set { second = value; } }

  public override string ToString()
    { return "first = " + first + " second = " + second; }
  private int first;               // not cannot initialize here
  private int second;
}
```

The output of this program is

```
testing struct
first = 2 second = 3
first = 5 second = 3
```

A struct type cannot have a user-defined default constructor. When such a type is passed as a parameter, it is passed by value, unless ref is used.

E.2.1   UNSAFE CODE

The type `struct` can be used in conjunction with pointer types. Pointers are an unsafe construct. They can be used to directly access memory. Such code, which is analogous to similar code in C programming, must be labeled with the keyword `unsafe`. We rewrite `Main()` to use a pointer type to manipulate the above `struct Pair` as follows:

In file UnsafePair.cs

```
// Example of the use of struct Pair
// compile as csc /unsafe  UnsafePair.cs

//Replace the previous Main()
unsafe public static void Main()
{
  Console.WriteLine("testing struct");
  Pair p1 = new Pair(2, 3);
  Pair* ptr = &p1;
  Console.WriteLine(p1);
  ptr->First = 5;
  Console.WriteLine(p1);
}
```

The output of this program is

```
testing struct
first = 2 second = 3
first = 5 second = 3
```

In order to compile this code, you need to set the unsafe compile option. You do this on the command line with the `/unsafe` option. In the IDE, you need to set the *Allow Unsafe Code* option in the *Project Configuration Build* options. Instructions for doing this are given in Section D.10, *Compile and Command-Line Options*, on page 556.

Use of pointers and the dereferencing operator is explained in detail in the companion volumes, *C by Dissection* and *C++ by Dissection*.

E.3 DELEGATES

A delegate is a type-safe function pointer. An object of this type can be used to invoke a method of like signature. An example would be

```
public delegate double fcn(double y);
```

This delegate could be used with any matching list of methods for computing a mathematical function, such as

```
static double f1(double y) { return y * y - 1; }
static double f2(double y) { return y * y * y - 27; }
```

Let us use this in a program that plots values of these functions.

In file Plot.cs

```
// using delegates
// plot a simple function in one variable

using System;

class Plot {
  public delegate double RealFun(double x);
  public static void Main()
  {
    RealFun f = new RealFun(Functions.F1);
    PlotIt(f, 0, 0.1, 100);
    f = new RealFun(Math.Sqrt);
    PlotIt(f, 0, 0.1, 100);
    f = new RealFun(Functions.F2);
    PlotIt(f, 0, 0.1, 100);
  }
```

```
    public static void PlotIt(RealFun f, double x0,
                               double incr, int n)
    {
      for (int i = 0; i < n ; ++i) {
        Console.WriteLine(" f({0:F4}) = {1:F4}", x0, f(x0));
        x0 += incr;
      }
    }
}

class Functions {
  public static double F1(double y) { return y * y - 1; }
  public static double F2(double y)
    { return y * y * y - 27; }
}
```

Partial output of this program is

```
f(0.1000) = -0.9900
f(0.2000) = -0.9600
f(0.3000) = -0.9100
f(0.4000) = -0.8400
f(0.5000) = -0.7500
f(0.6000) = -0.6400
f(0.7000) = -0.5100
f(0.8000) = -0.3600
f(0.9000) = -0.1900
f(1.0000) = 0.0000
f(1.1000) = 0.2100
f(1.2000) = 0.4400
f(1.3000) = 0.6900
f(1.4000) = 0.9600
f(1.5000) = 1.2500
```

The delegate declaration can be instantiated by methods from any class.
Here we have a special class `Functions` containing the functions we wish
to plot. But we used the `Math.Sqrt()` function as well.

E.4   THE params SIGNATURE

The keyword params specifies that an argument can be a comma-separated list of arguments of the same type or an array. This must be the last argument of a list of arguments. An example would be

```
public void Sum(params[] double data)
{
   double s = 0.0;
   foreach (double x in data)
     s = s + x;
   return s;
}
```

This method can be called as:

```
Sum(x, 8.9, y +3); // individual expressions that are double
Sum(w);                      // w is an array of double
```

This is somewhat akin to the C++ and C use of "..." as a function parameter argument. In C++ and C, however, the list of substituted actual parameters is not restricted as to type.

E.5   THREADING

C# has provisions for threading. A thread allows a program to run two or more processes concurrently. The major classes for threading and synchronization are in System.Threading. A simple way to use a thread is to create one and instantiate it using the delegate ThreadStart. We show a simple two-thread program using these constructs.

In file TwoThread.cs

```
using System;
using System.Threading;

class UseThread {
  public UseThread(int n, int threadNo)
    { this.n = n; this.threadNo = threadNo; }
```

```csharp
    public void TweedleDee()
    {
        for (int i = 0; i < n; ++i)
            Console.WriteLine("Thread "+ threadNo+ " Hee Hee ");
    }

    public void TweedleDum()
    {
        for (int i = 0; i < n; ++i)
            Console.WriteLine("Thread "+ threadNo+ " Tee Hee ");
    }

    private int n;
    private int threadNo;
}

class ThreadTest {
    public static void Main()
    {
        Console.WriteLine("Start Threads Program");
        UseThread t1 = new UseThread(20, 1);
        UseThread t2 = new UseThread(30, 2);
        ThreadStart s1 = new ThreadStart(t1.TweedleDee);
        ThreadStart s2 = new ThreadStart(t2.TweedleDum);
        Thread st1 = new Thread(s1);
        Thread st2 = new Thread(s2);
        st1.Start();
        st2.Start();
        Console.WriteLine(" End Threads Program");
    }
}
```

Partial output of this program is

```
Start Threads Program
 End Threads Program
Thread 1 Hee Hee
Thread 1 Hee Hee
      .....
Thread 1 Hee Hee
Thread 1 Hee Hee
Thread 2 Tee Hee
Thread 2 Tee Hee
Thread 2 Tee Hee
      .....
Thread 2 Tee Hee
```

The delegate declaration `public delegate void ThreadStart()` requires a method of no parameters returning `void`. We briefly dissect this program to explain each critical construct.

Dissection of the *TwoThread* Program

■`UseThread t1 = new UseThread(20, 1);`
`UseThread t2 = new UseThread(30, 2);`
`ThreadStart s1 = new ThreadStart(t1.TweedleDee);`
`ThreadStart s2 = new ThreadStart(t2.TweedleDum);`

Here we provide two `ThreadStart` declarations where we instantiate them with the `UseThread` methods `TweedleDee()` and `TweedleDum()`.

■`Thread st1 = new Thread(s1);`
`Thread st2 = new Thread(s2);`

Now each method is associated with a `Thread`. We can invoke the method through its `Thread`.

```
■st1.Start();
 st2.Start();
```

Here the two methods are started. The `Thread st1` starts the method `TweedleDee()`. The `Thread st2` starts the method `TweedleDum()`. The system is responsible for their execution. Conceptually the methods execute concurrently; on a multiprocessor system this would be feasible. How they are scheduled is up to the individual system.

E.5.1 CONTROLLING THREADS

Threads can be killed, suspended, prioritized, and joined. This gives a number of schemes for scheduling threads. Let us go back and modify `TweedleDum()` and `TweedleDee()`, by making each have a call to public static method `Thread.Sleep(timeInMilliseconds)`.

```
public void TweedleDee()
{
  for (int i = 0; i < n; ++i){
    Thread.Sleep(1);
    Console.WriteLine("Thread "+ threadNo+ " Hee Hee ");
   }
}

public void TweedleDum()
{
  for (int i = 0; i < n; ++i){
    Thread.Sleep(1);
    Console.WriteLine("Thread "+ threadNo+ " Tee Hee ");
  }
}
```

On most systems this changes the order of execution as each thread is suspended for one millisecond allowing the other thread to execute. You need to try this and compare the output to the previous version.

Now let us see what happens when we use a `Join()` to alter the thread scheduling.

```
public static void Main() {
  Console.WriteLine("Start Threads Program");
  UseThread t1 = new UseThread(20, 1);
  UseThread t2 = new UseThread(30, 2);
  ThreadStart s1 = new ThreadStart(t1.TweedleDee);
  ThreadStart s2 = new ThreadStart(t2.TweedleDum);
  Thread st1 = new Thread(s1);
  Thread st2 = new Thread(s2);
  st1.Start();
  st1.Join();                  // joins with the thread from Main()
  st2.Start();
  Console.WriteLine("End Threads Program");
}
```

To kill a thread you use *thread*.Interrupt(); where this method invocation throws a ThreadInterruptedException. Unless you want to actually interrupt the program and abort it, you need to write a catch for this exception that gracefully terminates it.

Threads can be given different levels of priority with SetThreadPriority(HANDLE thread, int priority). This is again system-dependent, and you should consult help and experiment on your local system.

E.5.2 SYNCHRONIZATION

We now write a classic threaded program, the producer-consumer program. This program is synchronized. The producer code generates a series of values. Each value is stored in a buffer. Once a value is generated, the consumer code is called to use the value stored in the buffer. The reading and writing from the buffer is synchronized so as not to overwrite existing produced values or consume from an empty buffer or repeatedly consume the same value. This is guaranteed by using a critical section. In the critical section only one thread at a time can be executed. The other threads are suspended. The critical section is introduced in C# by the keyword lock. We briefly examine some features of threading and class Monitor.

In file ProducerConsumer.cs

```
// A producer consumer using the Monitor class
// Monitor.Pulse(object) - notification a thread is done
// Monitor.Wait(object) - waiting on notification
using System;
using System.Threading;

public class ProducerConsumer
{
  public static void Main()
  {
    Buffer buf = new Buffer( );
    Producer prod = new Producer(buf, 15);
    Consumer cons = new Consumer(buf, 15);
    Thread producer = new Thread(new ThreadStart(prod.Run));
    Thread consumer = new Thread(new ThreadStart(cons.Run));
    try {
      producer.Start();
      consumer.Start();
      consumer.Join();           //syncs up with Main() thread
    }
    catch (Exception e) { Console.WriteLine(e); }
    Console.WriteLine(" Main() ended");
  }
}
```

Main() has three threads, the implicit starting thread for Main() and the
two explicit threads producer and consumer. Notice how the Join()
forces all threads to link up before executing the remaining code in
Main(). What would happen without this Join()?

```
public class Producer
{
  public Producer(Buffer buf, int howMany)
  {
    this.buf = buf;
    this.howMany = howMany;
  }
```

```
  public void Run()
  {
    for (int i = 0; i < howMany; ++i )
      buf.Produce(i);
  }

  private Buffer buf;
  private int howMany = 1;
}
```

The Producer class is used to generate howMany integer values written consecutively to the Buffer variable buf. Producer.Run() is what is used to instantiate the thread produce.

```
public class Consumer
{
  public Consumer(Buffer buf, int howMany)
  {
    this.buf = buf;
    this.howMany = howMany;
  }

  public void Run()
  {
    int v;

    for (int i = 0; i < howMany; ++i )
      v = buf.Consume();
  }
  private Buffer buf;
  private int howMany = 1;
}
```

The Consumer class is used to retrieve howMany values consecutively from the Buffer variable buf. Consumer.Run() is used to instantiate the thread consume.

```
public class Buffer
{
  public int Consume()
  {
    lock(this) {              //critical section -synchronized
      if (!flag) {            // Wait until Produce() is done
        try {
          Monitor.Wait(this);//Wait on Pulse() in Produce()
        }
        catch (Exception e) { Console.WriteLine(e); }
      }
      Console.WriteLine("Consume: " + v);
      flag = false;                    // Consume() is done
      Monitor.Pulse(this);            // notify Produce()
                                     //Consume() is done

      return v;
    }
  }

  public void Produce(int n)
  {
    lock(this) {
      if (flag) {              // Wait until Consume() is done
        try {
          Monitor.Wait(this);              // Wait on Pulse()
        }
        catch (Exception e) { Console.WriteLine(e); }
      }
      v = n;
      Console.WriteLine("Produce: " + v);
      flag = true;                    // Produce() is done
      Monitor.Pulse(this);            // notify Consume()
    }
  }
  private int v;                              // Buffer value
  private bool flag = false;        // tells Produce to Wait
}
```

The output of this program is

```
Produce: 0
Consume: 0
Produce: 1
Consume: 1
Produce: 2
Consume: 2
Produce: 3
Consume: 3
Produce: 4
Consume: 4
Produce: 5
Consume: 5
Produce: 6
Consume: 6
Produce: 7
Consume: 7
Produce: 8
Consume: 8
Produce: 9
Consume: 9
Produce: 10
Consume: 10
Produce: 11
Consume: 11
Produce: 12
Consume: 12
Produce: 13
Consume: 13
Produce: 14
Consume: 14
 Main() ended
```

Produce() and Consume() each have a code block that is a critical section
introduced by lock(this). A Buffer object stores an integer value in the
private member v. So buf.Produce(i) produces a value. After this happens flag is set to true and Pulse() notifies the waiting consumer
thread that it now can enter its critical section. The two threads strictly
take turns because of this synchronization.

INDEX